a Silent Voice

1

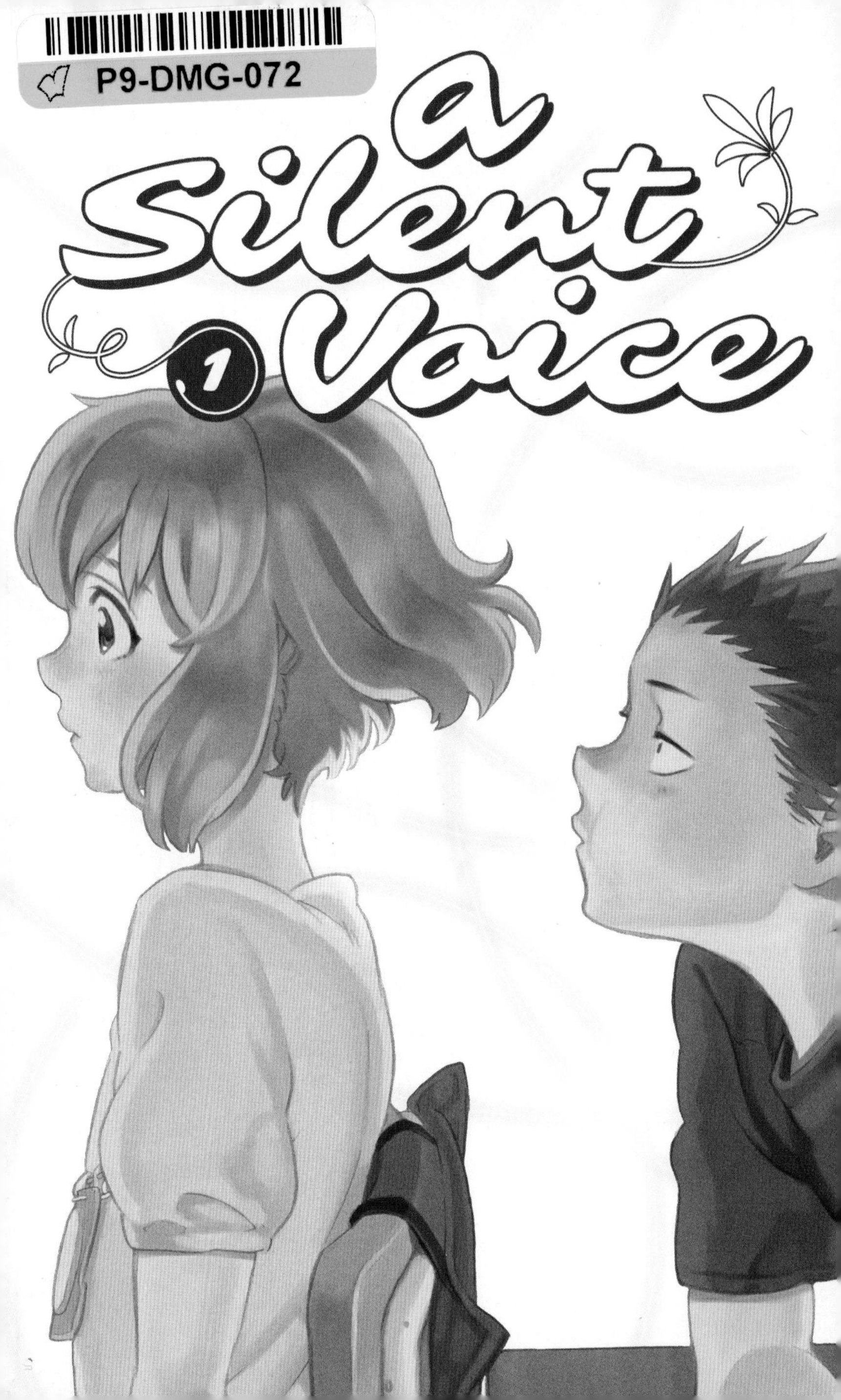

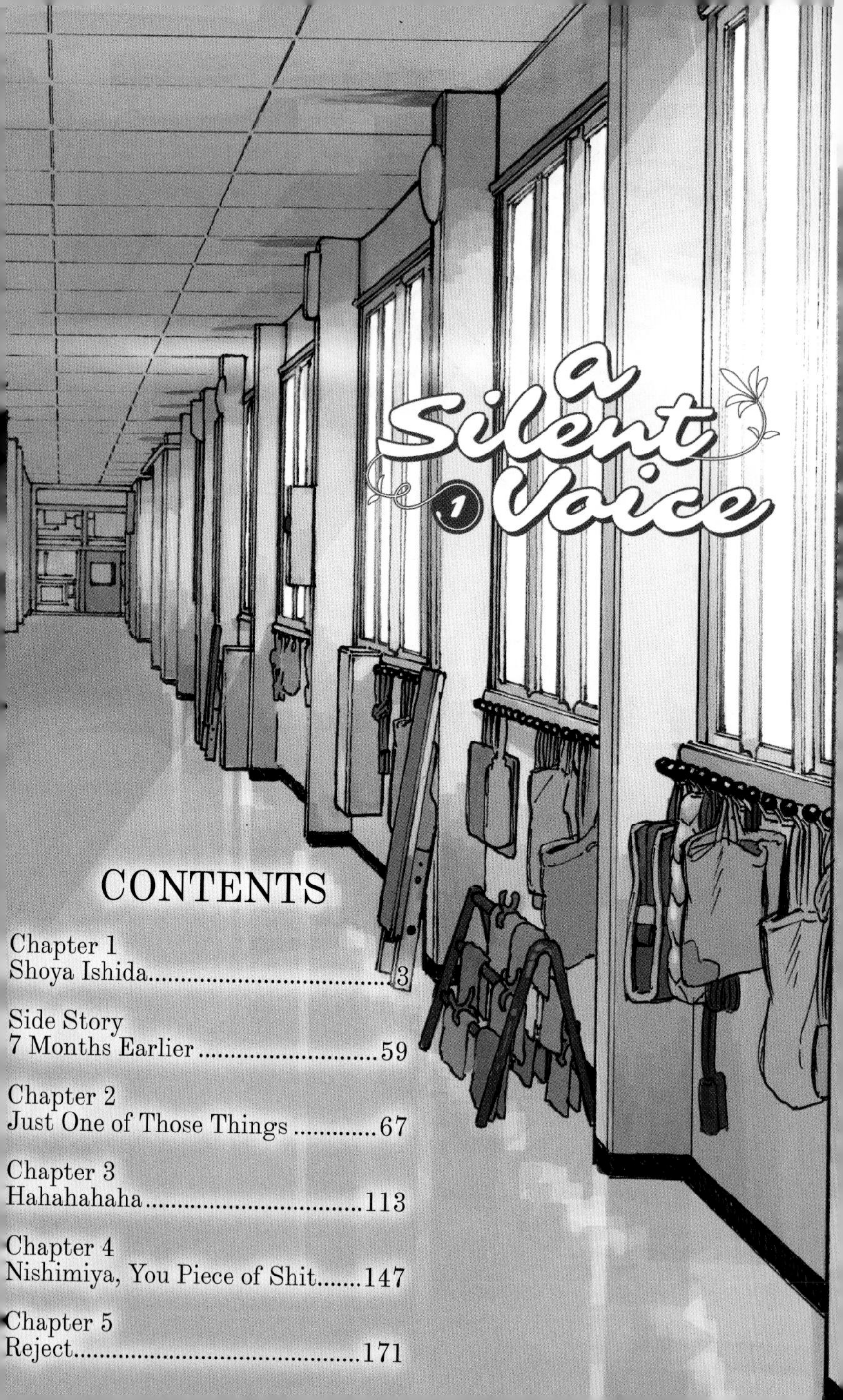
a Silent Voice
1

CONTENTS

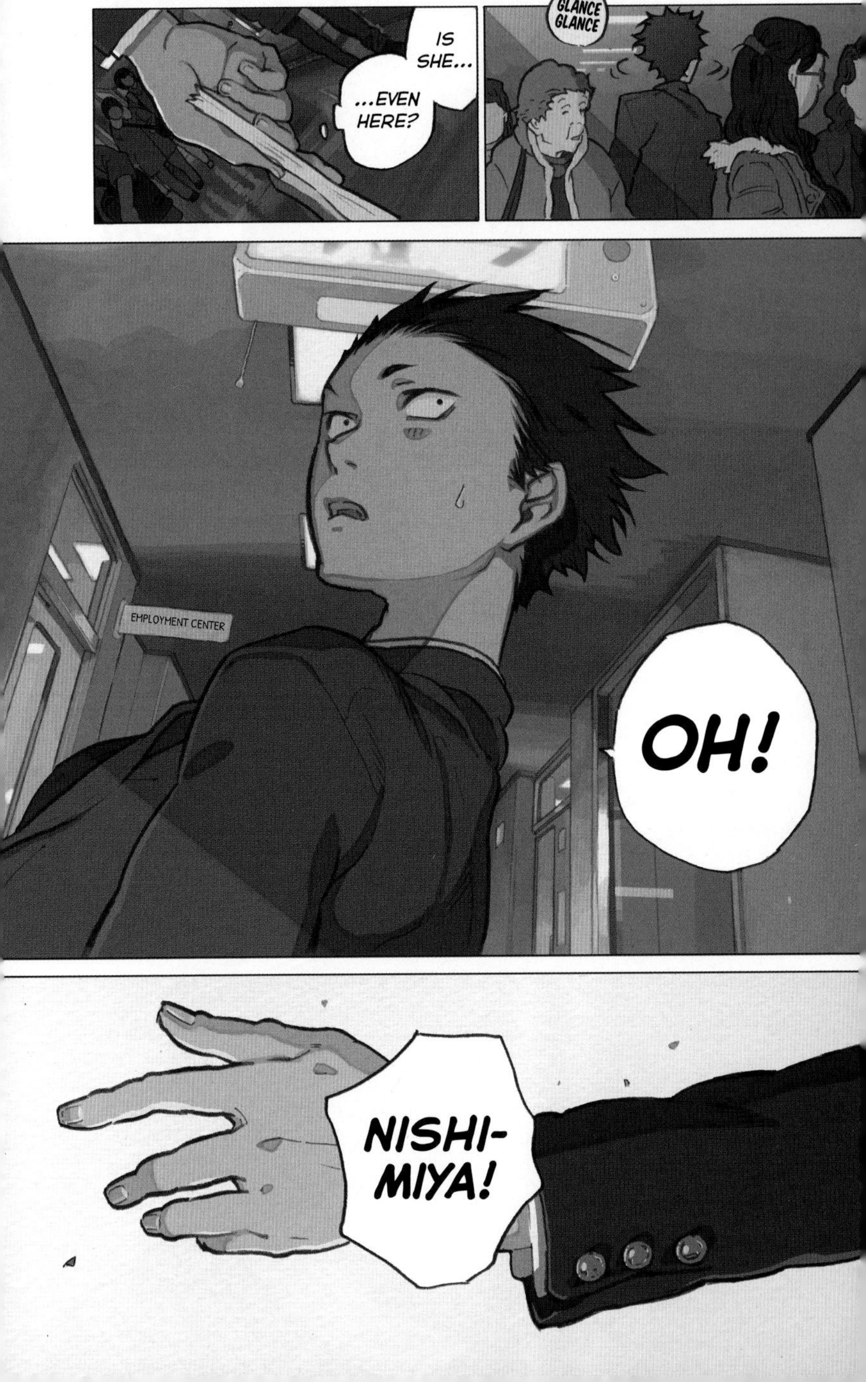
GLANCE GLANCE
IS SHE...
...EVEN HERE?
EMPLOYMENT CENTER
OH!
NISHI-MIYA!

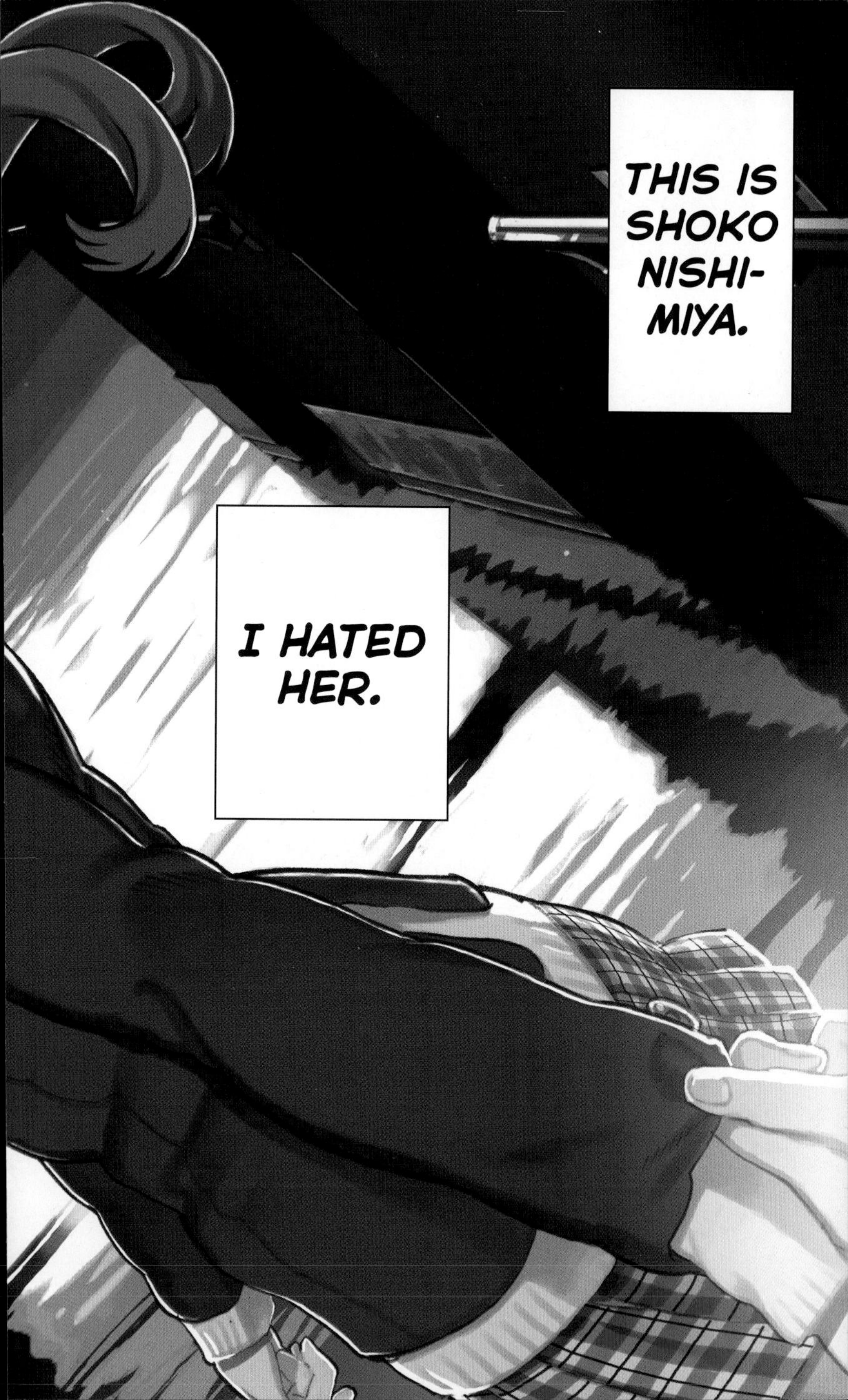
THIS IS SHOKO NISHI-MIYA.
I HATED HER.

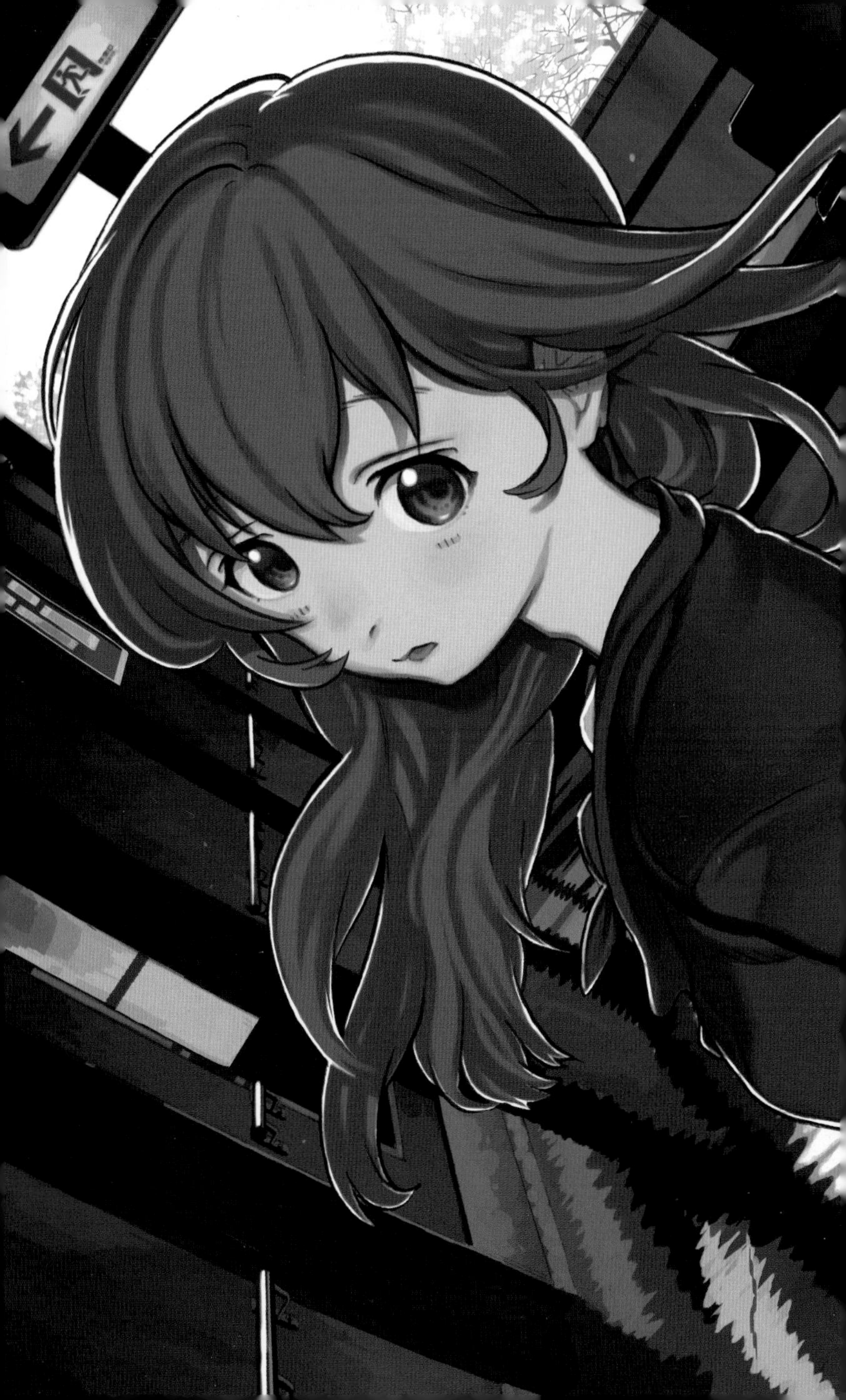

a Silent Voice

CHAPTER 1: SHOYA ISHIDA

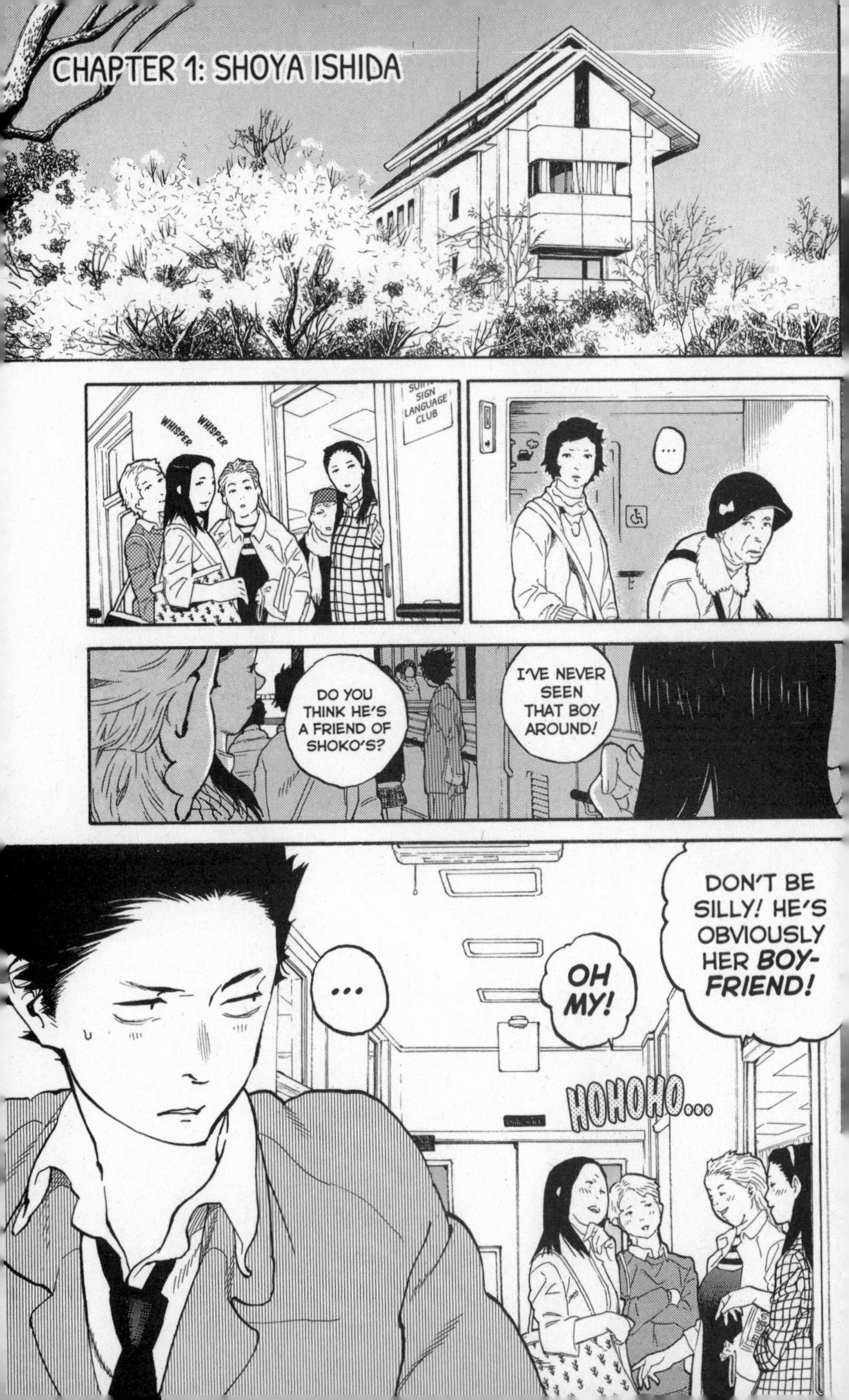

...
WHISPER
WHISPER
SIGN LANGUAGE CLUB
I'VE NEVER SEEN THAT BOY AROUND!
DO YOU THINK HE'S A FRIEND OF SHOKO'S?
DON'T BE SILLY! HE'S OBVIOUSLY HER BOY-FRIEND!
OH MY!
HOHOHO...
...

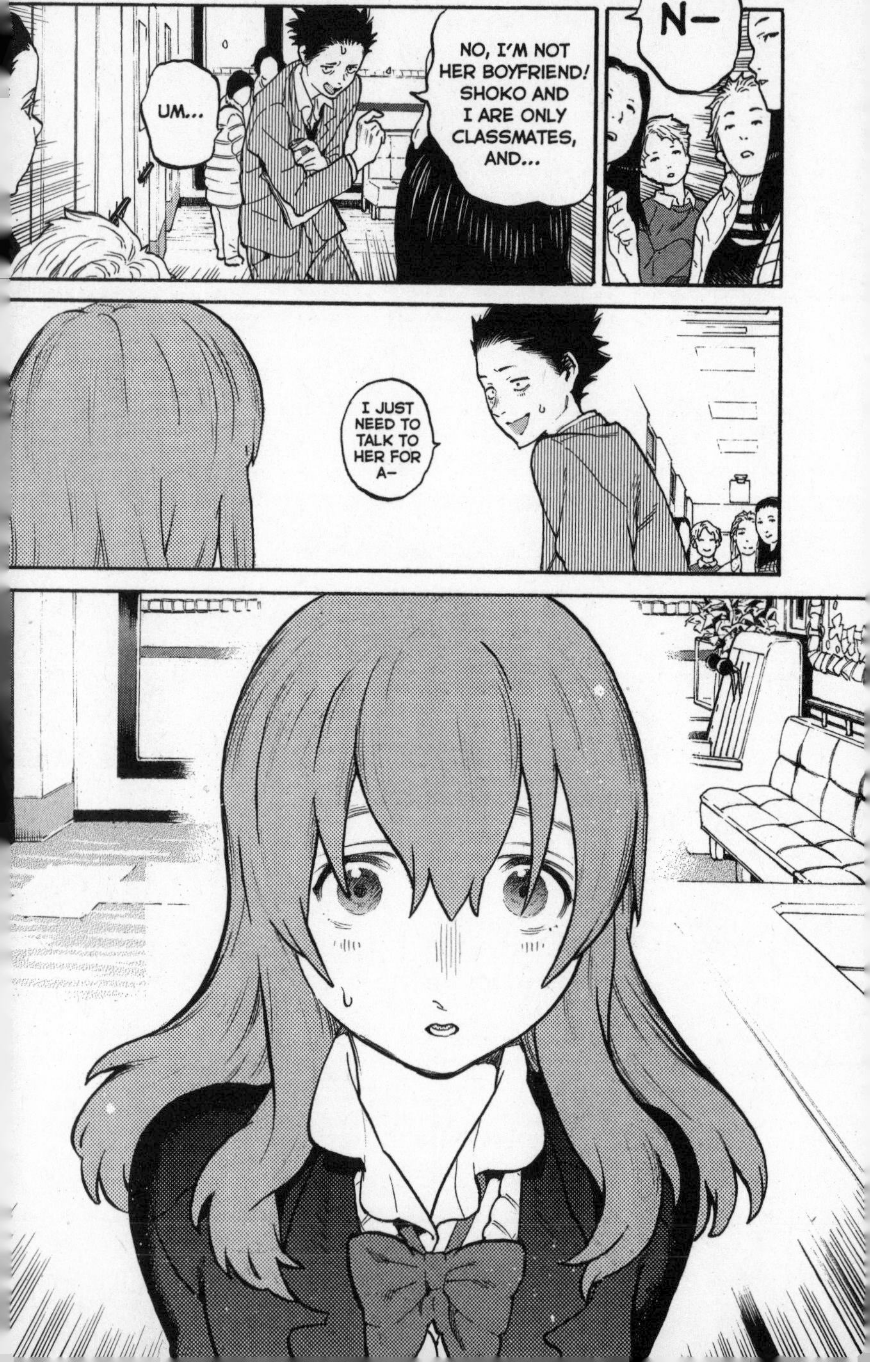
N-
NO, I'M NOT HER BOYFRIEND! SHOKO AND I ARE ONLY CLASSMATES, AND...
UM...
I JUST NEED TO TALK TO HER FOR A-

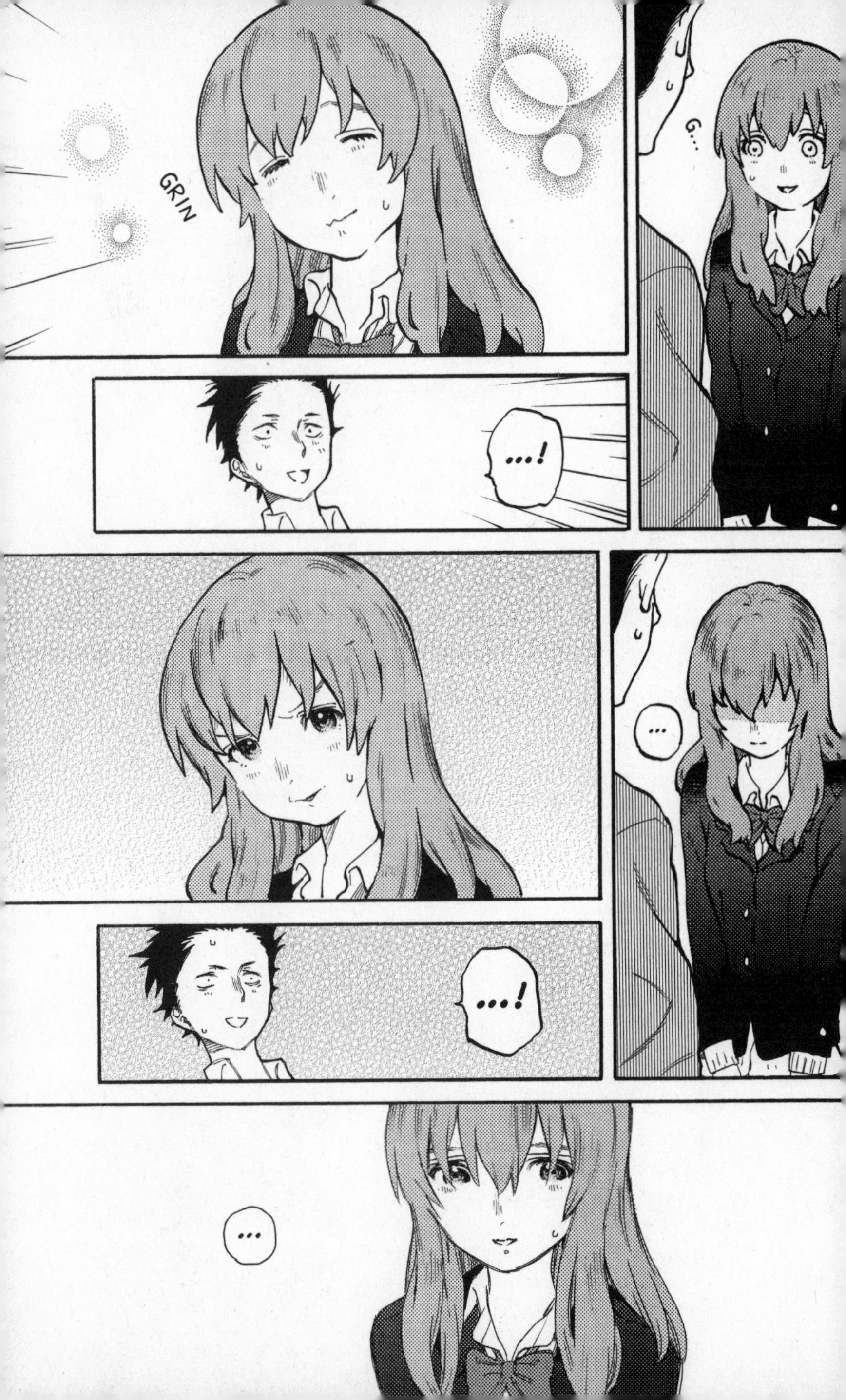
G...
GRIN
...!
...
...!
...

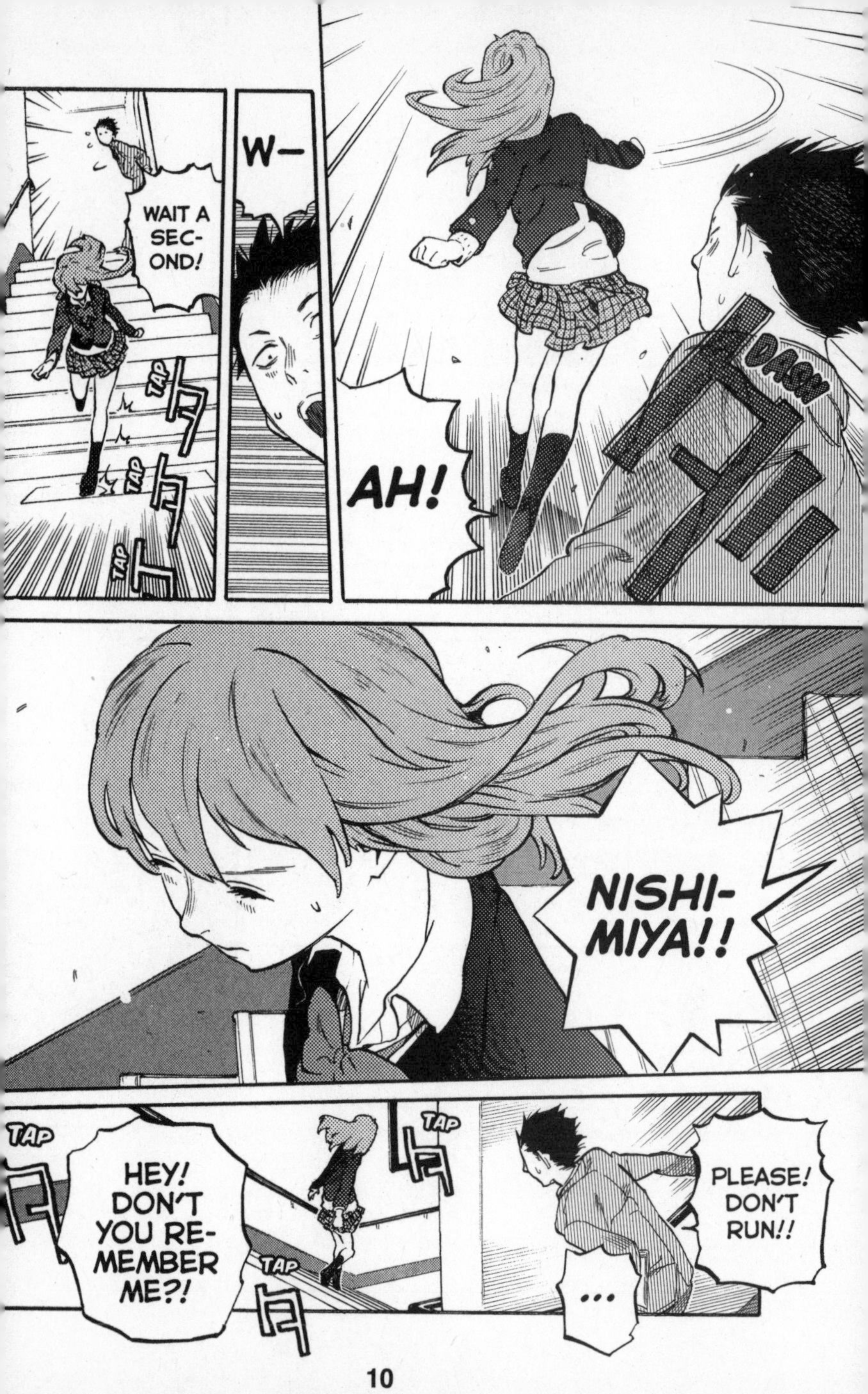
DASH
AH!
W—
WAIT A SEC- OND!
TAP
TAP
TAP
NISHI- MIYA!!
PLEASE! DON'T RUN!!
...
TAP
TAP
HEY! DON'T YOU RE- MEMBER ME?!
TAP

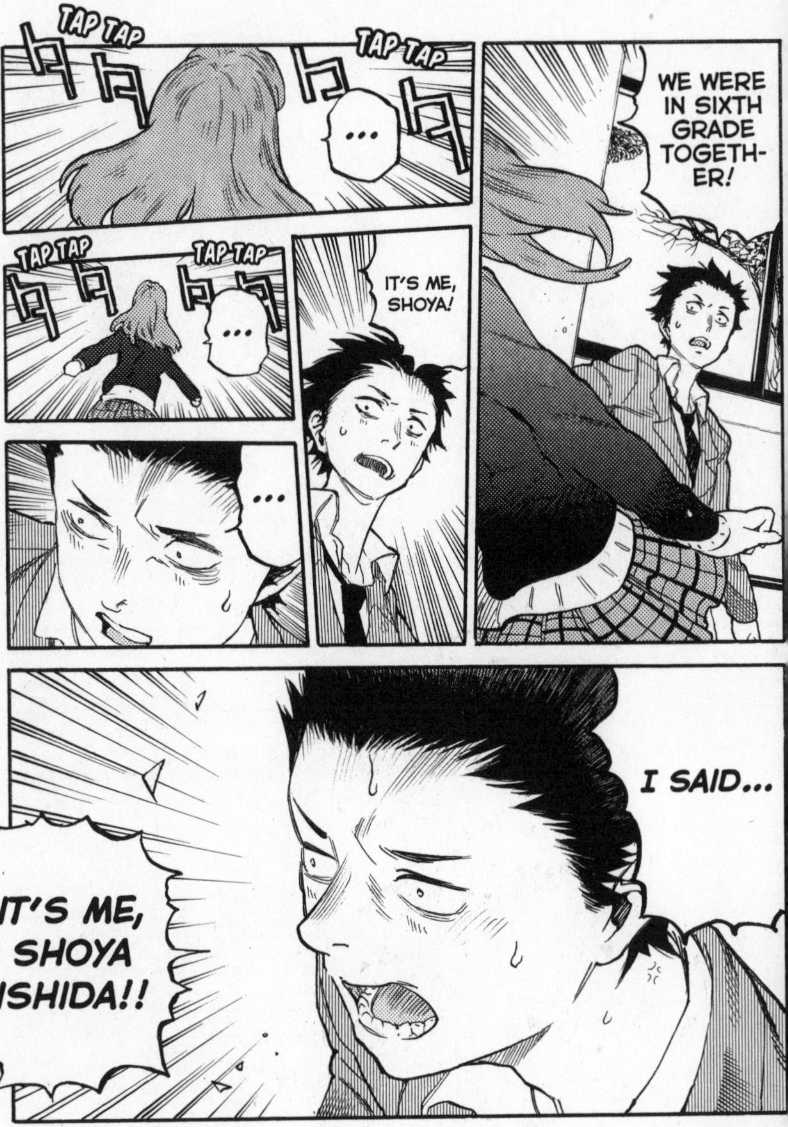
WE WERE IN SIXTH GRADE TOGETH-ER!
TAP TAP
...
TAP TAP
IT'S ME, SHOYA!
TAP TAP
...
TAP TAP
...
I SAID...
IT'S ME, SHOYA ISHIDA!!

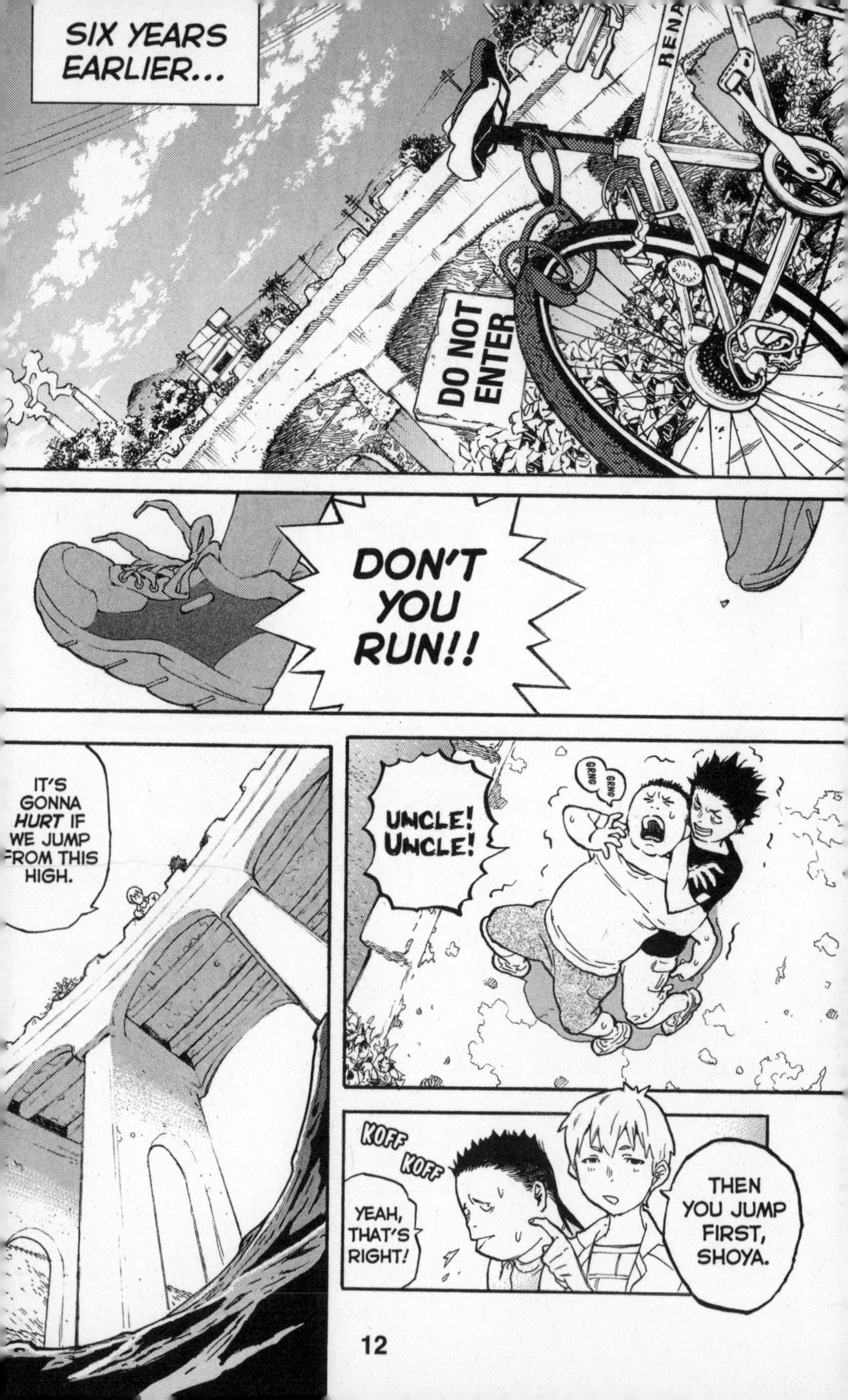
SIX YEARS EARLIER...
RENA
DO NOT ENTER
DON'T YOU RUN!!
GRNG GRNG
UNCLE! UNCLE!
THEN YOU JUMP FIRST, SHOYA.
KOFF KOFF
YEAH, THAT'S RIGHT!
IT'S GONNA *HURT* IF WE JUMP FROM THIS HIGH.

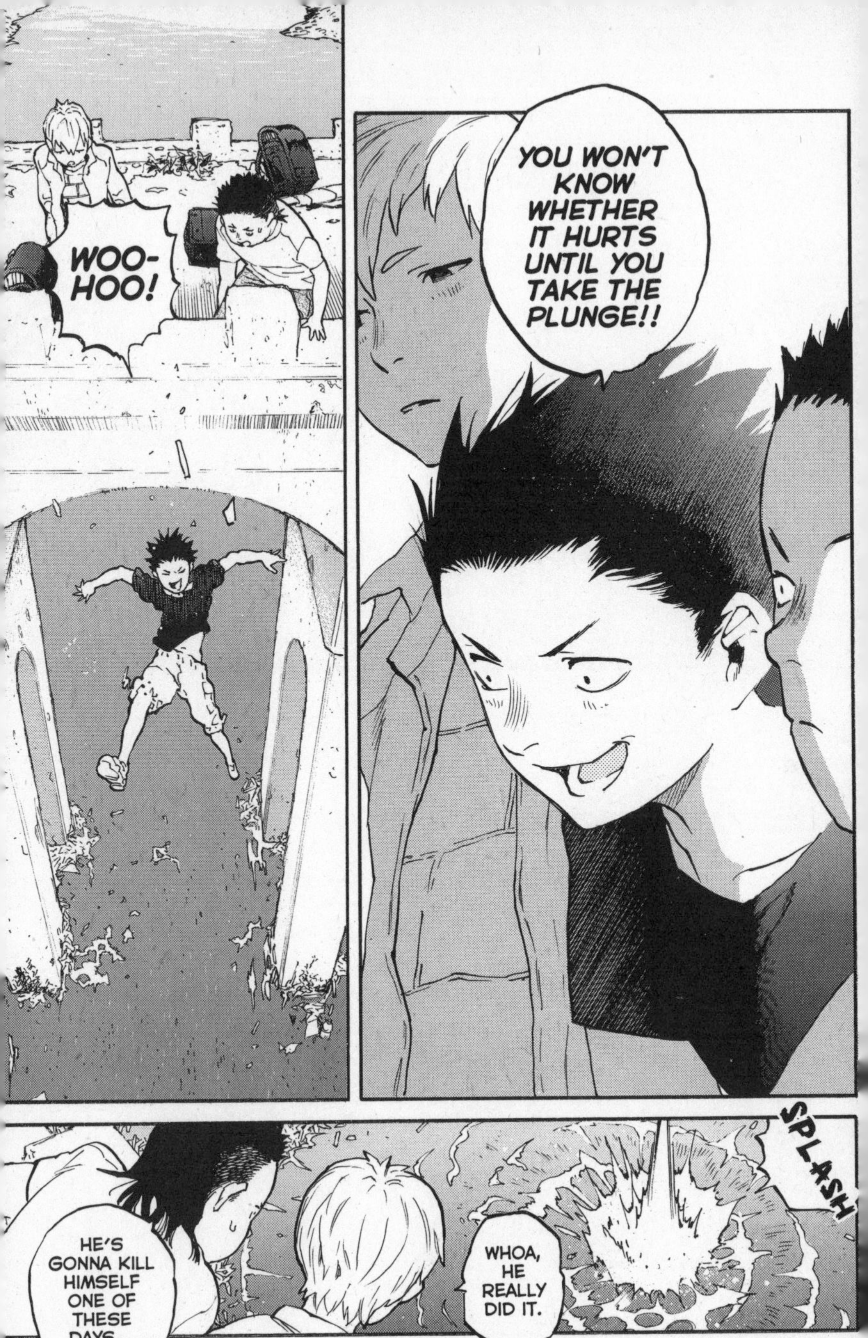
YOU WON'T KNOW WHETHER IT HURTS UNTIL YOU TAKE THE PLUNGE!!
WOO-HOO!
SPLASH
WHOA, HE REALLY DID IT.
HE'S GONNA KILL HIMSELF ONE OF THESE DAYS...

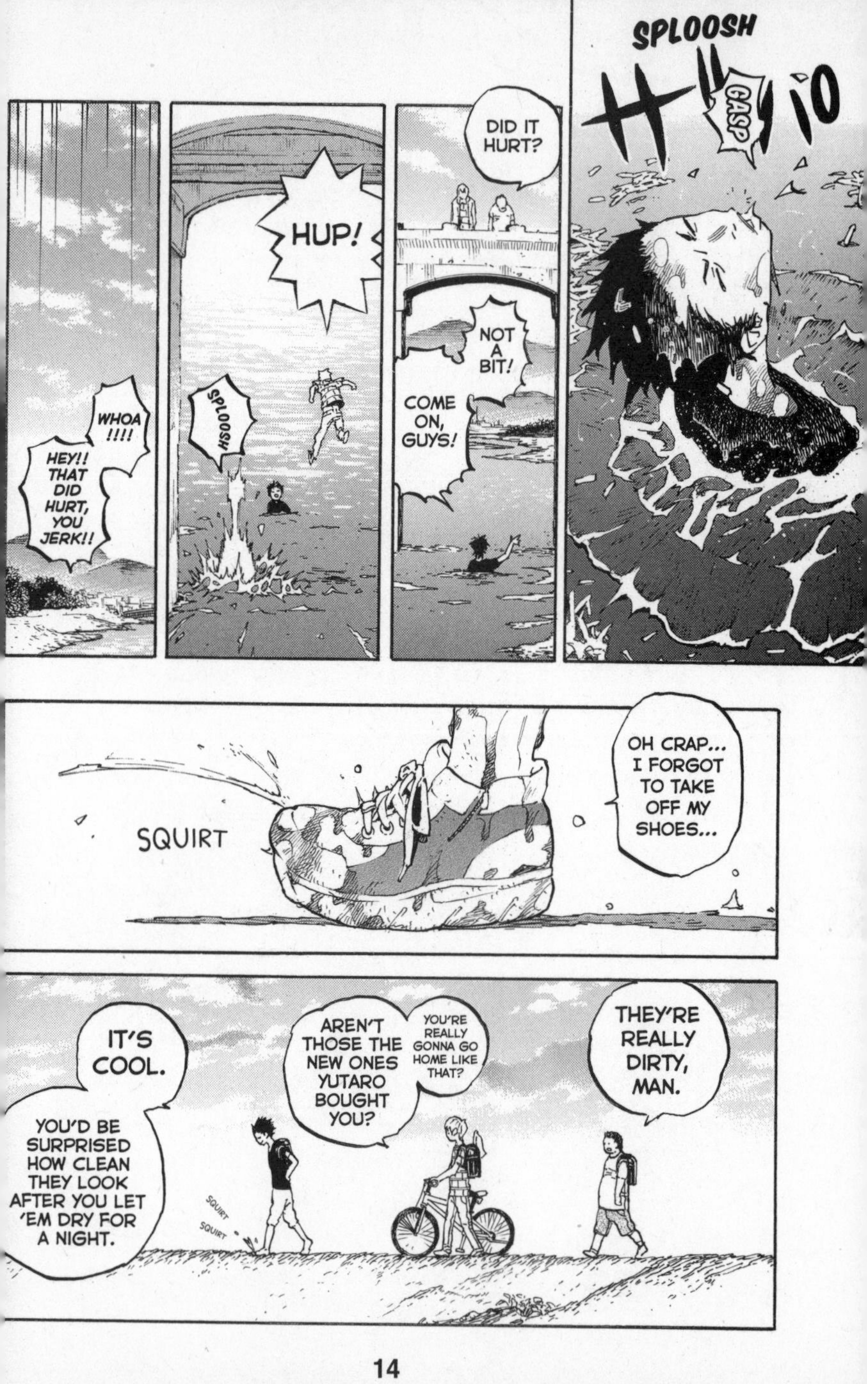
SPLOOSH
GASP
DID IT HURT?
NOT A BIT!
COME ON, GUYS!
HUP!
SPLOOSH
WHOA !!!!
HEY!! THAT DID HURT, YOU JERK!!
OH CRAP... I FORGOT TO TAKE OFF MY SHOES...
SQUIRT
THEY'RE REALLY DIRTY, MAN.
YOU'RE REALLY GONNA GO HOME LIKE THAT?
AREN'T THOSE THE NEW ONES YUTARO BOUGHT YOU?
IT'S COOL.
YOU'D BE SURPRISED HOW CLEAN THEY LOOK AFTER YOU LET 'EM DRY FOR A NIGHT.
SQUIRT
SQUIRT

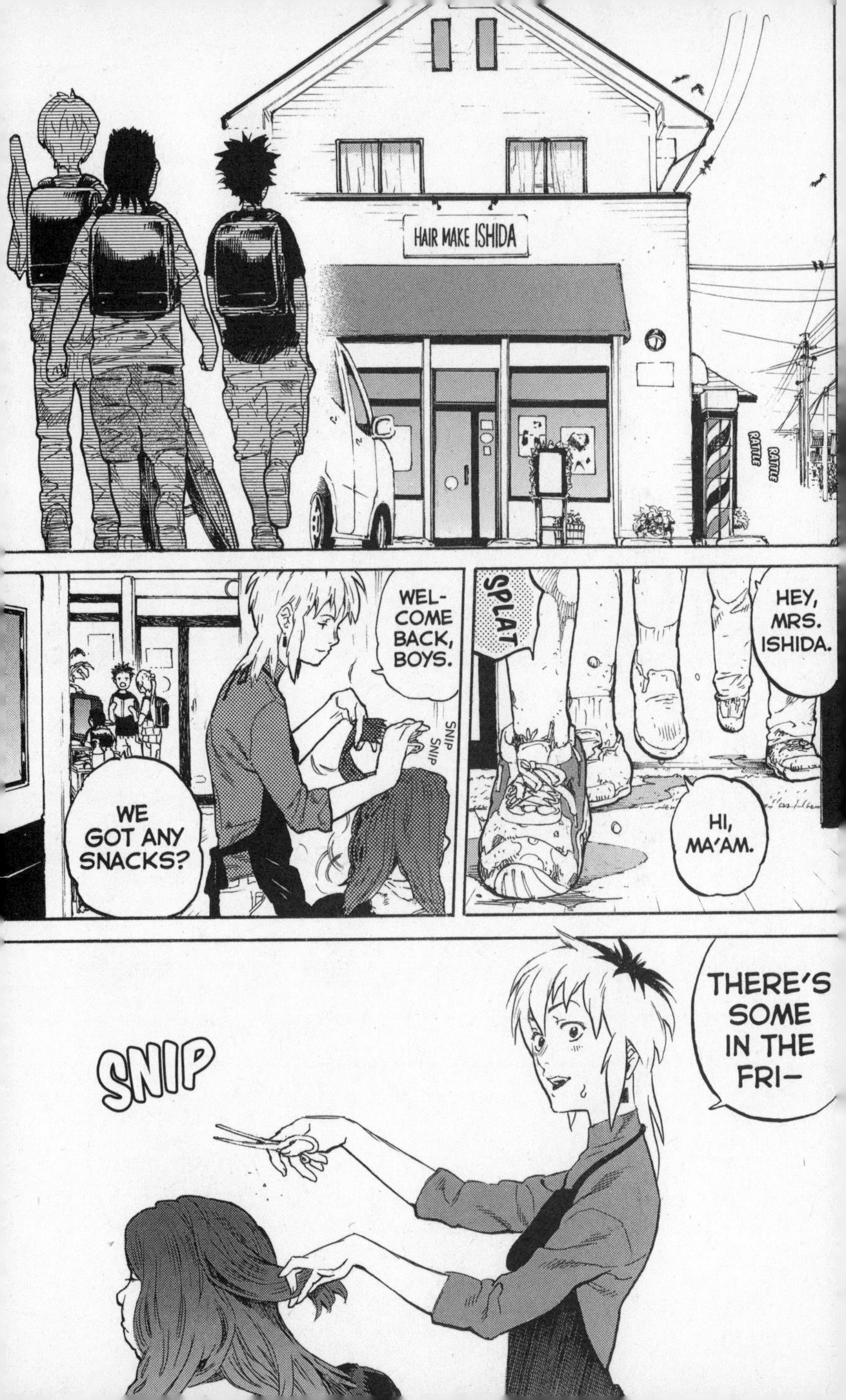

HAIR MAKE ISHIDA
RATTLE RATTLE
HEY, MRS. ISHIDA.
SPLAT
HI, MA'AM.
WEL-COME BACK, BOYS.
SNIP SNIP
WE GOT ANY SNACKS?
THERE'S SOME IN THE FRI-
SNIP

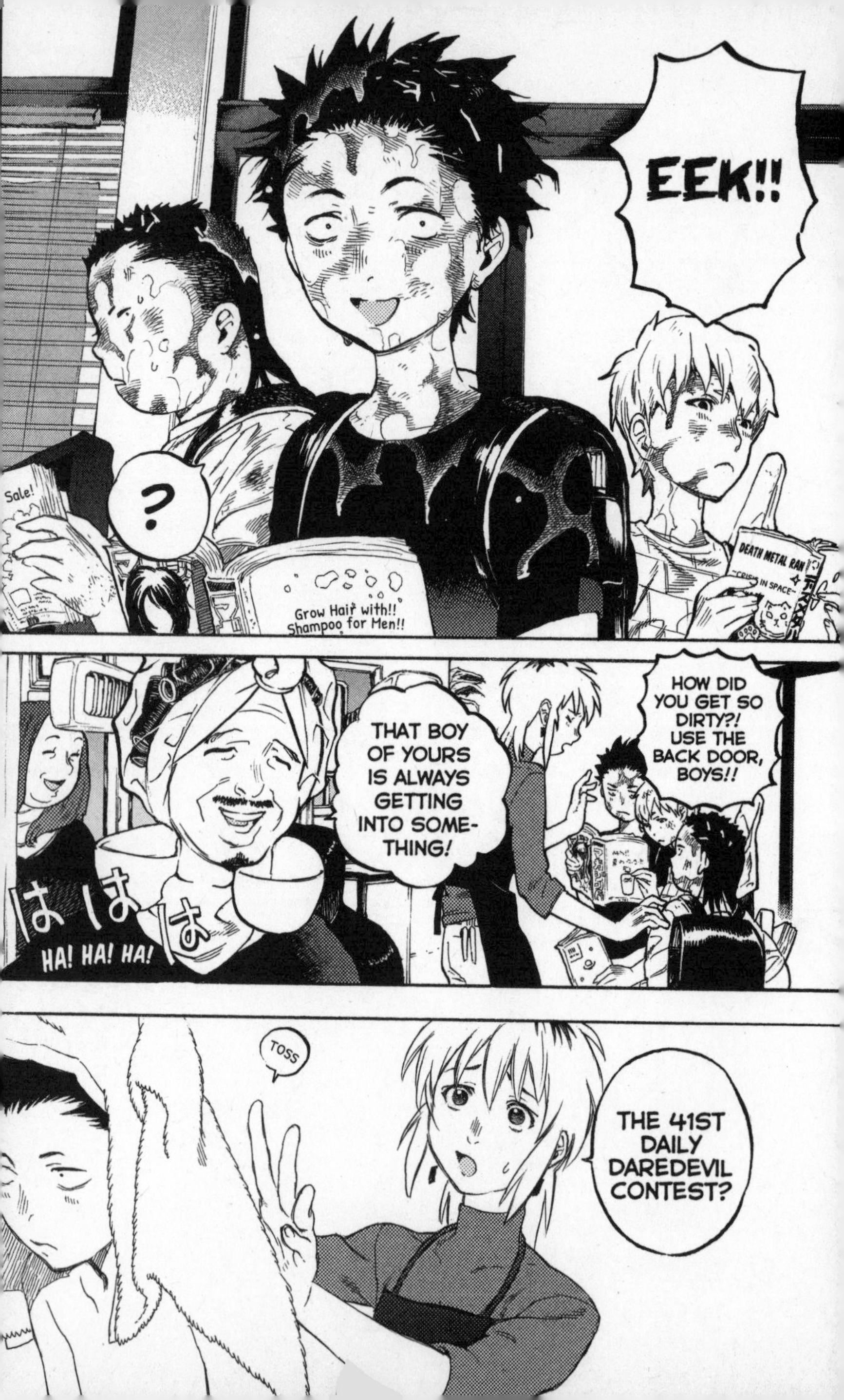
EEK!!
DEATH METAL RAN
Grow Hair with!! Shampoo for Men!!
?
Sale!
HOW DID YOU GET SO DIRTY?! USE THE BACK DOOR, BOYS!!
THAT BOY OF YOURS IS ALWAYS GETTING INTO SOME-THING!
はははは
HA! HA! HA!
THE 41ST DAILY DAREDEVIL CONTEST?
TOSS

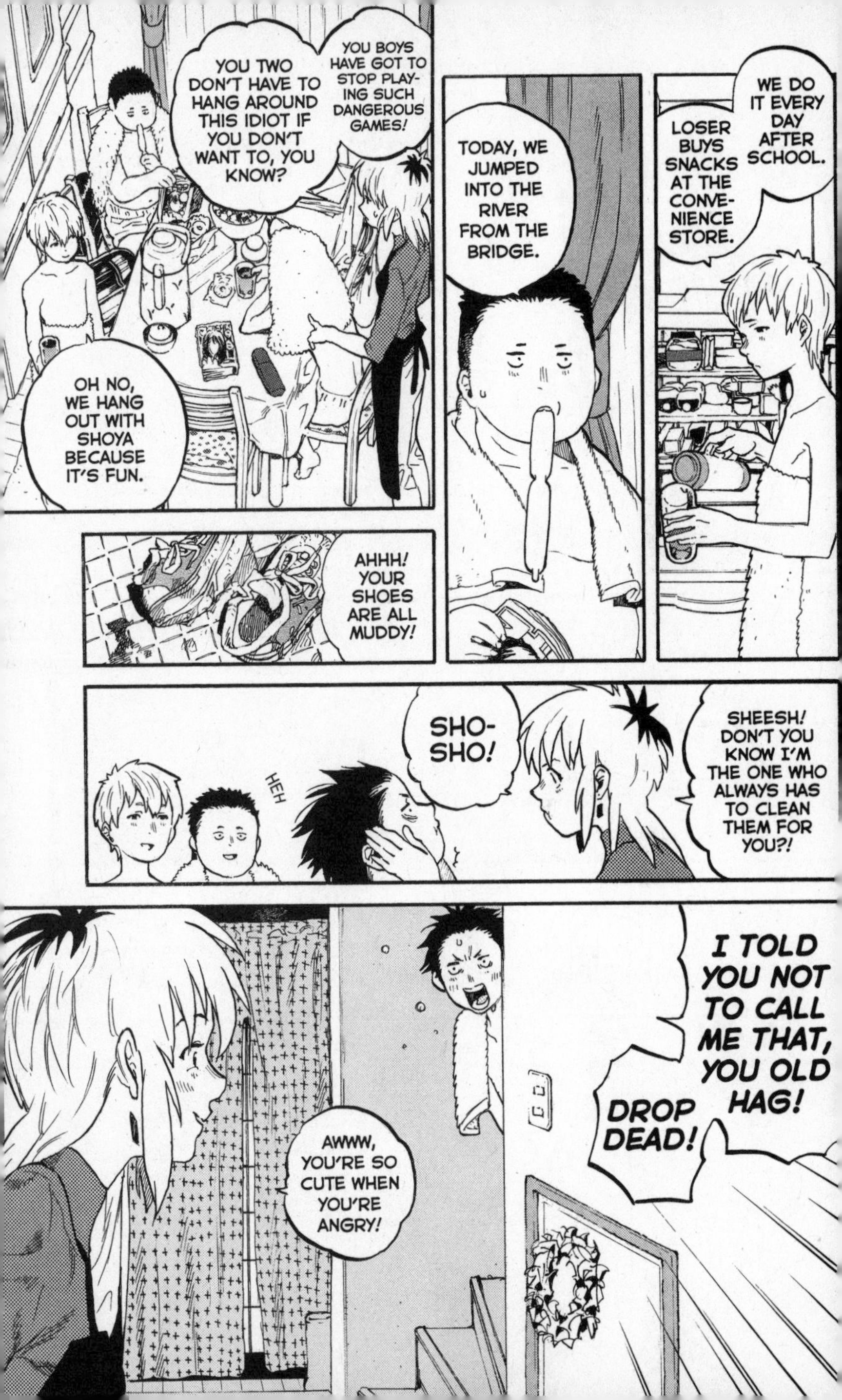

WE DO IT EVERY DAY AFTER SCHOOL.
LOSER BUYS SNACKS AT THE CONVE-NIENCE STORE.
TODAY, WE JUMPED INTO THE RIVER FROM THE BRIDGE.
YOU BOYS HAVE GOT TO STOP PLAY-ING SUCH DANGEROUS GAMES!
YOU TWO DON'T HAVE TO HANG AROUND THIS IDIOT IF YOU DON'T WANT TO, YOU KNOW?
OH NO, WE HANG OUT WITH SHOYA BECAUSE IT'S FUN.
AHHH! YOUR SHOES ARE ALL MUDDY!
SHEESH! DON'T YOU KNOW I'M THE ONE WHO ALWAYS HAS TO CLEAN THEM FOR YOU?!
SHO-SHO!
HEH
I TOLD YOU NOT TO CALL ME THAT, YOU OLD HAG!
DROP DEAD!
AWWW, YOU'RE SO CUTE WHEN YOU'RE ANGRY!

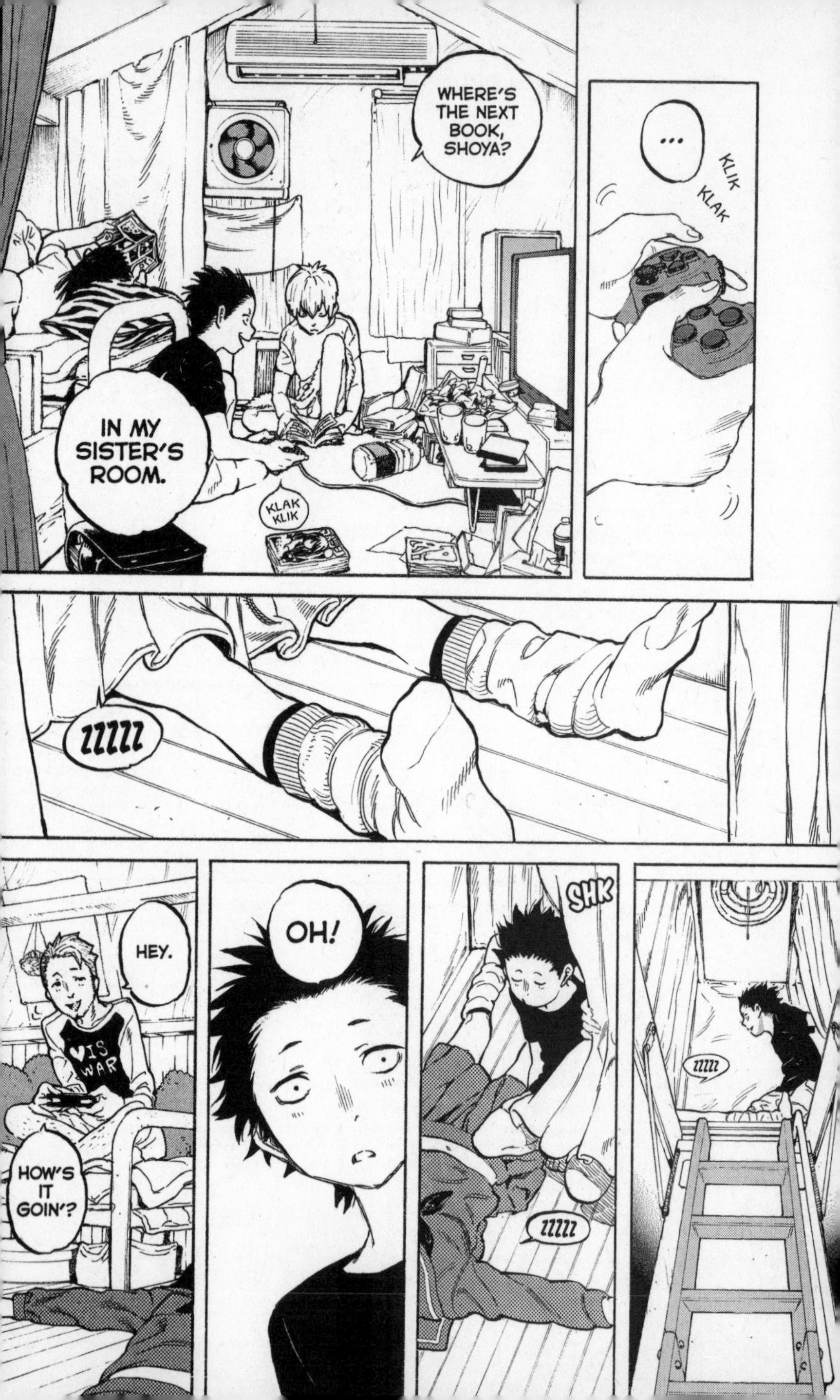
...
KLIK
KLAK
WHERE'S THE NEXT BOOK, SHOYA?
IN MY SISTER'S ROOM.
KLAK KLIK
ZZZZZ
ZZZZZ
SHK
ZZZZZ
OH!
HEY.
HOW'S IT GOIN'?

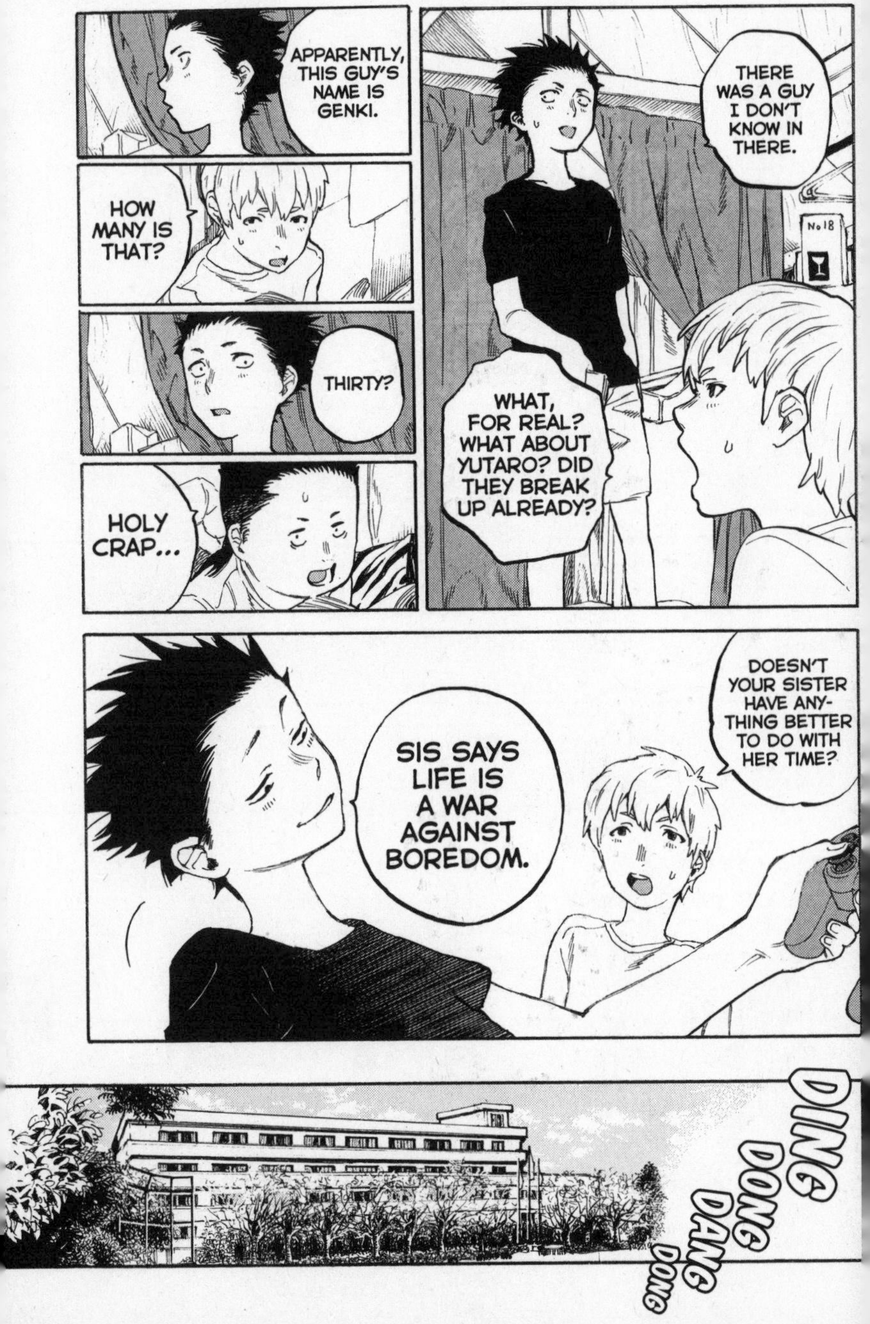
THERE WAS A GUY I DON'T KNOW IN THERE.
WHAT, FOR REAL? WHAT ABOUT YUTARO? DID THEY BREAK UP ALREADY?
No18
APPARENTLY, THIS GUY'S NAME IS GENKI.
HOW MANY IS THAT?
THIRTY?
HOLY CRAP...
DOESN'T YOUR SISTER HAVE ANY-THING BETTER TO DO WITH HER TIME?
SIS SAYS LIFE IS A WAR AGAINST BOREDOM.
DING DONG DANG DONG

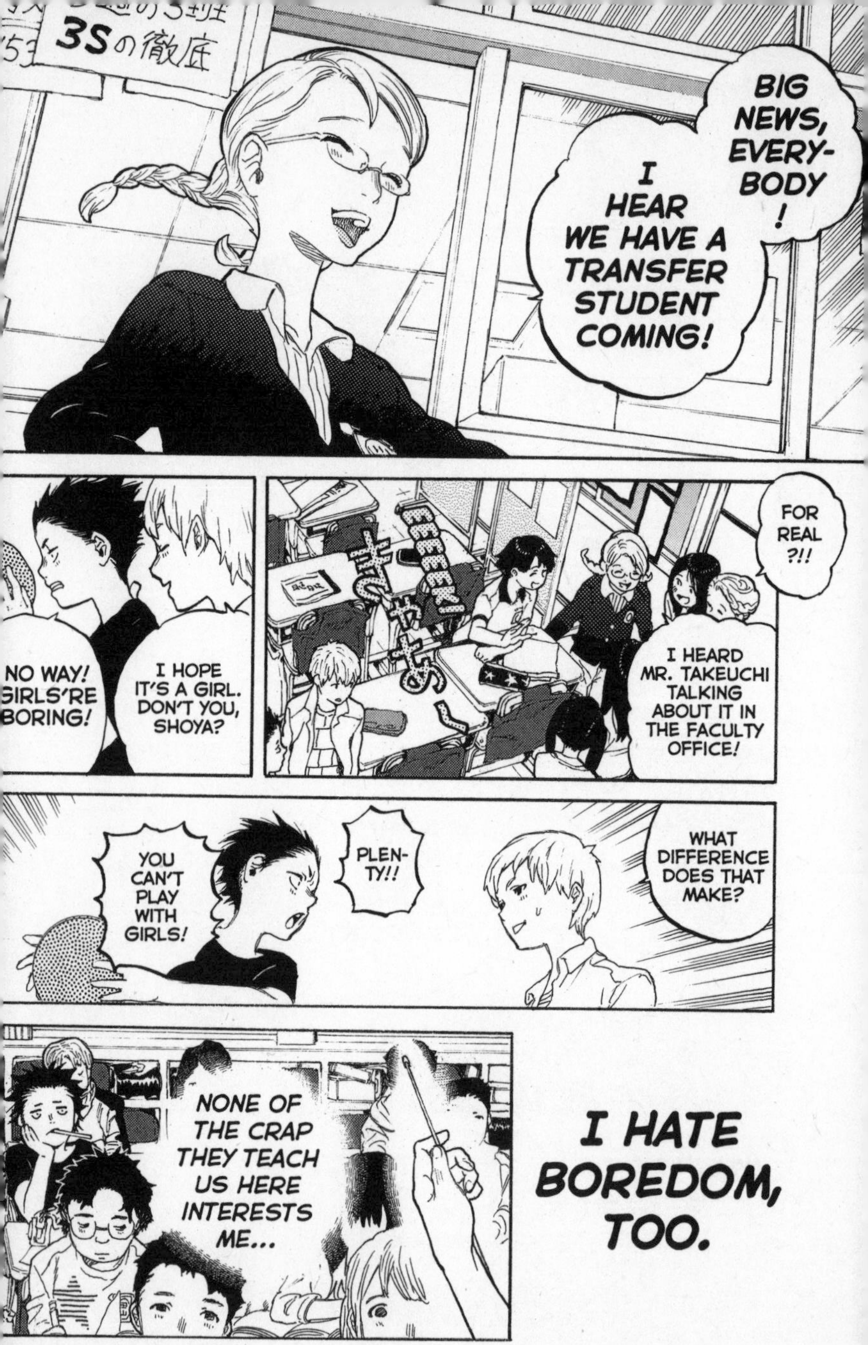
3Sの徹底
BIG NEWS, EVERYBODY!
I HEAR WE HAVE A TRANSFER STUDENT COMING!
FOR REAL?!!
I HEARD MR. TAKEUCHI TALKING ABOUT IT IN THE FACULTY OFFICE!
EEEEK!
きゃあ〜
I HOPE IT'S A GIRL. DON'T YOU, SHOYA?
NO WAY! GIRLS'RE BORING!
WHAT DIFFERENCE DOES THAT MAKE?
PLENTY!!
YOU CAN'T PLAY WITH GIRLS!
I HATE BOREDOM, TOO.
NONE OF THE CRAP THEY TEACH US HERE INTERESTS ME...

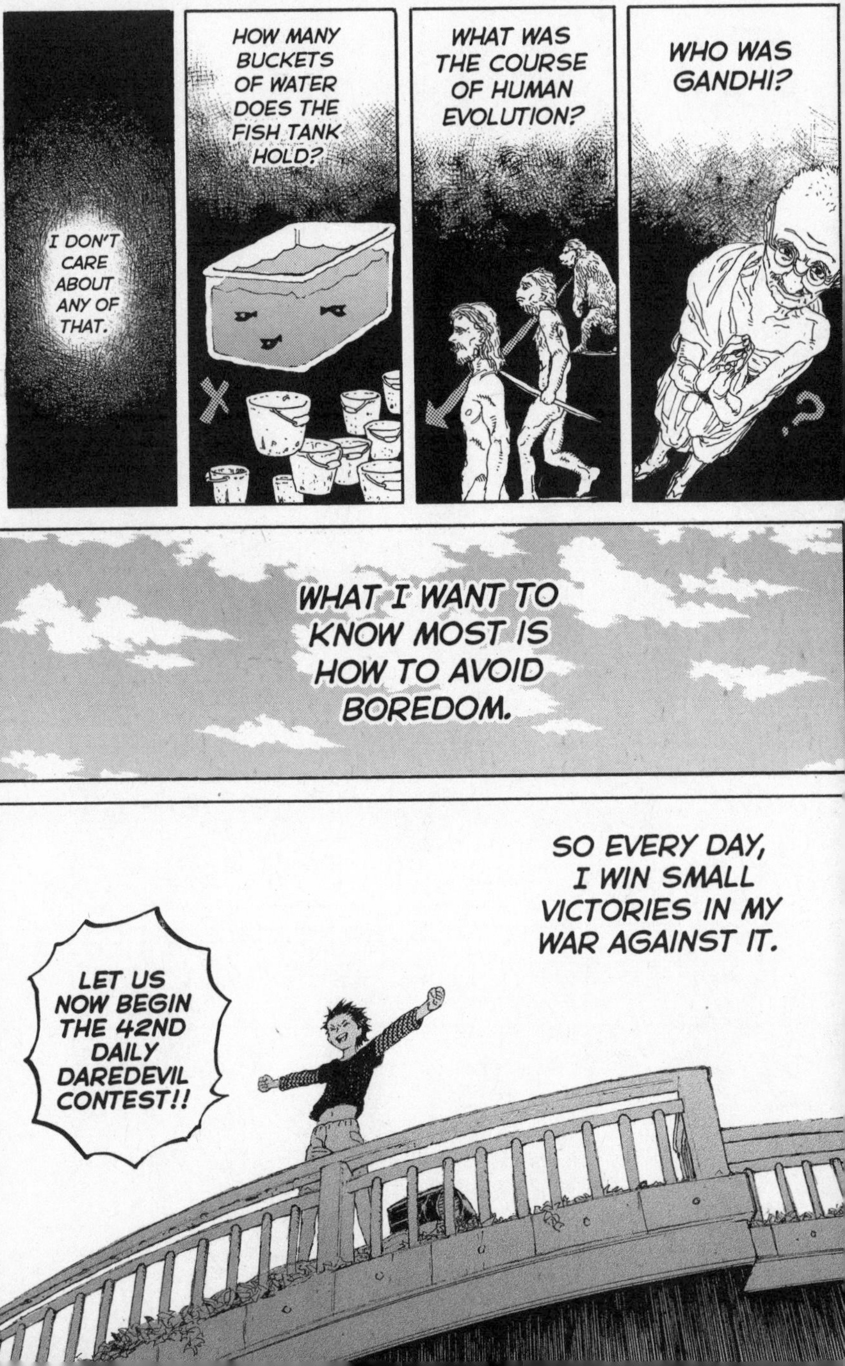
WHO WAS GANDHI?
WHAT WAS THE COURSE OF HUMAN EVOLUTION?
HOW MANY BUCKETS OF WATER DOES THE FISH TANK HOLD?
I DON'T CARE ABOUT ANY OF THAT.
WHAT I WANT TO KNOW MOST IS HOW TO AVOID BOREDOM.
SO EVERY DAY, I WIN SMALL VICTORIES IN MY WAR AGAINST IT.
LET US NOW BEGIN THE 42ND DAILY DAREDEVIL CONTEST!!

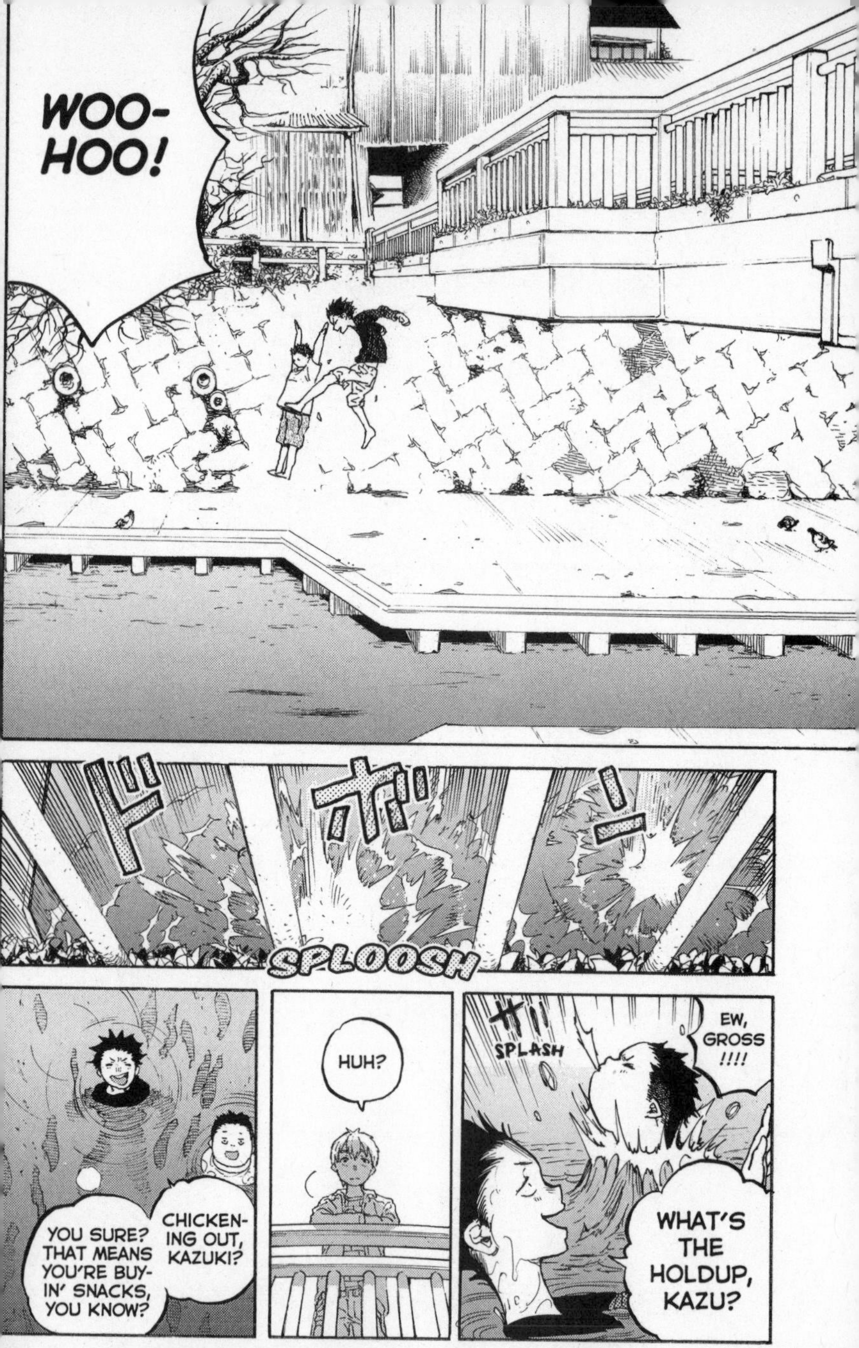
WOO-HOO!
ドボー
SPLOOSH
EW, GROSS!!!!
SPLASH
WHAT'S THE HOLDUP, KAZU?
HUH?
CHICKEN-ING OUT, KAZUKI?
YOU SURE? THAT MEANS YOU'RE BUY-IN' SNACKS, YOU KNOW?

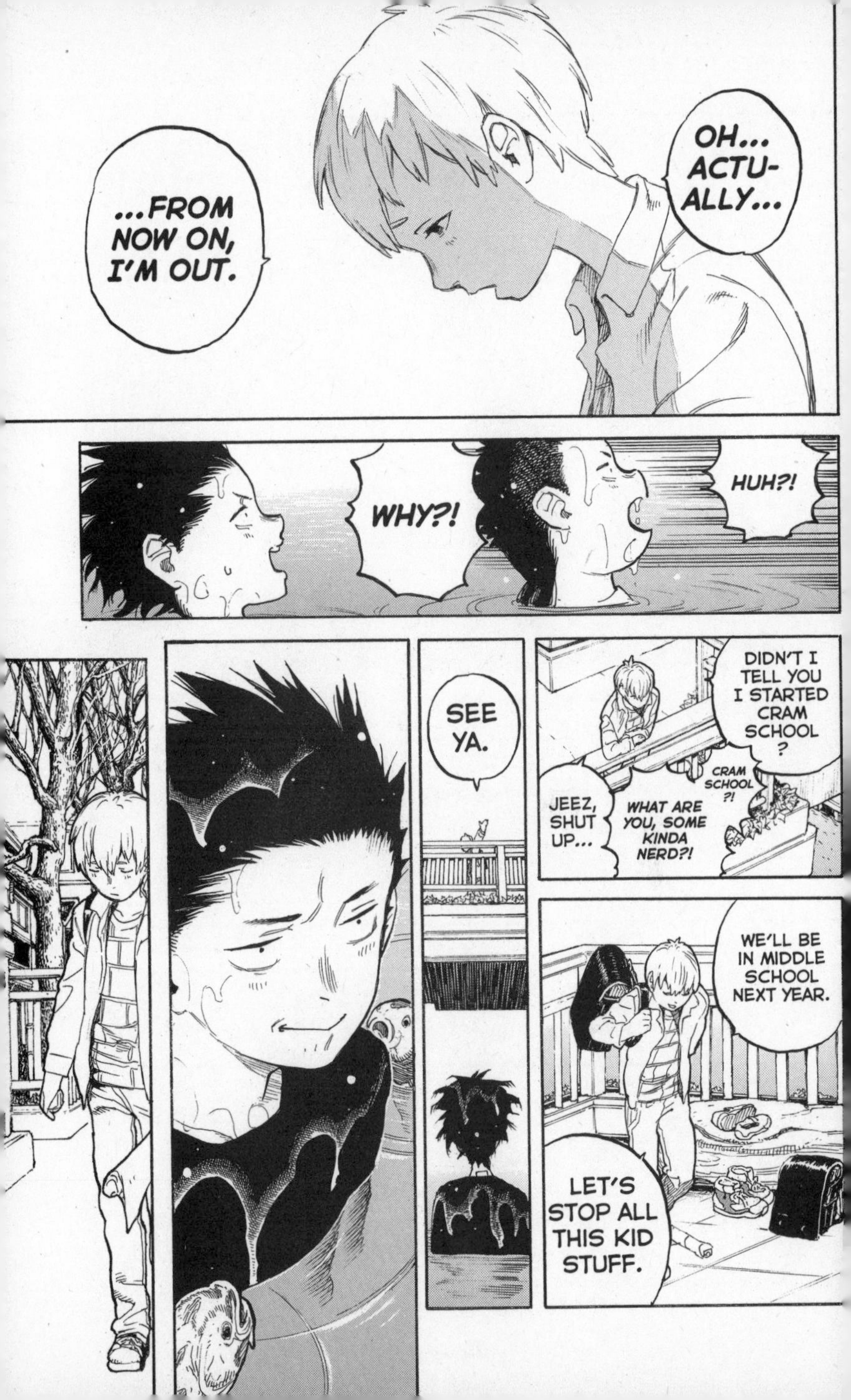
OH... ACTU-ALLY...
...FROM NOW ON, I'M OUT.
HUH?!
WHY?!
DIDN'T I TELL YOU I STARTED CRAM SCHOOL ?
CRAM SCHOOL ?!
WHAT ARE YOU, SOME KINDA NERD?!
JEEZ, SHUT UP...
WE'LL BE IN MIDDLE SCHOOL NEXT YEAR.
LET'S STOP ALL THIS KID STUFF.
SEE YA.

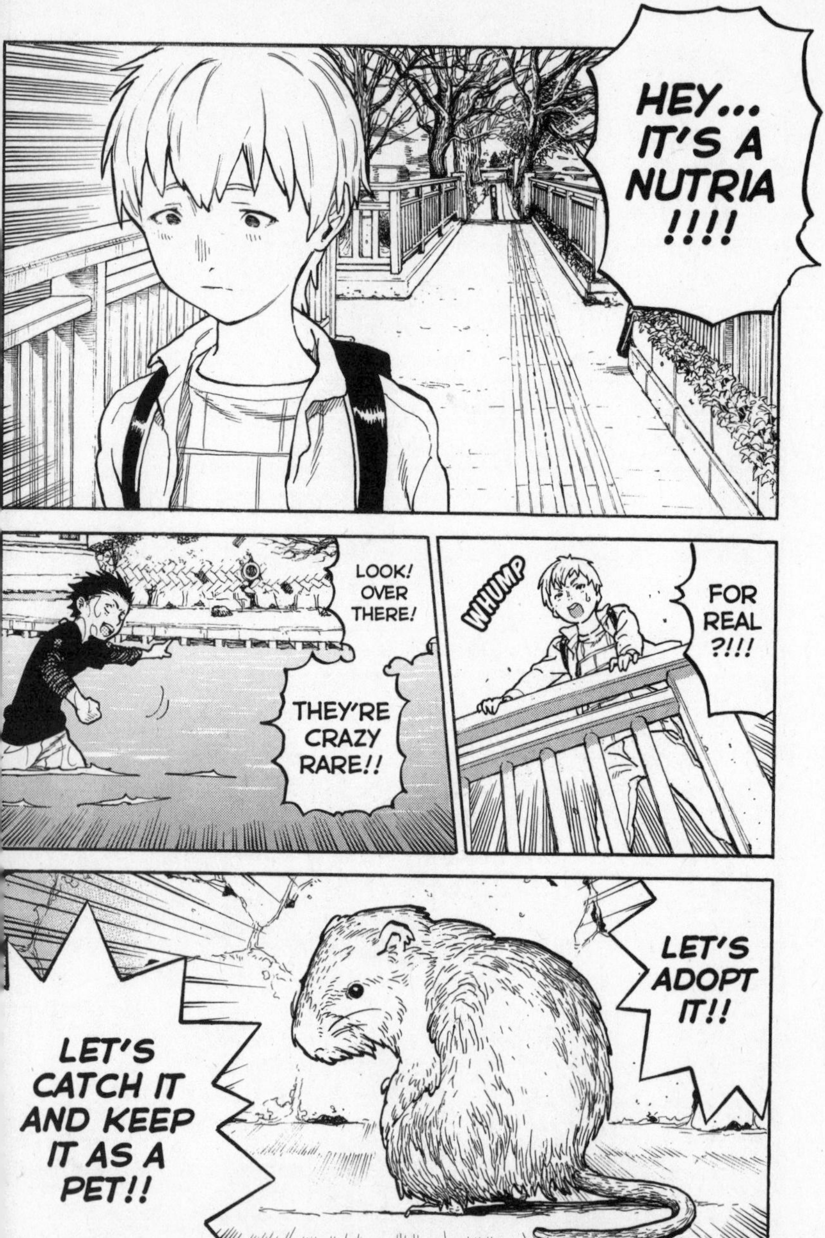
HEY... IT'S A NUTRIA !!!!
WHUMP
FOR REAL ?!!!
LOOK! OVER THERE!
THEY'RE CRAZY RARE!!
LET'S ADOPT IT!!
LET'S CATCH IT AND KEEP IT AS A PET!!

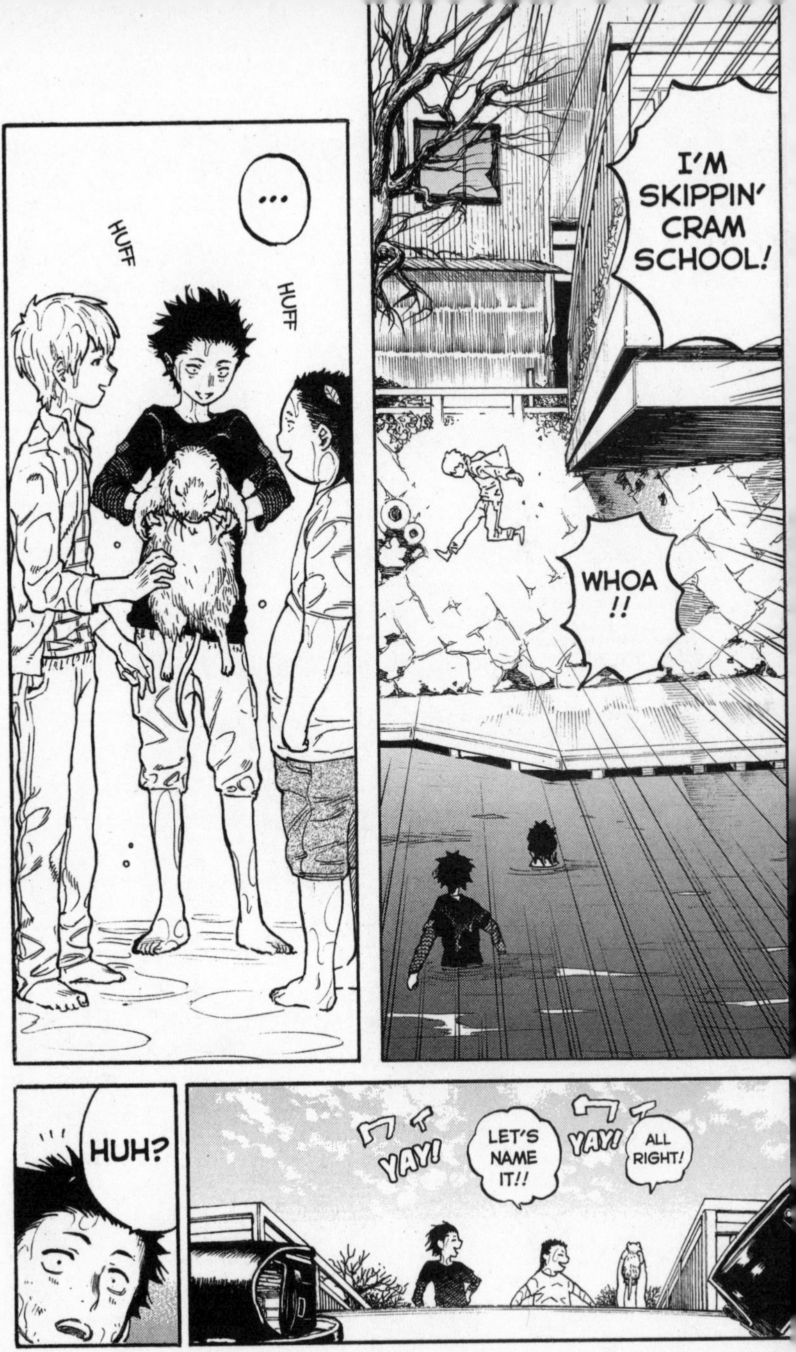
I'M SKIPPIN' CRAM SCHOOL!
WHOA !!
...
HUFF
HUFF
ALL RIGHT!
YAY!
LET'S NAME IT!!
YAY!
HUH?

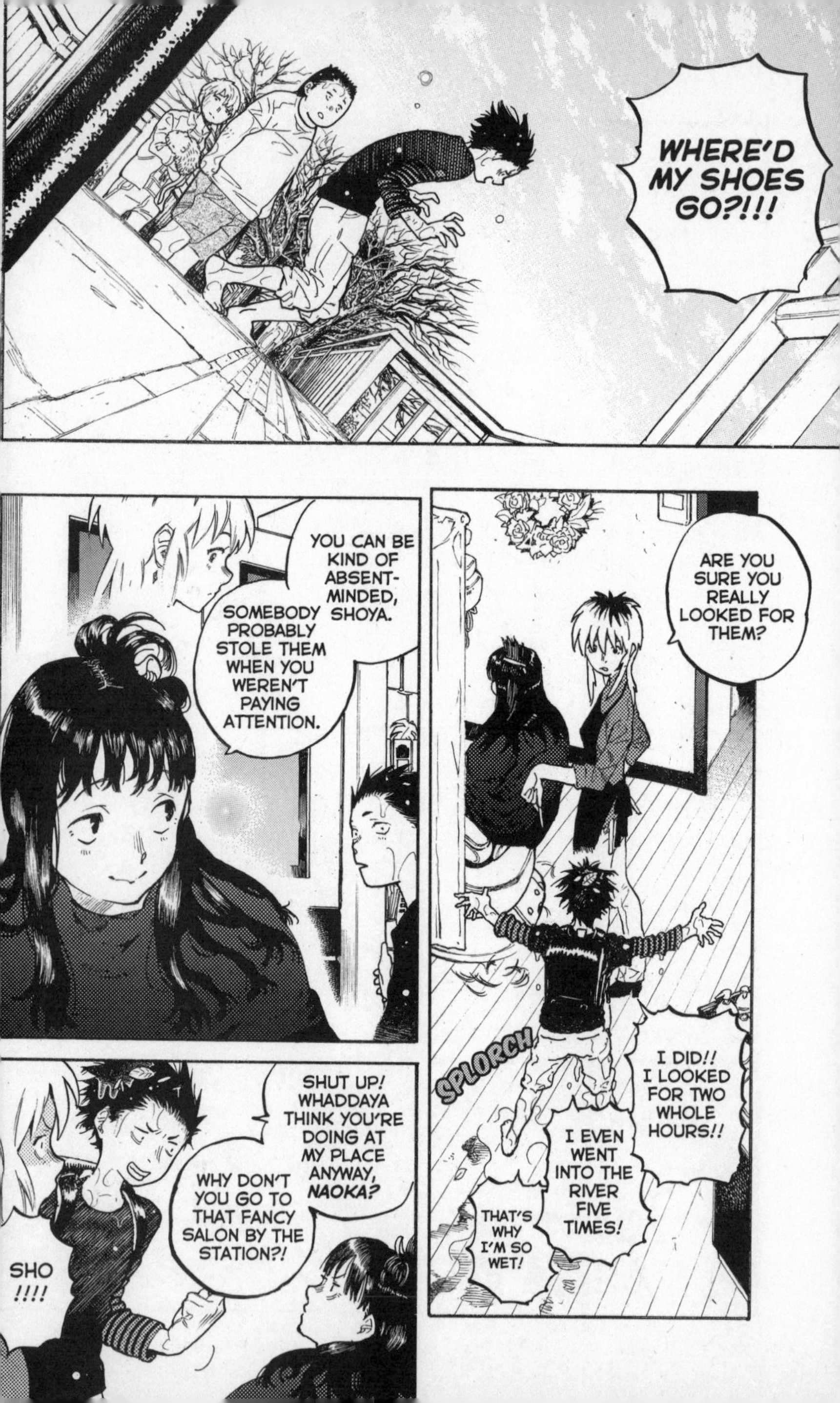
WHERE'D MY SHOES GO?!!!
ARE YOU SURE YOU REALLY LOOKED FOR THEM?
SPLORCH
I DID!! I LOOKED FOR TWO WHOLE HOURS!!
I EVEN WENT INTO THE RIVER FIVE TIMES!
THAT'S WHY I'M SO WET!
YOU CAN BE KIND OF ABSENT-MINDED, SHOYA.
SOMEBODY PROBABLY STOLE THEM WHEN YOU WEREN'T PAYING ATTENTION.
SHUT UP! WHADDAYA THINK YOU'RE DOING AT MY PLACE ANYWAY, *NAOKA?*
WHY DON'T YOU GO TO THAT FANCY SALON BY THE STATION?!
SHO !!!!

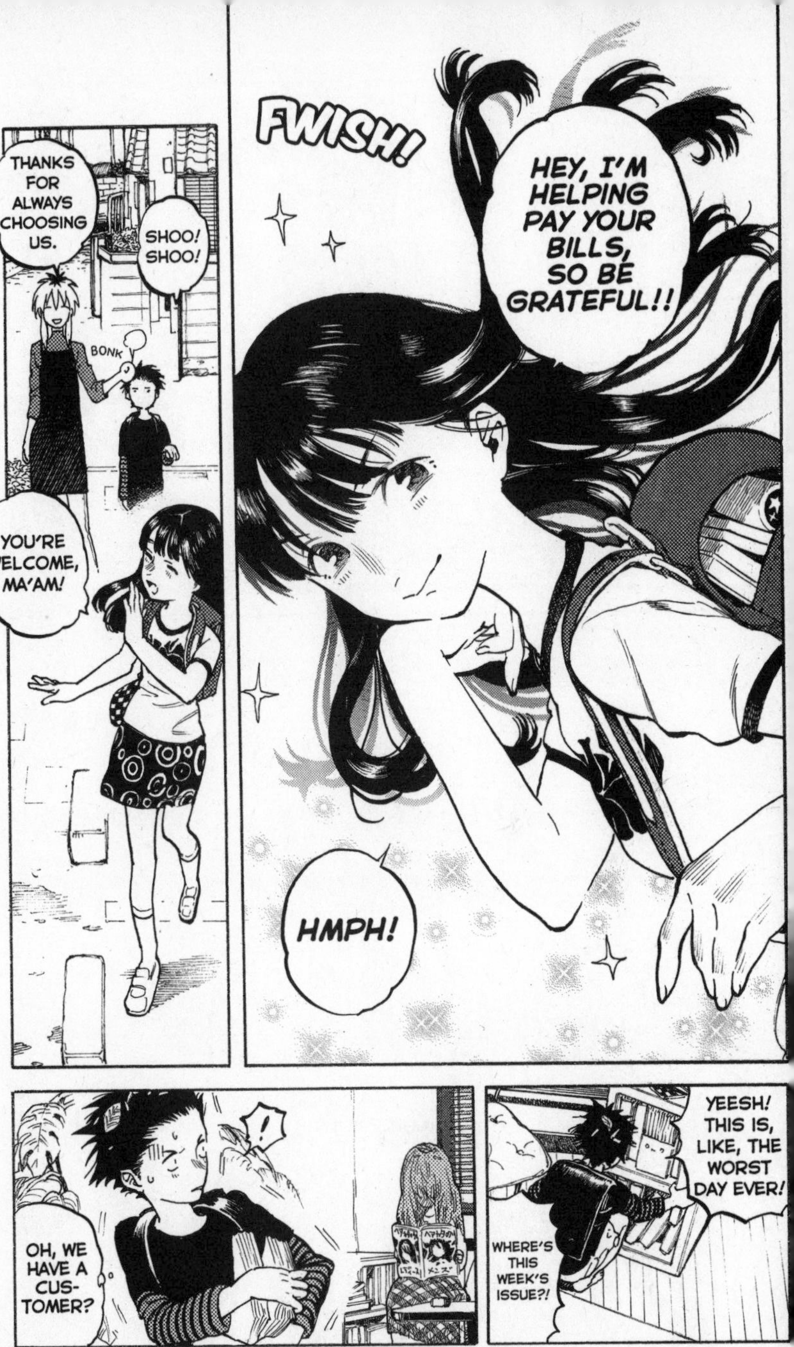
FWISH!
HEY, I'M HELPING PAY YOUR BILLS, SO BE GRATEFUL!!
HMPH!
THANKS FOR ALWAYS CHOOSING US.
SHOO! SHOO!
BONK
YOU'RE WELCOME, MA'AM!
YEESH! THIS IS, LIKE, THE WORST DAY EVER!
WHERE'S THIS WEEK'S ISSUE?!
!
OH, WE HAVE A CUS-TOMER?

*BOOK: "HAIR CATALOG MEN'S / LADIES'"

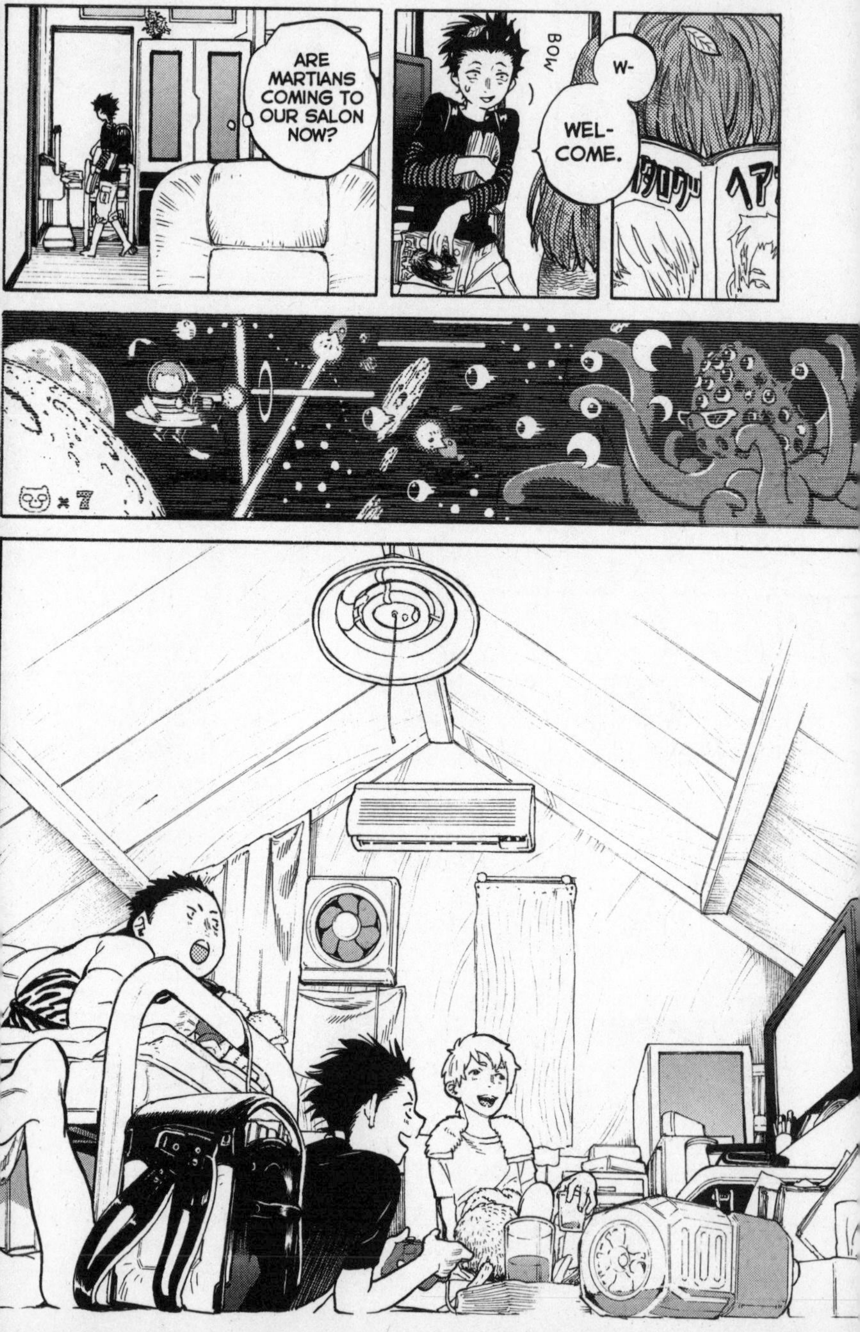
W-
WEL-
COME.
BOW
ARE MARTIANS COMING TO OUR SALON NOW?
×7

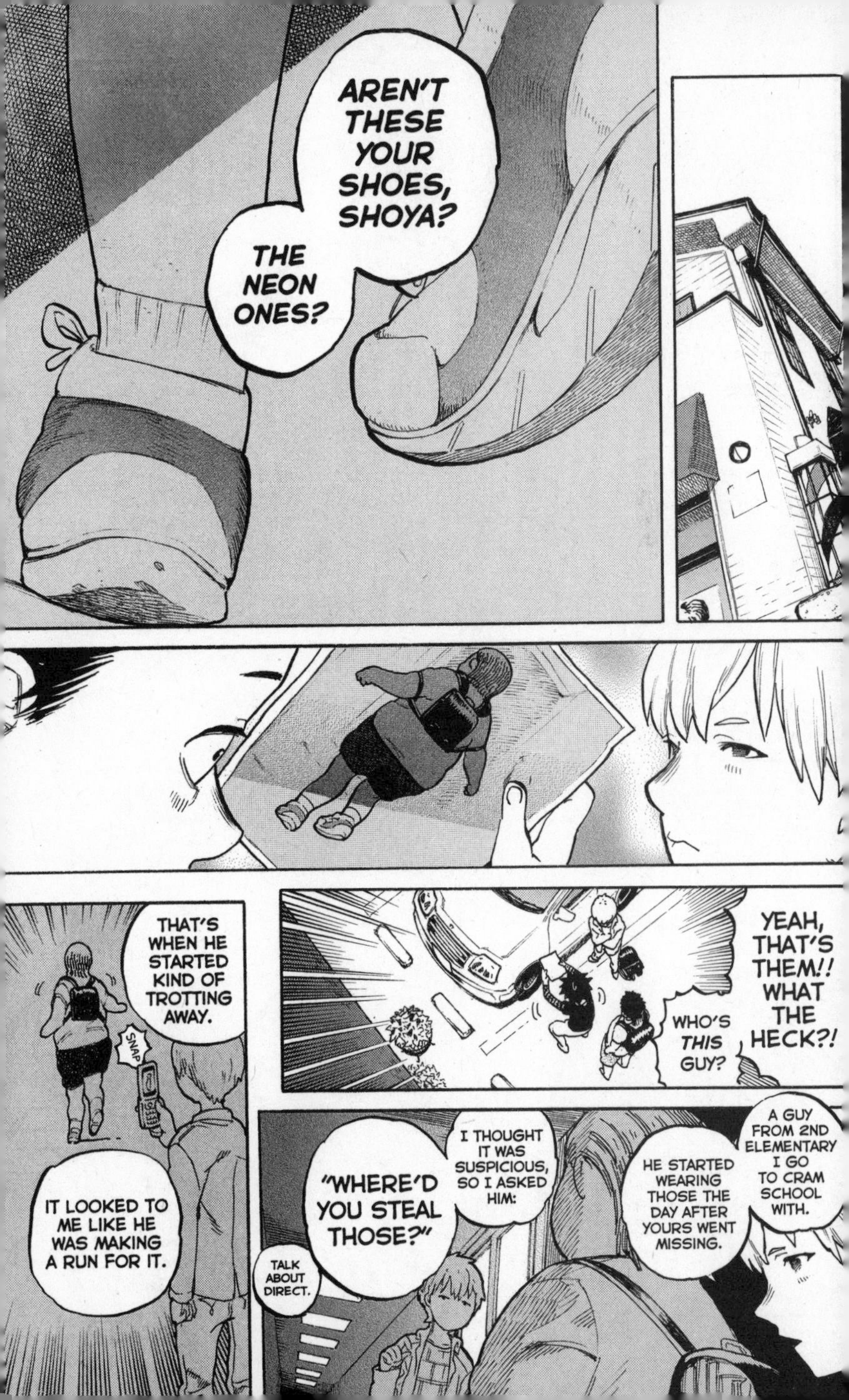
AREN'T THESE YOUR SHOES, SHOYA?
THE NEON ONES?
YEAH, THAT'S THEM!! WHAT THE HECK?!
WHO'S THIS GUY?
A GUY FROM 2ND ELEMENTARY I GO TO CRAM SCHOOL WITH.
HE STARTED WEARING THOSE THE DAY AFTER YOURS WENT MISSING.
I THOUGHT IT WAS SUSPICIOUS, SO I ASKED HIM:
"WHERE'D YOU STEAL THOSE?"
TALK ABOUT DIRECT.
THAT'S WHEN HE STARTED KIND OF TROTTING AWAY.
SNAP
IT LOOKED TO ME LIKE HE WAS MAKING A RUN FOR IT.

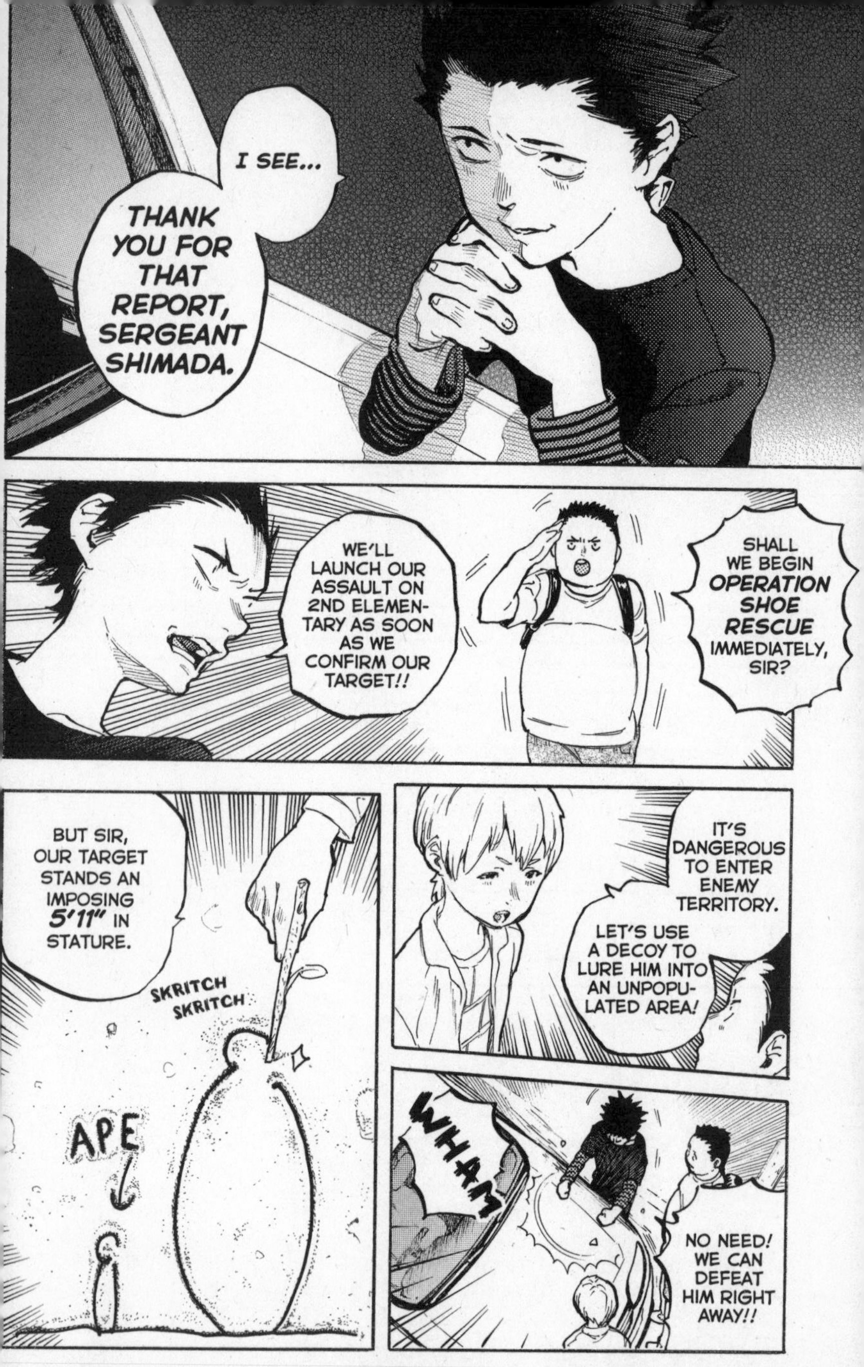
I SEE...
THANK YOU FOR THAT REPORT, SERGEANT SHIMADA.
SHALL WE BEGIN OPERATION SHOE RESCUE IMMEDIATELY, SIR?
WE'LL LAUNCH OUR ASSAULT ON 2ND ELEMENTARY AS SOON AS WE CONFIRM OUR TARGET!!
IT'S DANGEROUS TO ENTER ENEMY TERRITORY.
LET'S USE A DECOY TO LURE HIM INTO AN UNPOPULATED AREA!
WHAM
NO NEED! WE CAN DEFEAT HIM RIGHT AWAY!!
BUT SIR, OUR TARGET STANDS AN IMPOSING 5'11" IN STATURE.
SKRITCH SKRITCH
APE

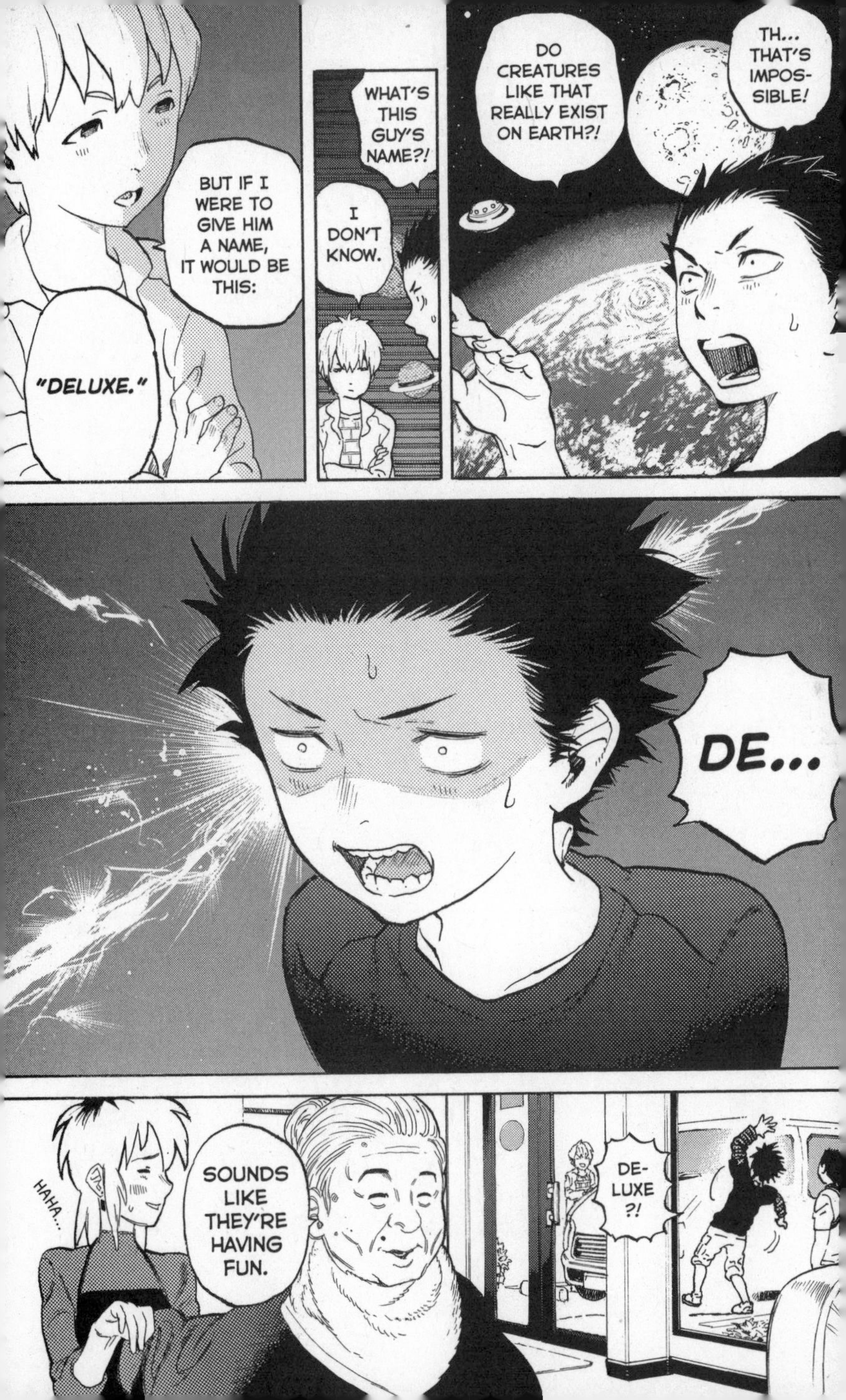
TH... THAT'S IMPOS-SIBLE!
DO CREATURES LIKE THAT REALLY EXIST ON EARTH?!
WHAT'S THIS GUY'S NAME?!
I DON'T KNOW.
BUT IF I WERE TO GIVE HIM A NAME, IT WOULD BE THIS:
"DELUXE."
DE...
DE-LUXE ?!
SOUNDS LIKE THEY'RE HAVING FUN.
HAHA...

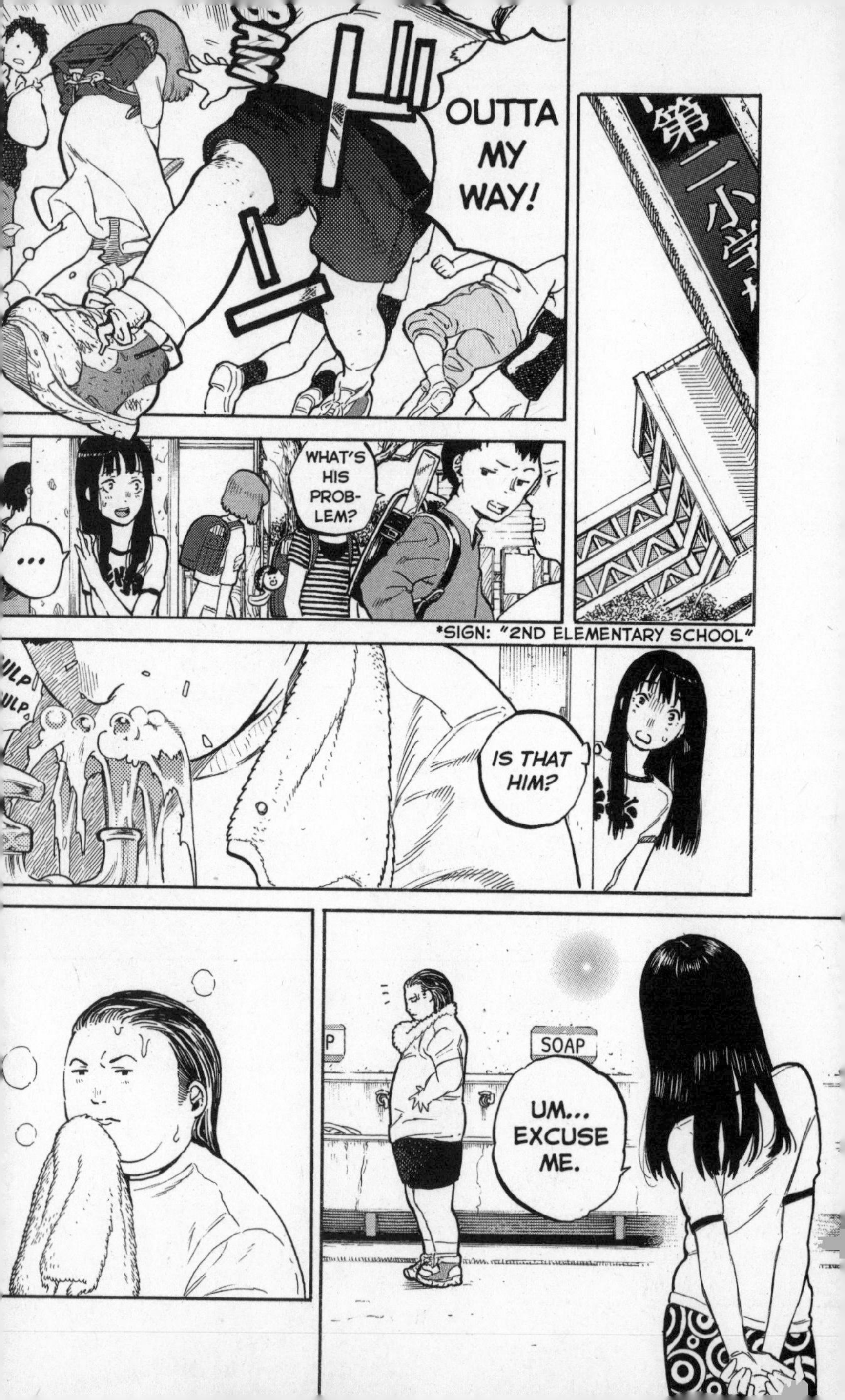
第二小学
BAM
OUTTA MY WAY!
WHAT'S HIS PROB-LEM?
...
*SIGN: "2ND ELEMENTARY SCHOOL"
IS THAT HIM?
ULP
ULP
SOAP
UM... EXCUSE ME.

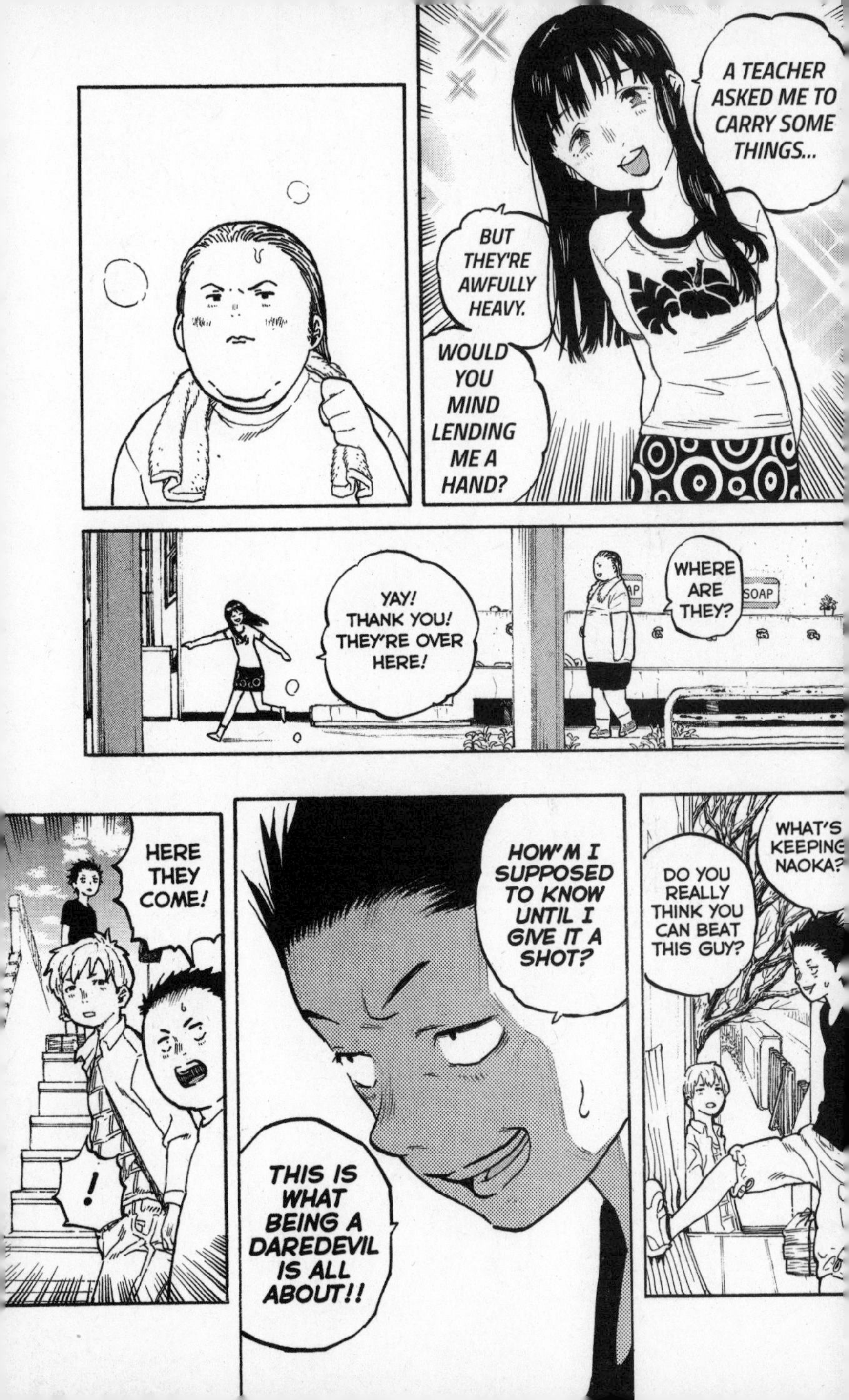
A TEACHER ASKED ME TO CARRY SOME THINGS...
BUT THEY'RE AWFULLY HEAVY.
WOULD YOU MIND LENDING ME A HAND?
WHERE ARE THEY?
SOAP
YAY! THANK YOU! THEY'RE OVER HERE!
WHAT'S KEEPING NAOKA?
DO YOU REALLY THINK YOU CAN BEAT THIS GUY?
HOW'M I SUPPOSED TO KNOW UNTIL I GIVE IT A SHOT?
THIS IS WHAT BEING A DAREDEVIL IS ALL ABOUT!!
HERE THEY COME!
!

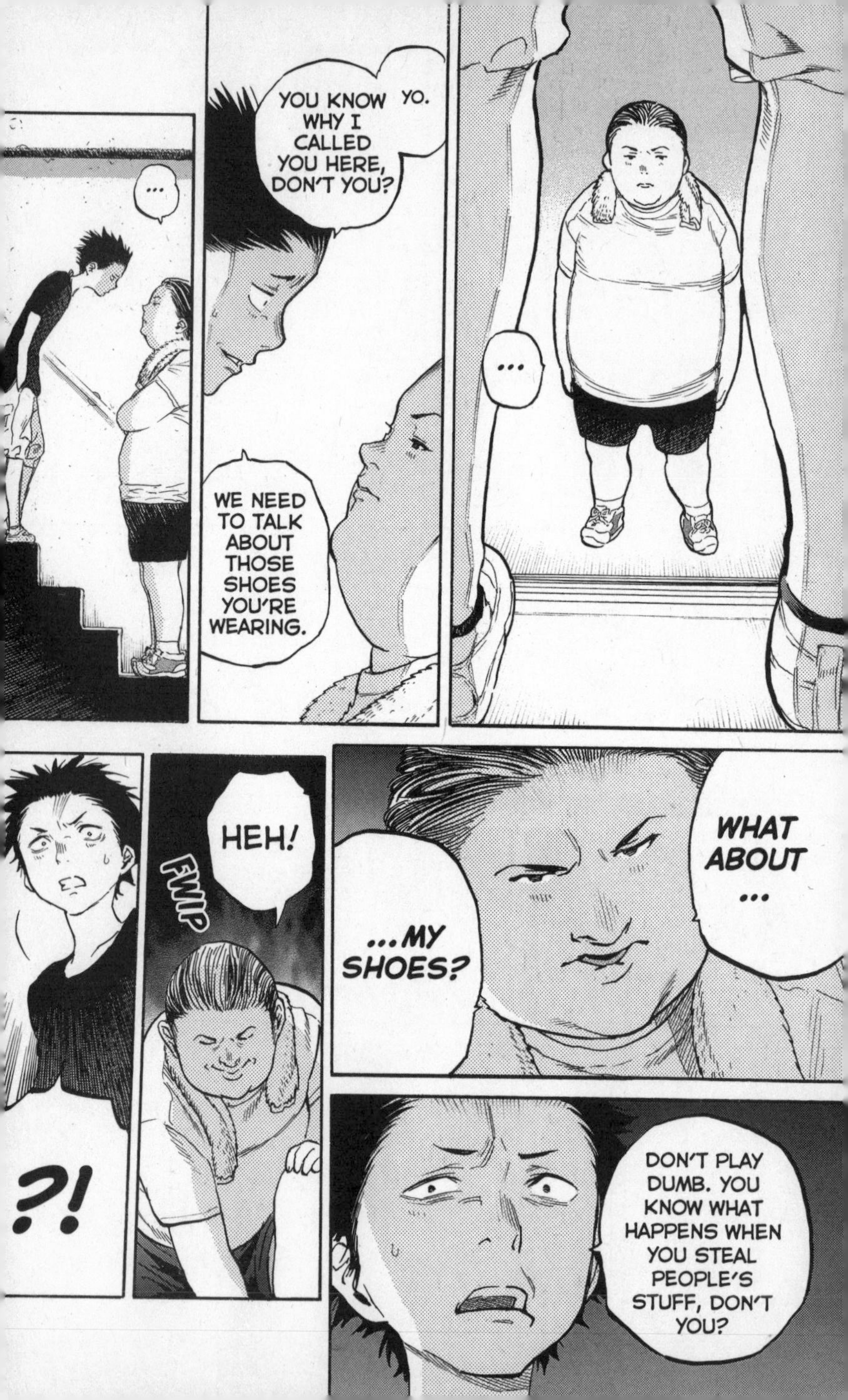
...
YO.
YOU KNOW WHY I CALLED YOU HERE, DON'T YOU?
WE NEED TO TALK ABOUT THOSE SHOES YOU'RE WEARING.
...
WHAT ABOUT ...
...MY SHOES?
DON'T PLAY DUMB. YOU KNOW WHAT HAPPENS WHEN YOU STEAL PEOPLE'S STUFF, DON'T YOU?
HEH!
FWIP
?!

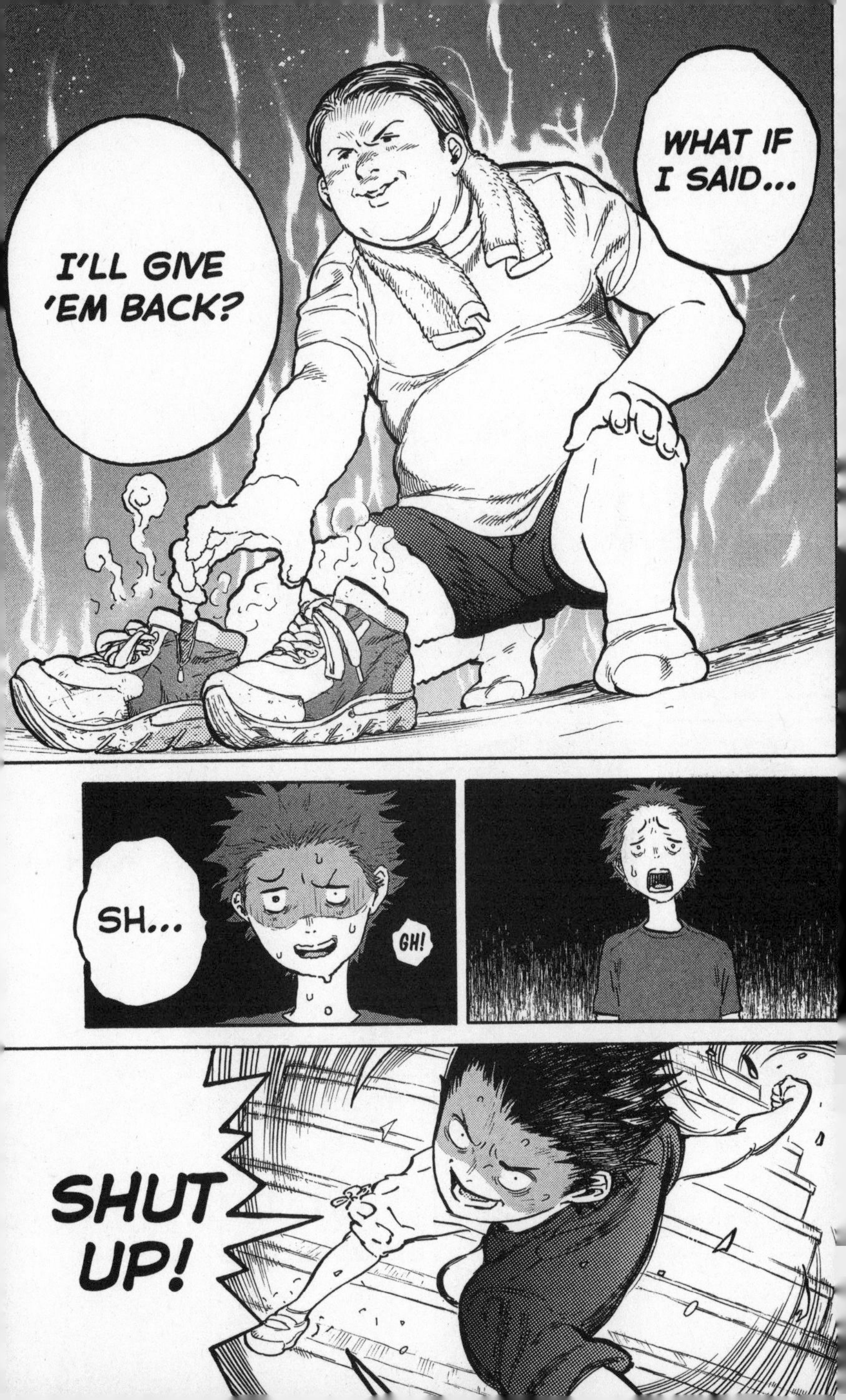
WHAT IF I SAID...
I'LL GIVE 'EM BACK?
SH...
GH!
SHUT UP!

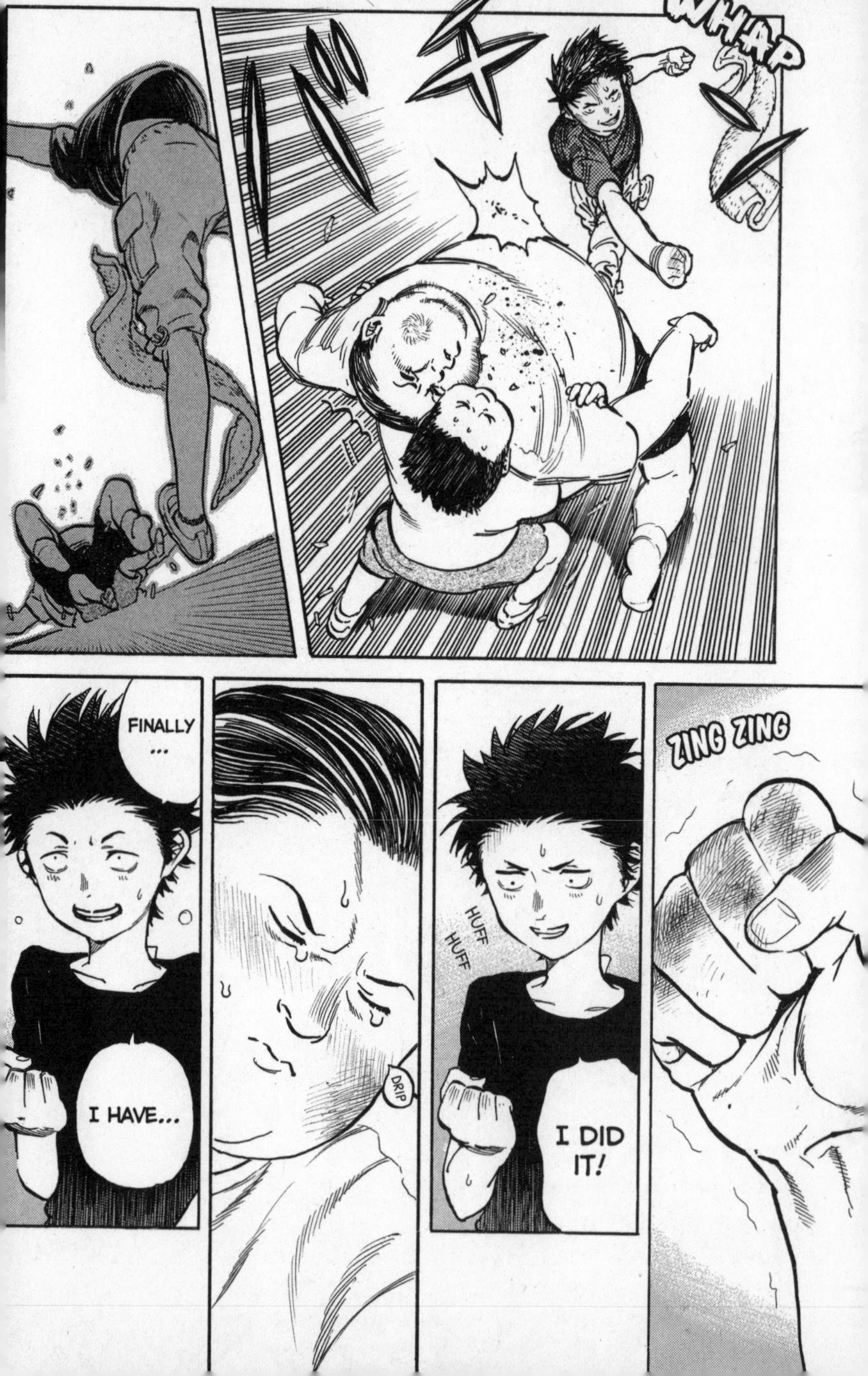
WHAP
ZING ZING
HUFF HUFF
I DID IT!
DRIP
FINALLY ...
I HAVE...

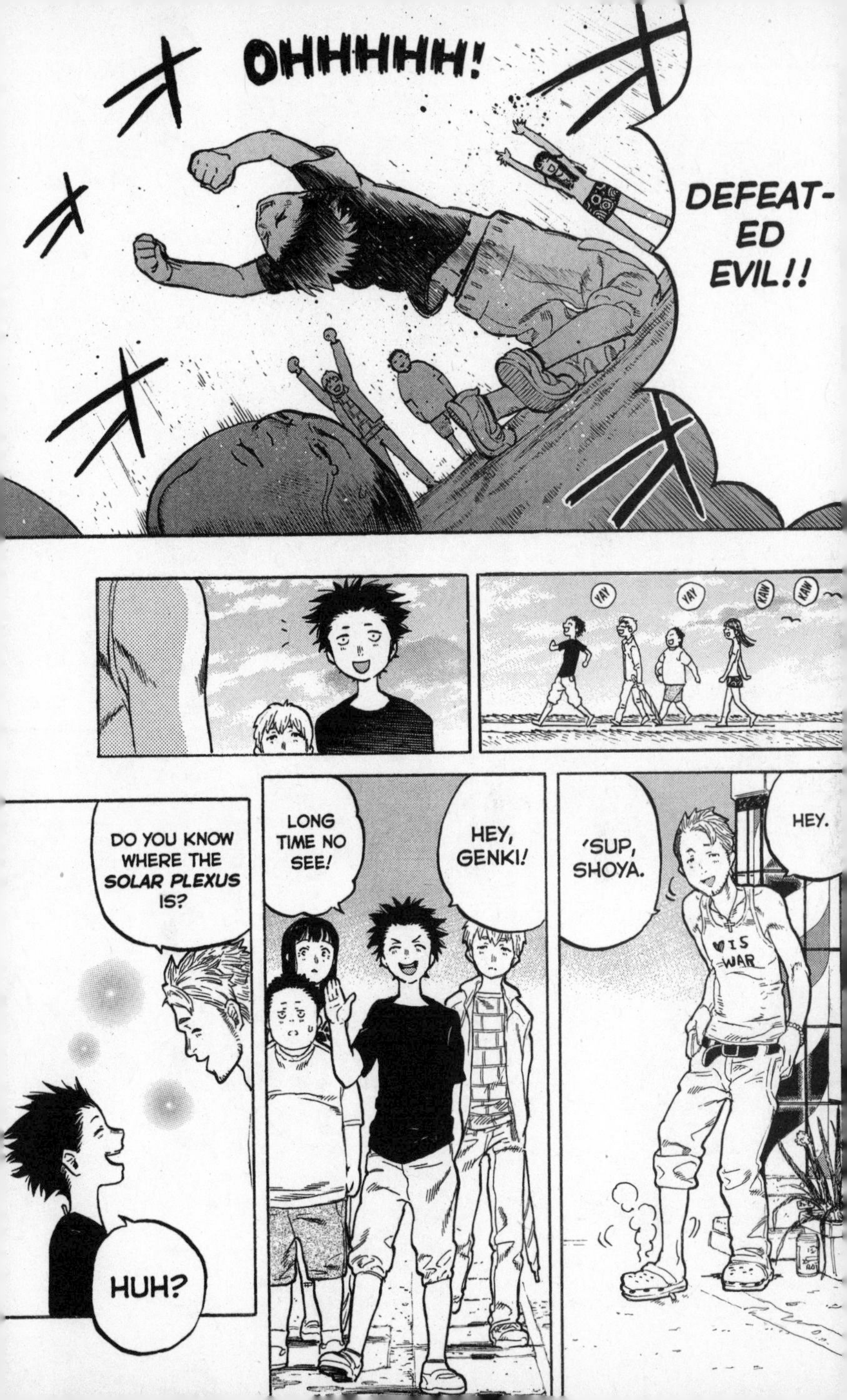
OHHHHHH!
DEFEAT-ED EVIL!!
YAY
YAY
KAW
KAW
HEY.
'SUP, SHOYA.
HEY, GENKI!
LONG TIME NO SEE!
DO YOU KNOW WHERE THE SOLAR PLEXUS IS?
HUH?

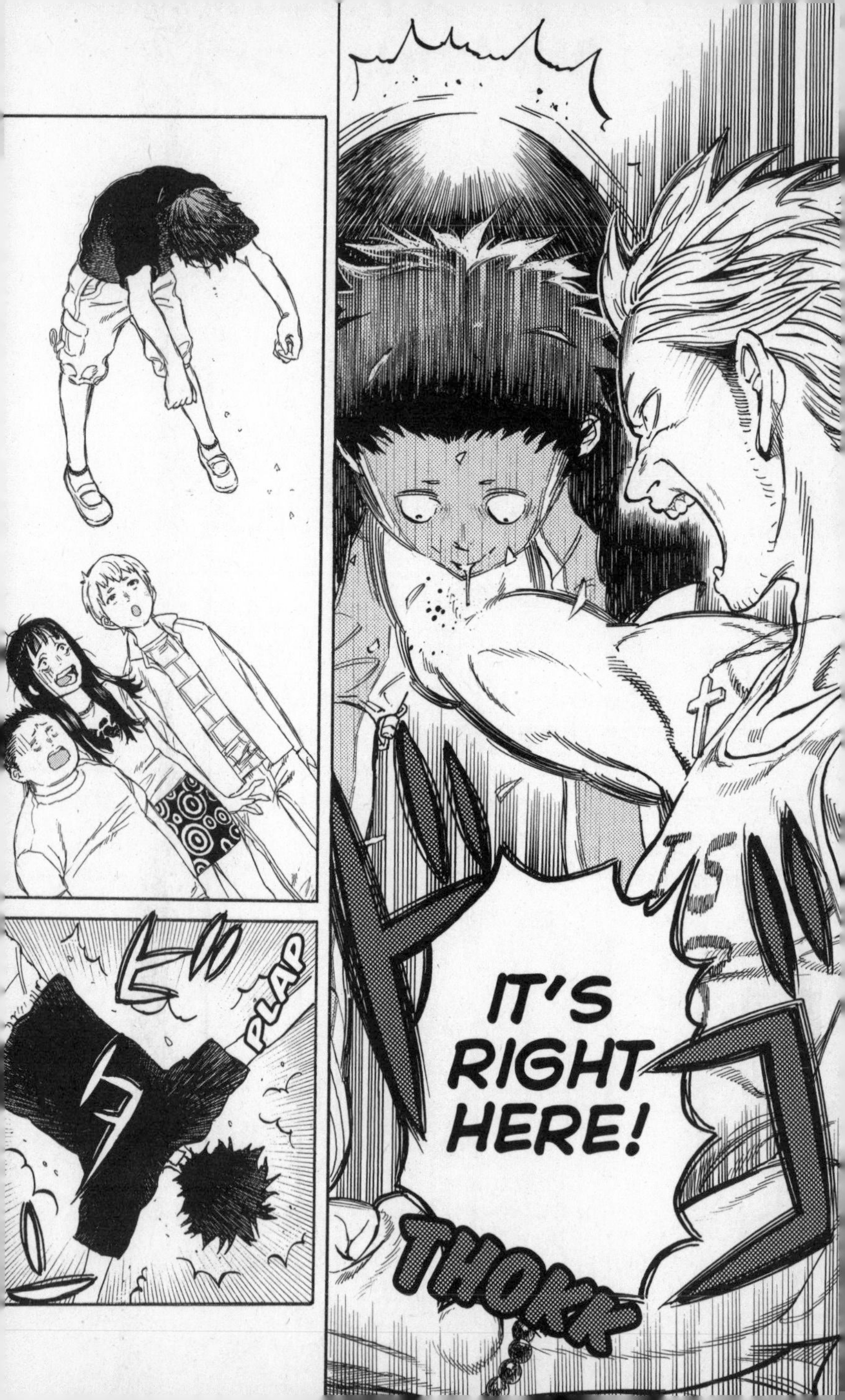
IT'S RIGHT HERE!
THOKK
PLAP

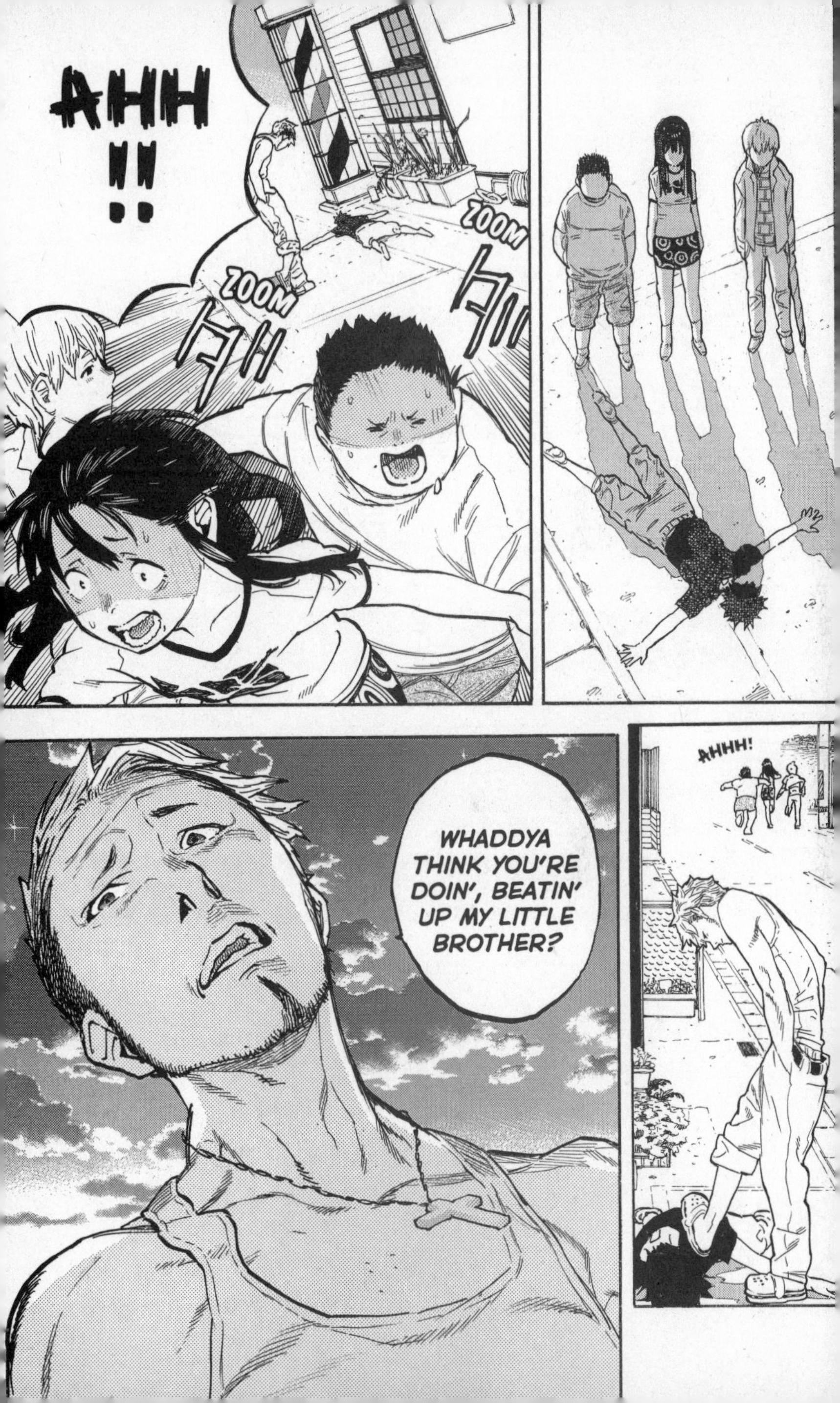
AHH !!
ZOOM
ZOOM
AHHH!
WHADDYA THINK YOU'RE DOIN', BEATIN' UP MY LITTLE BROTHER?

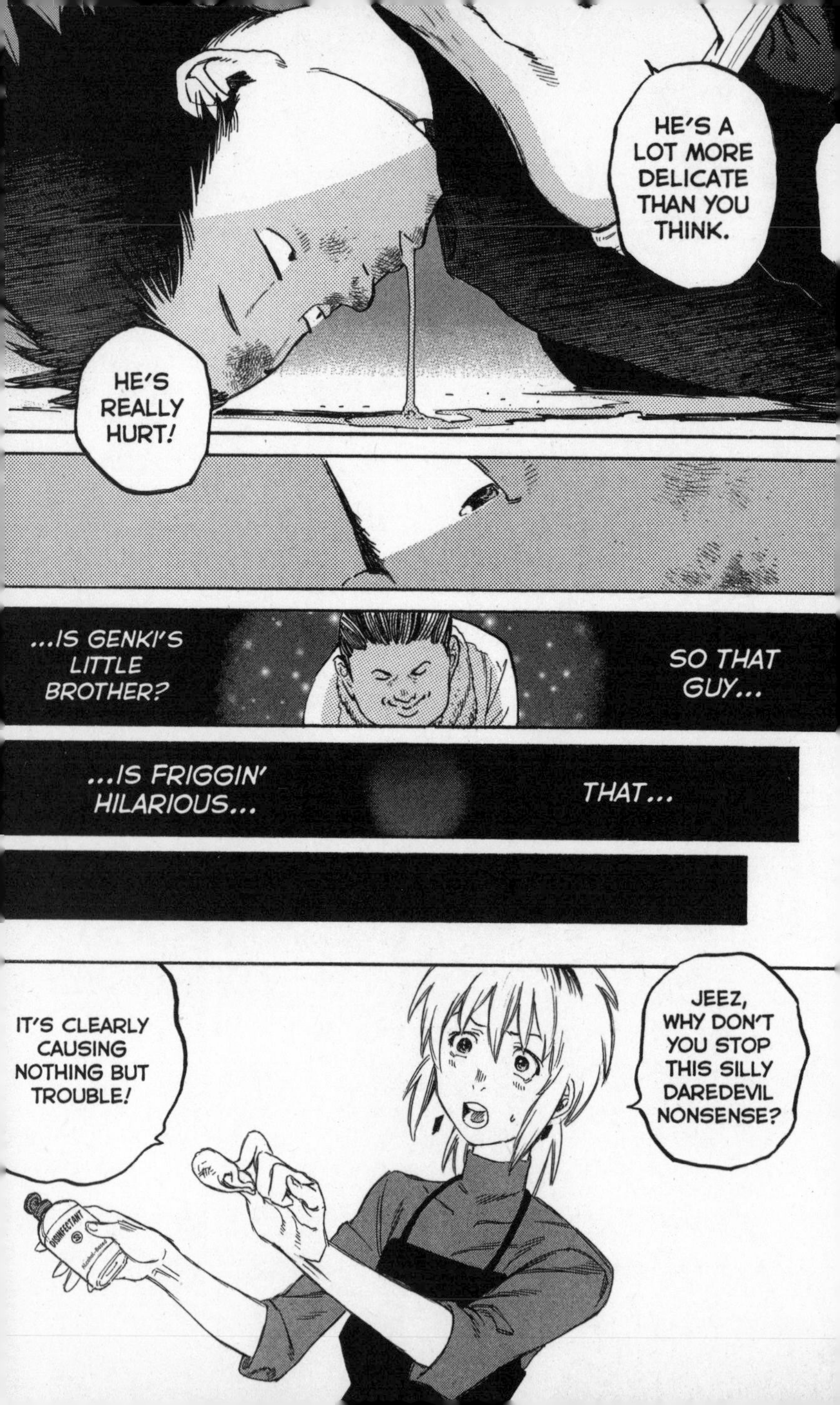
HE'S A LOT MORE DELICATE THAN YOU THINK.
HE'S REALLY HURT!
SO THAT GUY...
...IS GENKI'S LITTLE BROTHER?
THAT...
...IS FRIGGIN' HILARIOUS...
JEEZ, WHY DON'T YOU STOP THIS SILLY DAREDEVIL NONSENSE?
IT'S CLEARLY CAUSING NOTHING BUT TROUBLE!
DISINFECTANT

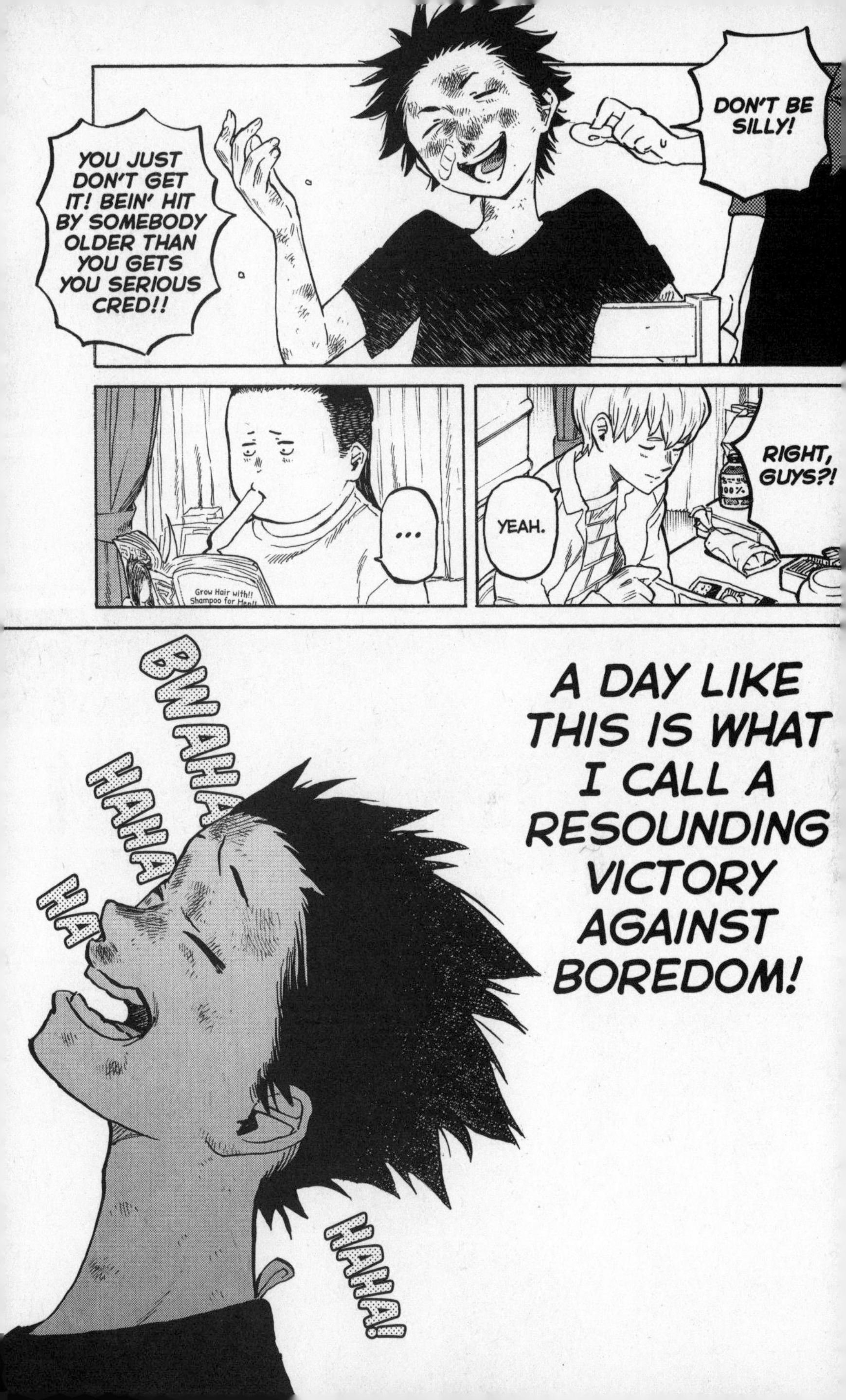
DON'T BE SILLY!
YOU JUST DON'T GET IT! BEIN' HIT BY SOMEBODY OLDER THAN YOU GETS YOU SERIOUS CRED!!
RIGHT, GUYS?!
YEAH.
...
Grow Hair with!! Shampoo for Men!!
A DAY LIKE THIS IS WHAT I CALL A RESOUNDING VICTORY AGAINST BOREDOM!
BWAHAHAHAHA HA
HAHA!

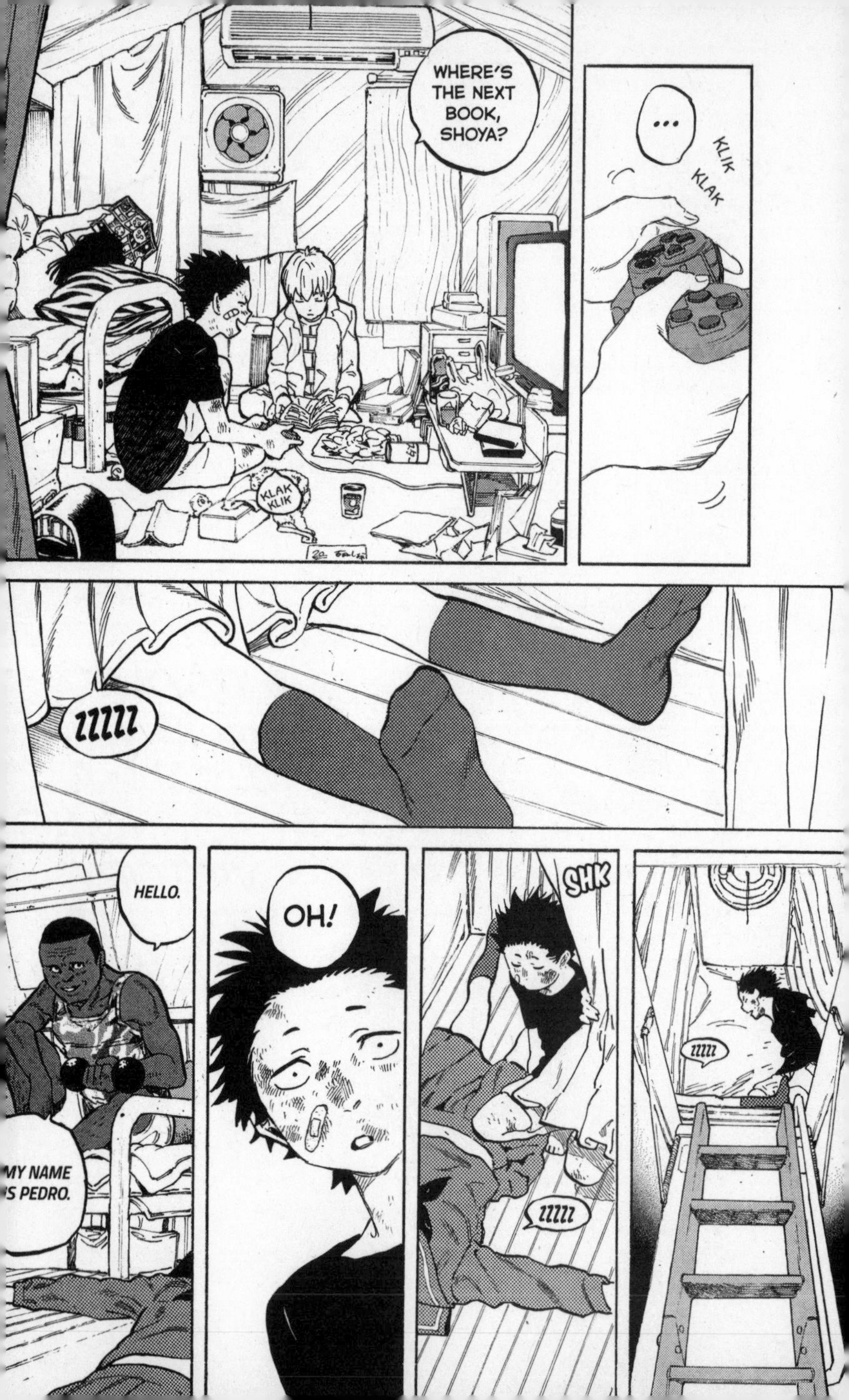
...
KLIK KLAK
WHERE'S THE NEXT BOOK, SHOYA?
KLAK KLIK
ZZZZZ
ZZZZZ
SHK
ZZZZZ
OH!
HELLO.
MY NAME
S PEDRO.

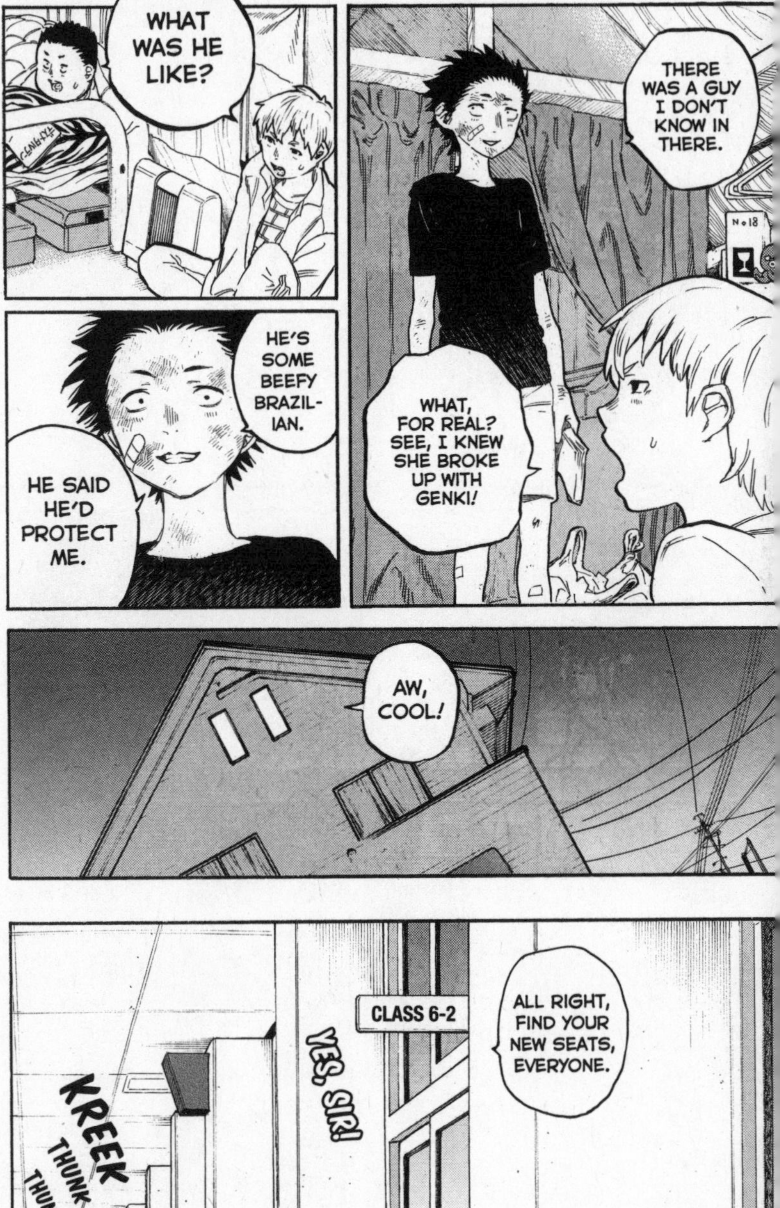
THERE WAS A GUY I DON'T KNOW IN THERE.
N o 18
WHAT, FOR REAL? SEE, I KNEW SHE BROKE UP WITH GENKI!
WHAT WAS HE LIKE?
HE'S SOME BEEFY BRAZIL-IAN.
HE SAID HE'D PROTECT ME.
AW, COOL!
ALL RIGHT, FIND YOUR NEW SEATS, EVERYONE.
CLASS 6-2
YES, SIR!
KREEK
THUNK
THUNK

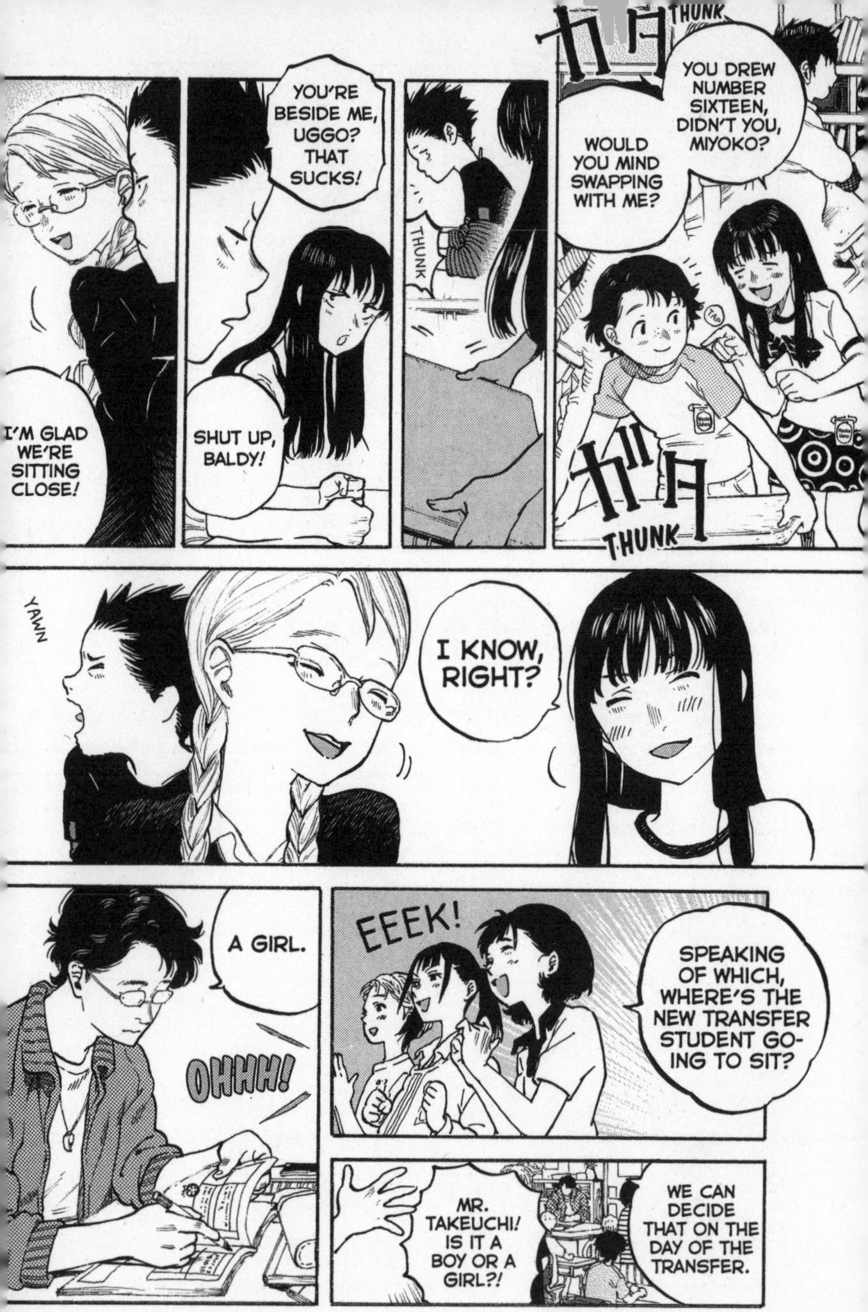
THUNK
YOU DREW NUMBER SIXTEEN, DIDN'T YOU, MIYOKO?
WOULD YOU MIND SWAPPING WITH ME?
TAP
THUNK
THUNK
YOU'RE BESIDE ME, UGGO? THAT SUCKS!
SHUT UP, BALDY!
I'M GLAD WE'RE SITTING CLOSE!
I KNOW, RIGHT?
YAWN
SPEAKING OF WHICH, WHERE'S THE NEW TRANSFER STUDENT GO-ING TO SIT?
EEEK!
WE CAN DECIDE THAT ON THE DAY OF THE TRANSFER.
MR. TAKEUCHI! IS IT A BOY OR A GIRL?!
A GIRL.
OHHH!

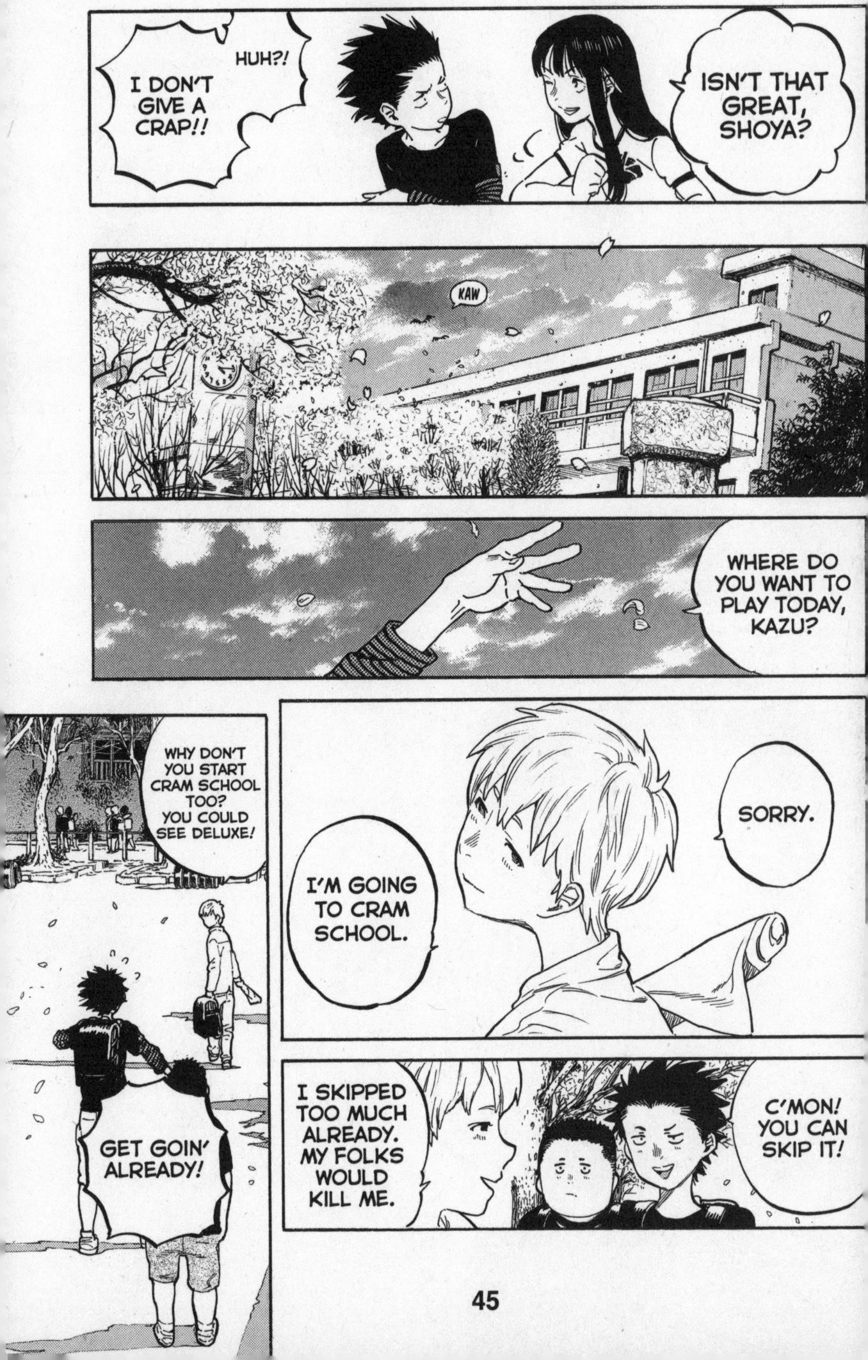
ISN'T THAT GREAT, SHOYA?
HUH?!
I DON'T GIVE A CRAP!!
KAW
WHERE DO YOU WANT TO PLAY TODAY, KAZU?
SORRY.
I'M GOING TO CRAM SCHOOL.
C'MON! YOU CAN SKIP IT!
I SKIPPED TOO MUCH ALREADY. MY FOLKS WOULD KILL ME.
WHY DON'T YOU START CRAM SCHOOL TOO? YOU COULD SEE DELUXE!
GET GOIN' ALREADY!

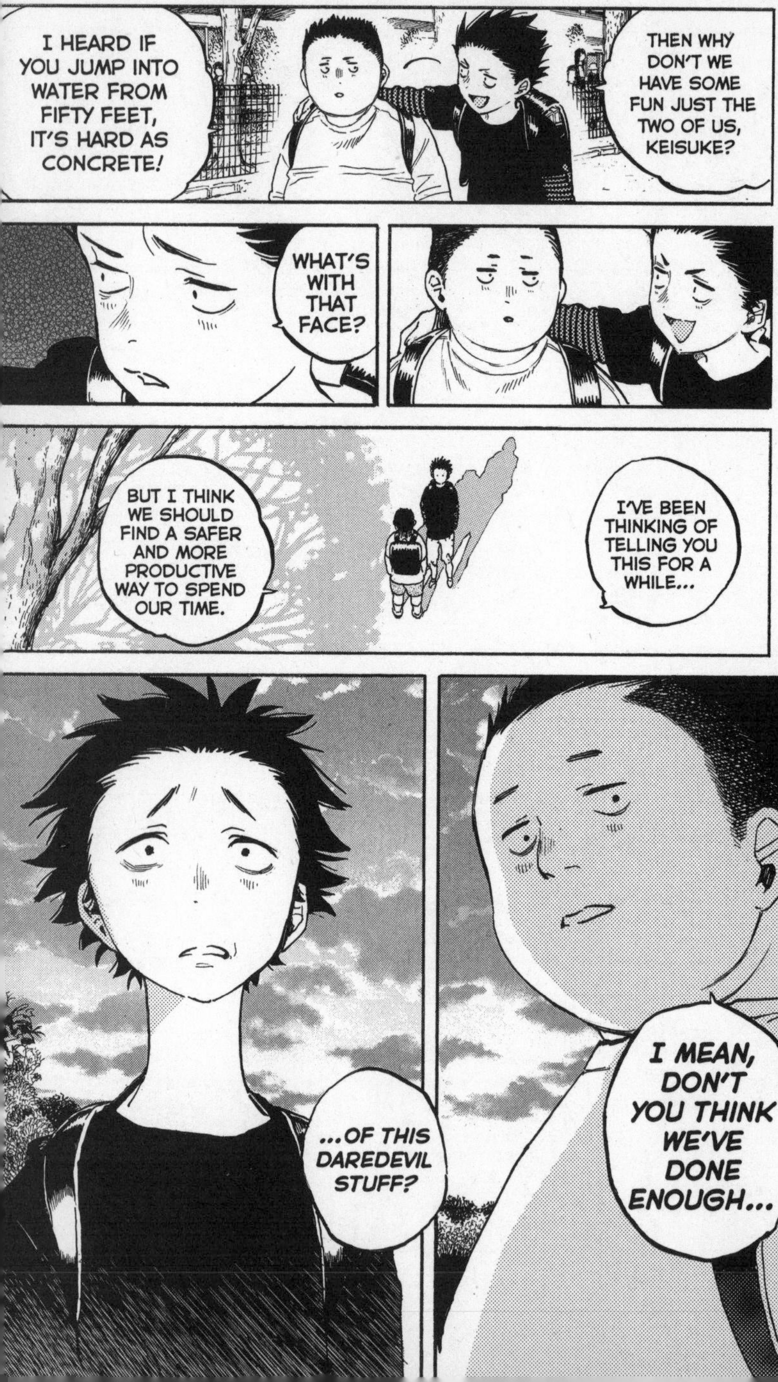
THEN WHY DON'T WE HAVE SOME FUN JUST THE TWO OF US, KEISUKE?
I HEARD IF YOU JUMP INTO WATER FROM FIFTY FEET, IT'S HARD AS CONCRETE!
WHAT'S WITH THAT FACE?
I'VE BEEN THINKING OF TELLING YOU THIS FOR A WHILE...
BUT I THINK WE SHOULD FIND A SAFER AND MORE PRODUCTIVE WAY TO SPEND OUR TIME.
I MEAN, DON'T YOU THINK WE'VE DONE ENOUGH...
...OF THIS DAREDEVIL STUFF?

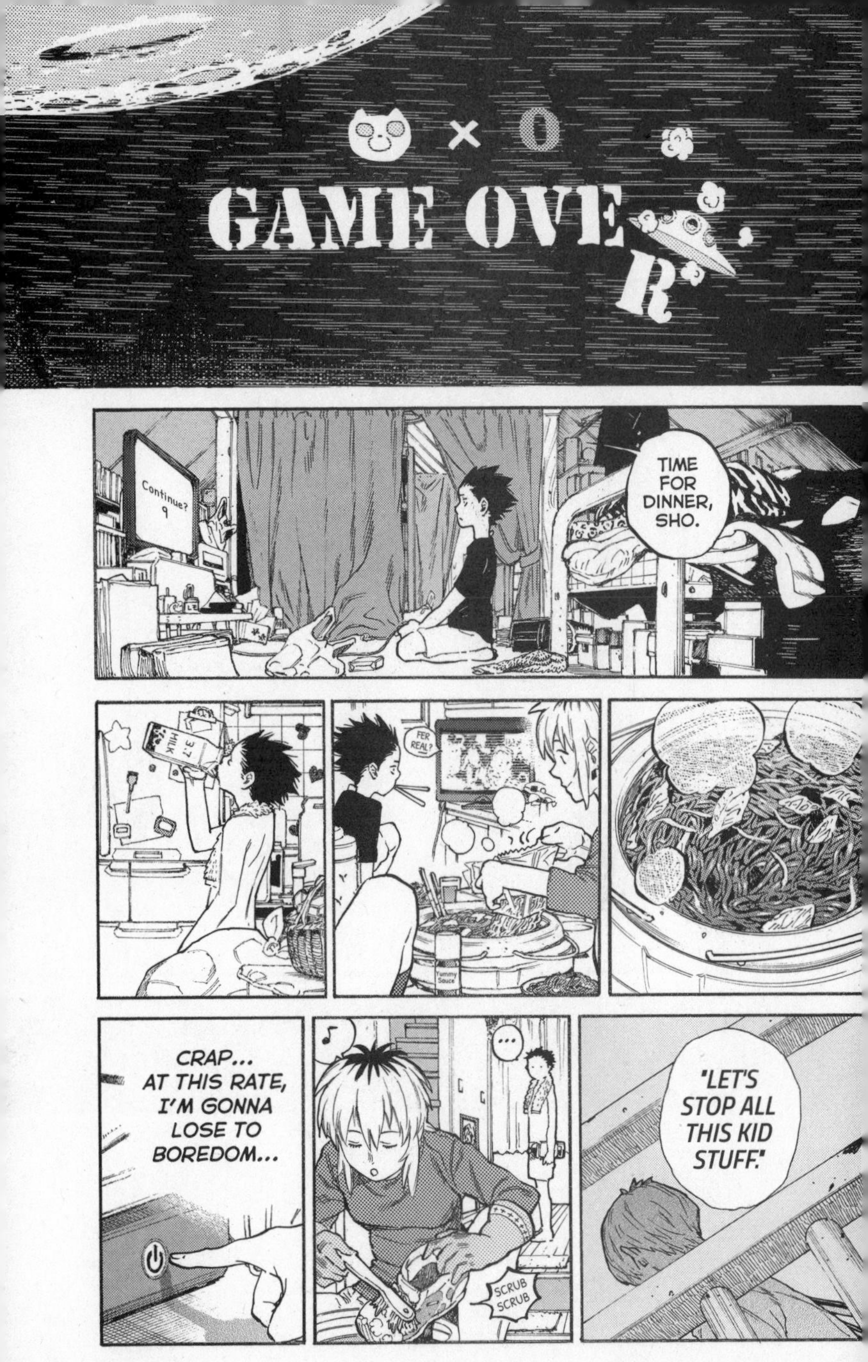
GAME OVER
Continue?
9
TIME FOR DINNER, SHO.
FER REAL?
Yummy Sauce
3.7 MILK
"LET'S STOP ALL THIS KID STUFF."
...
SCRUB SCRUB
CRAP... AT THIS RATE, I'M GONNA LOSE TO BOREDOM...

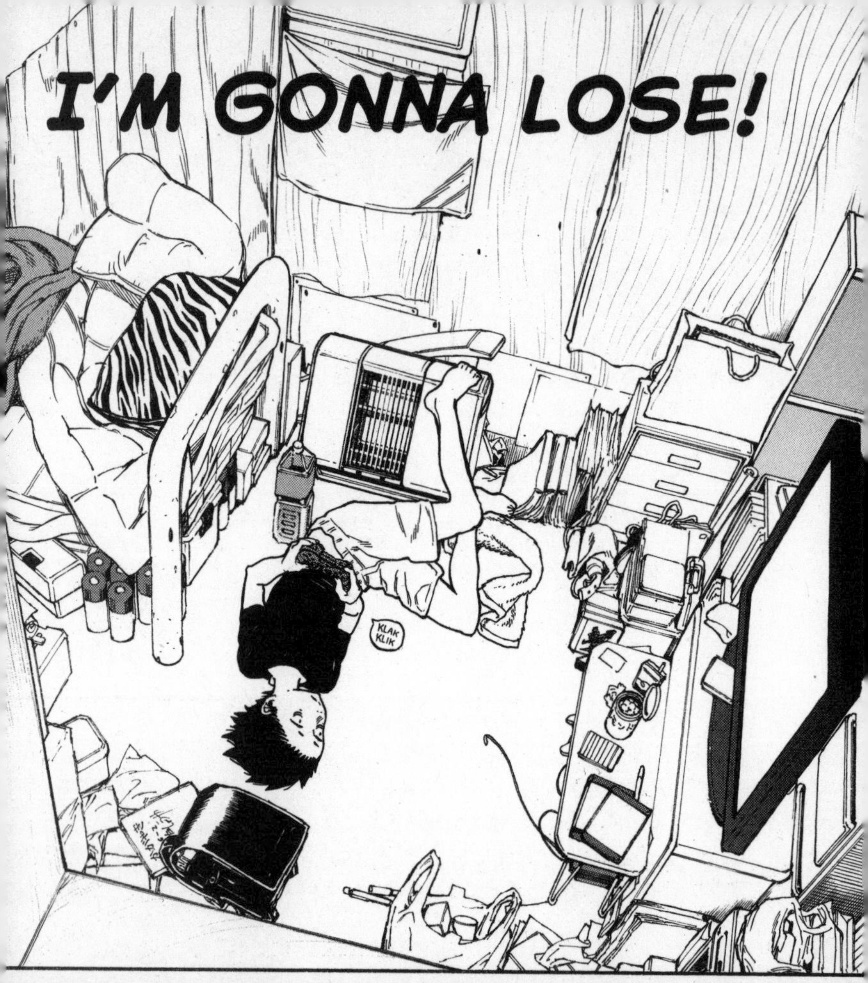
I'M GONNA LOSE!
KLAK KLIK
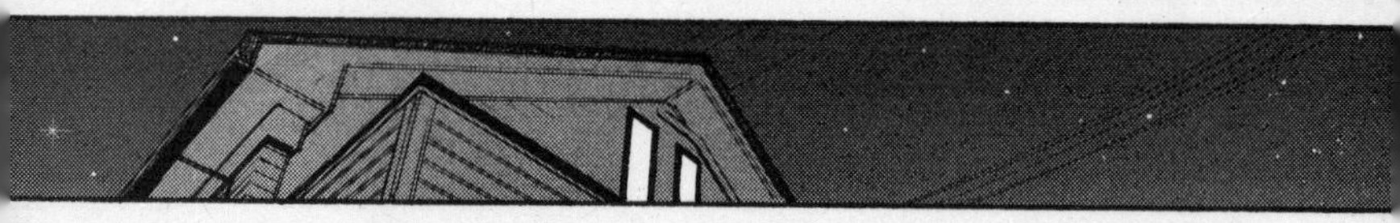
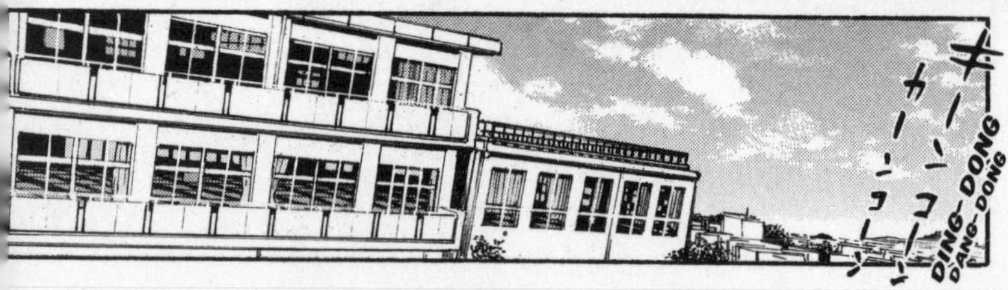
DING-DONG
DANG-DONG

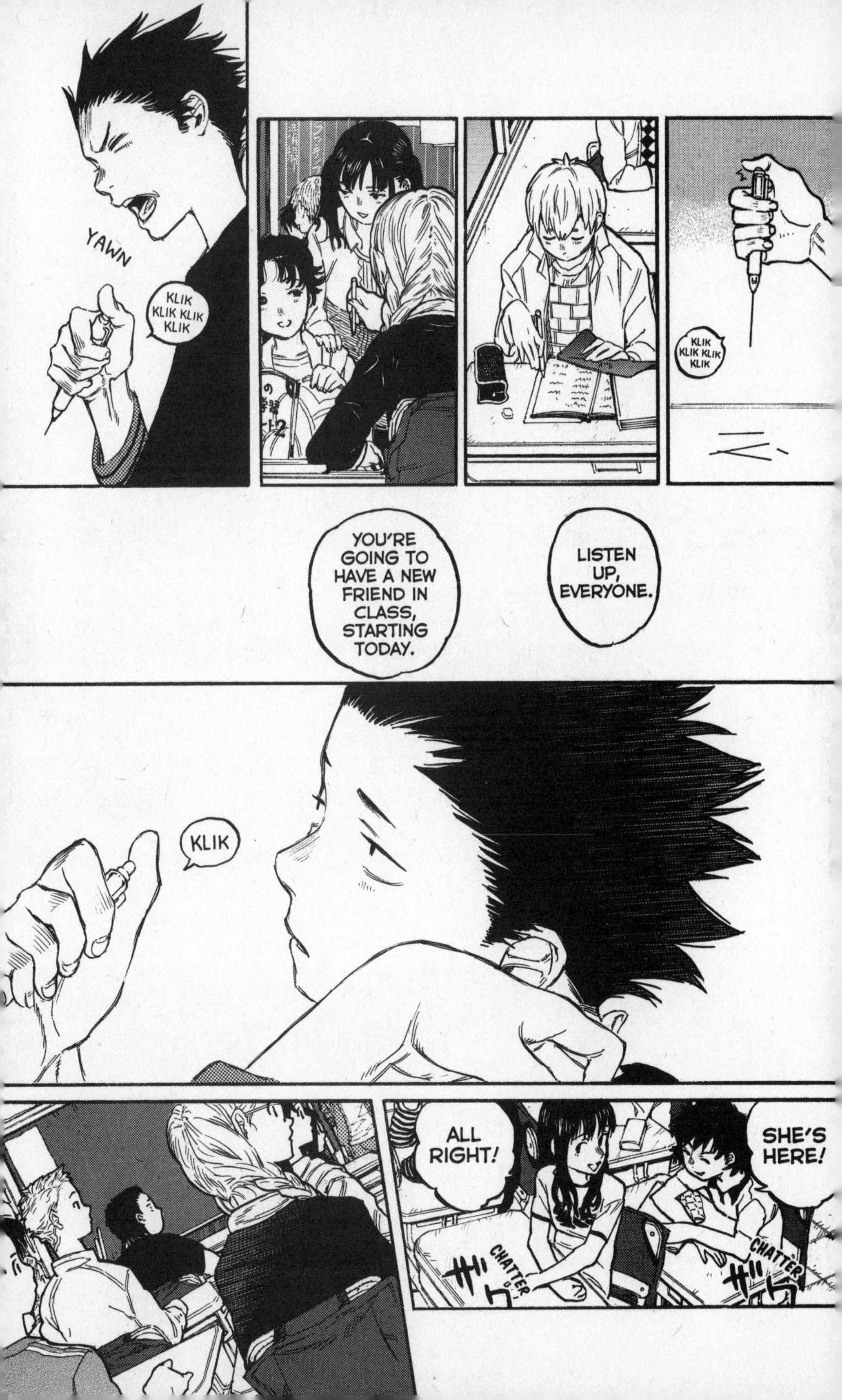
KLIK KLIK KLIK KLIK
YAWN
KLIK KLIK KLIK KLIK
LISTEN UP, EVERYONE.
YOU'RE GOING TO HAVE A NEW FRIEND IN CLASS, STARTING TODAY.
KLIK
SHE'S HERE!
CHATTER
ALL RIGHT!
CHATTER

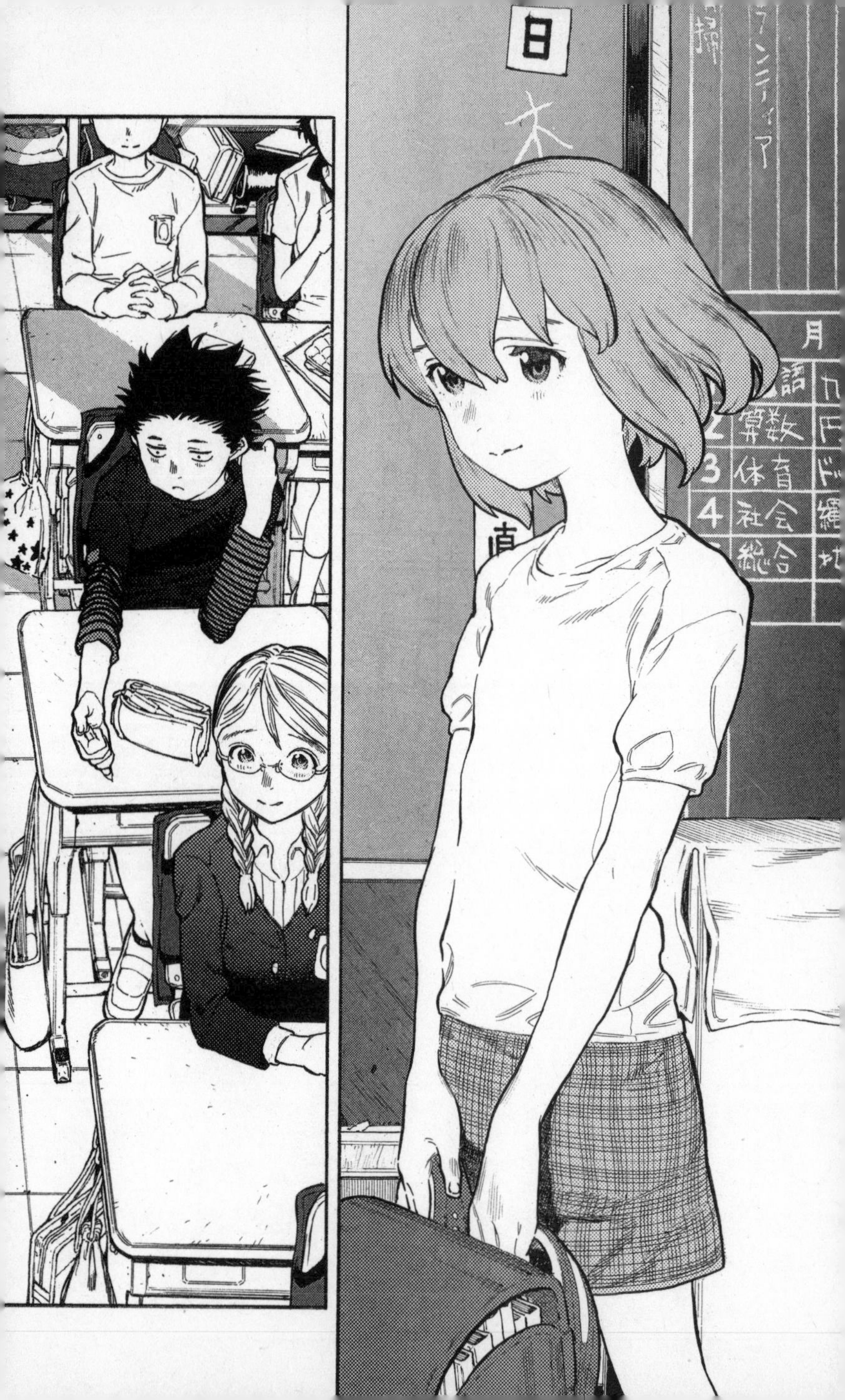
日
月
2 算数
3 体育
4 社会
総合

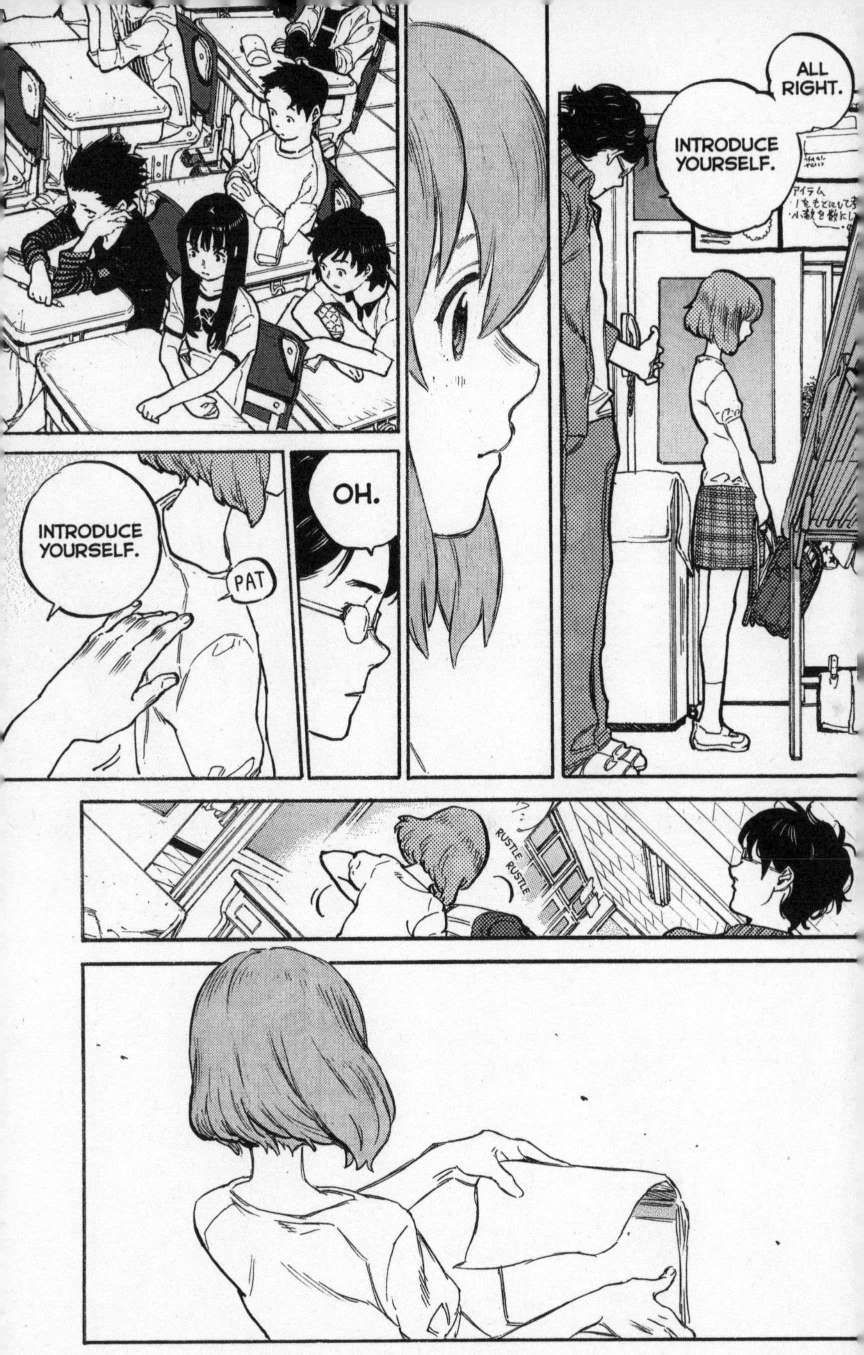
ALL RIGHT.
INTRODUCE YOURSELF.
OH.
INTRODUCE YOURSELF.
PAT
RUSTLE
RUSTLE

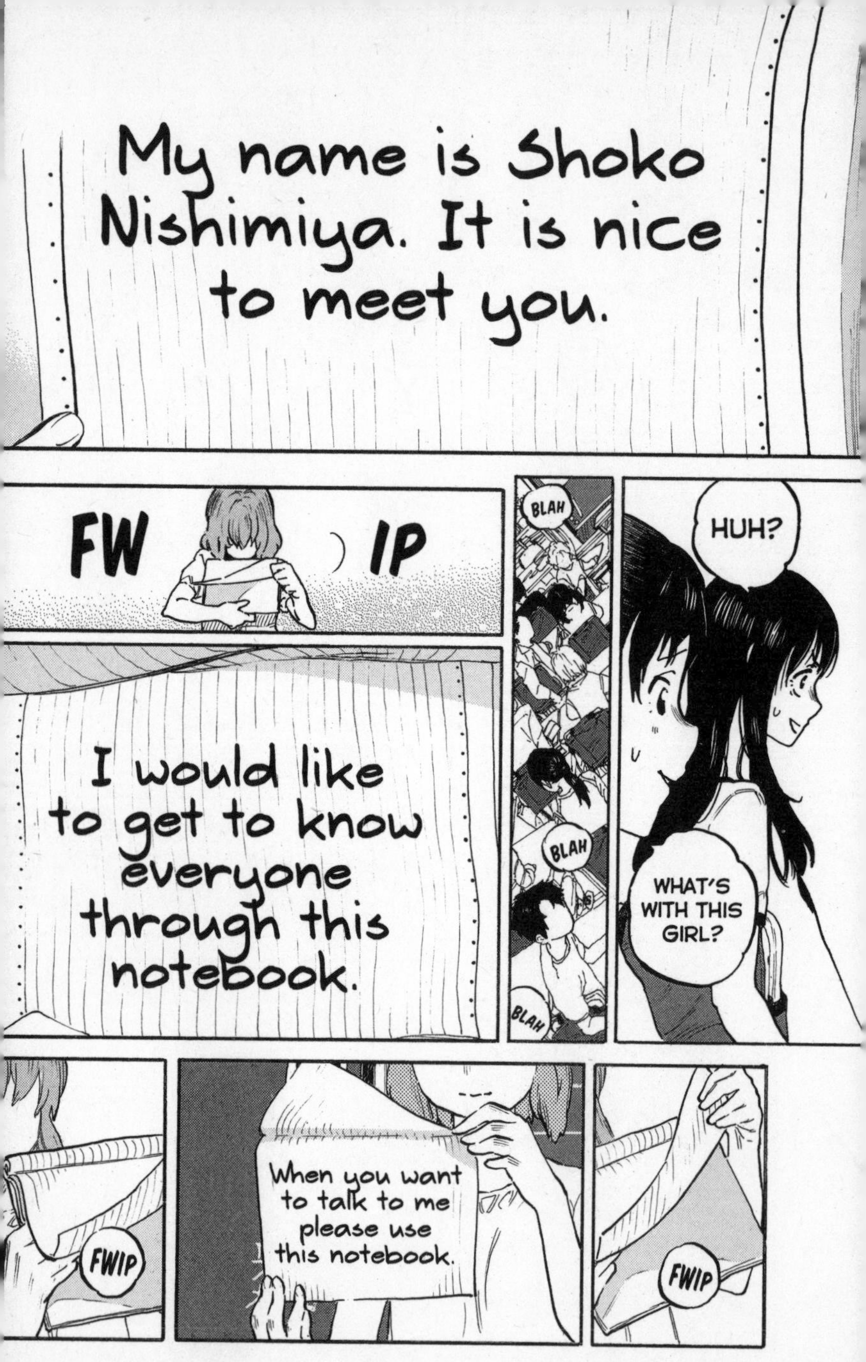
My name is Shoko Nishimiya. It is nice to meet you.
HUH?
WHAT'S WITH THIS GIRL?
BLAH
BLAH
BLAH
FWIP
I would like to get to know everyone through this notebook.
FWIP
When you want to talk to me please use this notebook.
FWIP

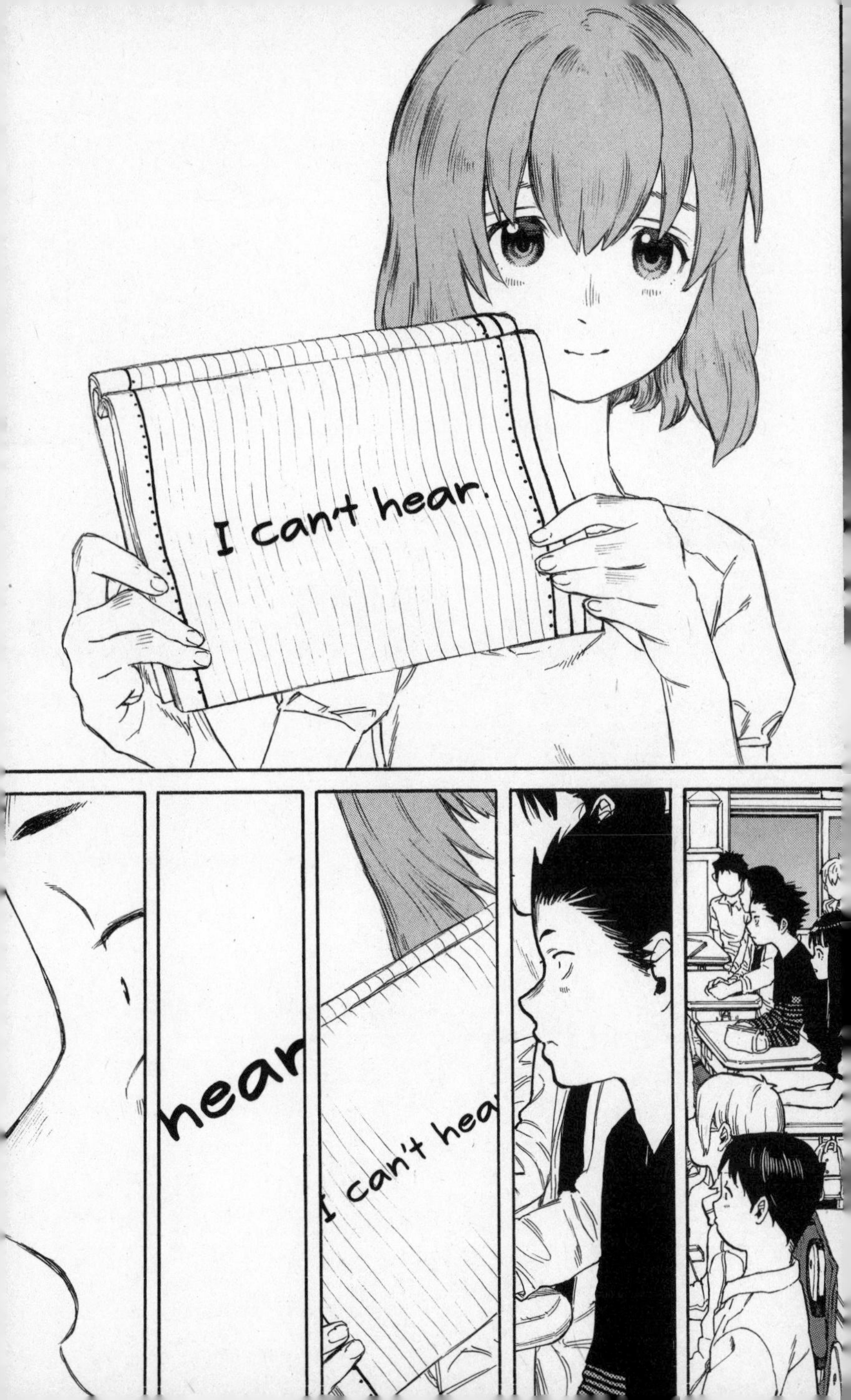
I can't hear.
I can't hea
hear

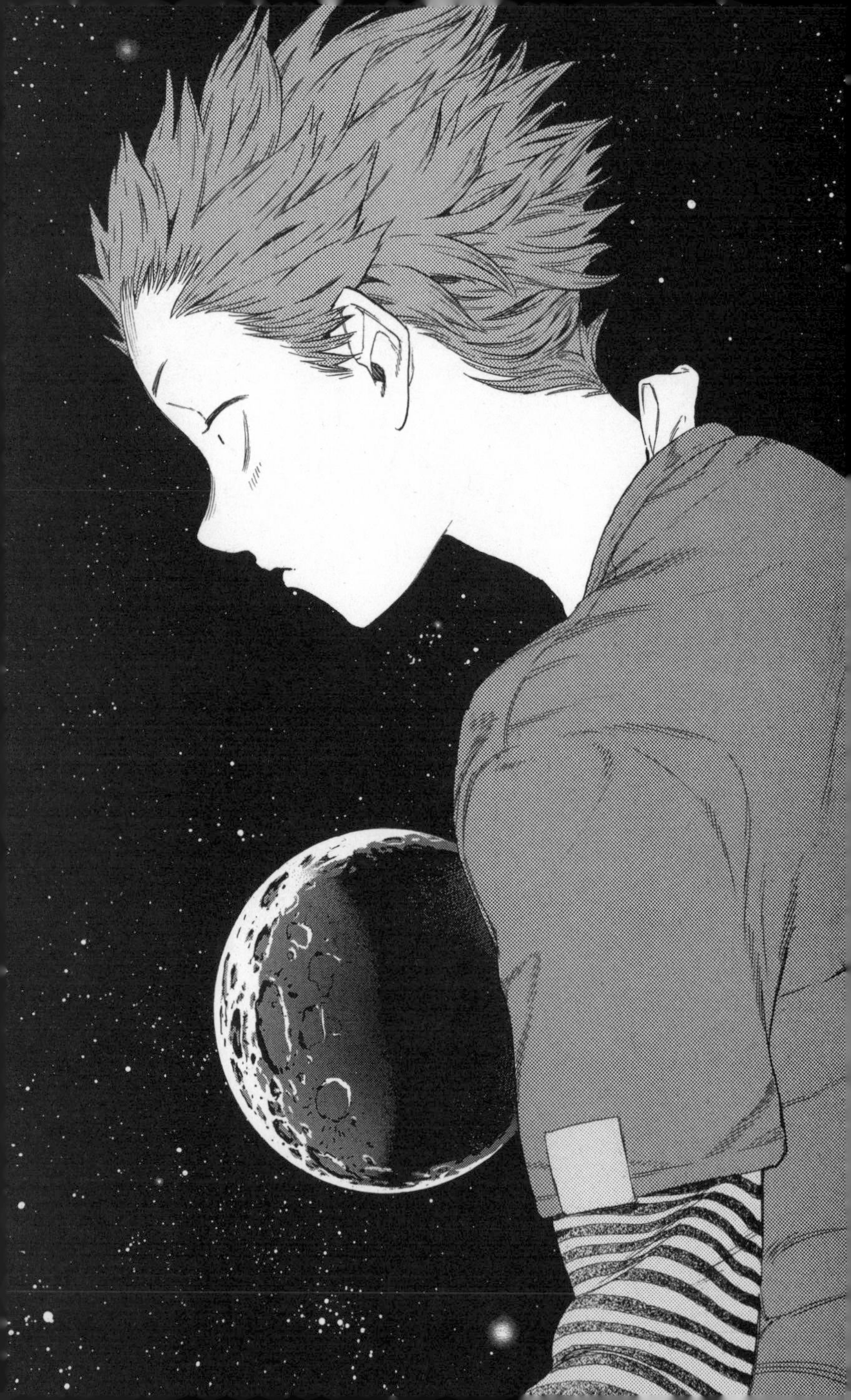

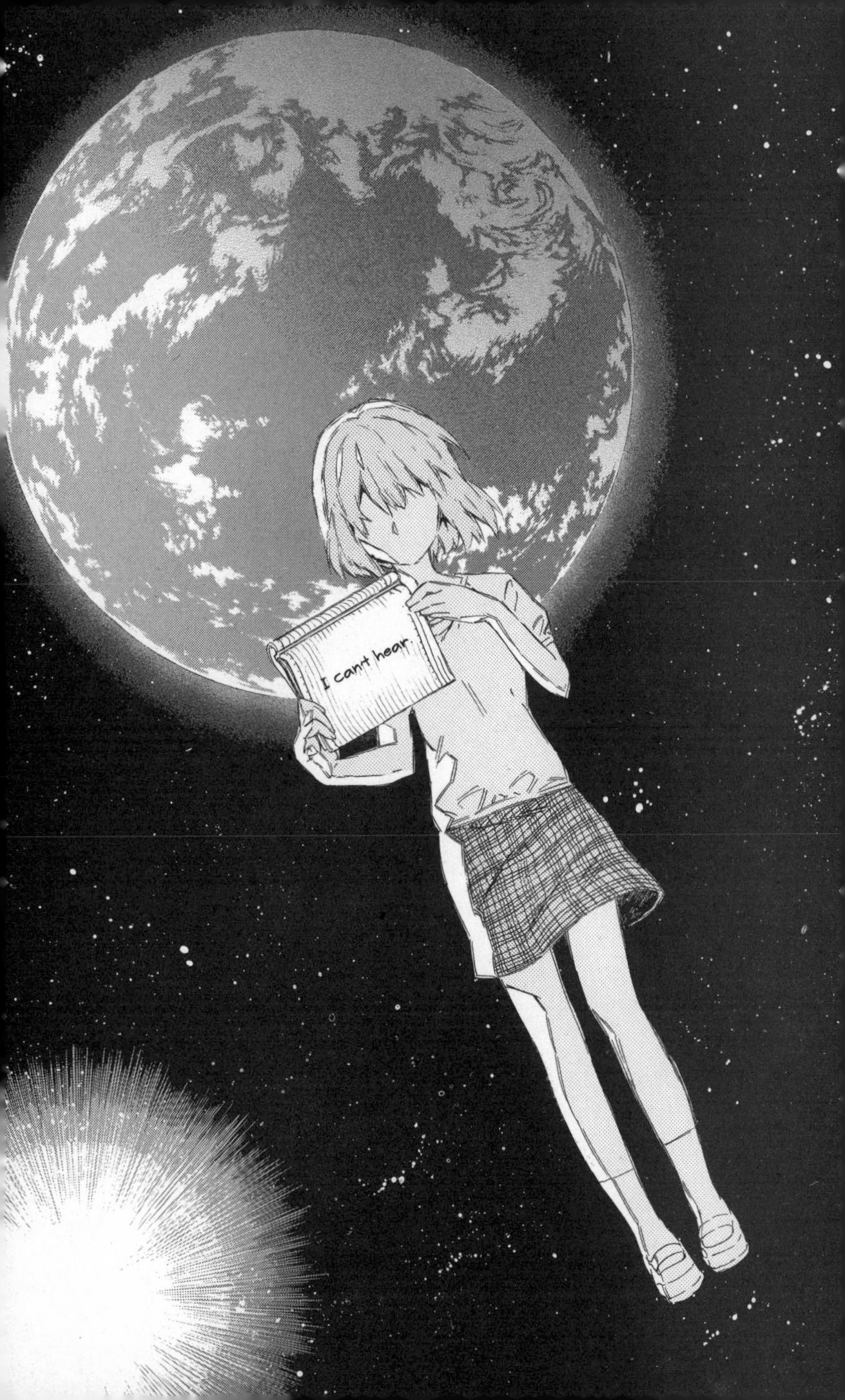
I can't hear.

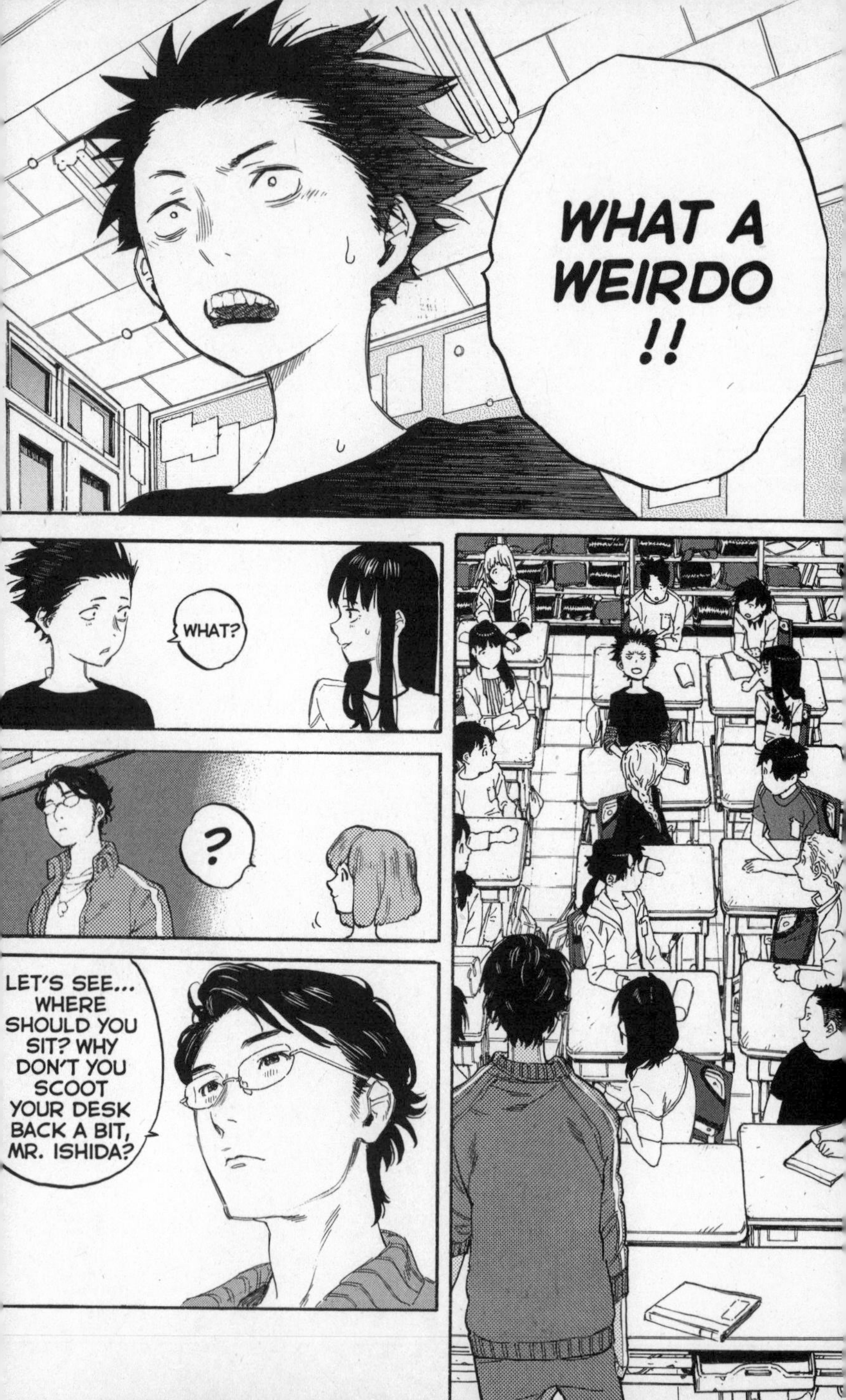
WHAT A WEIRDO !!
WHAT?
?
LET'S SEE... WHERE SHOULD YOU SIT? WHY DON'T YOU SCOOT YOUR DESK BACK A BIT, MR. ISHIDA?

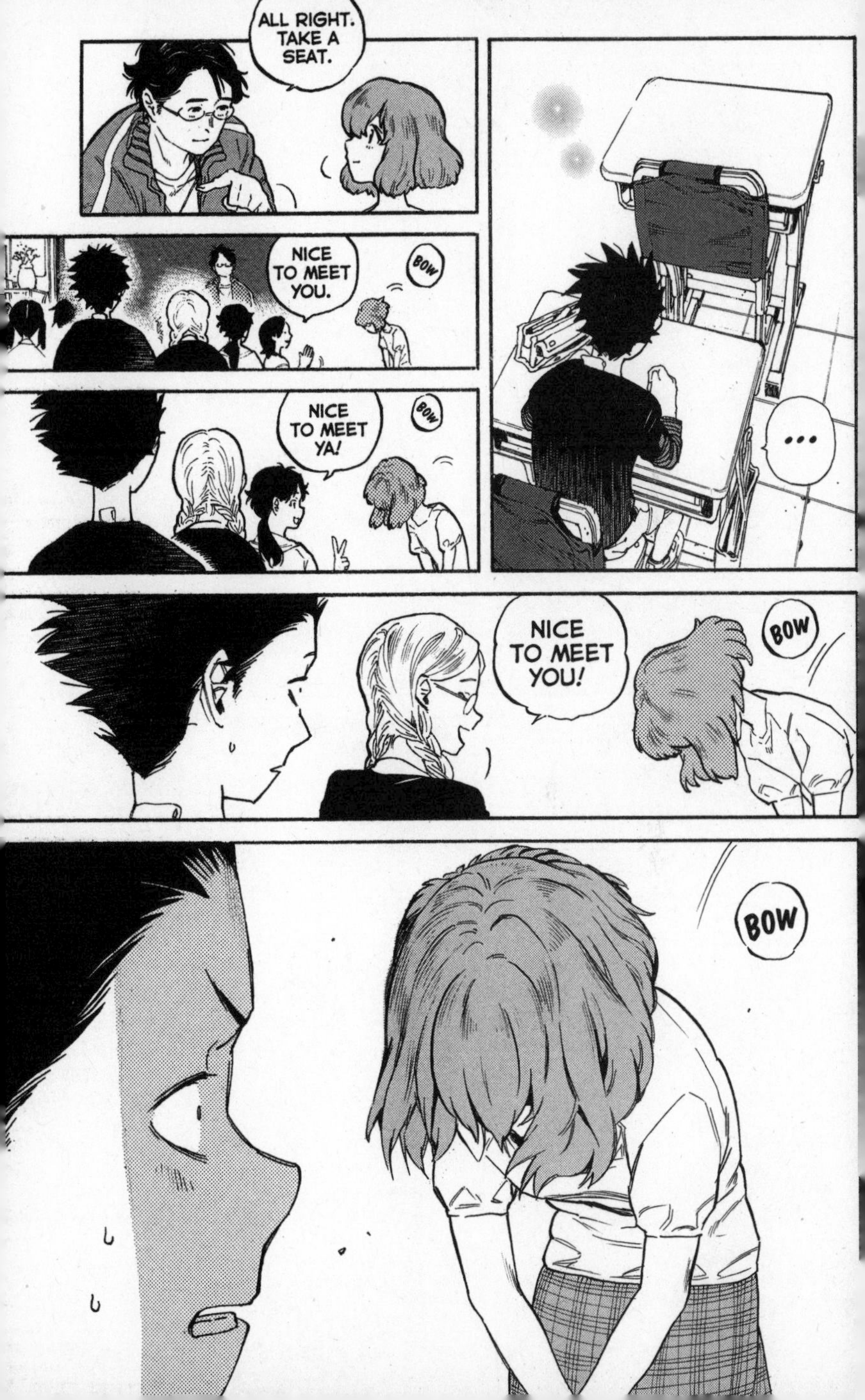
...
ALL RIGHT. TAKE A SEAT.
BOW
NICE TO MEET YOU.
BOW
NICE TO MEET YA!
BOW
NICE TO MEET YOU!
BOW

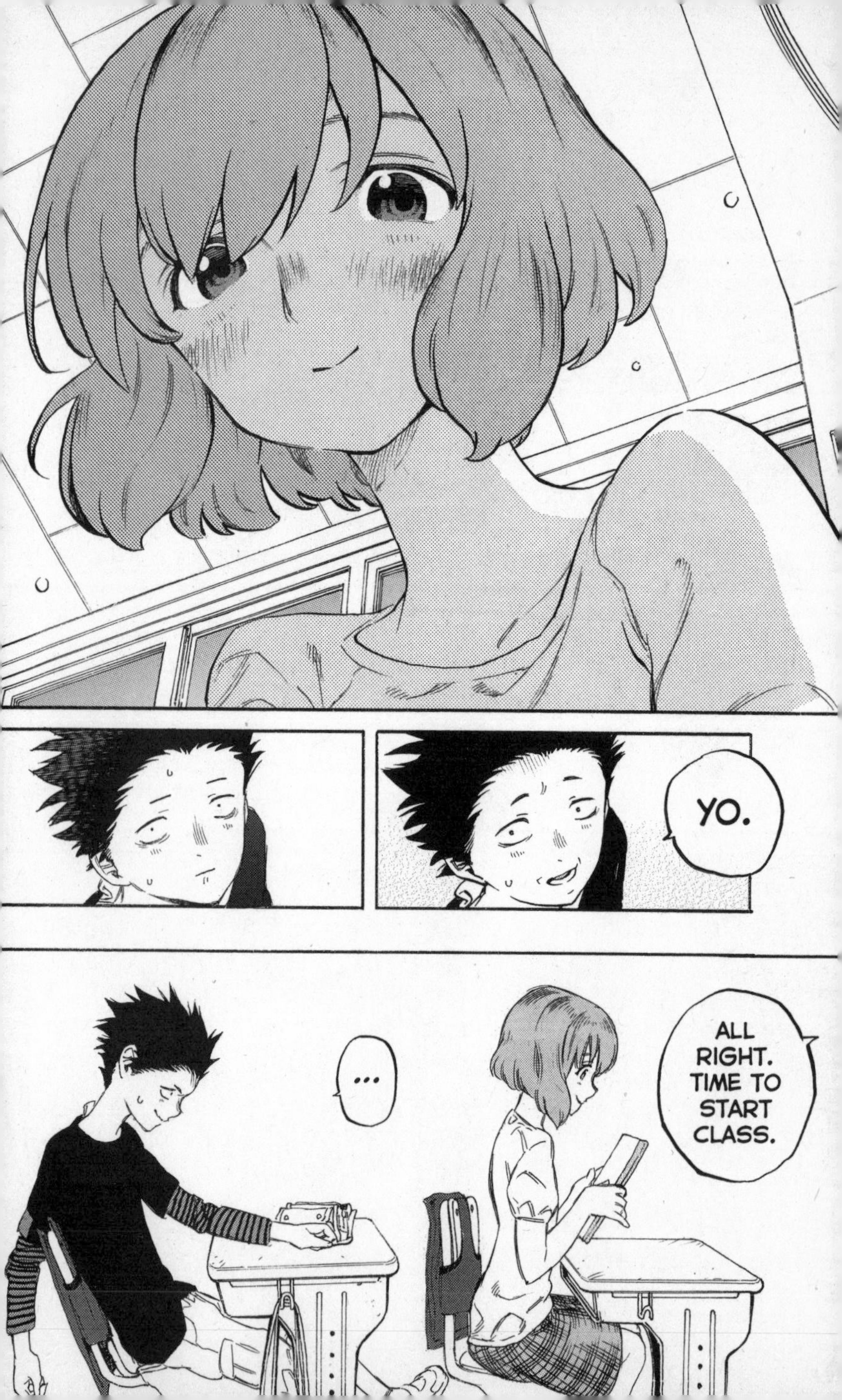
YO.
ALL RIGHT. TIME TO START CLASS.
...

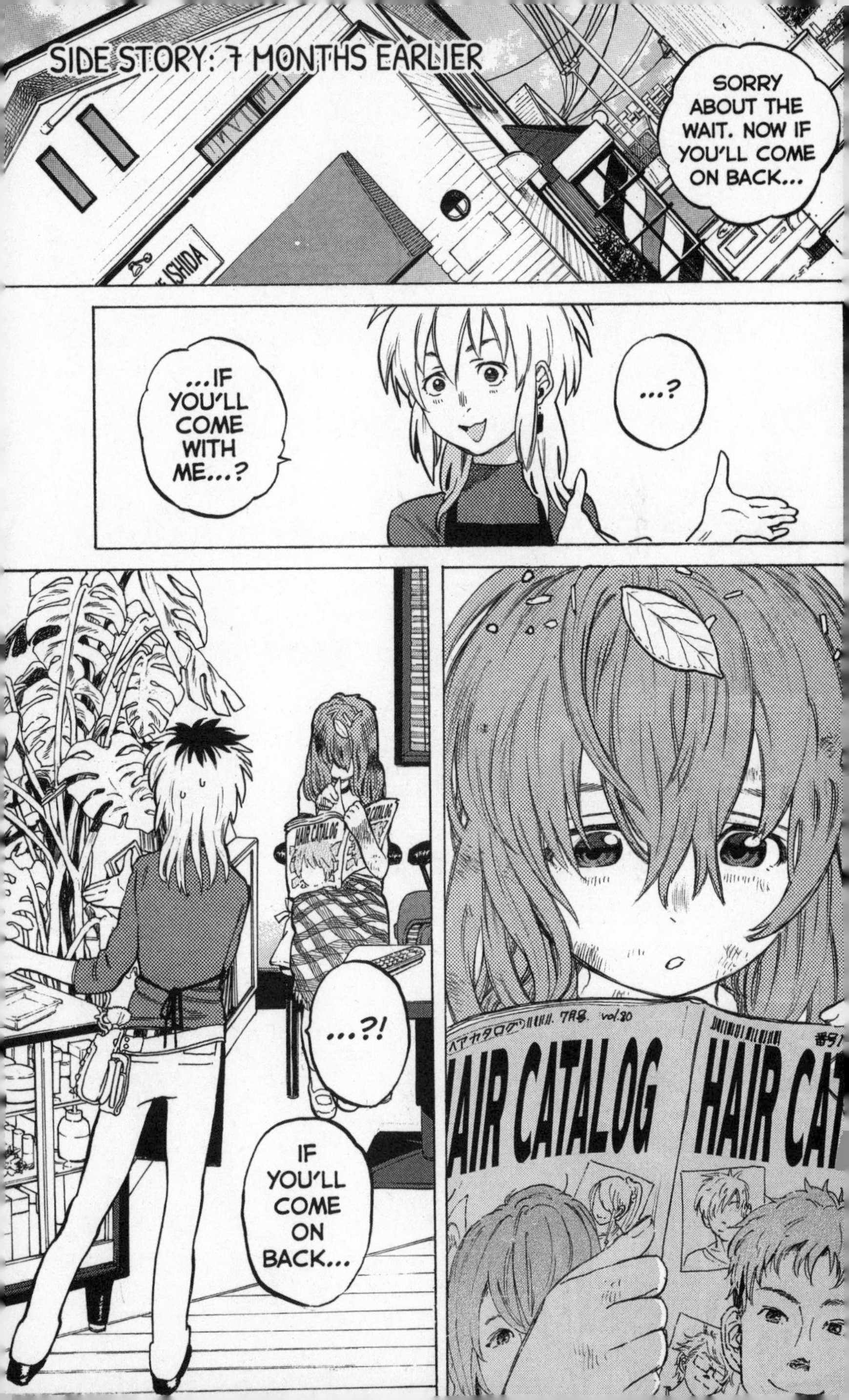
SIDE STORY: 7 MONTHS EARLIER
ISHIDA
SORRY ABOUT THE WAIT. NOW IF YOU'LL COME ON BACK...
...?
...IF YOU'LL COME WITH ME...?
HAIR CATALOG
HAIR CATALOG
HAIR CA
...?!
IF YOU'LL COME ON BACK...

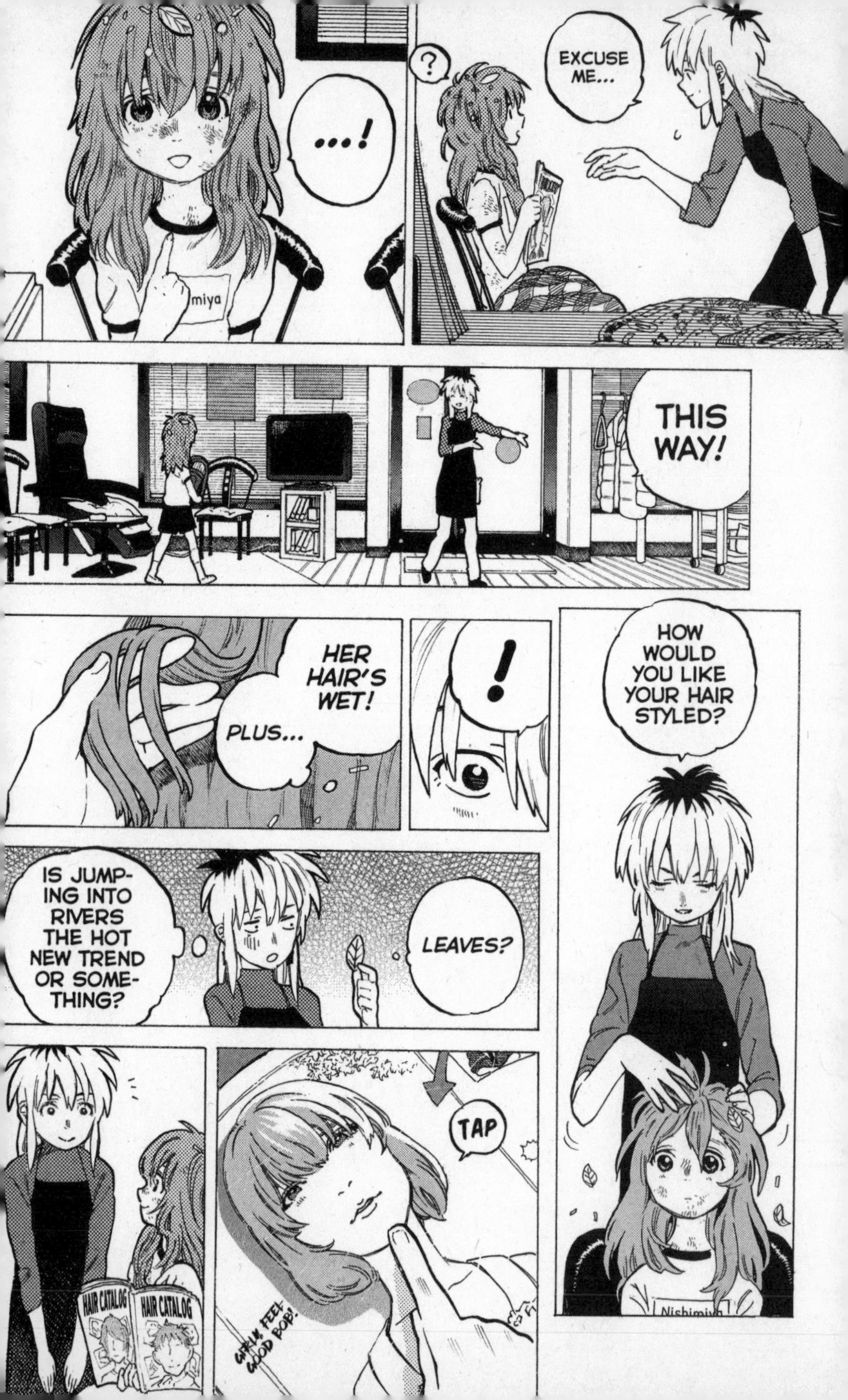
?
EXCUSE ME...
...!
miya
THIS WAY!
HOW WOULD YOU LIKE YOUR HAIR STYLED?
!
HER HAIR'S WET!
PLUS...
LEAVES?
IS JUMPING INTO RIVERS THE HOT NEW TREND OR SOMETHING?
TAP
CURLY, FEEL-GOOD BOB!
HAIR CATALOG
HAIR CATALOG

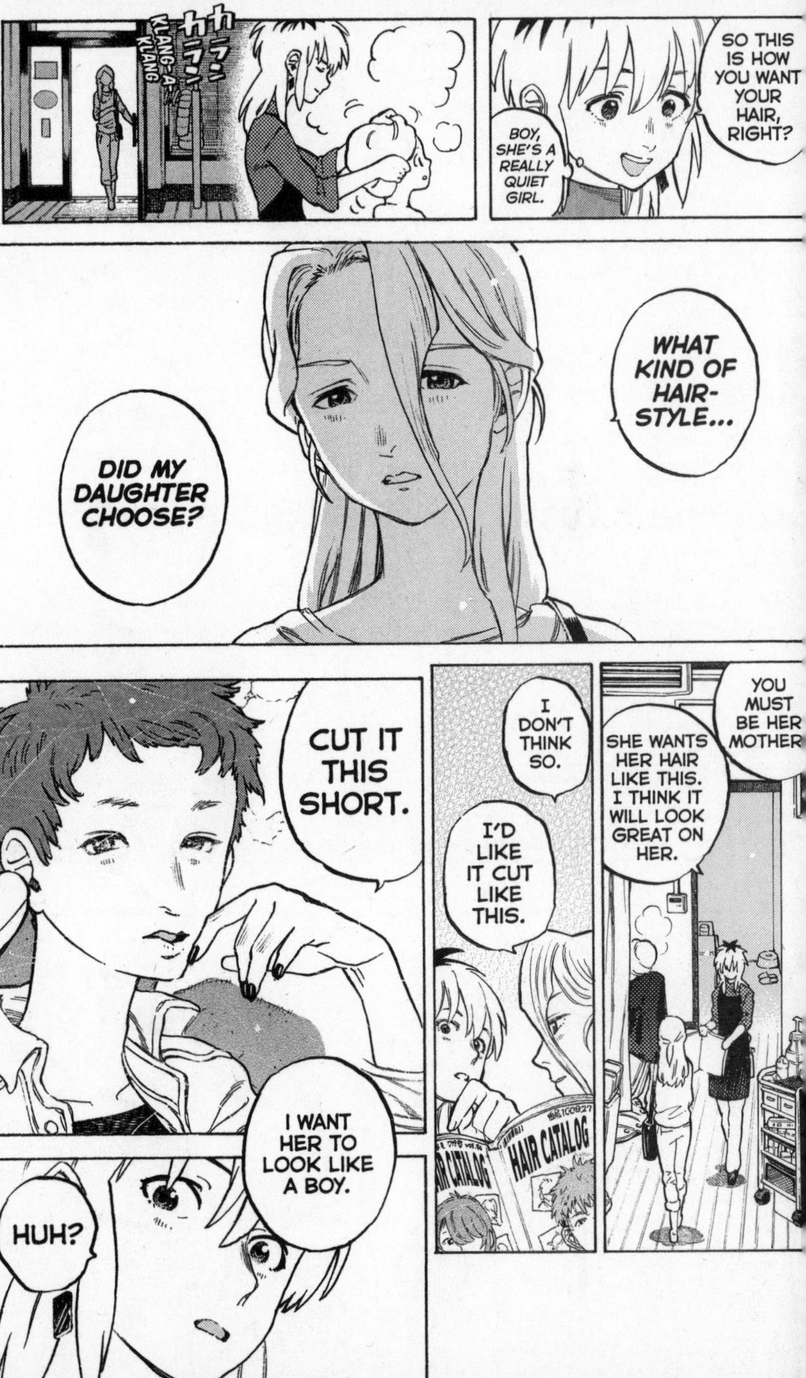
SO THIS IS HOW YOU WANT YOUR HAIR, RIGHT?
BOY, SHE'S A REALLY QUIET GIRL.
KLANG-A-KLANG
WHAT KIND OF HAIR-STYLE...
DID MY DAUGHTER CHOOSE?
YOU MUST BE HER MOTHER
SHE WANTS HER HAIR LIKE THIS. I THINK IT WILL LOOK GREAT ON HER.
I DON'T THINK SO.
I'D LIKE IT CUT LIKE THIS.
HAIR CATALOG
HAIR CATALOG
CUT IT THIS SHORT.
I WANT HER TO LOOK LIKE A BOY.
HUH?

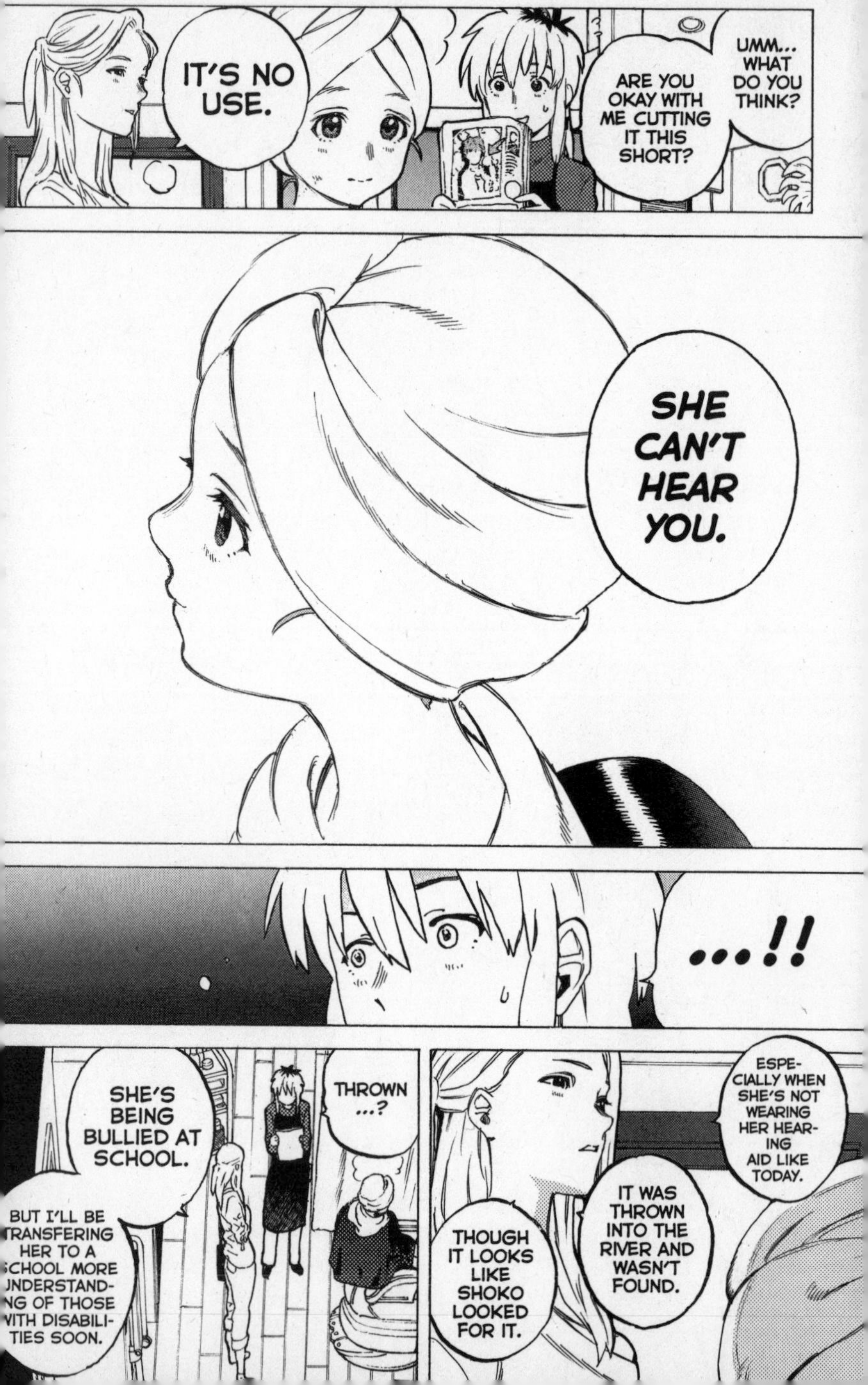
UMM... WHAT DO YOU THINK?
ARE YOU OKAY WITH ME CUTTING IT THIS SHORT?
IT'S NO USE.
SHE CAN'T HEAR YOU.
...!!
ESPECIALLY WHEN SHE'S NOT WEARING HER HEARING AID LIKE TODAY.
IT WAS THROWN INTO THE RIVER AND WASN'T FOUND.
THOUGH IT LOOKS LIKE SHOKO LOOKED FOR IT.
THROWN ...?
SHE'S BEING BULLIED AT SCHOOL.
BUT I'LL BE TRANSFERING HER TO A SCHOOL MORE UNDERSTANDING OF THOSE WITH DISABILITIES SOON.

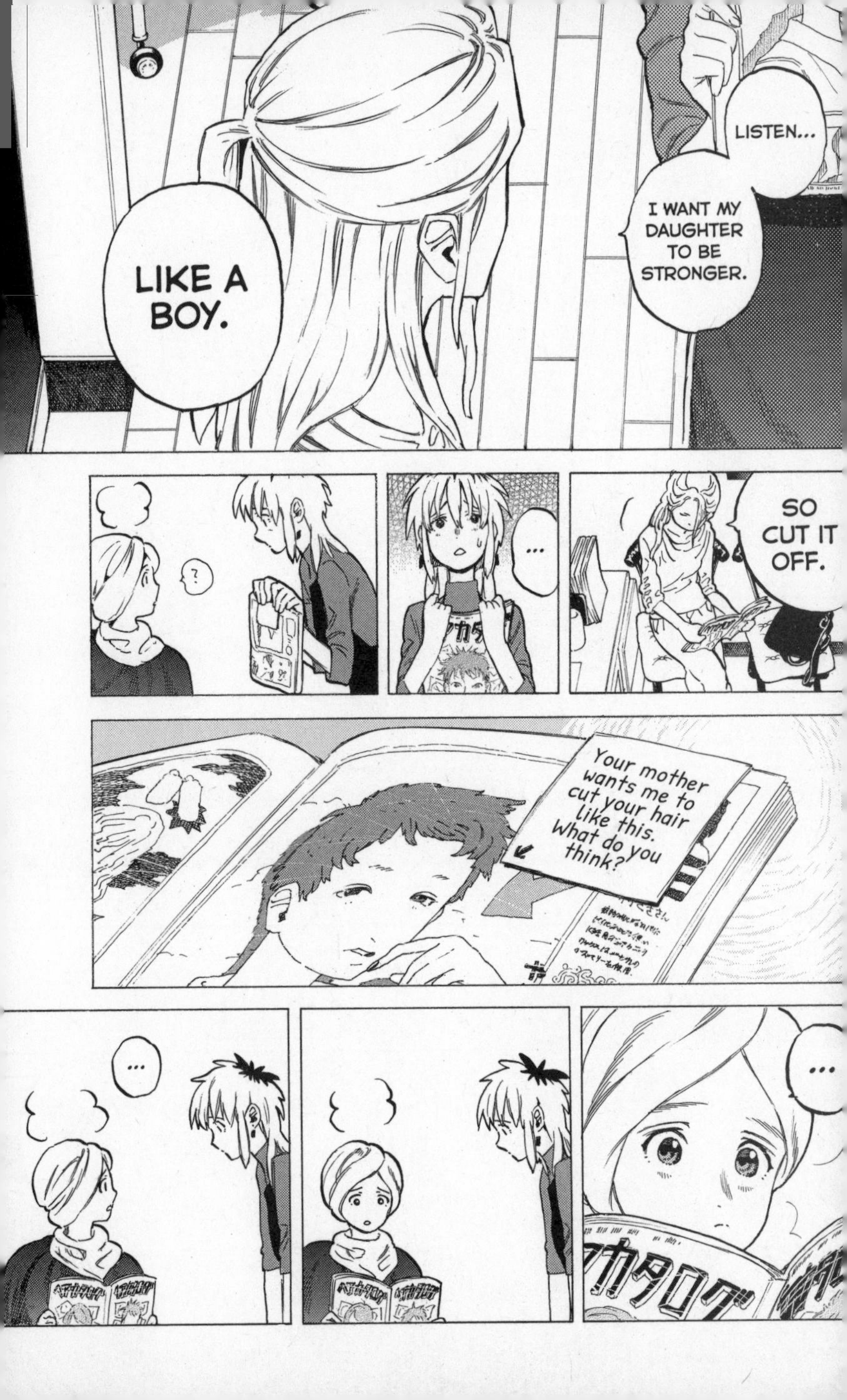
LISTEN...
I WANT MY DAUGHTER TO BE STRONGER.
LIKE A BOY.
SO CUT IT OFF.
...
?
Your mother wants me to cut your hair like this. What do you think?
...
...

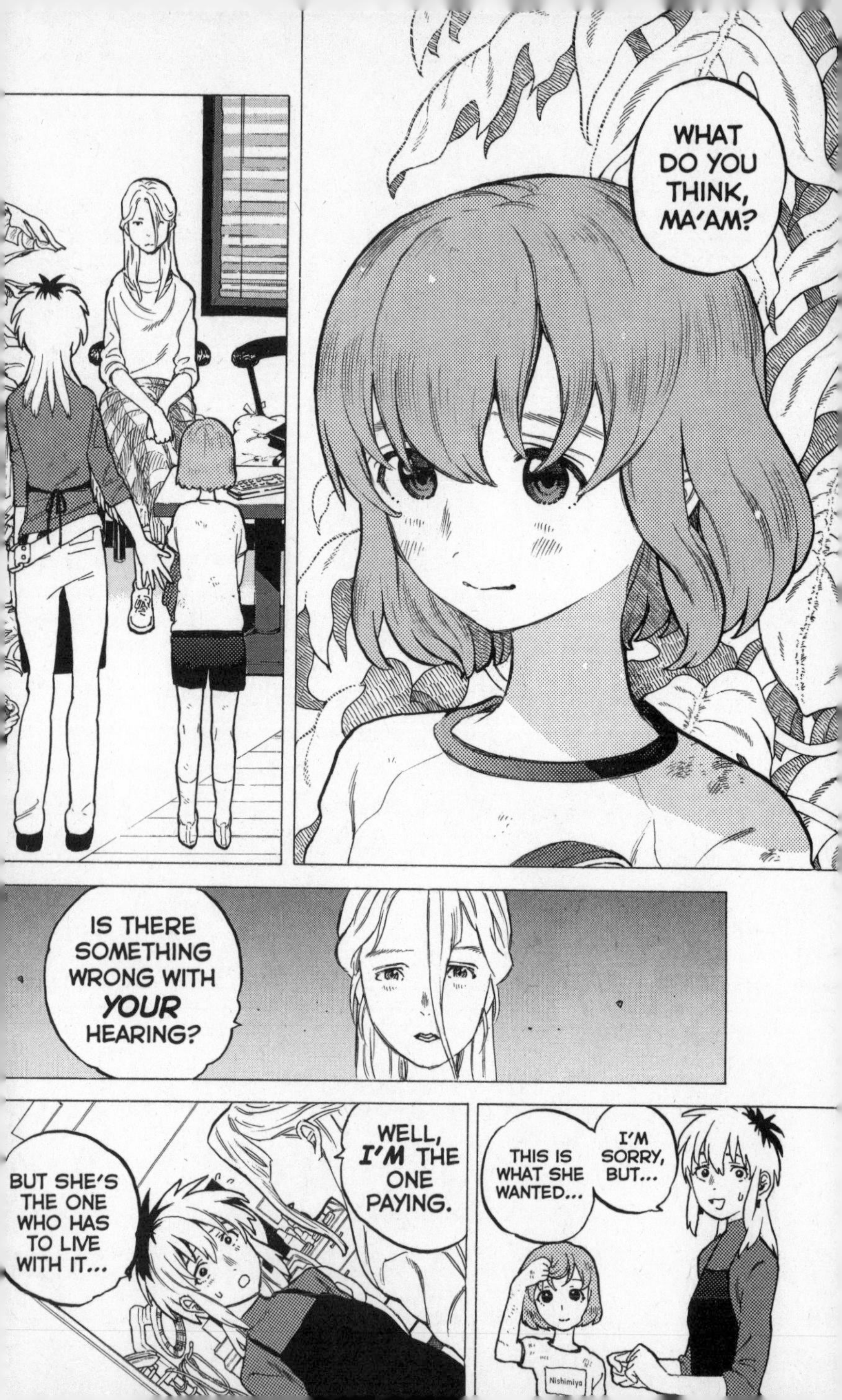
WHAT DO YOU THINK, MA'AM?
IS THERE SOMETHING WRONG WITH *YOUR* HEARING?
I'M SORRY, BUT...
THIS IS WHAT SHE WANTED...
Nishimiya
WELL, *I'M* THE ONE PAYING.
BUT SHE'S THE ONE WHO HAS TO LIVE WITH IT...

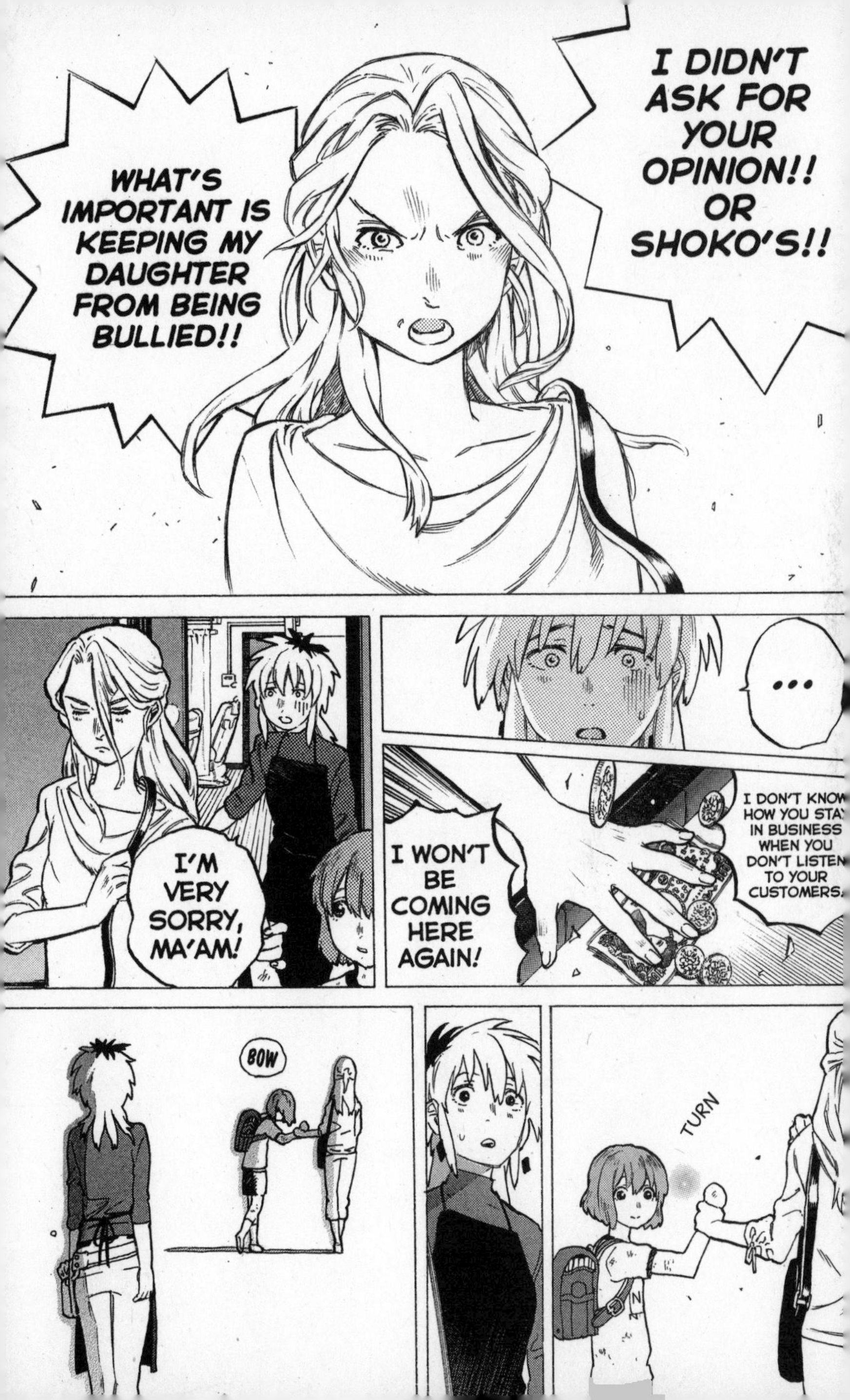
I DIDN'T ASK FOR YOUR OPINION!! OR SHOKO'S!!
WHAT'S IMPORTANT IS KEEPING MY DAUGHTER FROM BEING BULLIED!!
...
I DON'T KNOW HOW YOU STAY IN BUSINESS WHEN YOU DON'T LISTEN TO YOUR CUSTOMERS.
I WON'T BE COMING HERE AGAIN!
I'M VERY SORRY, MA'AM!
TURN
BOW

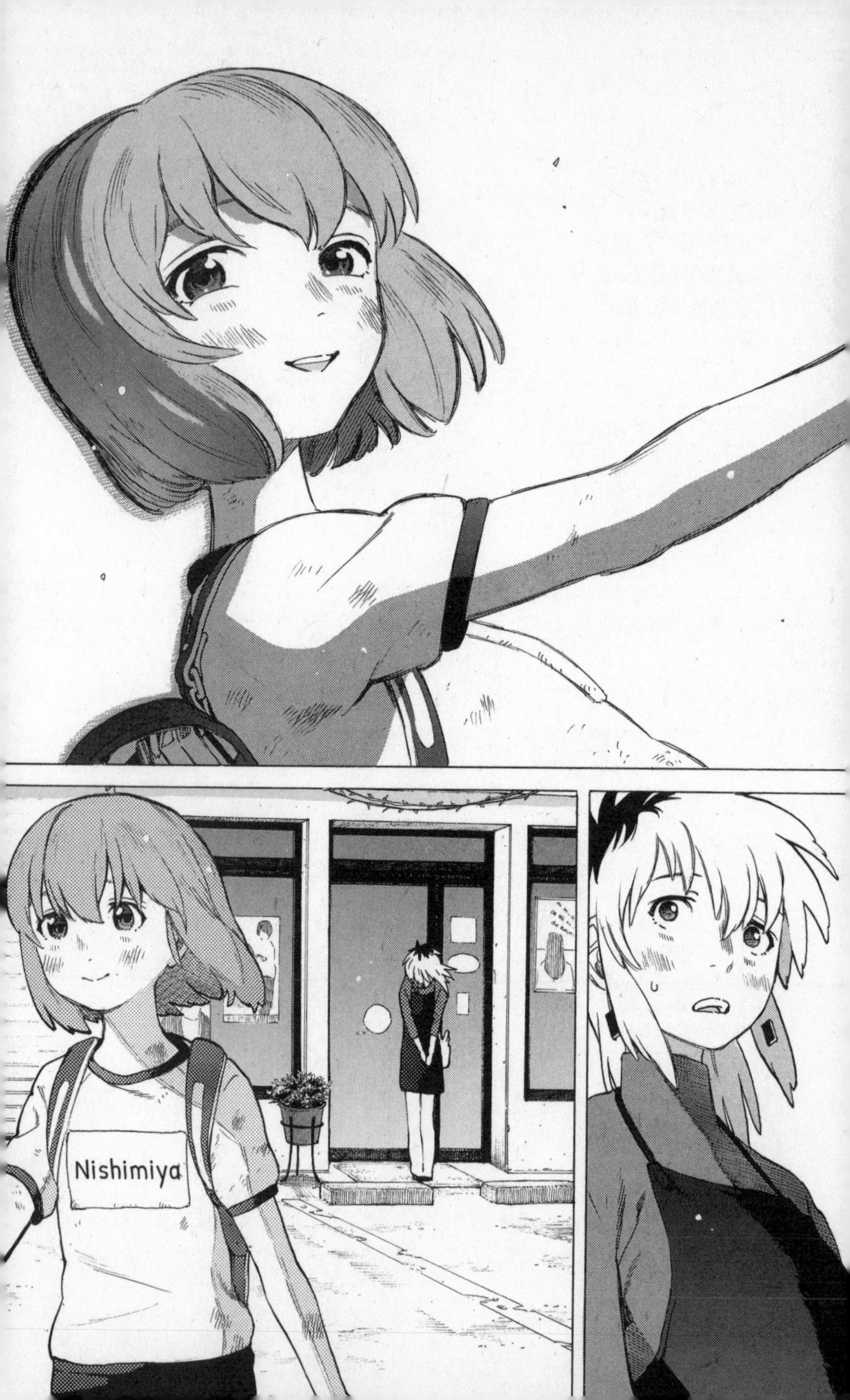
Nishimiya

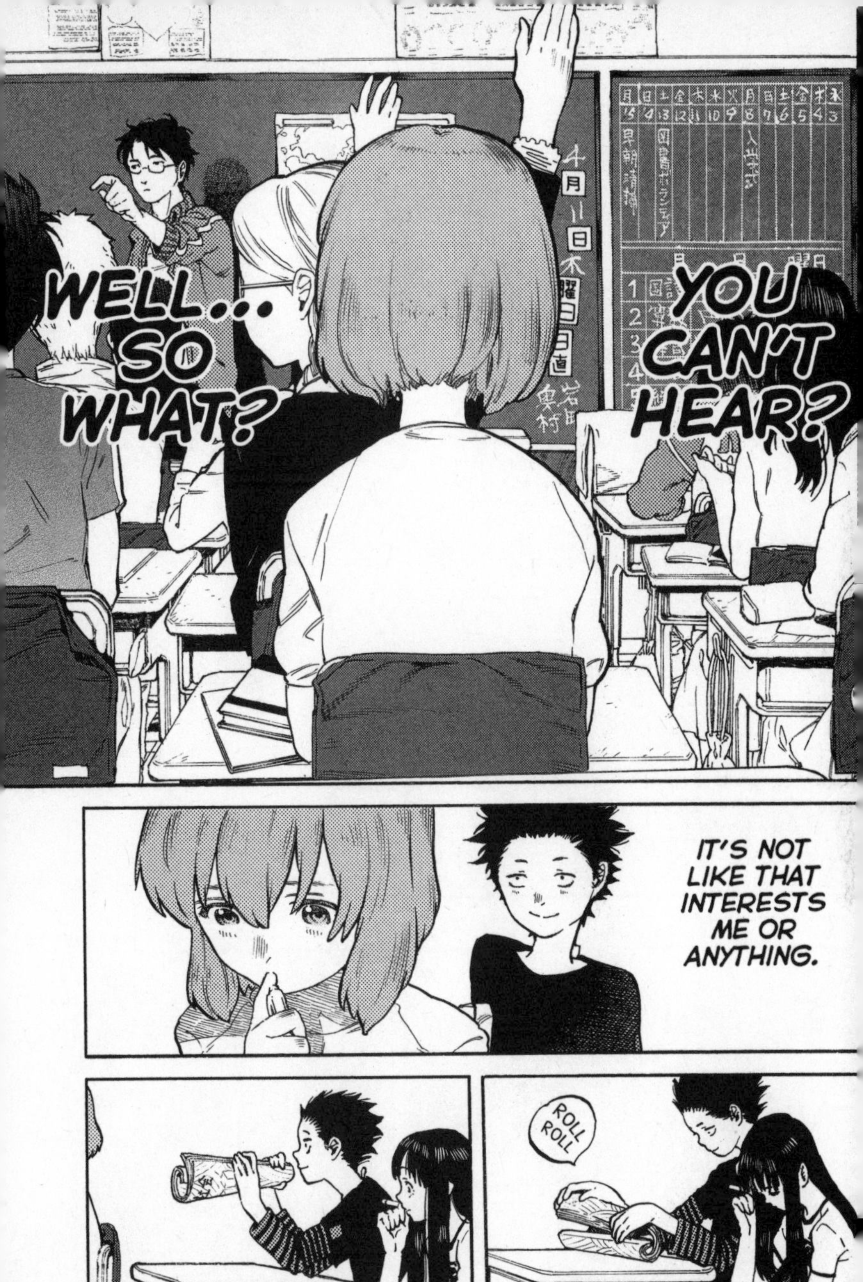
YOU CAN'T HEAR?
WELL... SO WHAT?
IT'S NOT LIKE THAT INTERESTS ME OR ANYTHING.
ROLL ROLL

CHAPTER 2: JUST ONE OF THOSE THINGS

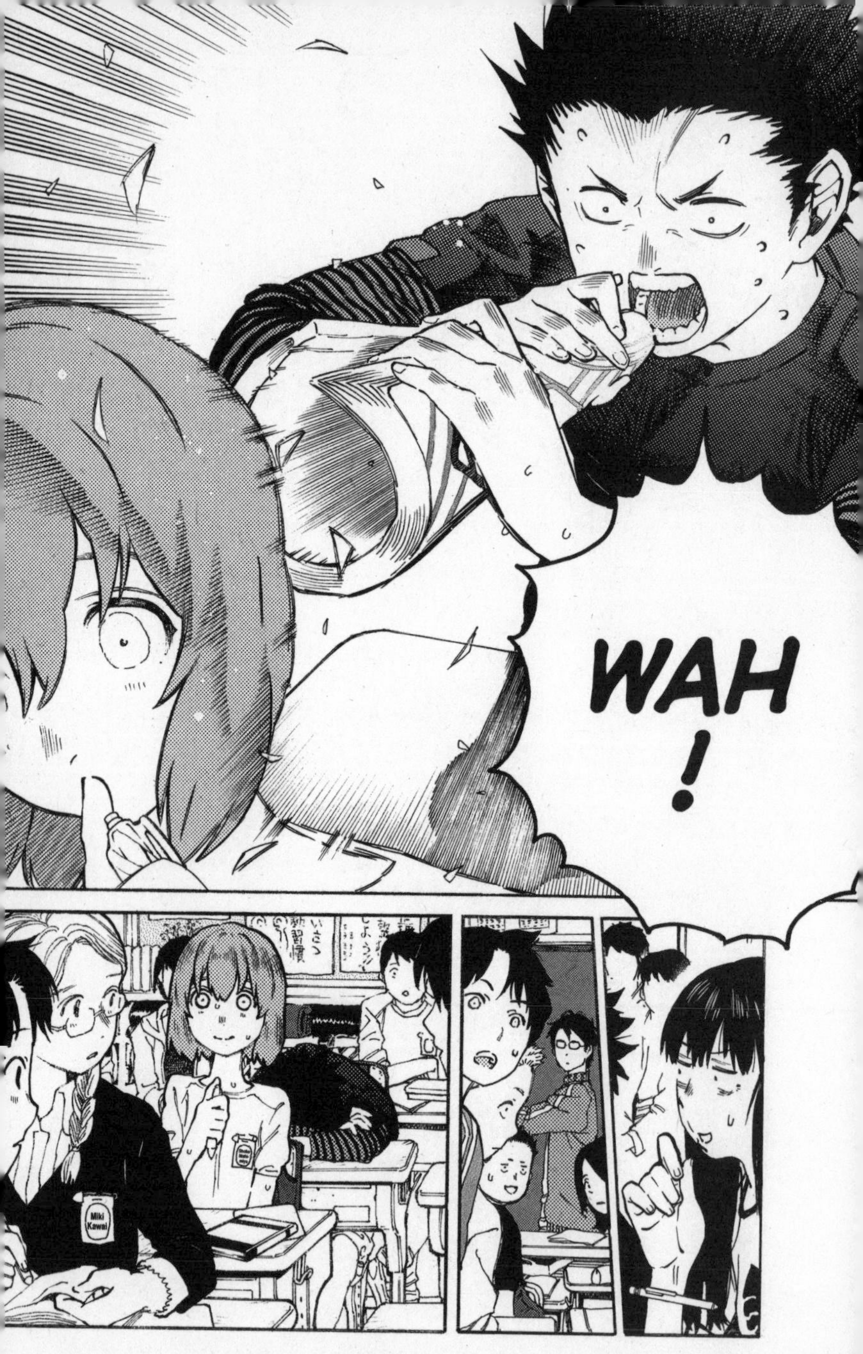
WAH !
Miki Kawai

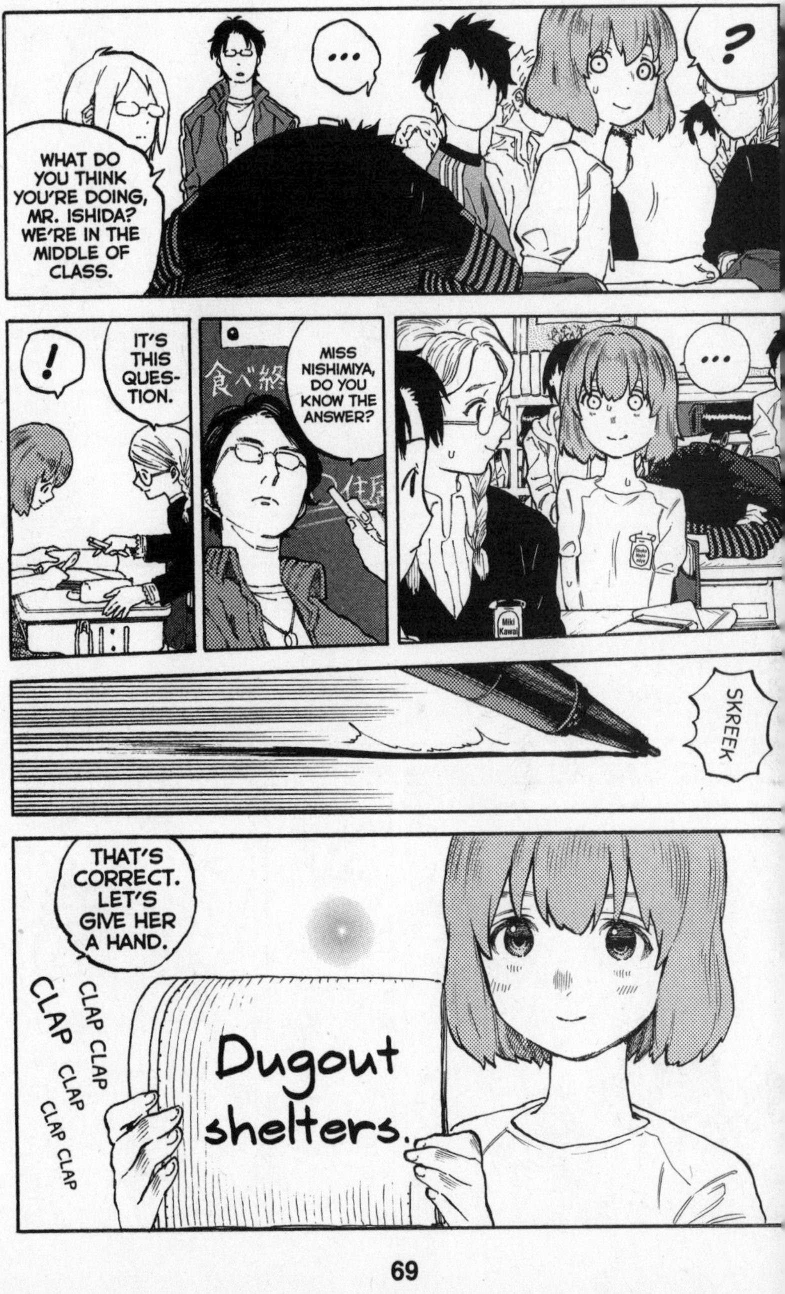
?
...
WHAT DO YOU THINK YOU'RE DOING, MR. ISHIDA? WE'RE IN THE MIDDLE OF CLASS.
...
MISS NISHIMIYA, DO YOU KNOW THE ANSWER?
食べ終
IT'S THIS QUESTION.
!
Miki Kawai
SKREEK
THAT'S CORRECT. LET'S GIVE HER A HAND.
Dugout shelters.
CLAP CLAP
CLAP
CLAP
CLAP
CLAP CLAP

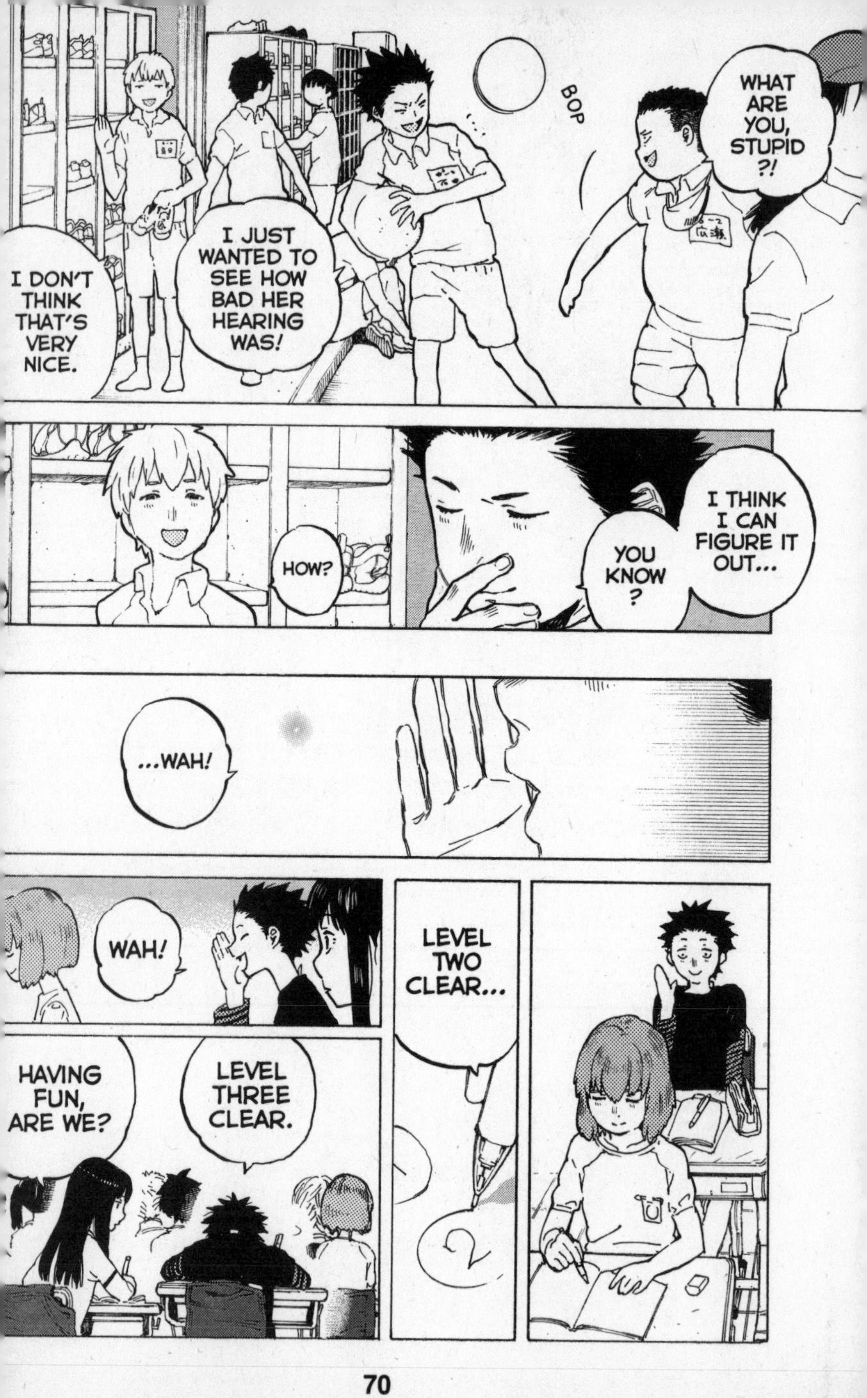
WHAT ARE YOU, STUPID?!
BOP
I JUST WANTED TO SEE HOW BAD HER HEARING WAS!
I DON'T THINK THAT'S VERY NICE.
I THINK I CAN FIGURE IT OUT...
YOU KNOW?
HOW?
...WAH!
LEVEL TWO CLEAR...
WAH!
LEVEL THREE CLEAR.
HAVING FUN, ARE WE?

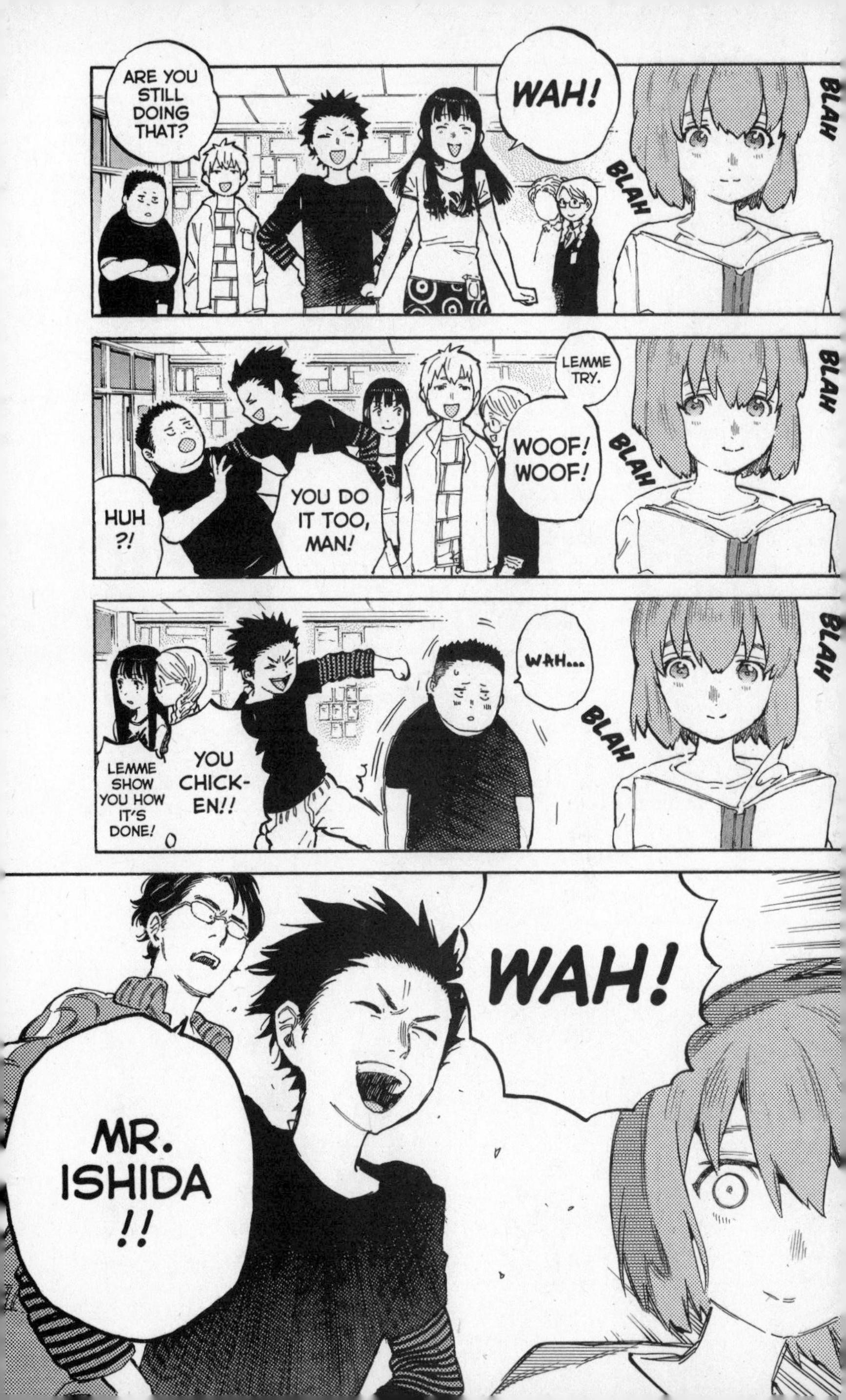

BLAH
BLAH
WAH!
ARE YOU STILL DOING THAT?
BLAH
BLAH
LEMME TRY.
WOOF! WOOF!
YOU DO IT TOO, MAN!
HUH ?!
BLAH
BLAH
WAH...
YOU CHICKEN!!
LEMME SHOW YOU HOW IT'S DONE!
WAH!
MR. ISHIDA !!

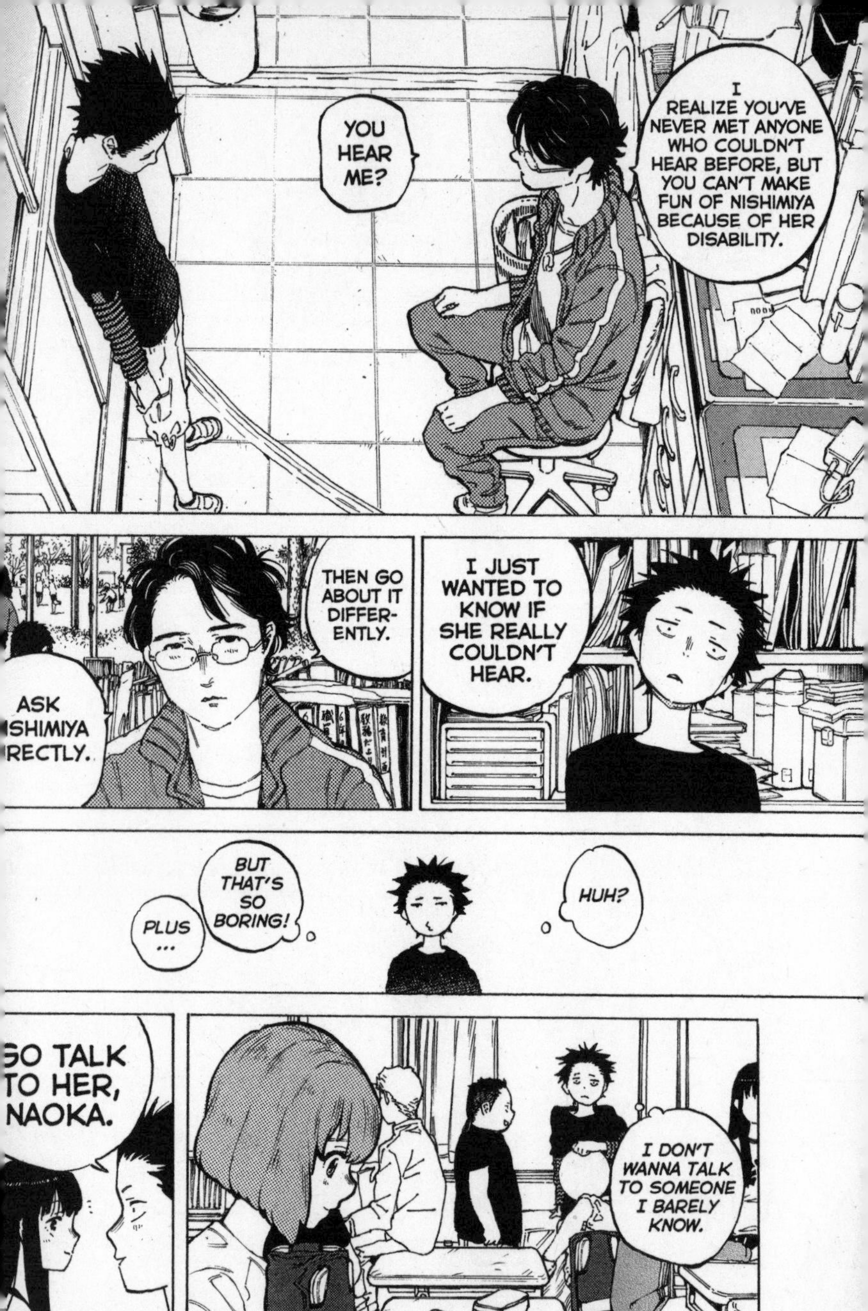
I REALIZE YOU'VE NEVER MET ANYONE WHO COULDN'T HEAR BEFORE, BUT YOU CAN'T MAKE FUN OF NISHIMIYA BECAUSE OF HER DISABILITY.
YOU HEAR ME?
I JUST WANTED TO KNOW IF SHE REALLY COULDN'T HEAR.
THEN GO ABOUT IT DIFFER-ENTLY.
ASK SHIMIYA RECTLY.
HUH?
BUT THAT'S SO BORING!
PLUS ...
I DON'T WANNA TALK TO SOMEONE I BARELY KNOW.
GO TALK TO HER, NAOKA.

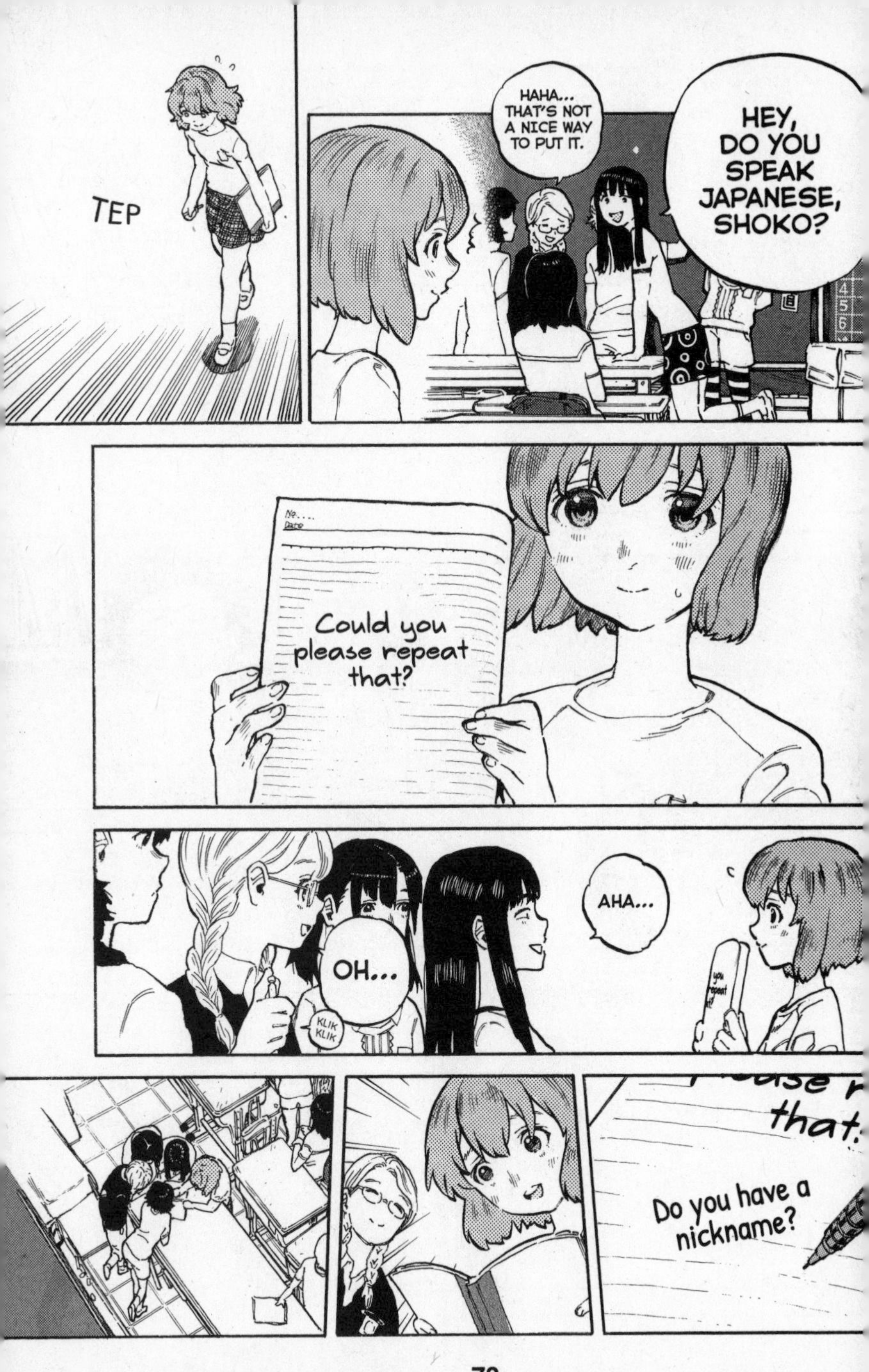
HEY, DO YOU SPEAK JAPANESE, SHOKO?
HAHA... THAT'S NOT A NICE WAY TO PUT IT.
TEP
Could you please repeat that?
AHA...
OH...
KLIK KLIK
Do you have a nickname?

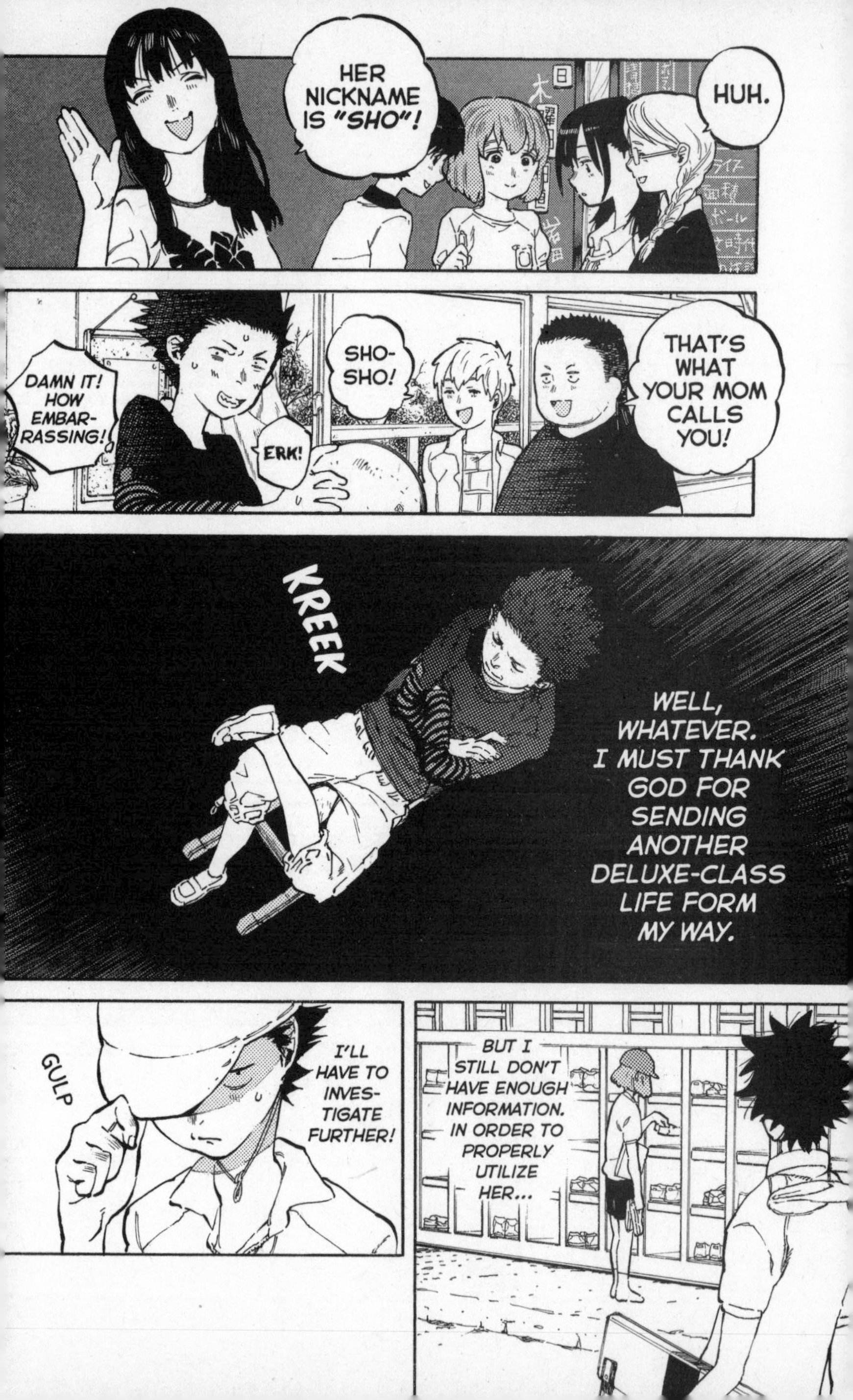
HUH.
HER NICKNAME IS "SHO"!
THAT'S WHAT YOUR MOM CALLS YOU!
SHO-SHO!
ERK!
DAMN IT! HOW EMBARRASSING!
KREEK
WELL, WHATEVER. I MUST THANK GOD FOR SENDING ANOTHER DELUXE-CLASS LIFE FORM MY WAY.
BUT I STILL DON'T HAVE ENOUGH INFORMATION. IN ORDER TO PROPERLY UTILIZE HER...
I'LL HAVE TO INVESTIGATE FURTHER!
GULP

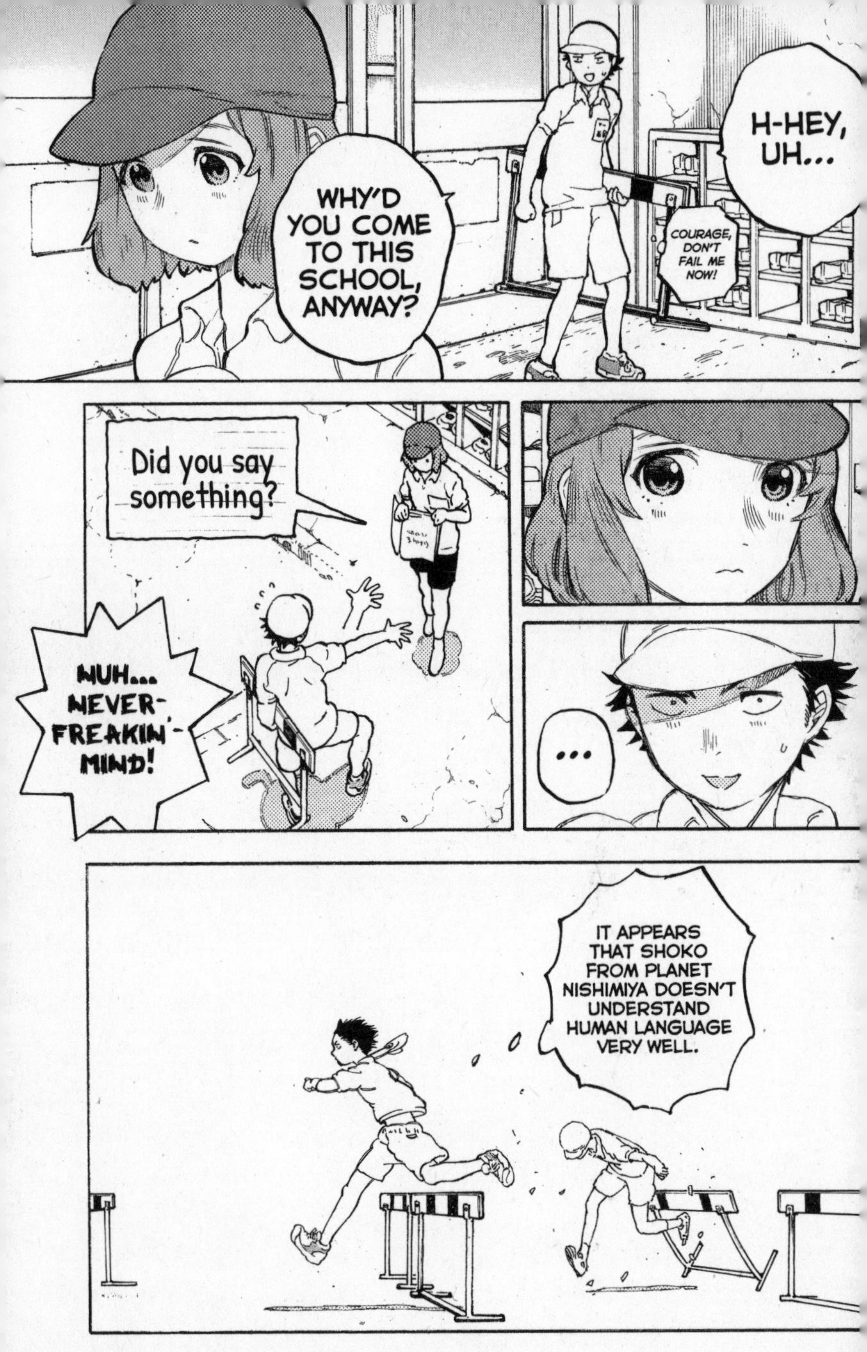
H-HEY, UH...
COURAGE, DON'T FAIL ME NOW!
WHY'D YOU COME TO THIS SCHOOL, ANYWAY?
...
Did you say something?
NUH... NEVER-FREAKIN'-MIND!
IT APPEARS THAT SHOKO FROM PLANET NISHIMIYA DOESN'T UNDERSTAND HUMAN LANGUAGE VERY WELL.

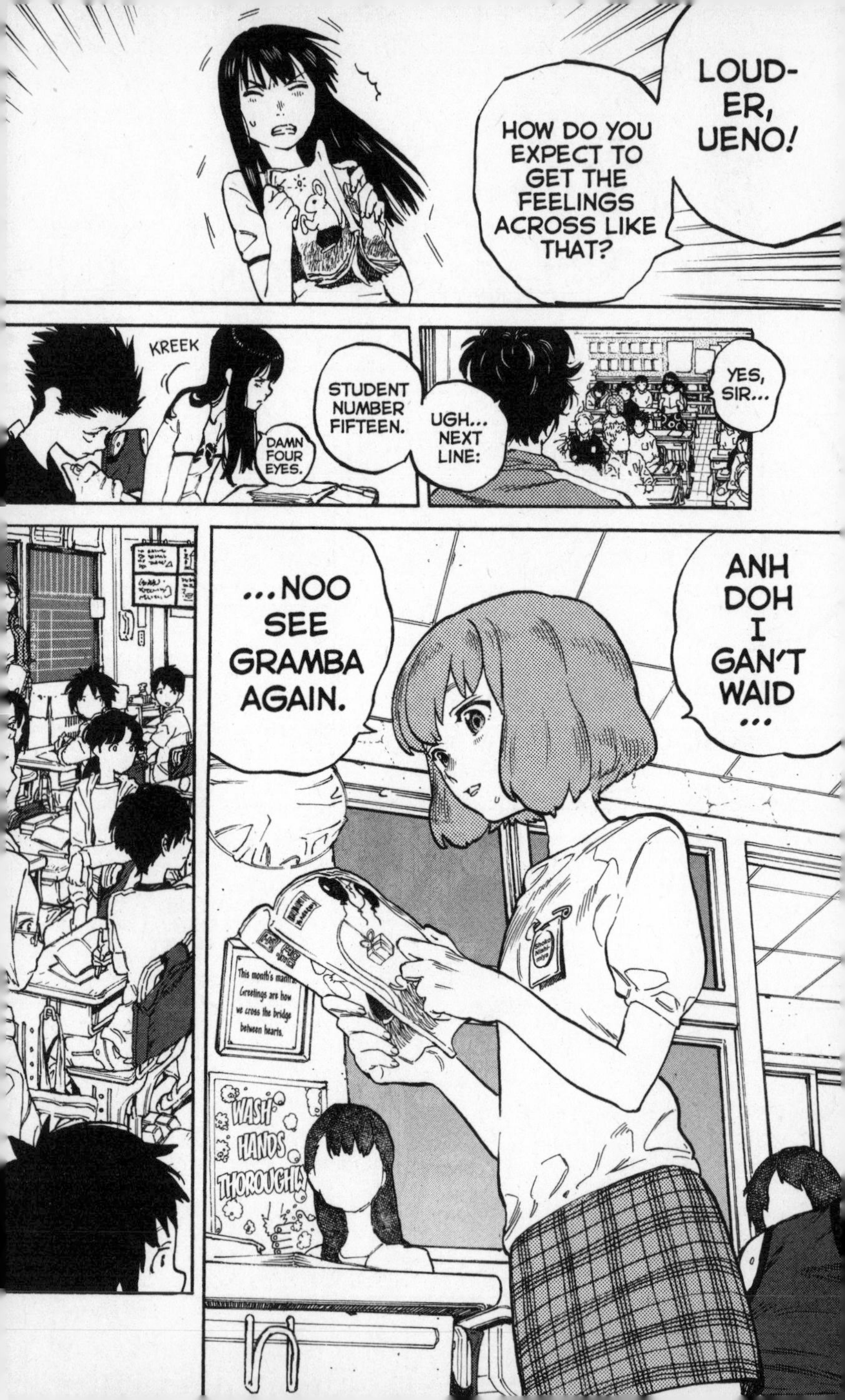
LOUD-ER, UENO!
HOW DO YOU EXPECT TO GET THE FEELINGS ACROSS LIKE THAT?
YES, SIR...
UGH... NEXT LINE:
STUDENT NUMBER FIFTEEN.
KREEK
DAMN FOUR EYES.
ANH DOH I GAN'T WAID ...
...NOO SEE GRAMBA AGAIN.
Shoko Nishimiya
This month's mantra: Greetings are how we cross the bridge between hearts.
WASH HANDS THOROUGHLY!

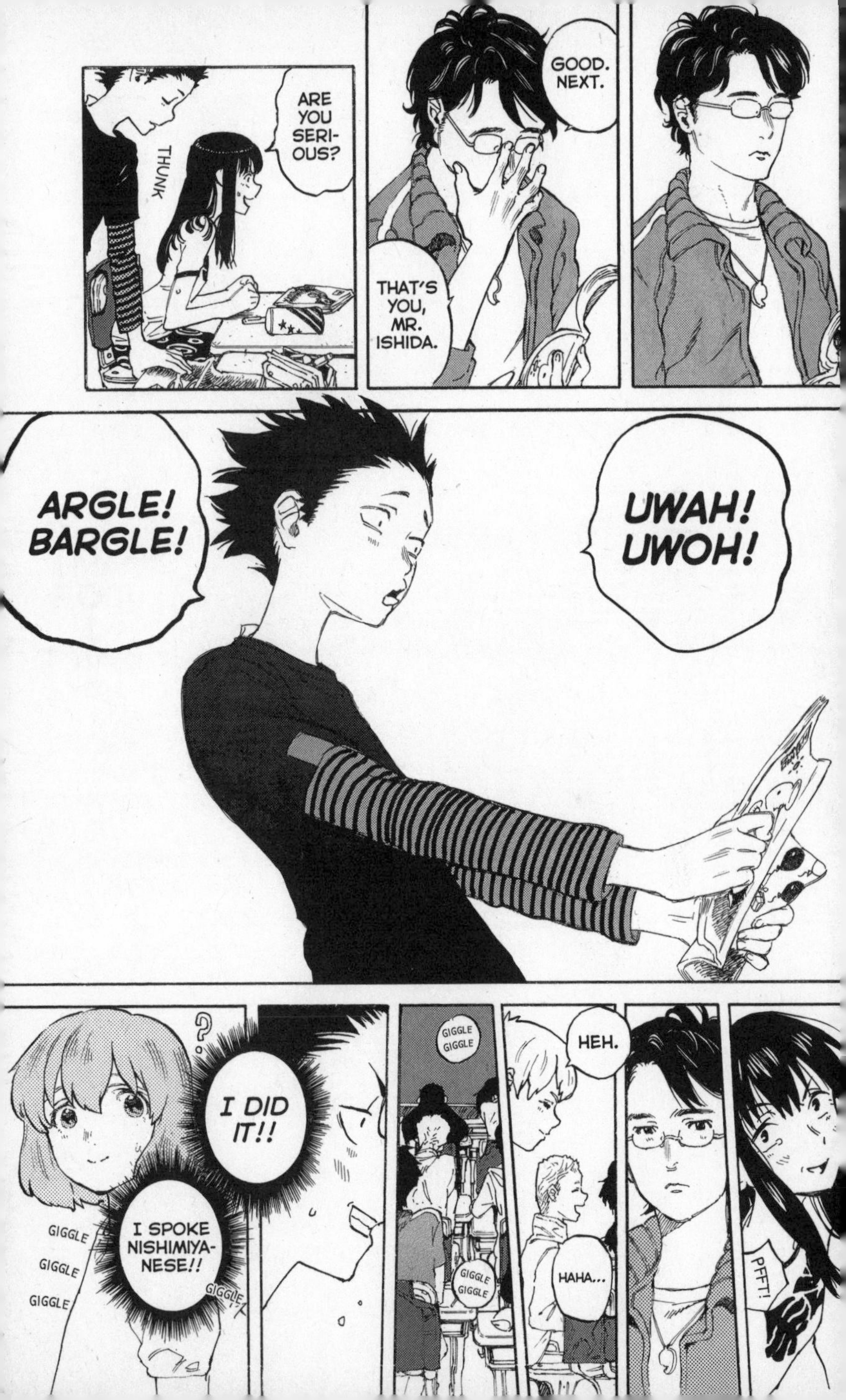
GOOD. NEXT.
THAT'S YOU, MR. ISHIDA.
ARE YOU SERIOUS?
THUNK
UWAH! UWOH!
ARGLE! BARGLE!
PFFT!
HEH.
HAHA...
GIGGLE GIGGLE
GIGGLE GIGGLE
I DID IT!!
I SPOKE NISHIMIYA-NESE!!
GIGGLE
?
GIGGLE
GIGGLE
GIGGLE

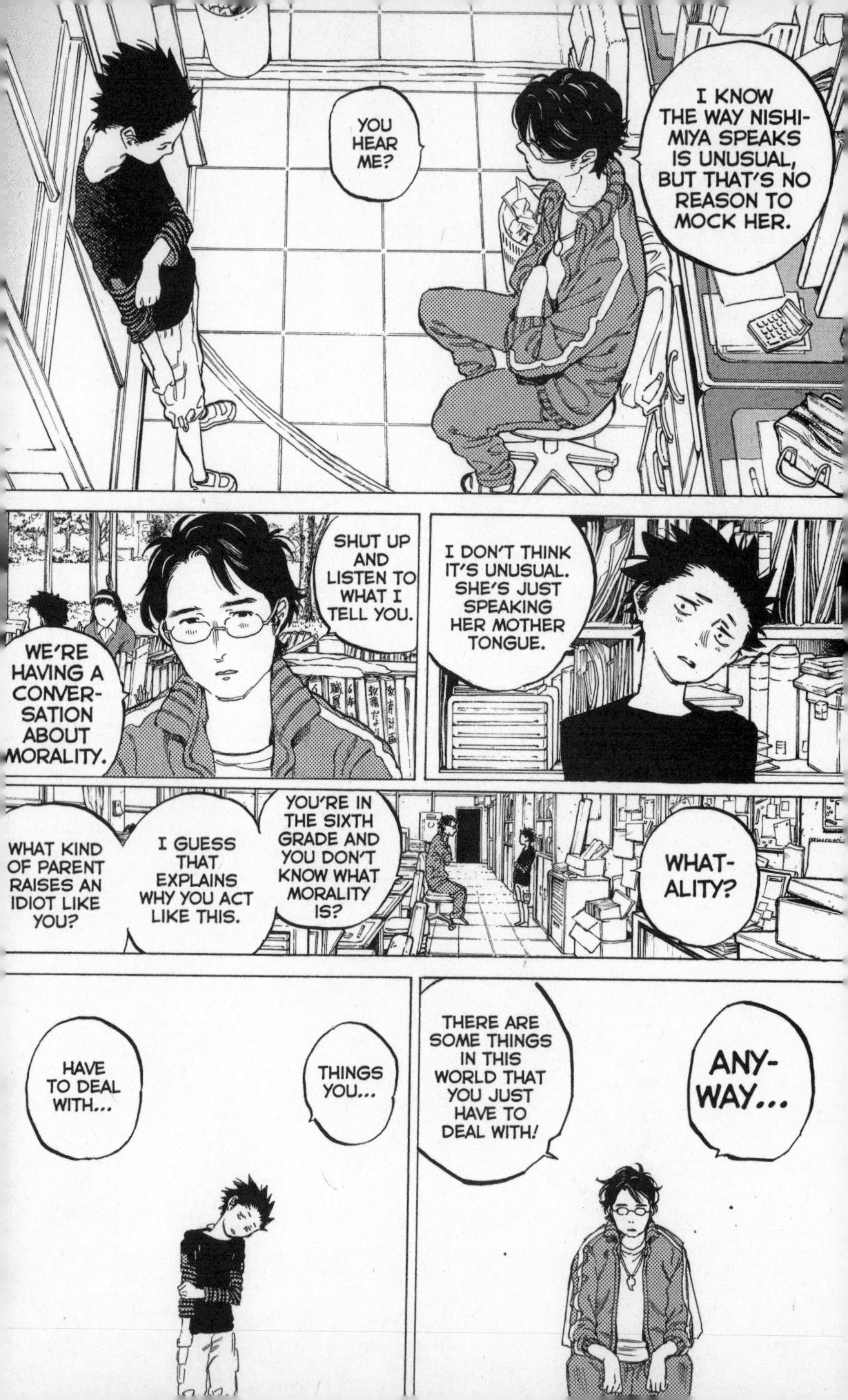

I KNOW THE WAY NISHI-MIYA SPEAKS IS UNUSUAL, BUT THAT'S NO REASON TO MOCK HER.
YOU HEAR ME?
I DON'T THINK IT'S UNUSUAL. SHE'S JUST SPEAKING HER MOTHER TONGUE.
SHUT UP AND LISTEN TO WHAT I TELL YOU.
WE'RE HAVING A CONVER-SATION ABOUT MORALITY.
WHAT-ALITY?
YOU'RE IN THE SIXTH GRADE AND YOU DON'T KNOW WHAT MORALITY IS?
I GUESS THAT EXPLAINS WHY YOU ACT LIKE THIS.
WHAT KIND OF PARENT RAISES AN IDIOT LIKE YOU?
ANY-WAY...
THERE ARE SOME THINGS IN THIS WORLD THAT YOU JUST HAVE TO DEAL WITH!
THINGS YOU...
HAVE TO DEAL WITH...

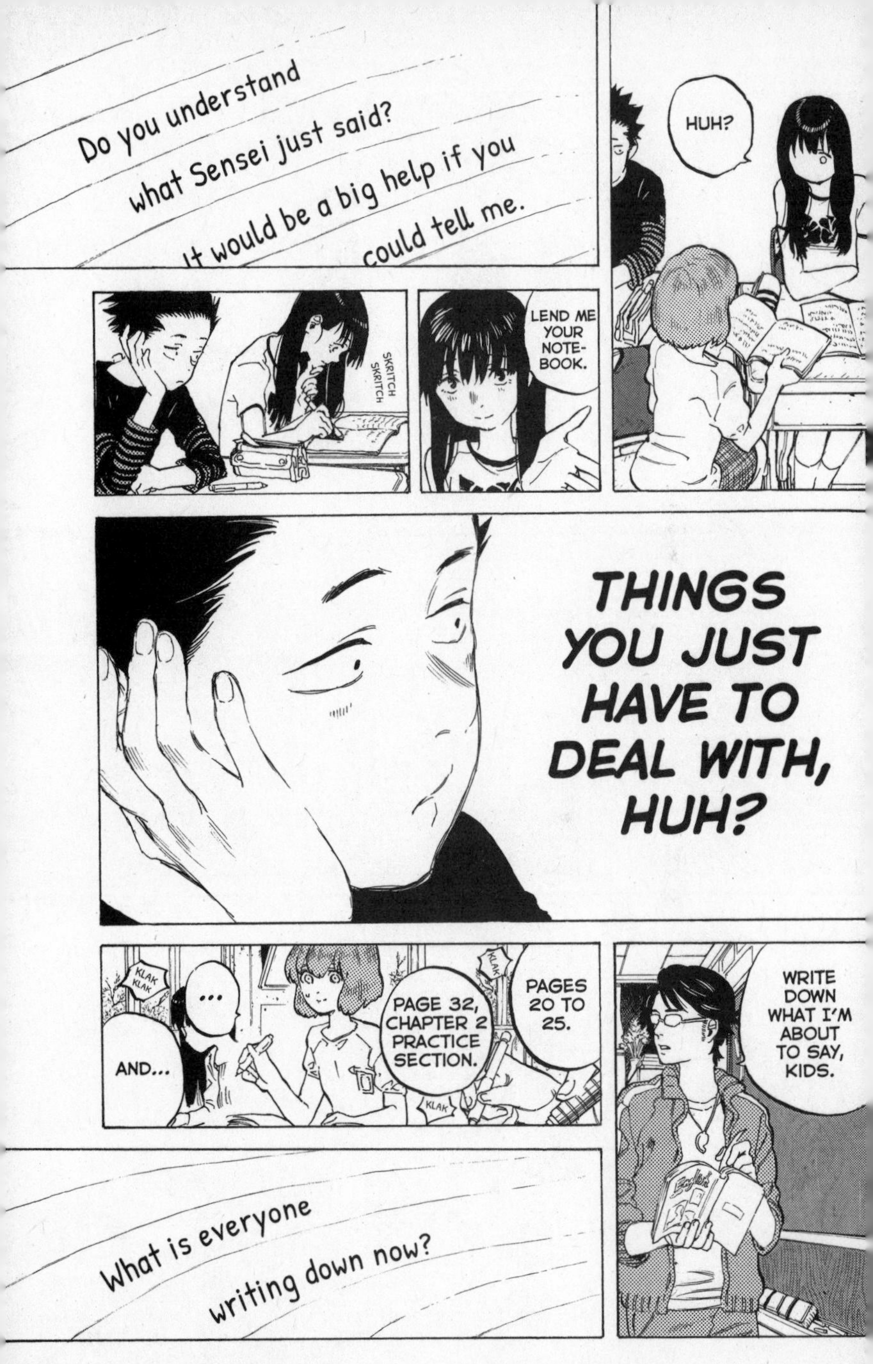
HUH?
Do you understand what Sensei just said?
It would be a big help if you could tell me.
LEND ME YOUR NOTE-BOOK.
SKRITCH SKRITCH
THINGS YOU JUST HAVE TO DEAL WITH, HUH?
WRITE DOWN WHAT I'M ABOUT TO SAY, KIDS.
PAGES 20 TO 25.
KLAK
PAGE 32, CHAPTER 2 PRACTICE SECTION.
KLAK KLAK
...
AND...
KLAK
What is everyone writing down now?

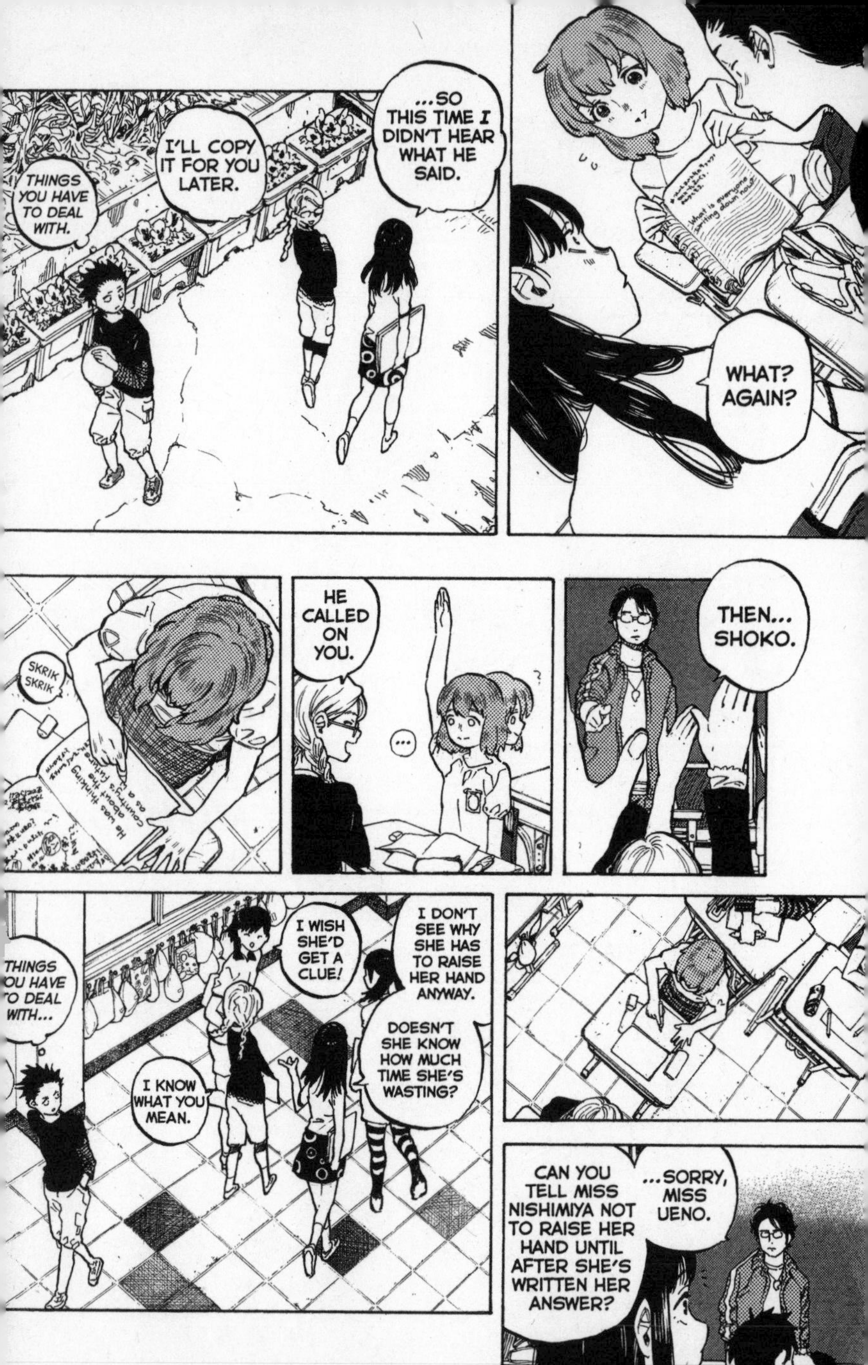
What is everyone writing down now?
WHAT? AGAIN?
...SO THIS TIME I DIDN'T HEAR WHAT HE SAID.
I'LL COPY IT FOR YOU LATER.
THINGS YOU HAVE TO DEAL WITH.
THEN... SHOKO.
HE CALLED ON YOU.
...
SKRIK SKRIK
...SORRY, MISS UENO.
CAN YOU TELL MISS NISHIMIYA NOT TO RAISE HER HAND UNTIL AFTER SHE'S WRITTEN HER ANSWER?
I DON'T SEE WHY SHE HAS TO RAISE HER HAND ANYWAY.
I WISH SHE'D GET A CLUE!
DOESN'T SHE KNOW HOW MUCH TIME SHE'S WASTING?
I KNOW WHAT YOU MEAN.
THINGS OU HAVE O DEAL WITH...

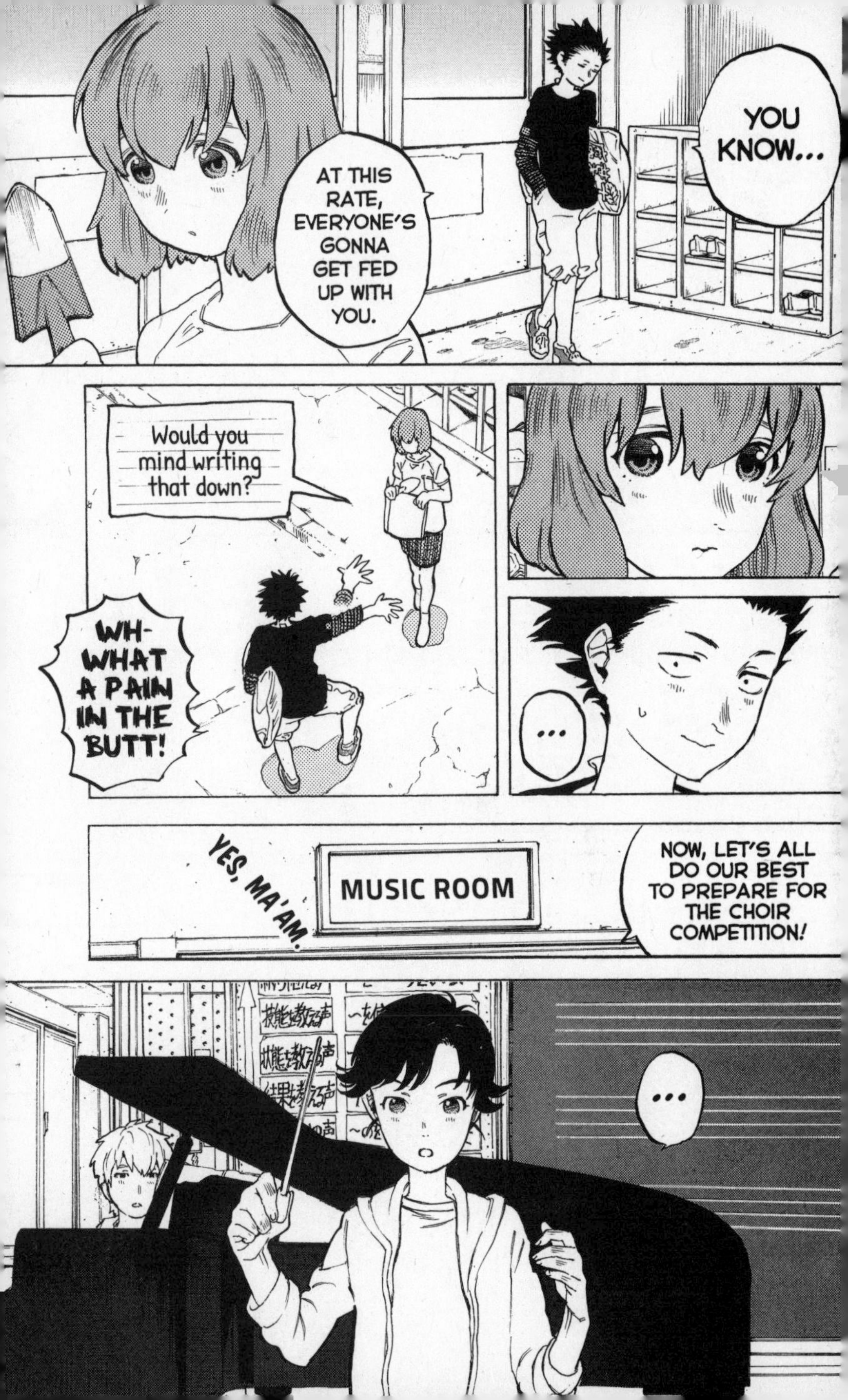
YOU KNOW...
AT THIS RATE, EVERYONE'S GONNA GET FED UP WITH YOU.
...
Would you mind writing that down?
WH-WHAT A PAIN IN THE BUTT!
NOW, LET'S ALL DO OUR BEST TO PREPARE FOR THE CHOIR COMPETITION!
MUSIC ROOM
YES, MA'AM.
...

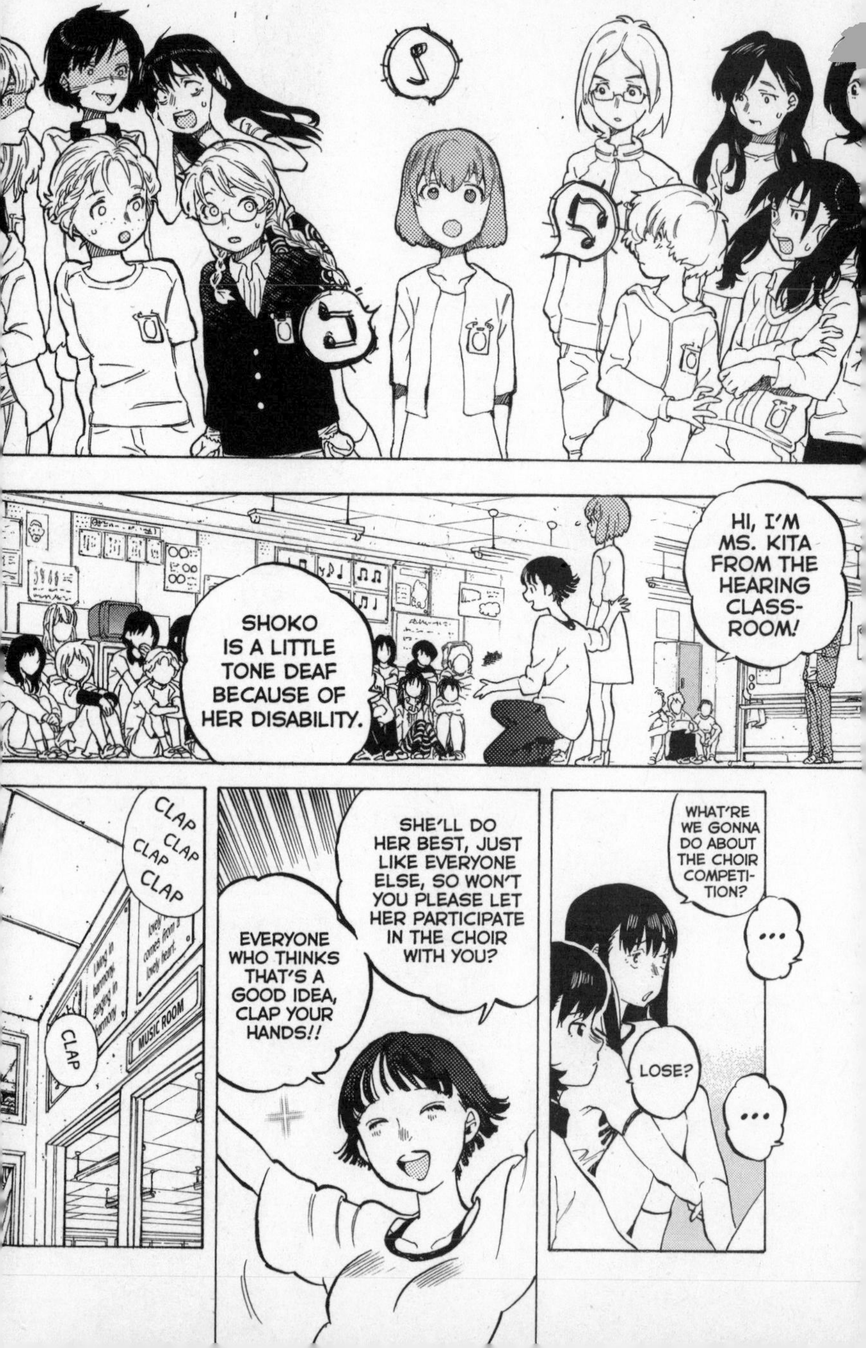
HI, I'M MS. KITA FROM THE HEARING CLASS-ROOM!
SHOKO IS A LITTLE TONE DEAF BECAUSE OF HER DISABILITY.
WHAT'RE WE GONNA DO ABOUT THE CHOIR COMPETITION?
...
LOSE?
...
SHE'LL DO HER BEST, JUST LIKE EVERYONE ELSE, SO WON'T YOU PLEASE LET HER PARTICIPATE IN THE CHOIR WITH YOU?
EVERYONE WHO THINKS THAT'S A GOOD IDEA, CLAP YOUR HANDS!!
CLAP CLAP CLAP CLAP
Living in harmony, singing in harmony
MUSIC ROOM
CLAP

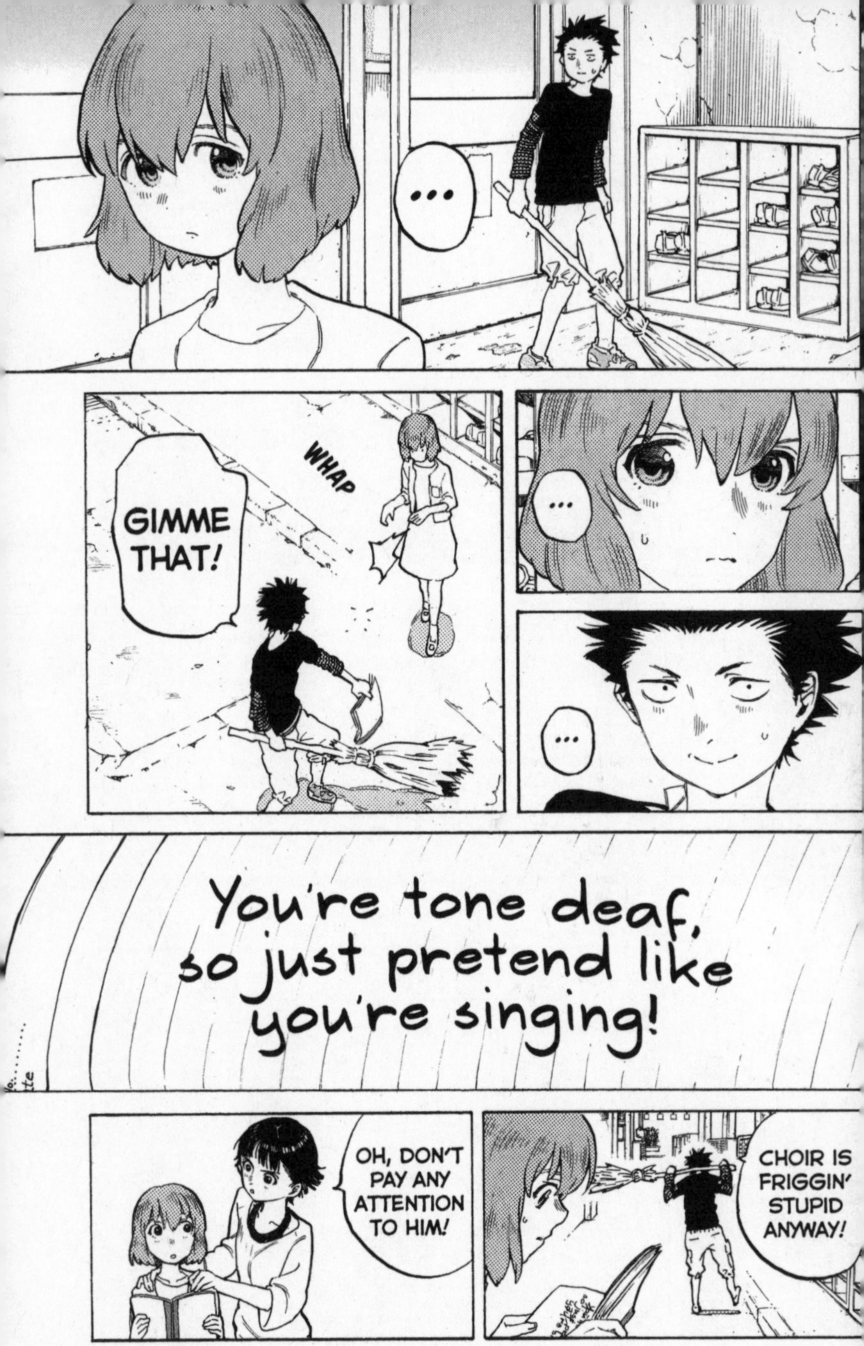
...
...
...
GIMME THAT!
WHAP
You're tone deaf, so just pretend like you're singing!
CHOIR IS FRIGGIN' STUPID ANYWAY!
OH, DON'T PAY ANY ATTENTION TO HIM!

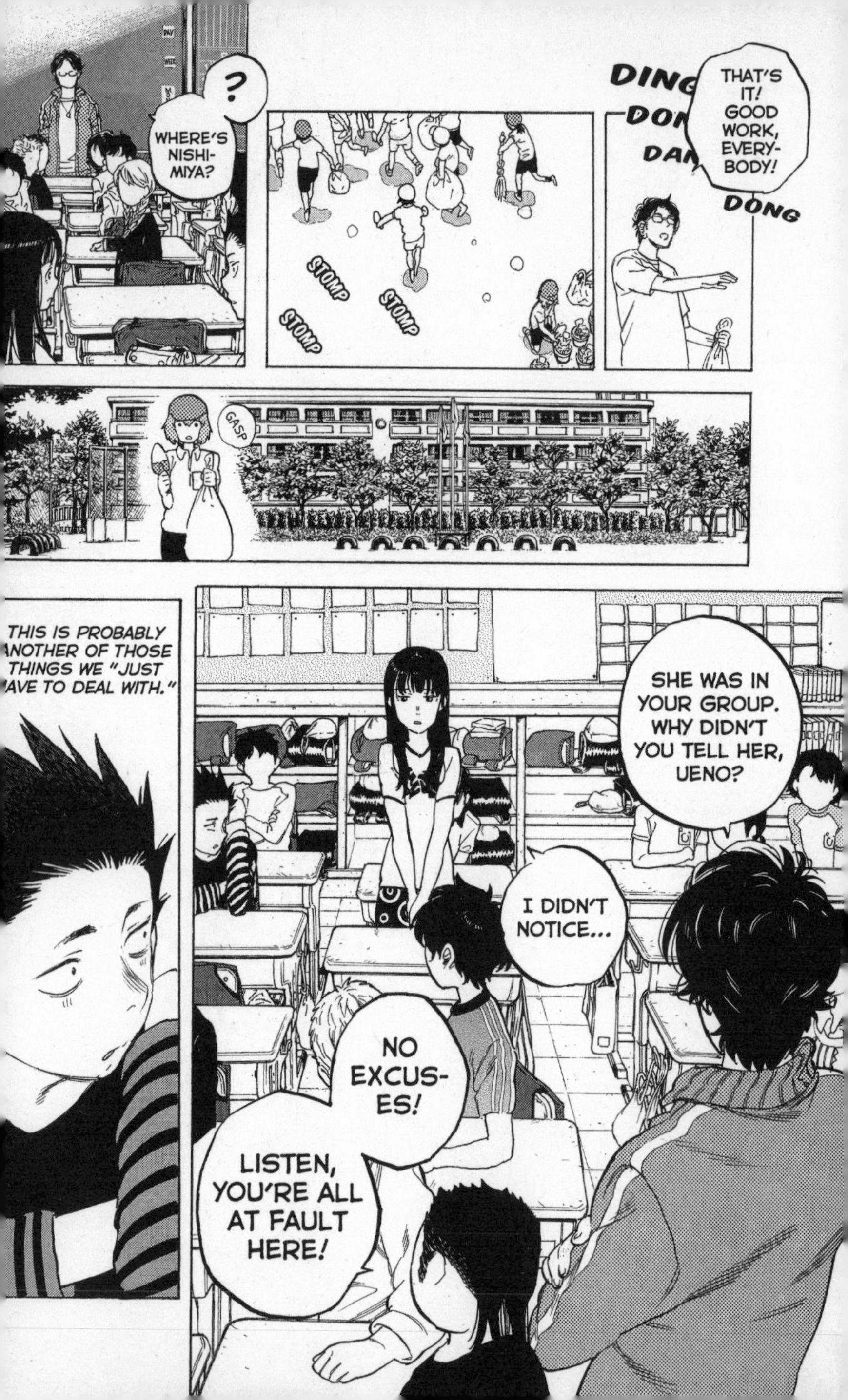
DING
DON
DAN
THAT'S IT! GOOD WORK, EVERY-BODY!
DONG
STOMP
STOMP
STOMP
?
WHERE'S NISHI-MIYA?
GASP
SHE WAS IN YOUR GROUP. WHY DIDN'T YOU TELL HER, UENO?
I DIDN'T NOTICE...
NO EXCUS-ES!
LISTEN, YOU'RE ALL AT FAULT HERE!
THIS IS PROBABLY ANOTHER OF THOSE THINGS WE "JUST AVE TO DEAL WITH."

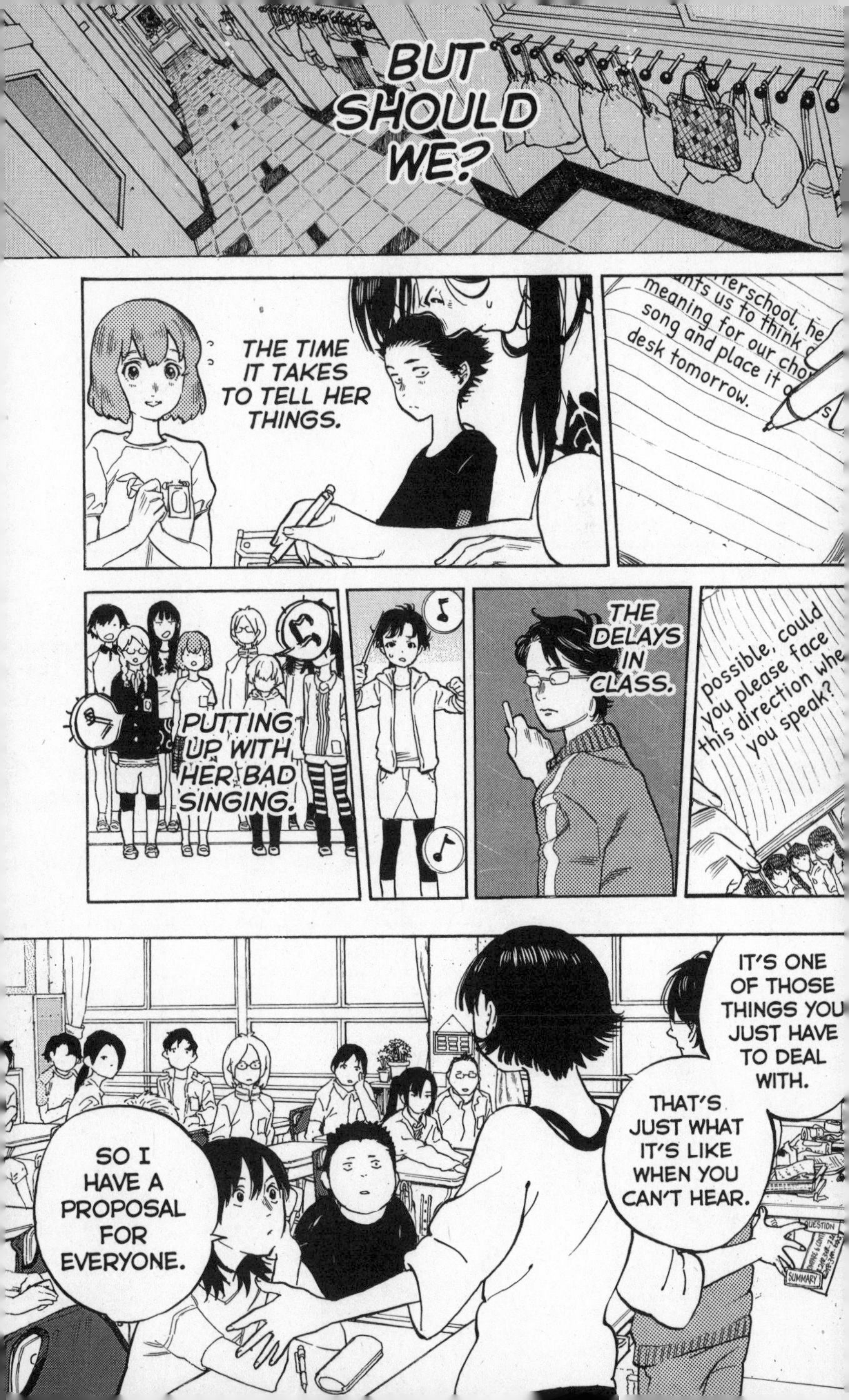
BUT SHOULD WE?
fterschool, he
nts us to think
meaning for our cho
song and place it
desk tomorrow.
THE TIME IT TAKES TO TELL HER THINGS.
possible, could you please face this direction whe you speak?
THE DELAYS IN CLASS.
PUTTING UP WITH HER BAD SINGING.
IT'S ONE OF THOSE THINGS YOU JUST HAVE TO DEAL WITH.
THAT'S JUST WHAT IT'S LIKE WHEN YOU CAN'T HEAR.
QUESTION
SUMMARY
SO I HAVE A PROPOSAL FOR EVERYONE.

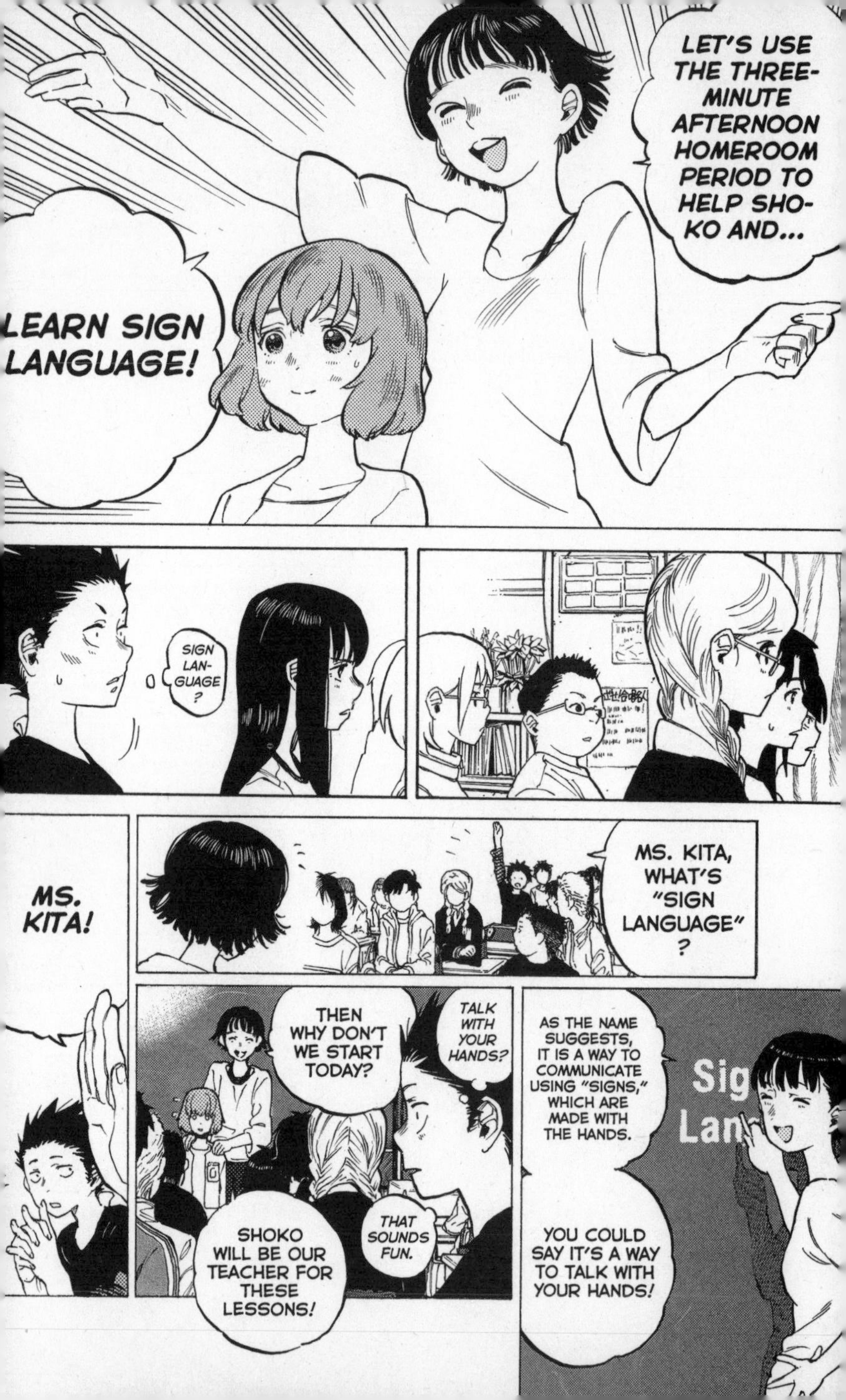
LET'S USE THE THREE-MINUTE AFTERNOON HOMEROOM PERIOD TO HELP SHOKO AND...
LEARN SIGN LANGUAGE!
SIGN LANGUAGE?
MS. KITA, WHAT'S "SIGN LANGUAGE"?
MS. KITA!
AS THE NAME SUGGESTS, IT IS A WAY TO COMMUNICATE USING "SIGNS," WHICH ARE MADE WITH THE HANDS.
YOU COULD SAY IT'S A WAY TO TALK WITH YOUR HANDS!
TALK WITH YOUR HANDS?
THEN WHY DON'T WE START TODAY?
THAT SOUNDS FUN.
SHOKO WILL BE OUR TEACHER FOR THESE LESSONS!

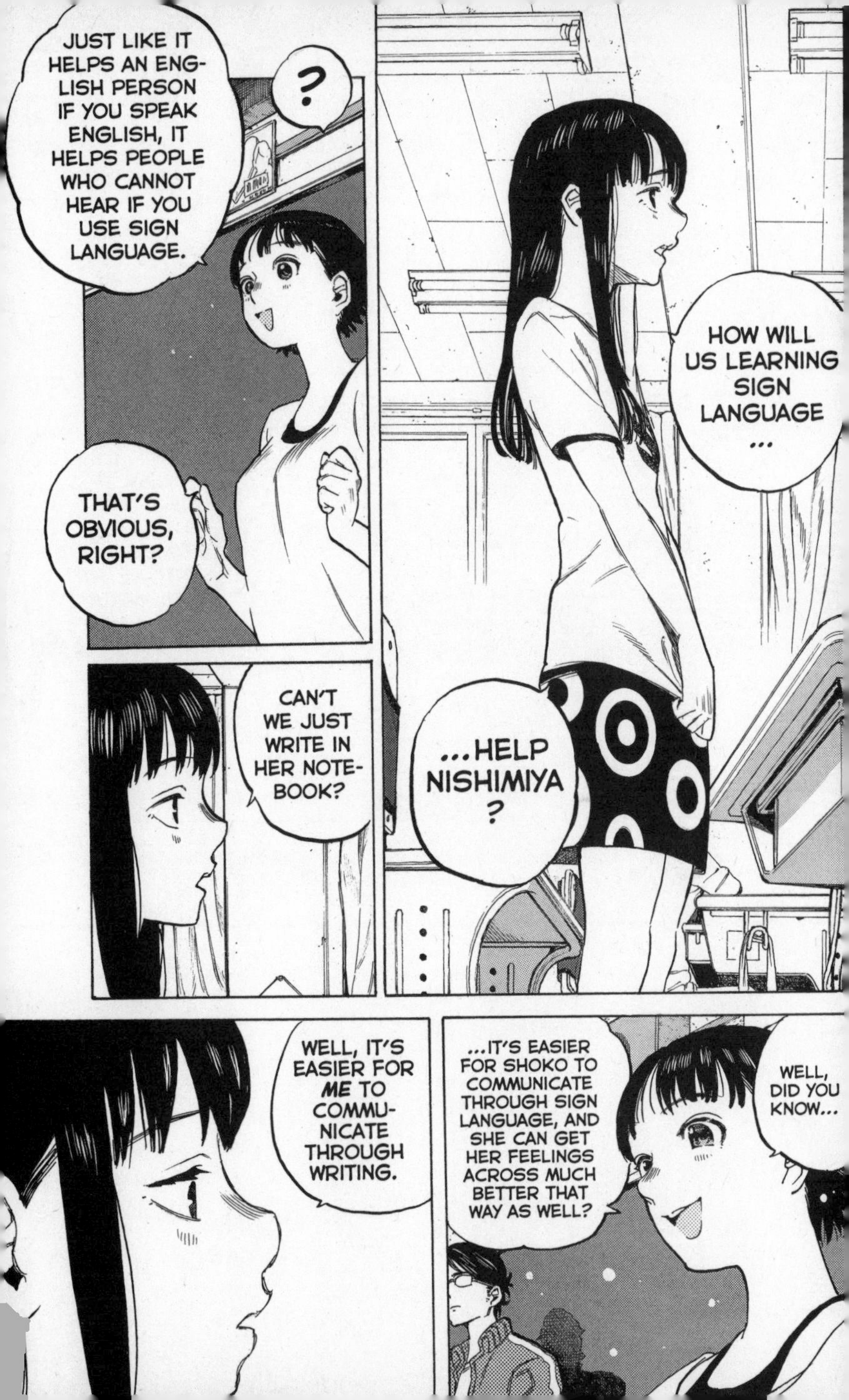
HOW WILL US LEARNING SIGN LANGUAGE ...
...HELP NISHIMIYA ?
?
JUST LIKE IT HELPS AN ENGLISH PERSON IF YOU SPEAK ENGLISH, IT HELPS PEOPLE WHO CANNOT HEAR IF YOU USE SIGN LANGUAGE.
THAT'S OBVIOUS, RIGHT?
CAN'T WE JUST WRITE IN HER NOTEBOOK?
WELL, DID YOU KNOW...
...IT'S EASIER FOR SHOKO TO COMMUNICATE THROUGH SIGN LANGUAGE, AND SHE CAN GET HER FEELINGS ACROSS MUCH BETTER THAT WAY AS WELL?
WELL, IT'S EASIER FOR *ME* TO COMMUNICATE THROUGH WRITING.

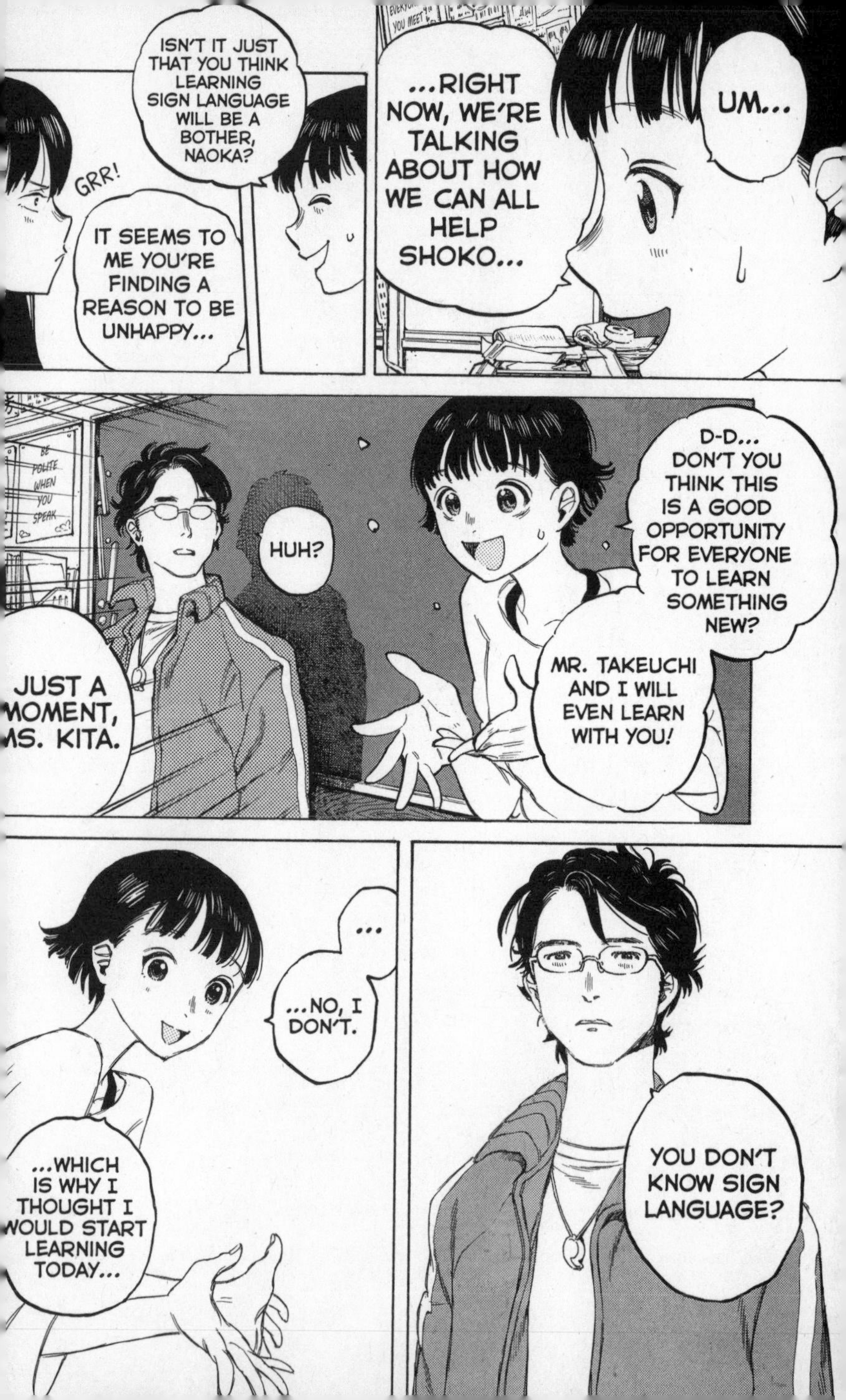
UM...
...RIGHT NOW, WE'RE TALKING ABOUT HOW WE CAN ALL HELP SHOKO...
ISN'T IT JUST THAT YOU THINK LEARNING SIGN LANGUAGE WILL BE A BOTHER, NAOKA?
GRR!
IT SEEMS TO ME YOU'RE FINDING A REASON TO BE UNHAPPY...
D-D... DON'T YOU THINK THIS IS A GOOD OPPORTUNITY FOR EVERYONE TO LEARN SOMETHING NEW?
MR. TAKEUCHI AND I WILL EVEN LEARN WITH YOU!
HUH?
BE POLITE WHEN YOU SPEAK
JUST A MOMENT, MS. KITA.
YOU DON'T KNOW SIGN LANGUAGE?
...
...NO, I DON'T.
...WHICH IS WHY I THOUGHT I WOULD START LEARNING TODAY...

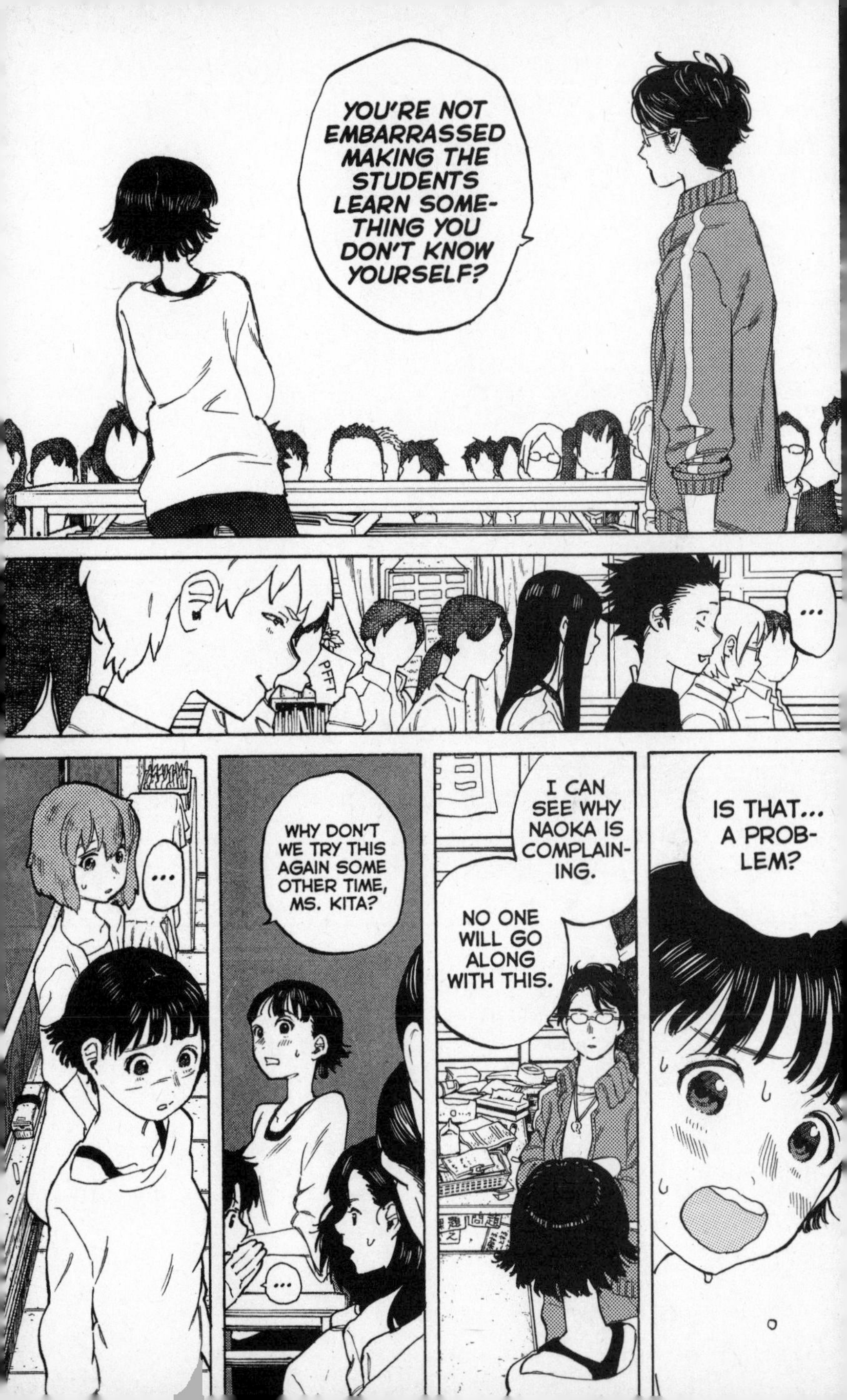
YOU'RE NOT EMBARRASSED MAKING THE STUDENTS LEARN SOMETHING YOU DON'T KNOW YOURSELF?
...
PFFT
IS THAT... A PROBLEM?
I CAN SEE WHY NAOKA IS COMPLAINING.
NO ONE WILL GO ALONG WITH THIS.
WHY DON'T WE TRY THIS AGAIN SOME OTHER TIME, MS. KITA?
...
...

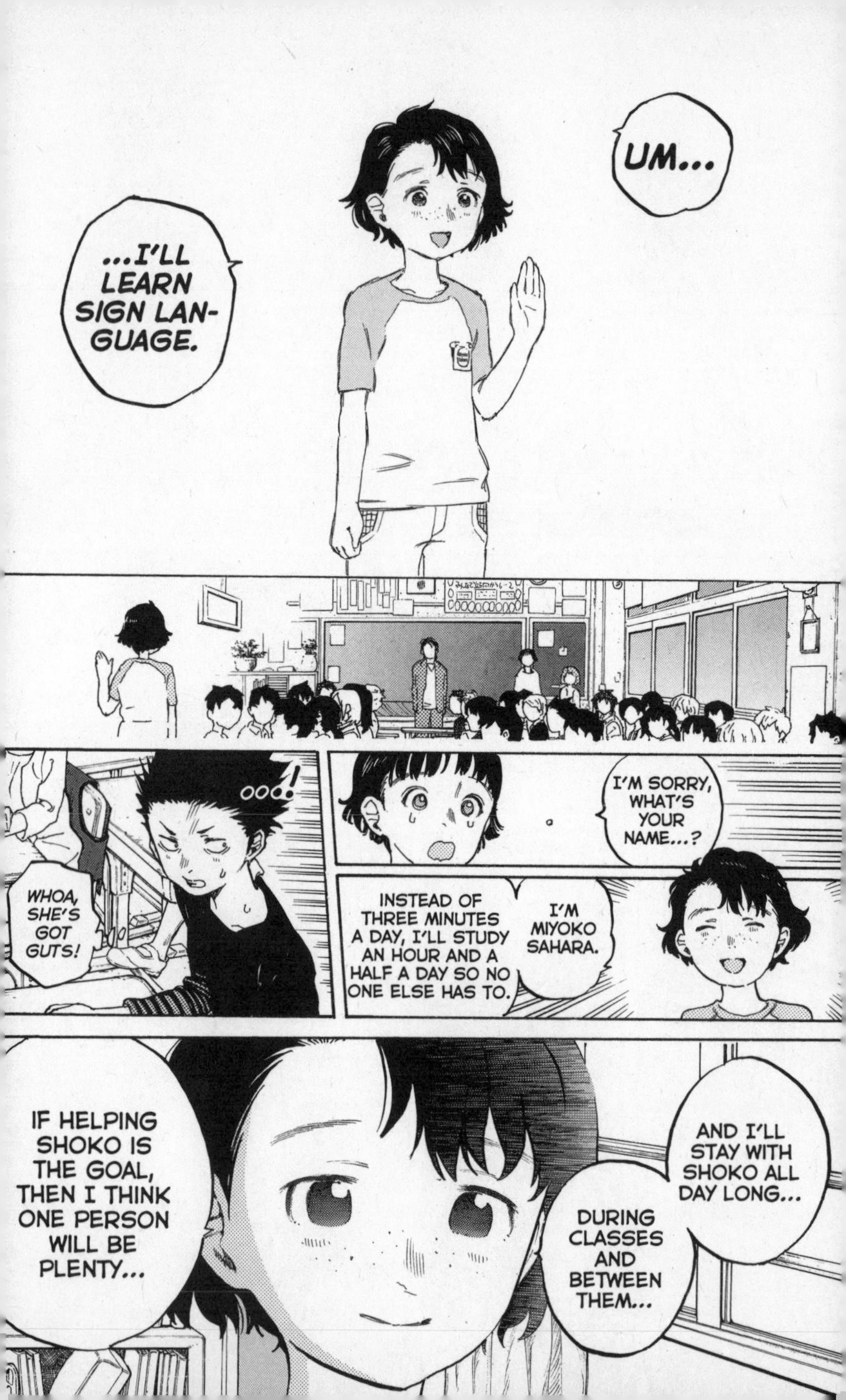
UM...
...I'LL LEARN SIGN LANGUAGE.
I'M SORRY, WHAT'S YOUR NAME...?
I'M MIYOKO SAHARA.
INSTEAD OF THREE MINUTES A DAY, I'LL STUDY AN HOUR AND A HALF A DAY SO NO ONE ELSE HAS TO.
OOO!
WHOA, SHE'S GOT GUTS!
AND I'LL STAY WITH SHOKO ALL DAY LONG...
DURING CLASSES AND BETWEEN THEM...
IF HELPING SHOKO IS THE GOAL, THEN I THINK ONE PERSON WILL BE PLENTY...

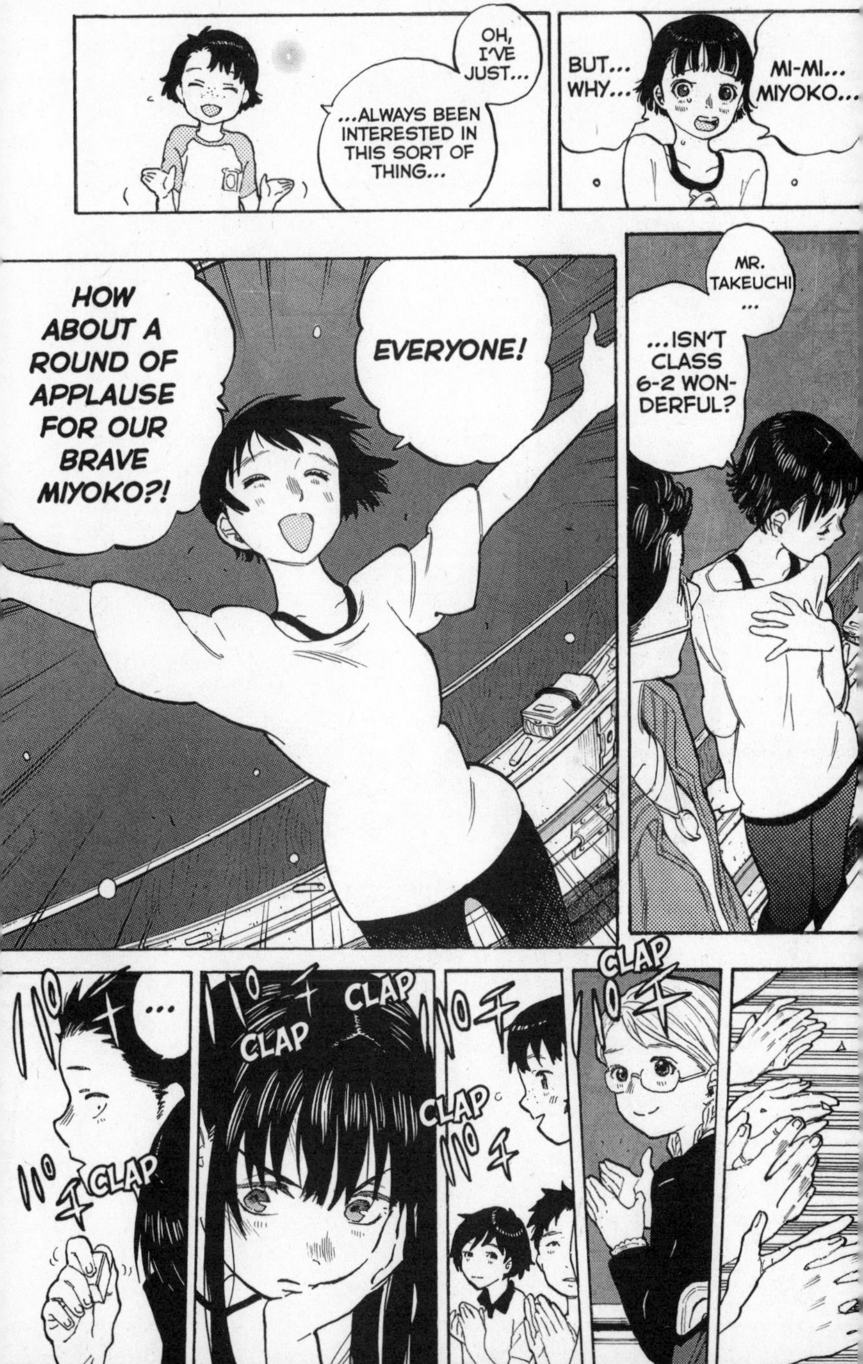
MI-MI... MIYOKO...
BUT... WHY...
OH, I'VE JUST...
...ALWAYS BEEN INTERESTED IN THIS SORT OF THING...
MR. TAKEUCHI...
...ISN'T CLASS 6-2 WONDERFUL?
EVERYONE!
HOW ABOUT A ROUND OF APPLAUSE FOR OUR BRAVE MIYOKO?!
CLAP
CLAP
CLAP
CLAP
CLAP
...
CLAP

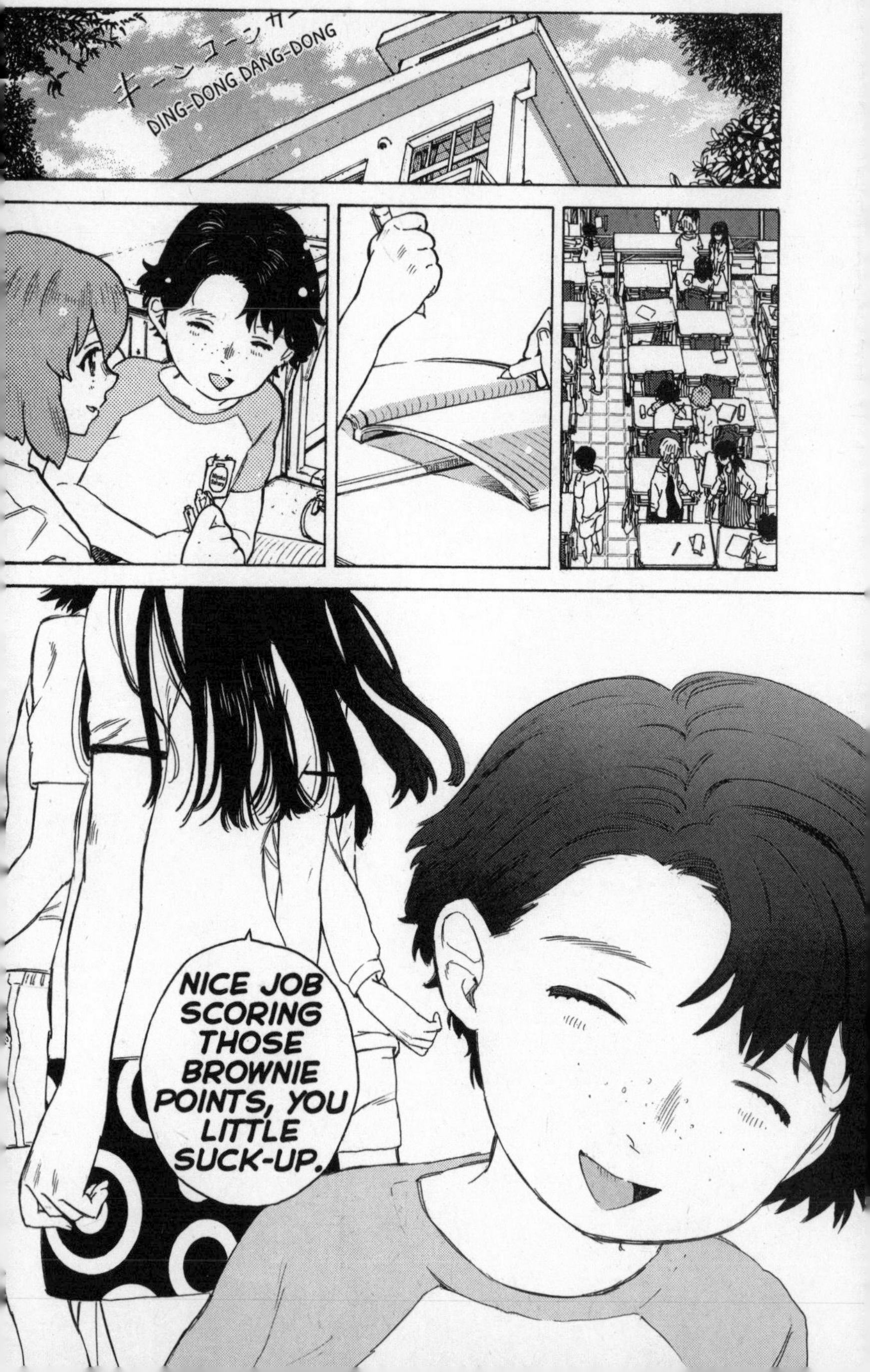
キーンコーンカー
DING-DONG DANG-DONG
NICE JOB SCORING THOSE BROWNIE POINTS, YOU LITTLE SUCK-UP.

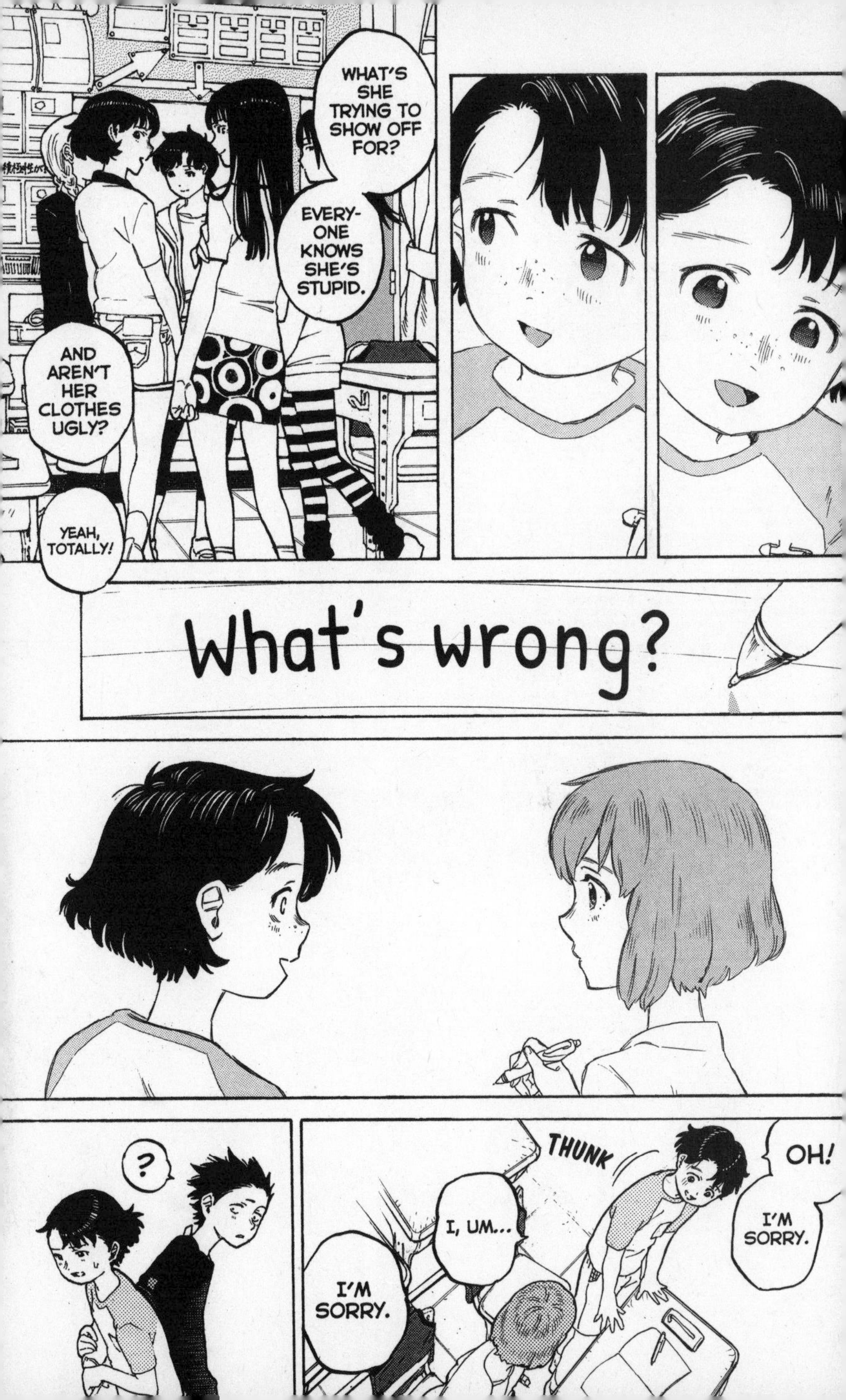
WHAT'S SHE TRYING TO SHOW OFF FOR?
EVERY-ONE KNOWS SHE'S STUPID.
AND AREN'T HER CLOTHES UGLY?
YEAH, TOTALLY!
What's wrong?
OH!
I'M SORRY.
THUNK
I, UM...
I'M SORRY.
?

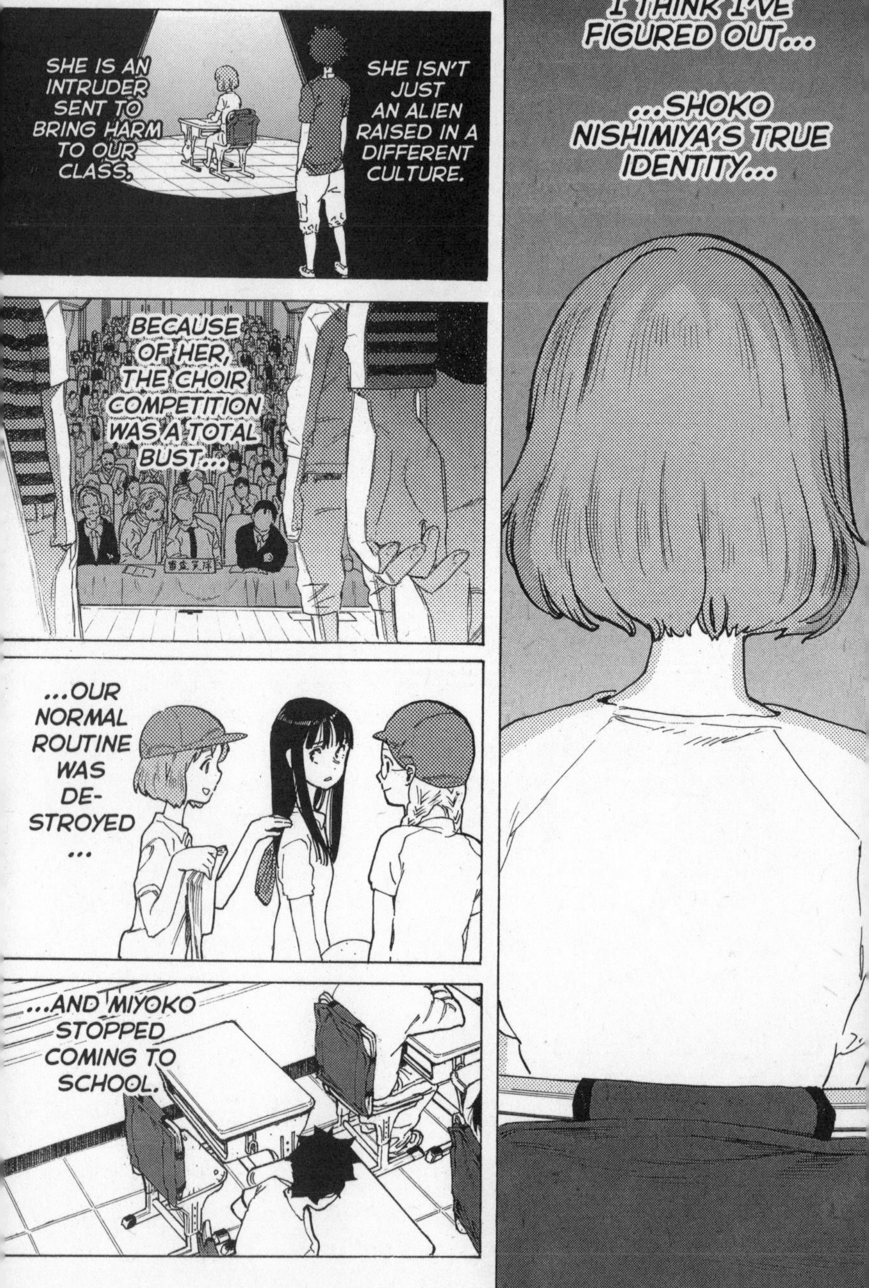
I THINK I'VE FIGURED OUT...
...SHOKO NISHIMIYA'S TRUE IDENTITY...
SHE ISN'T JUST AN ALIEN RAISED IN A DIFFERENT CULTURE.
SHE IS AN INTRUDER SENT TO BRING HARM TO OUR CLASS.
BECAUSE OF HER, THE CHOIR COMPETITION WAS A TOTAL BUST...
...OUR NORMAL ROUTINE WAS DE-STROYED ...
...AND MIYOKO STOPPED COMING TO SCHOOL.

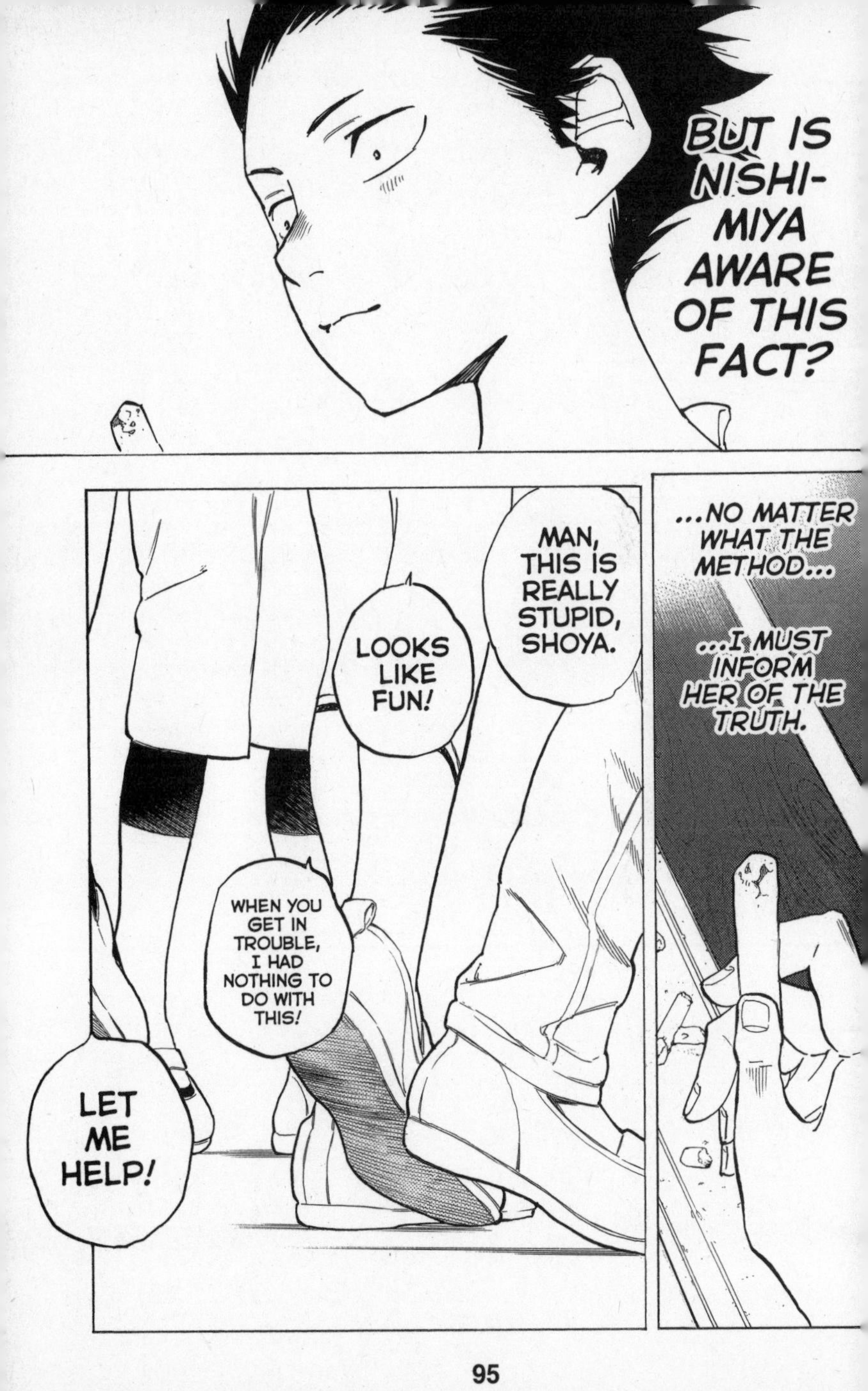
BUT IS NISHI-MIYA AWARE OF THIS FACT?
...NO MATTER WHAT THE METHOD...
...I MUST INFORM HER OF THE TRUTH.
MAN, THIS IS REALLY STUPID, SHOYA.
LOOKS LIKE FUN!
WHEN YOU GET IN TROUBLE, I HAD NOTHING TO DO WITH THIS!
LET ME HELP!

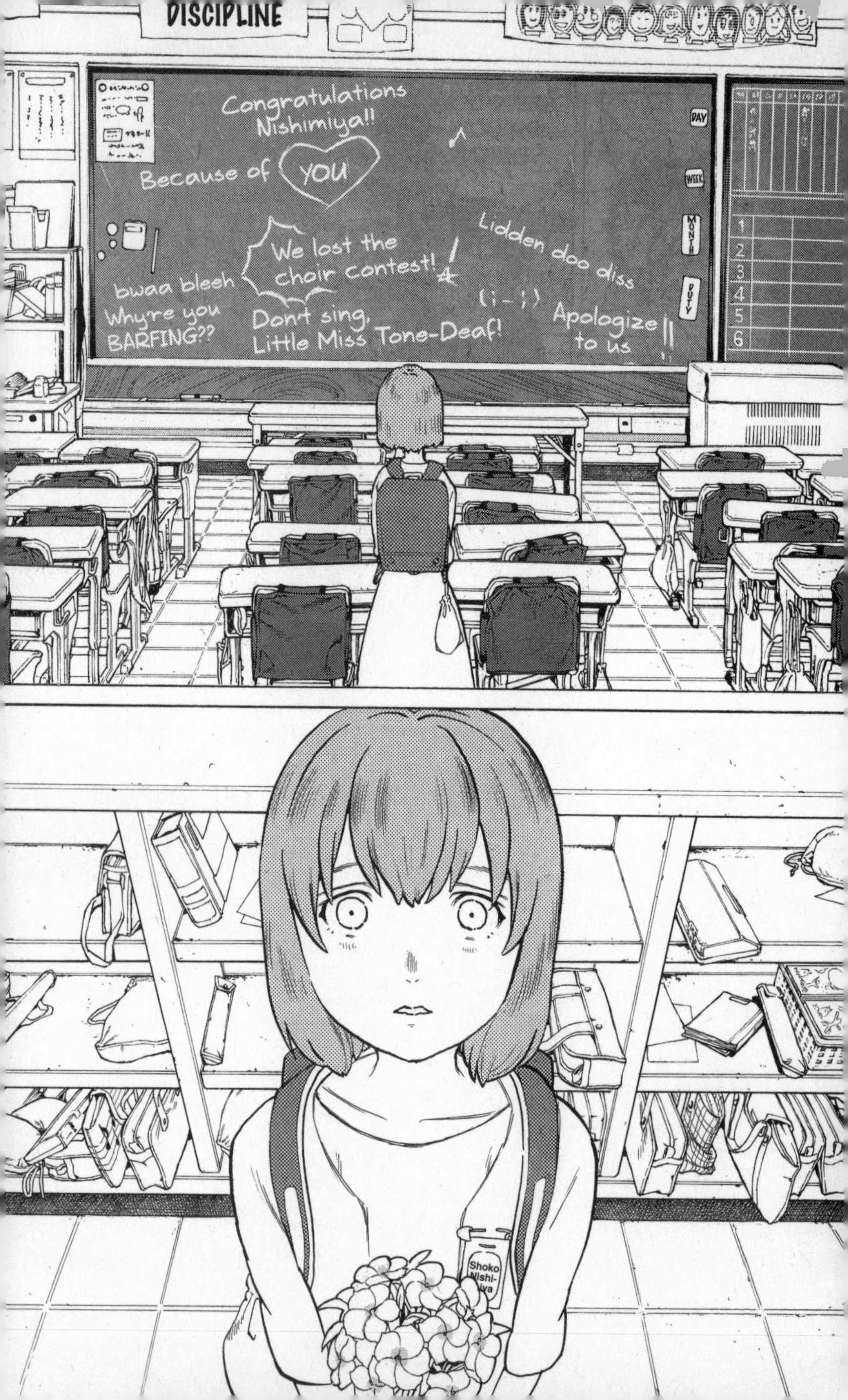
DISCIPLINE
Congratulations Nishimiya!!
Because of YOU
We lost the choir contest!
Lidden doo diss
bwaa bleeh
Why're you BARFING??
Don't sing, Little Miss Tone-Deaf!
(;_;)
Apologize to us!!
DAY
WEEK
MONTH
DUTY
Shoko Nishi-miya

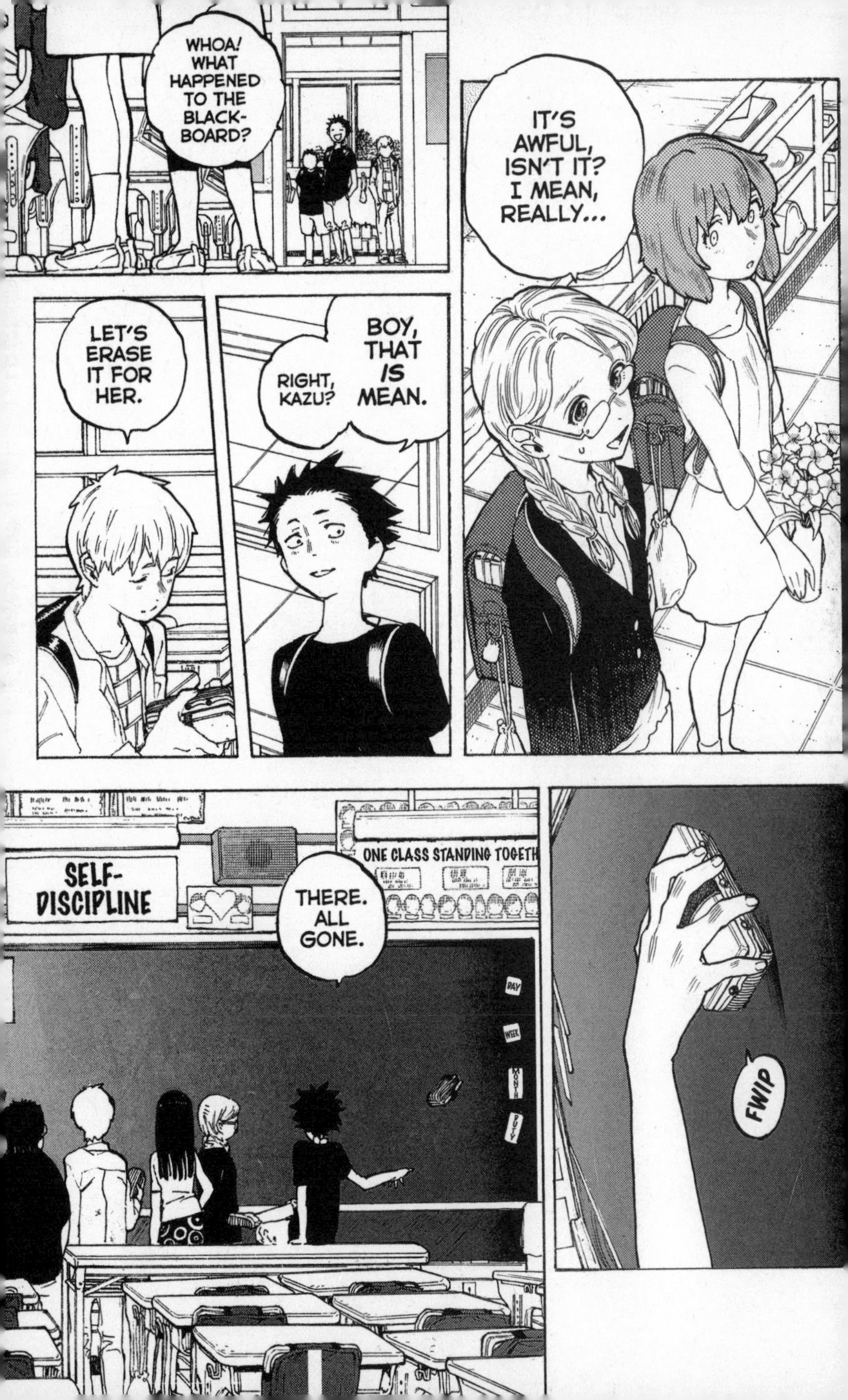
IT'S AWFUL, ISN'T IT? I MEAN, REALLY...
WHOA! WHAT HAPPENED TO THE BLACK-BOARD?
BOY, THAT *IS* MEAN.
RIGHT, KAZU?
LET'S ERASE IT FOR HER.
FWIP
SELF-DISCIPLINE
ONE CLASS STANDING TOGETH
THERE. ALL GONE.
DAY
WEEK
MONTH
DUTY

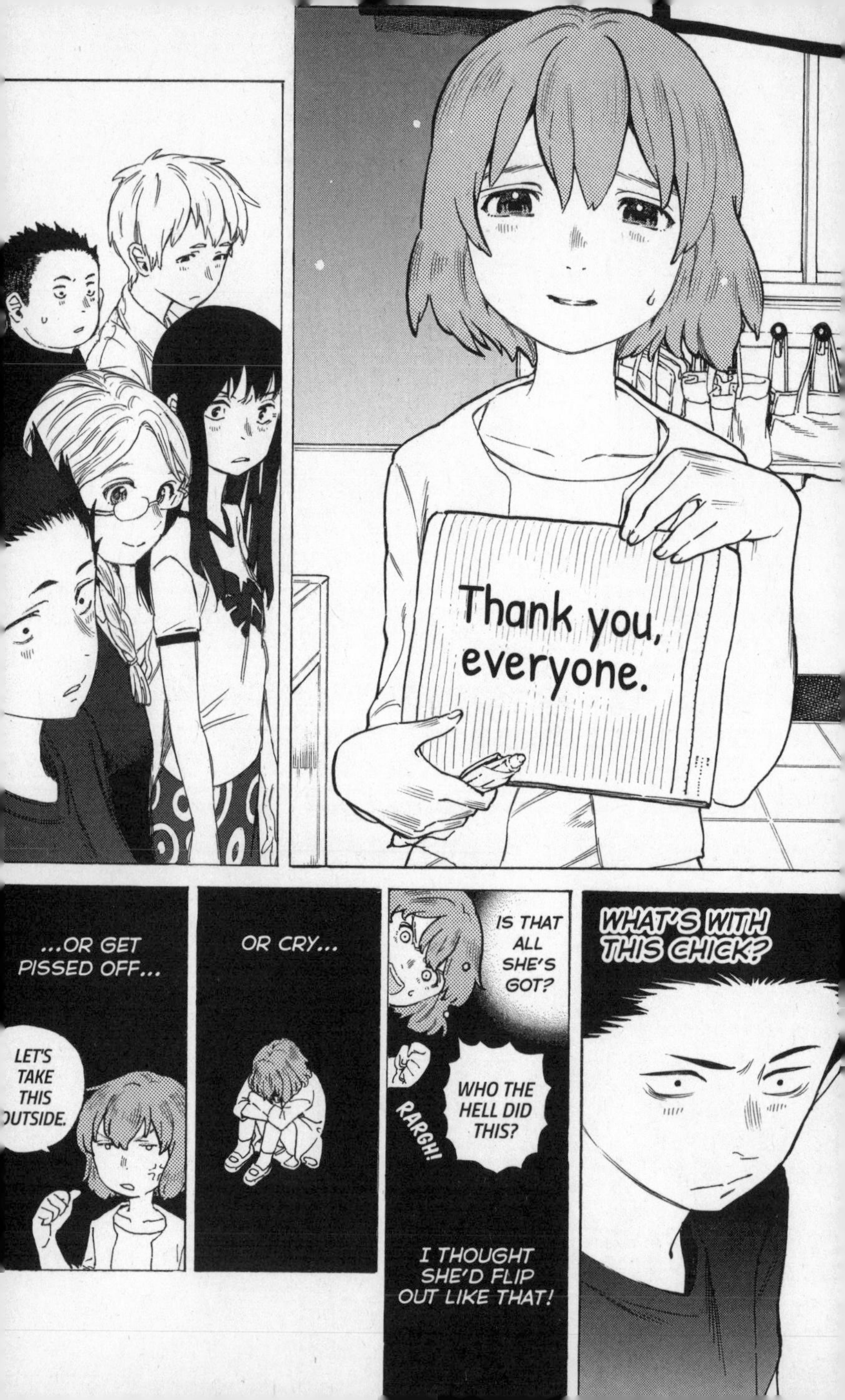
Thank you, everyone.
WHAT'S WITH THIS CHICK?
IS THAT ALL SHE'S GOT?
WHO THE HELL DID THIS?
RARGH!
I THOUGHT SHE'D FLIP OUT LIKE THAT!
OR CRY...
...OR GET PISSED OFF...
LET'S TAKE THIS OUTSIDE.

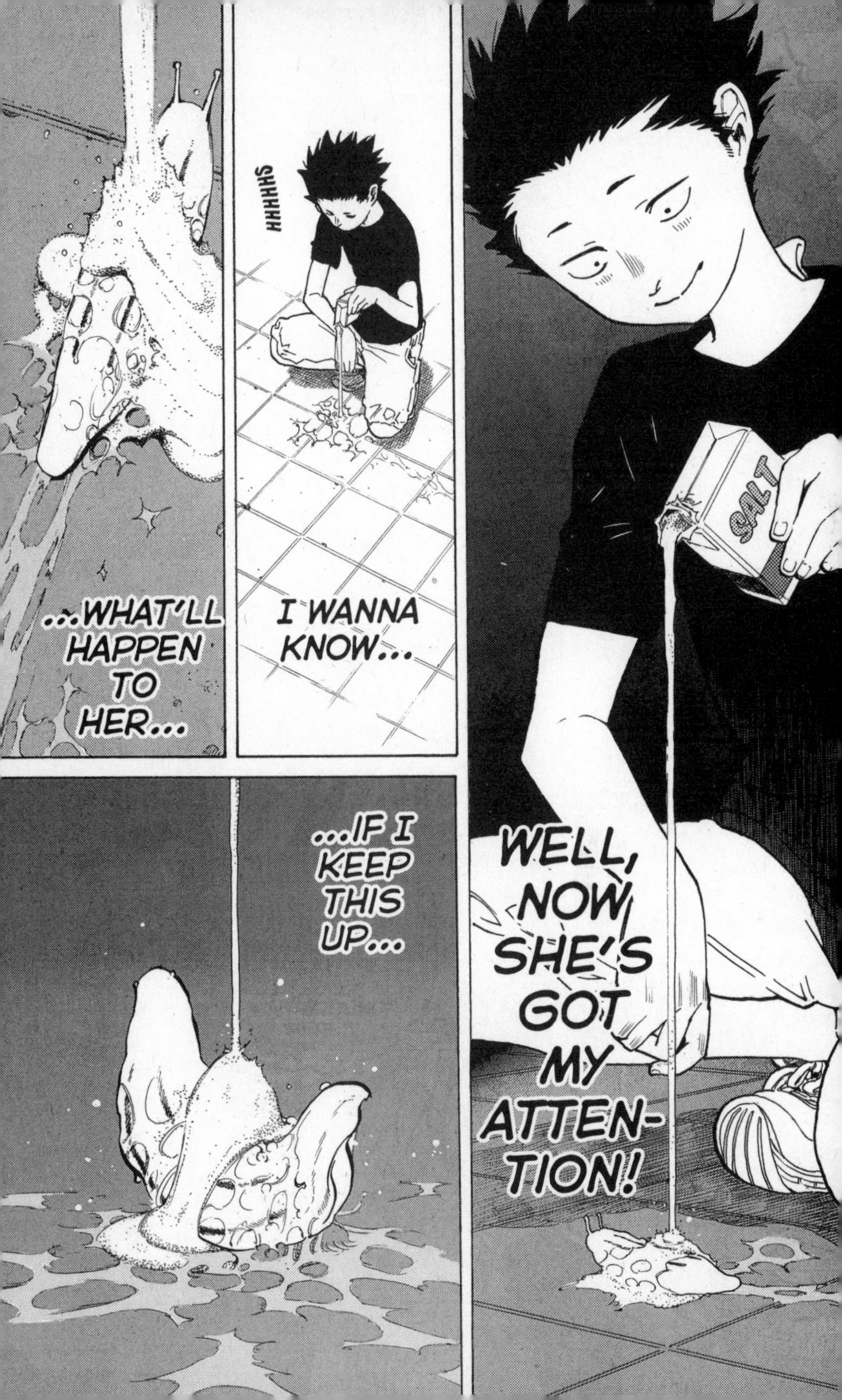
WELL, NOW SHE'S GOT MY ATTENTION!
SALT
SHHHHH
I WANNA KNOW...
...WHAT'LL HAPPEN TO HER...
...IF I KEEP THIS UP...

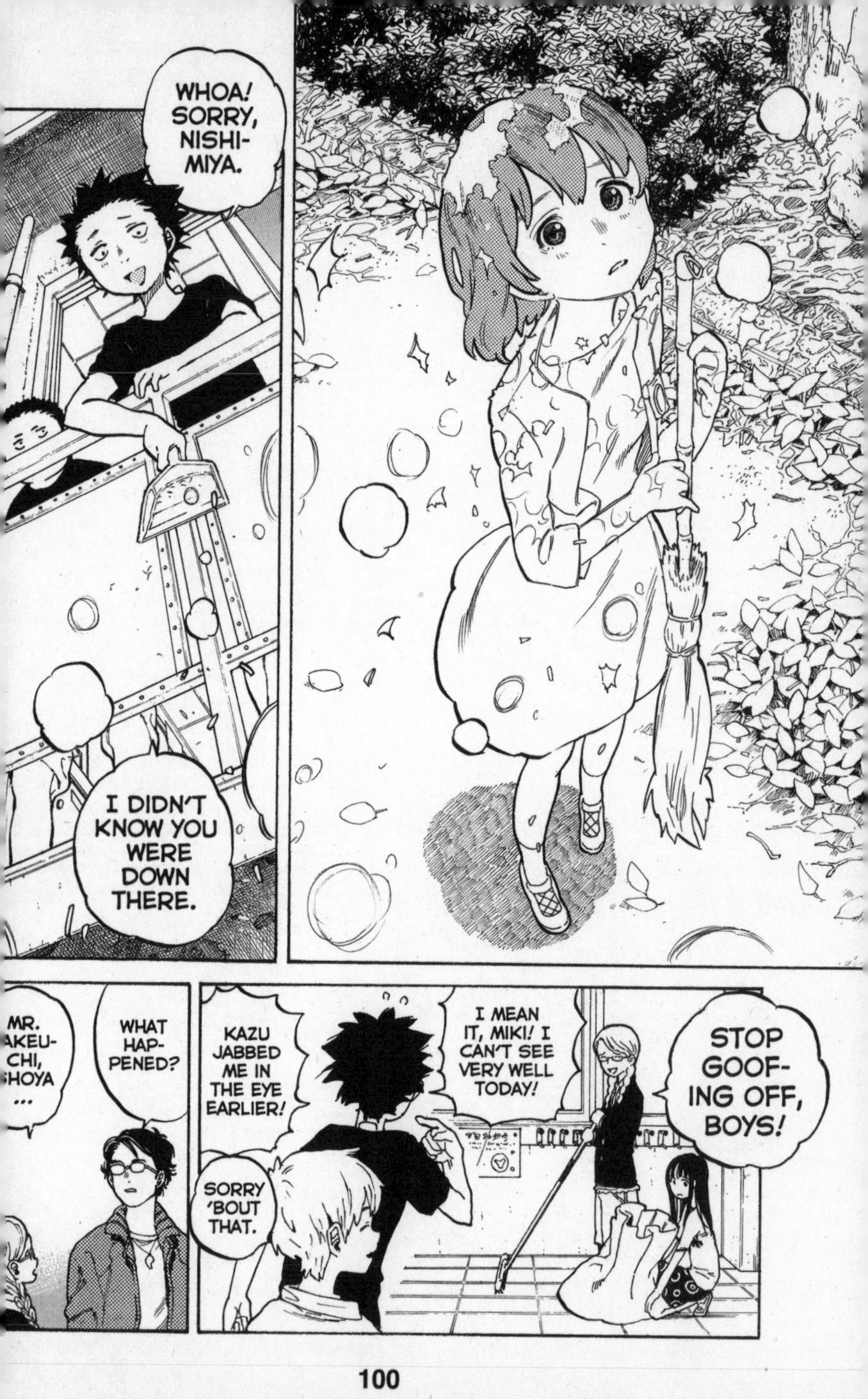
WHOA! SORRY, NISHI-MIYA.
I DIDN'T KNOW YOU WERE DOWN THERE.
STOP GOOF-ING OFF, BOYS!
I MEAN IT, MIKI! I CAN'T SEE VERY WELL TODAY!
KAZU JABBED ME IN THE EYE EARLIER!
SORRY 'BOUT THAT.
WHAT HAP-PENED?
MR. AKEU-CHI, HOYA ...

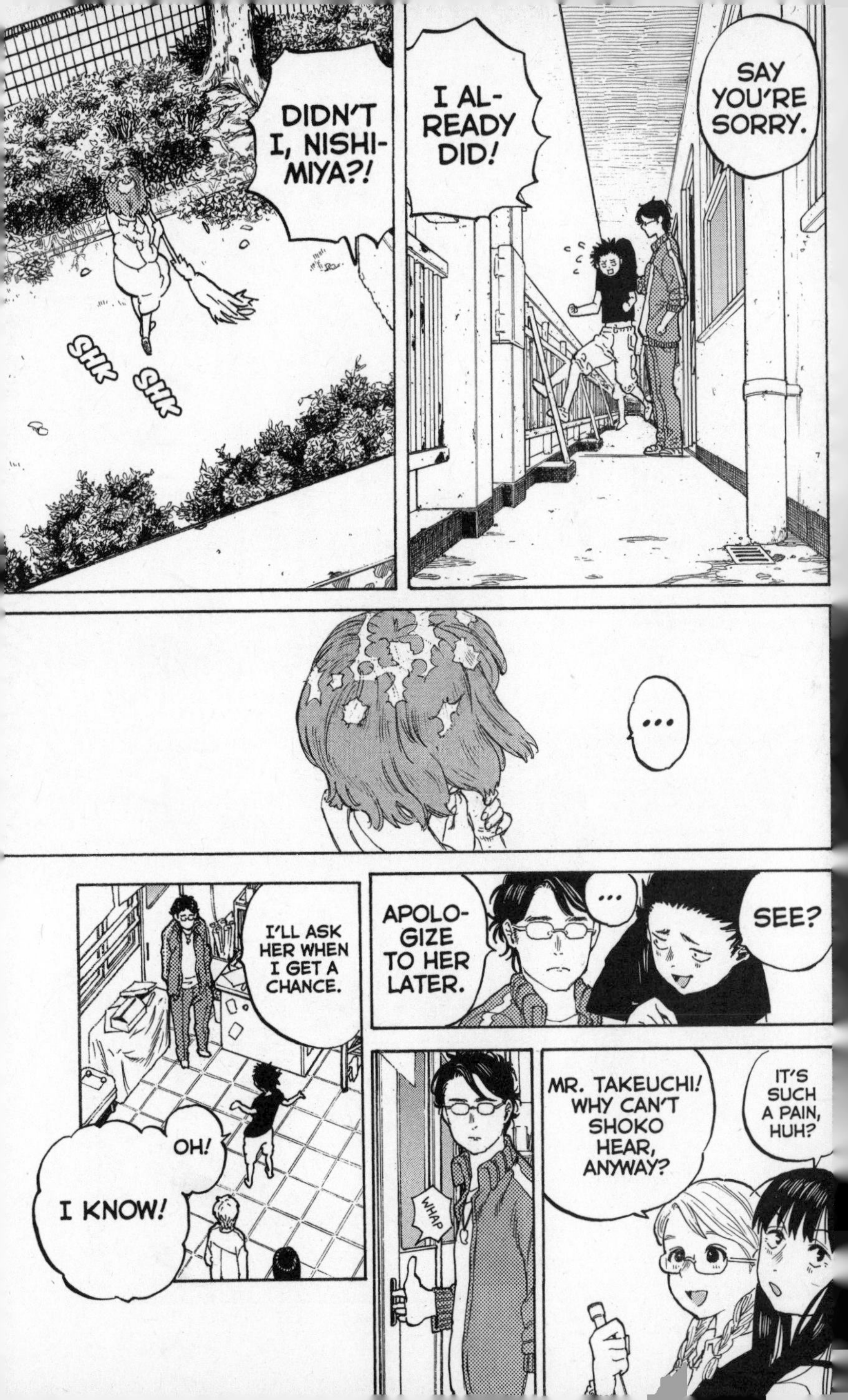
SAY YOU'RE SORRY.
I AL-READY DID!
DIDN'T I, NISHI-MIYA?!
SHK
SHK
...
SEE?
...
APOLO-GIZE TO HER LATER.
IT'S SUCH A PAIN, HUH?
MR. TAKEUCHI! WHY CAN'T SHOKO HEAR, ANYWAY?
WHAP
I'LL ASK HER WHEN I GET A CHANCE.
OH!
I KNOW!

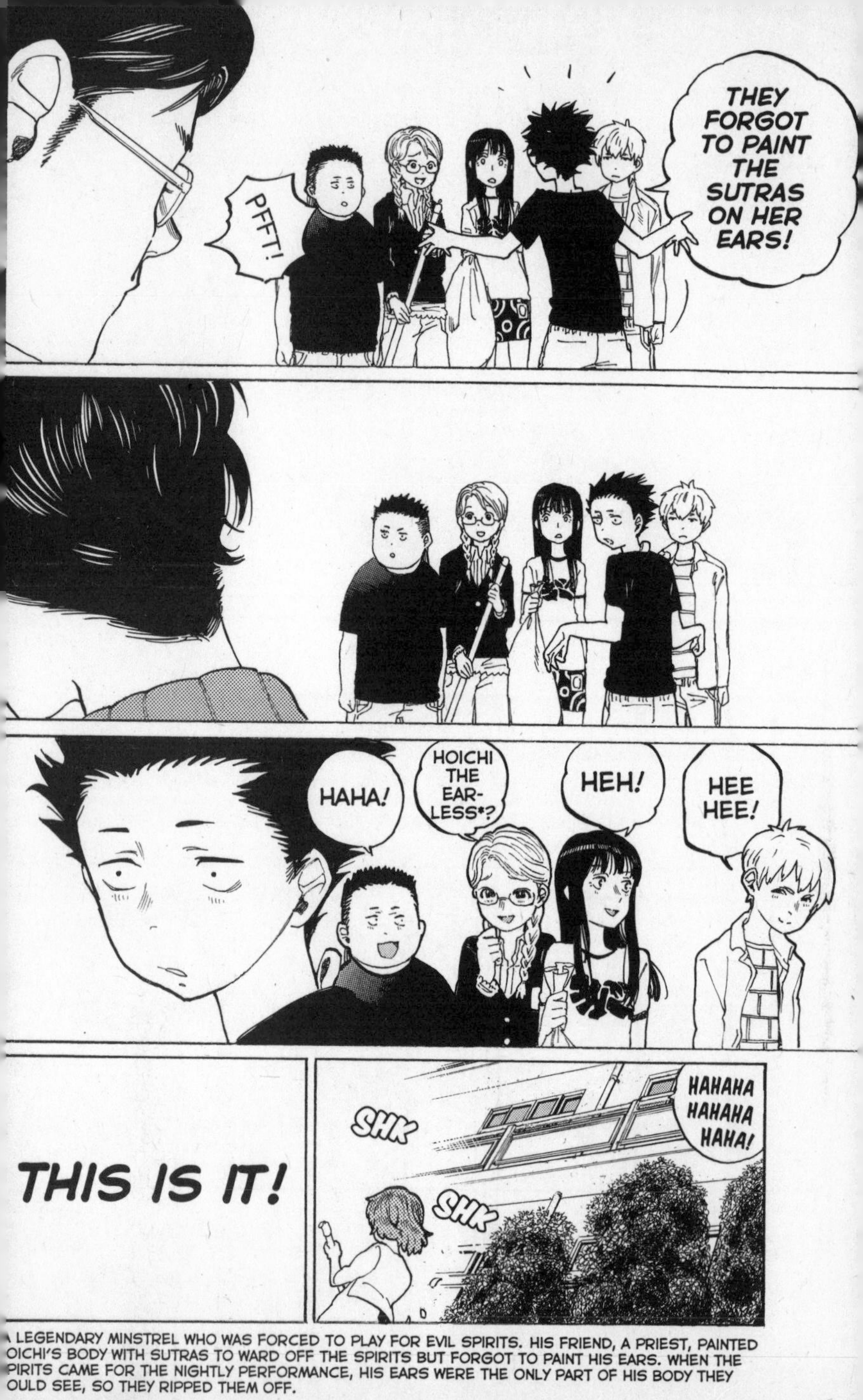
THEY FORGOT TO PAINT THE SUTRAS ON HER EARS!
PFFT!
HEE HEE!
HEH!
HOICHI THE EAR-LESS*?
HAHA!
HAHAHA HAHAHA HAHA!
SHK
SHK
THIS IS IT!

A LEGENDARY MINSTREL WHO WAS FORCED TO PLAY FOR EVIL SPIRITS. HIS FRIEND, A PRIEST, PAINTED OICHI'S BODY WITH SUTRAS TO WARD OFF THE SPIRITS BUT FORGOT TO PAINT HIS EARS. WHEN THE PIRITS CAME FOR THE NIGHTLY PERFORMANCE, HIS EARS WERE THE ONLY PART OF HIS BODY THEY OULD SEE, SO THEY RIPPED THEM OFF.

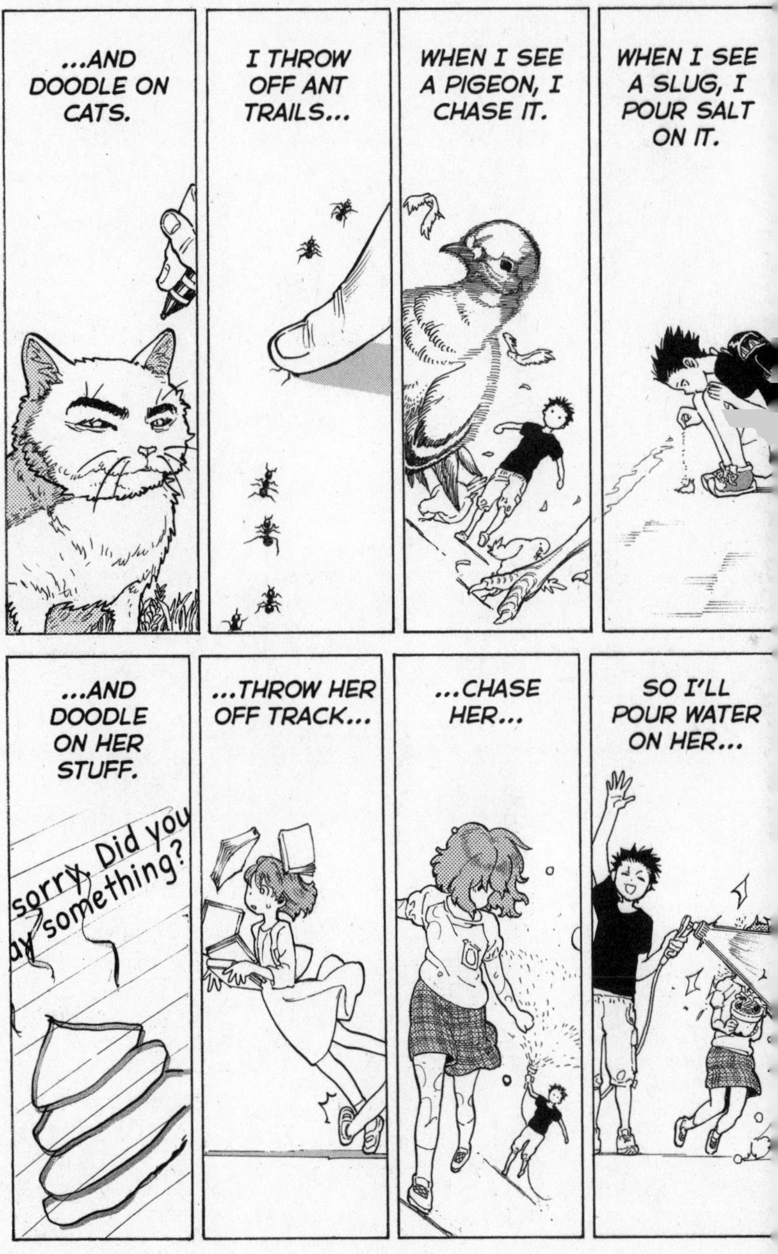
WHEN I SEE A SLUG, I POUR SALT ON IT.
WHEN I SEE A PIGEON, I CHASE IT.
I THROW OFF ANT TRAILS...
...AND DOODLE ON CATS.
SO I'LL POUR WATER ON HER...
...CHASE HER...
...THROW HER OFF TRACK...
...AND DOODLE ON HER STUFF.
sorry. Did you
ay something?

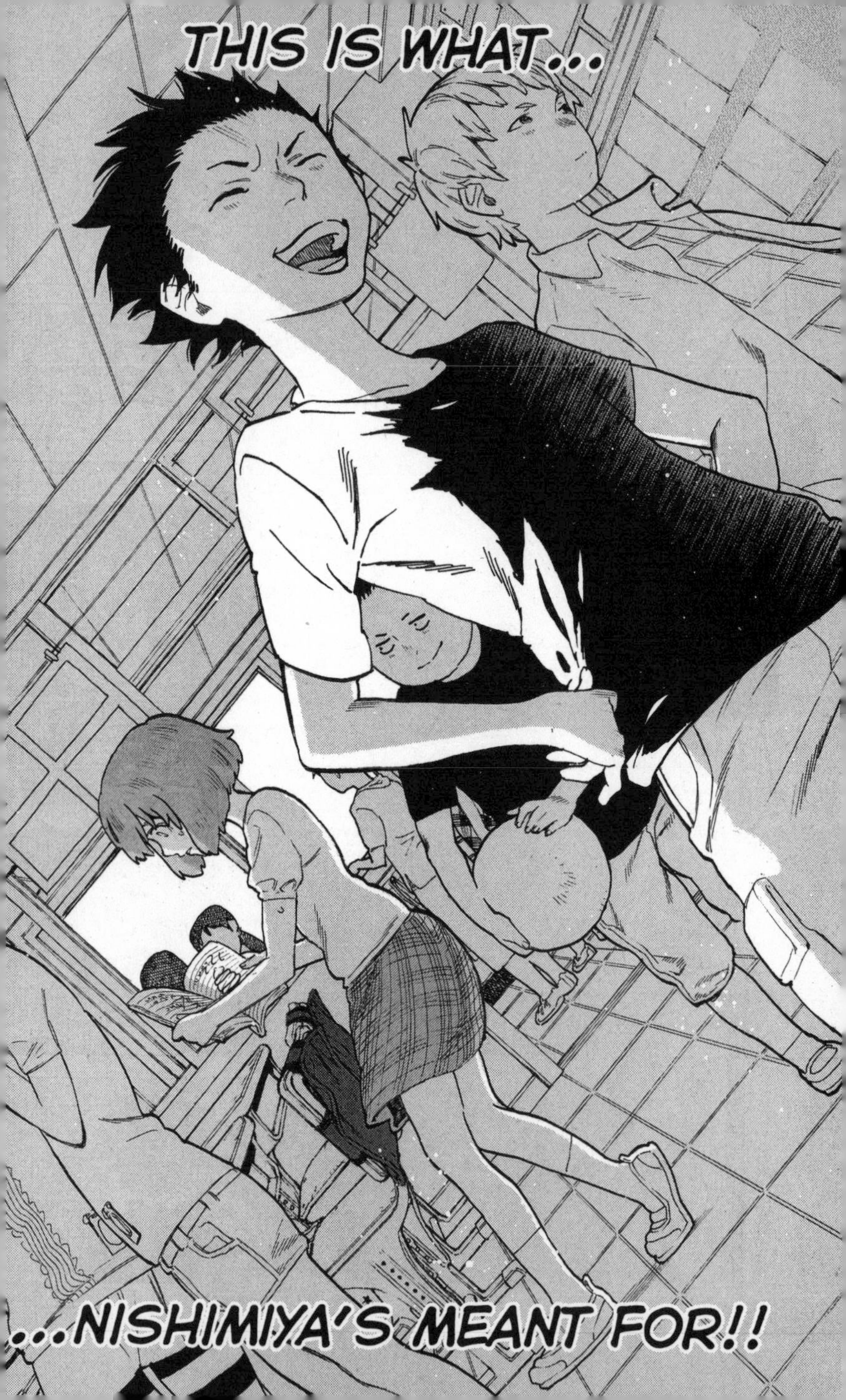
THIS IS WHAT...
...NISHIMIYA'S MEANT FOR!!

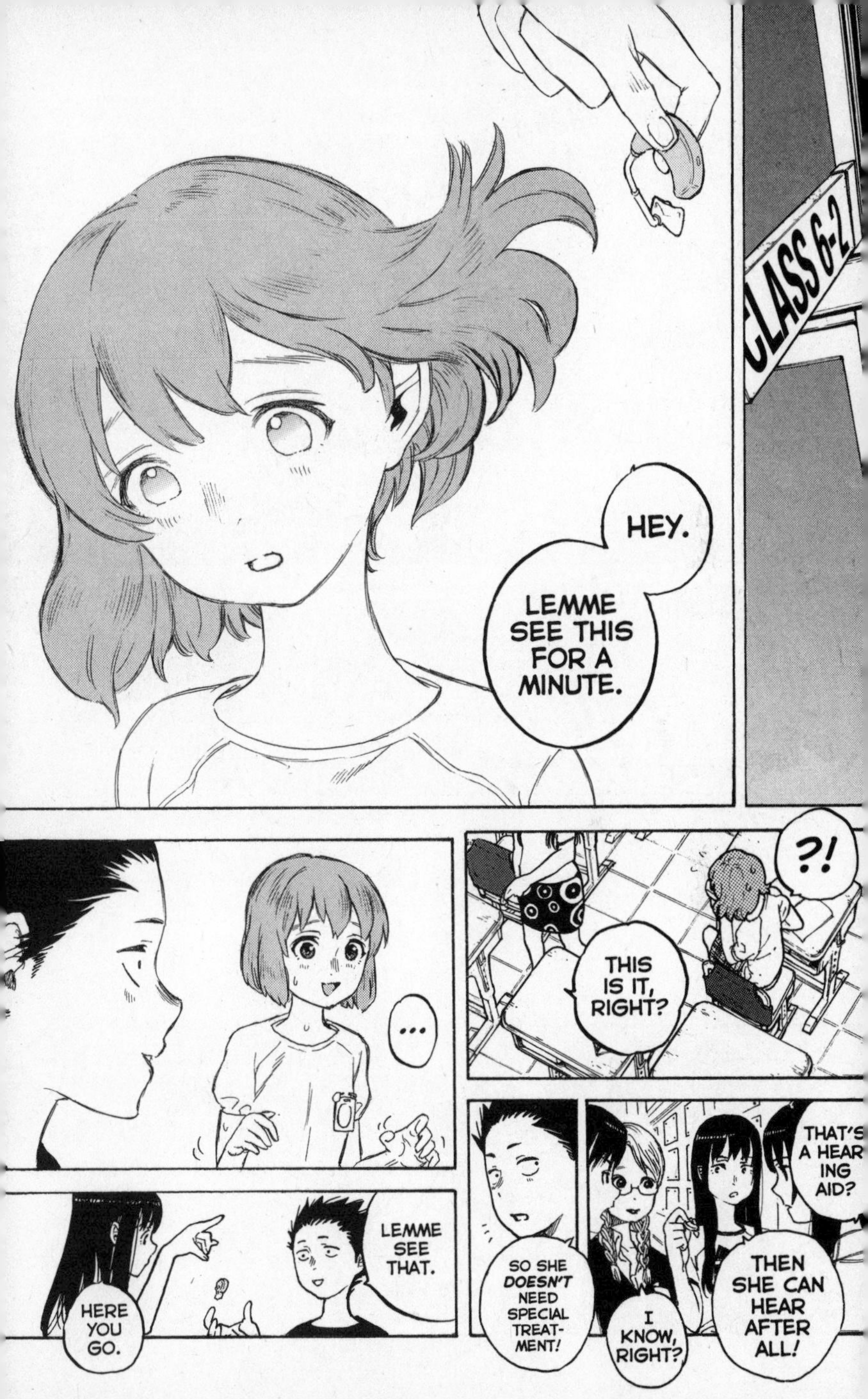
CLASS 6-2
HEY.
LEMME SEE THIS FOR A MINUTE.
?!
THIS IS IT, RIGHT?
...
THAT'S A HEAR ING AID?
THEN SHE CAN HEAR AFTER ALL!
I KNOW, RIGHT?
SO SHE *DOESN'T* NEED SPECIAL TREAT-MENT!
LEMME SEE THAT.
HERE YOU GO.

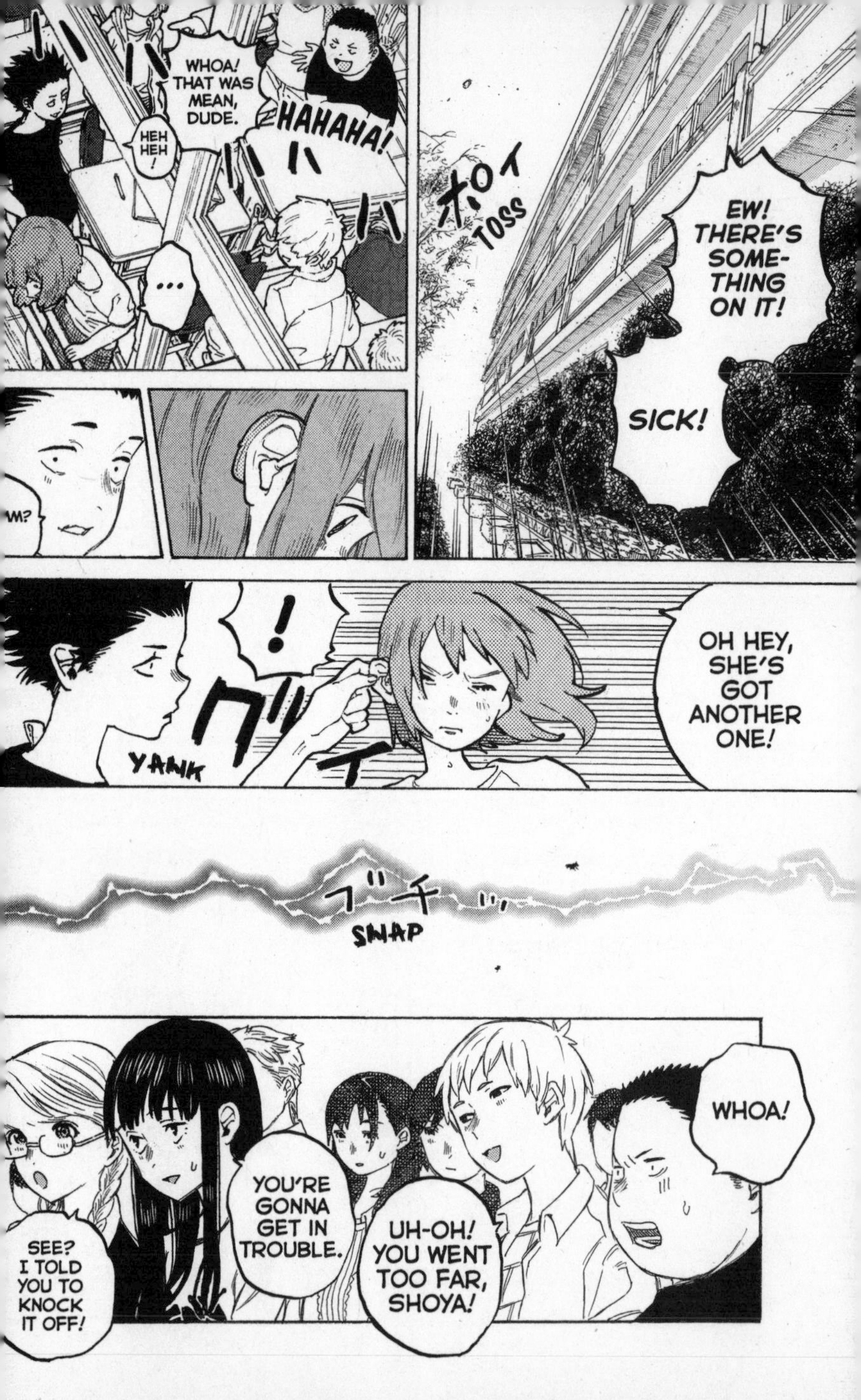
TOSS
EW! THERE'S SOMETHING ON IT!
SICK!
HAHAHA!
WHOA! THAT WAS MEAN, DUDE.
HEH HEH!
...
M?
OH HEY, SHE'S GOT ANOTHER ONE!
!
YANK
SNAP
WHOA!
UH-OH! YOU WENT TOO FAR, SHOYA!
YOU'RE GONNA GET IN TROUBLE.
SEE? I TOLD YOU TO KNOCK IT OFF!

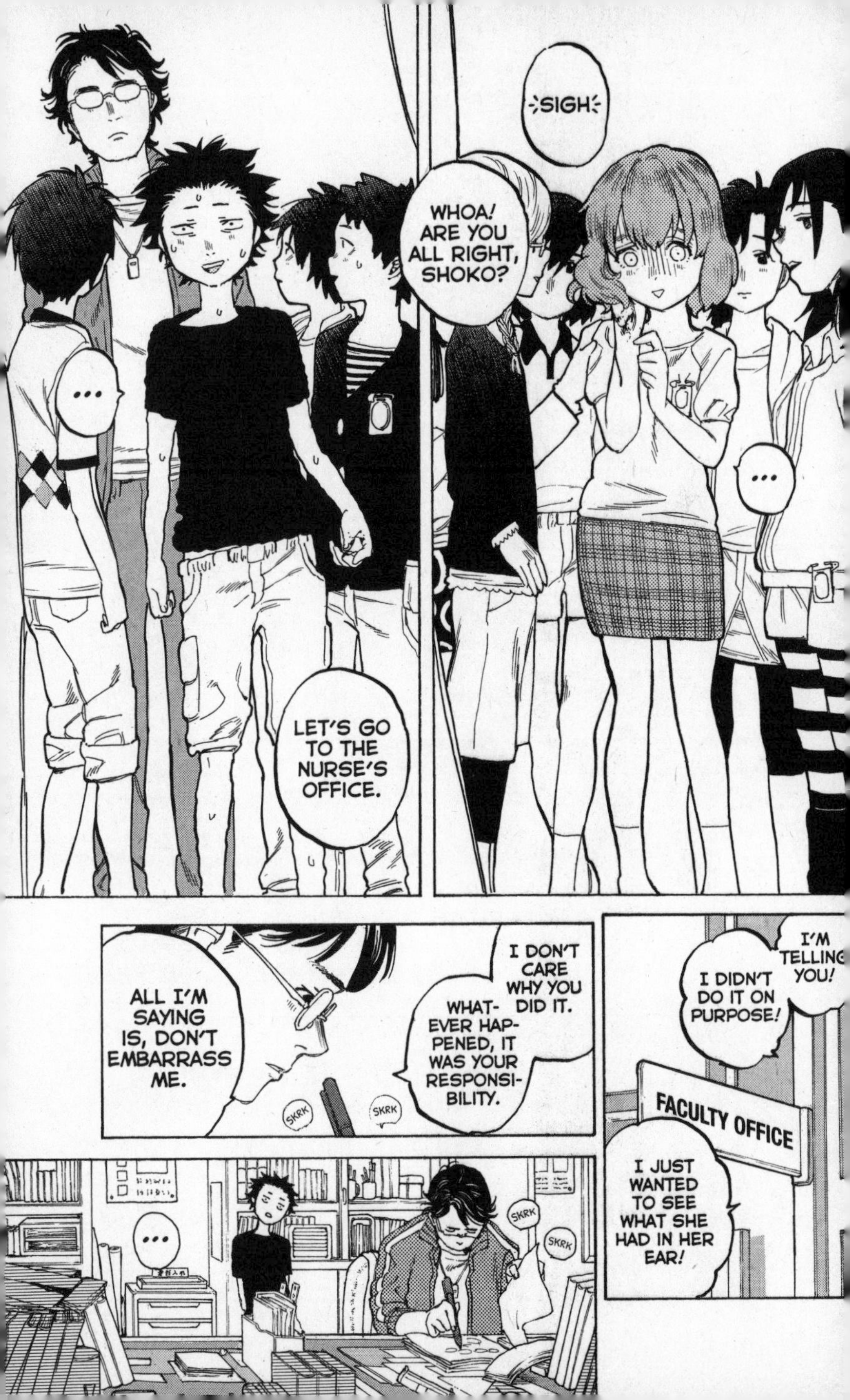
SIGH
WHOA! ARE YOU ALL RIGHT, SHOKO?
...
...
LET'S GO TO THE NURSE'S OFFICE.
I'M TELLING YOU!
I DIDN'T DO IT ON PURPOSE!
FACULTY OFFICE
I JUST WANTED TO SEE WHAT SHE HAD IN HER EAR!
I DON'T CARE WHY YOU DID IT.
WHATEVER HAPPENED, IT WAS YOUR RESPONSIBILITY.
ALL I'M SAYING IS, DON'T EMBARRASS ME.
SKRK
SKRK
SKRK
SKRK
...

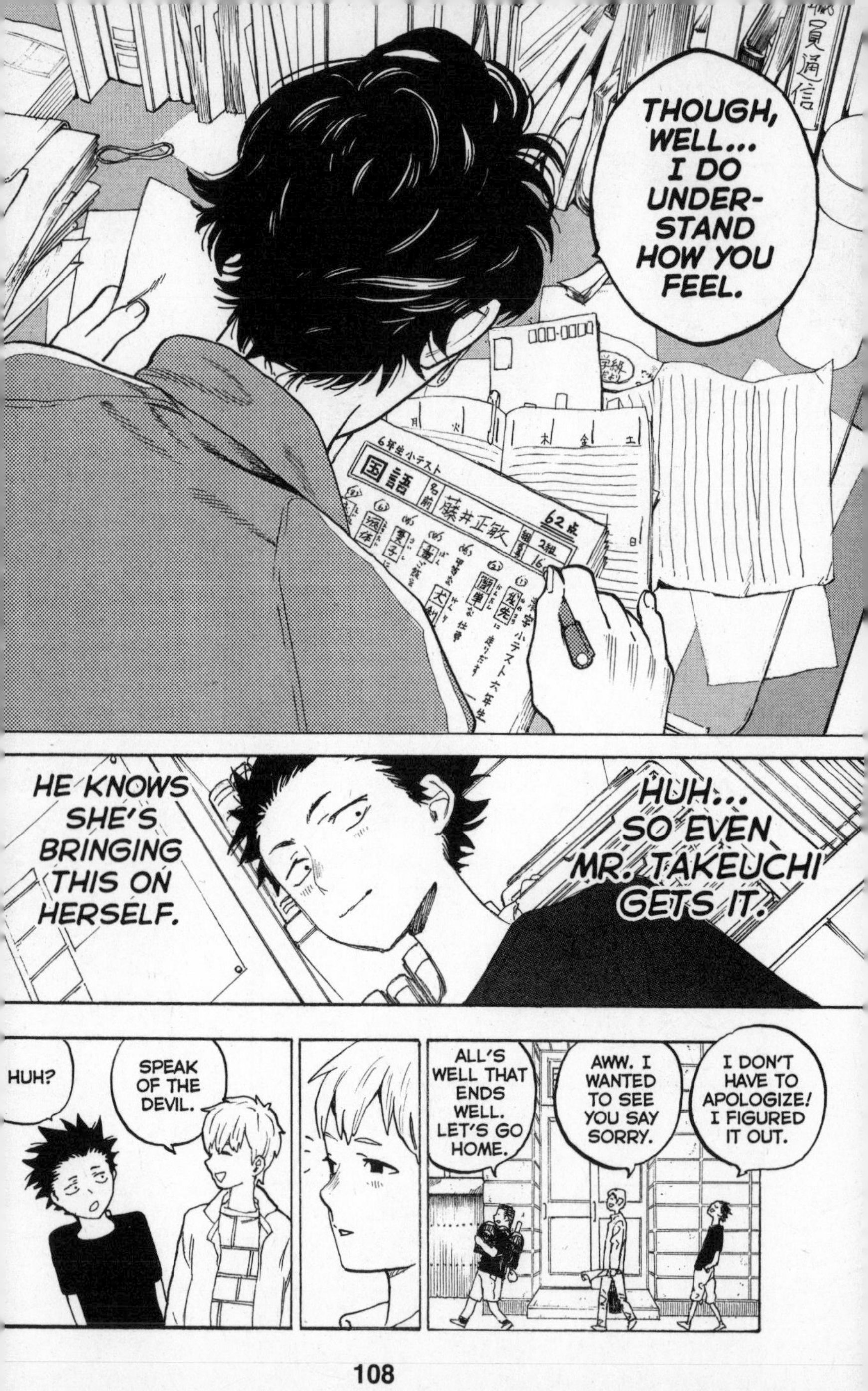
THOUGH, WELL... I DO UNDER-STAND HOW YOU FEEL.
HUH... SO EVEN MR. TAKEUCHI GETS IT.
HE KNOWS SHE'S BRINGING THIS ON HERSELF.
I DON'T HAVE TO APOLOGIZE! I FIGURED IT OUT.
AWW. I WANTED TO SEE YOU SAY SORRY.
ALL'S WELL THAT ENDS WELL. LET'S GO HOME.
SPEAK OF THE DEVIL.
HUH?

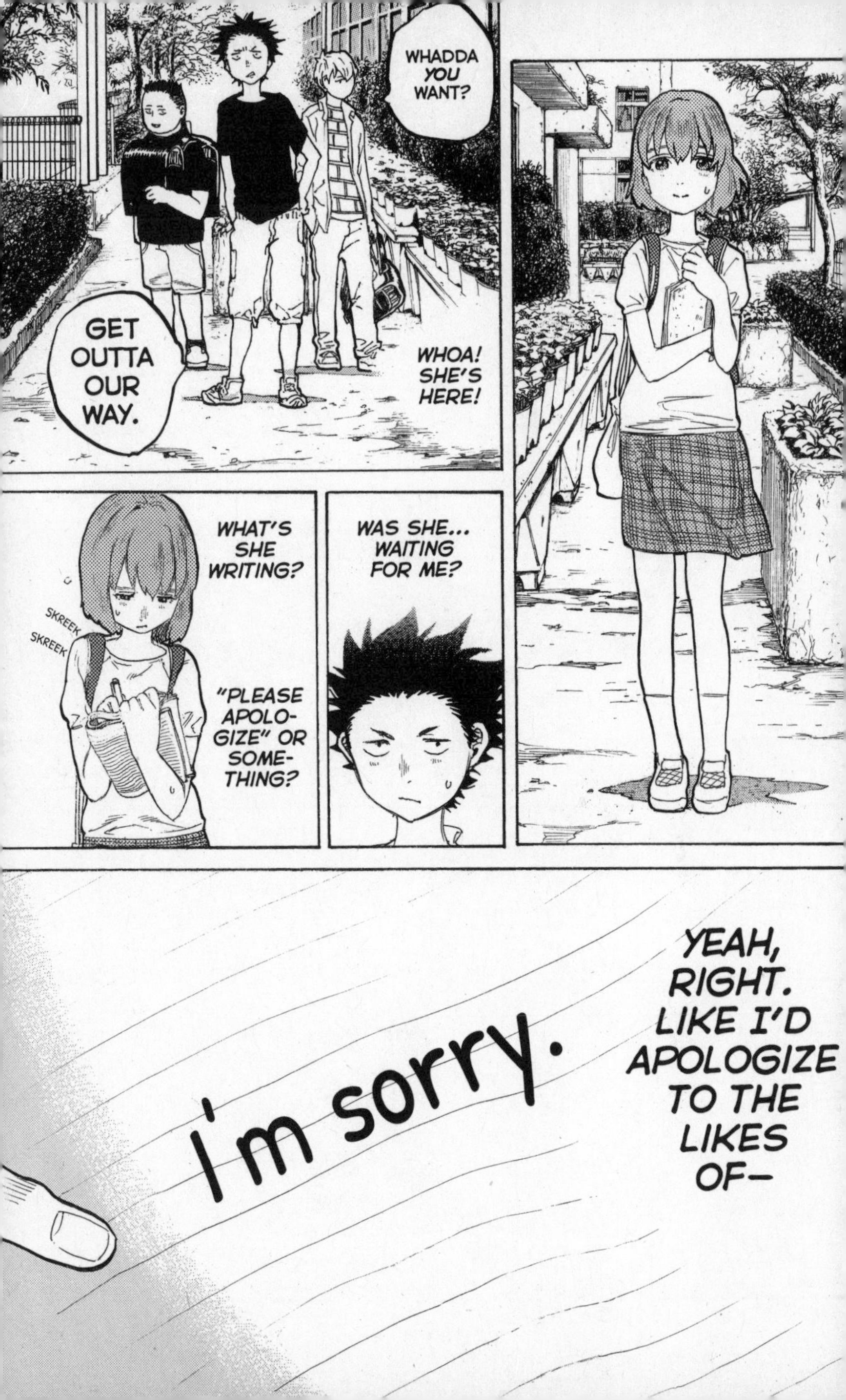
WHOA! SHE'S HERE!
WHADDA YOU WANT?
GET OUTTA OUR WAY.
WAS SHE... WAITING FOR ME?
WHAT'S SHE WRITING?
SKREEK
SKREEK
"PLEASE APOLOGIZE" OR SOMETHING?
YEAH, RIGHT. LIKE I'D APOLOGIZE TO THE LIKES OF—
i'm sorry.

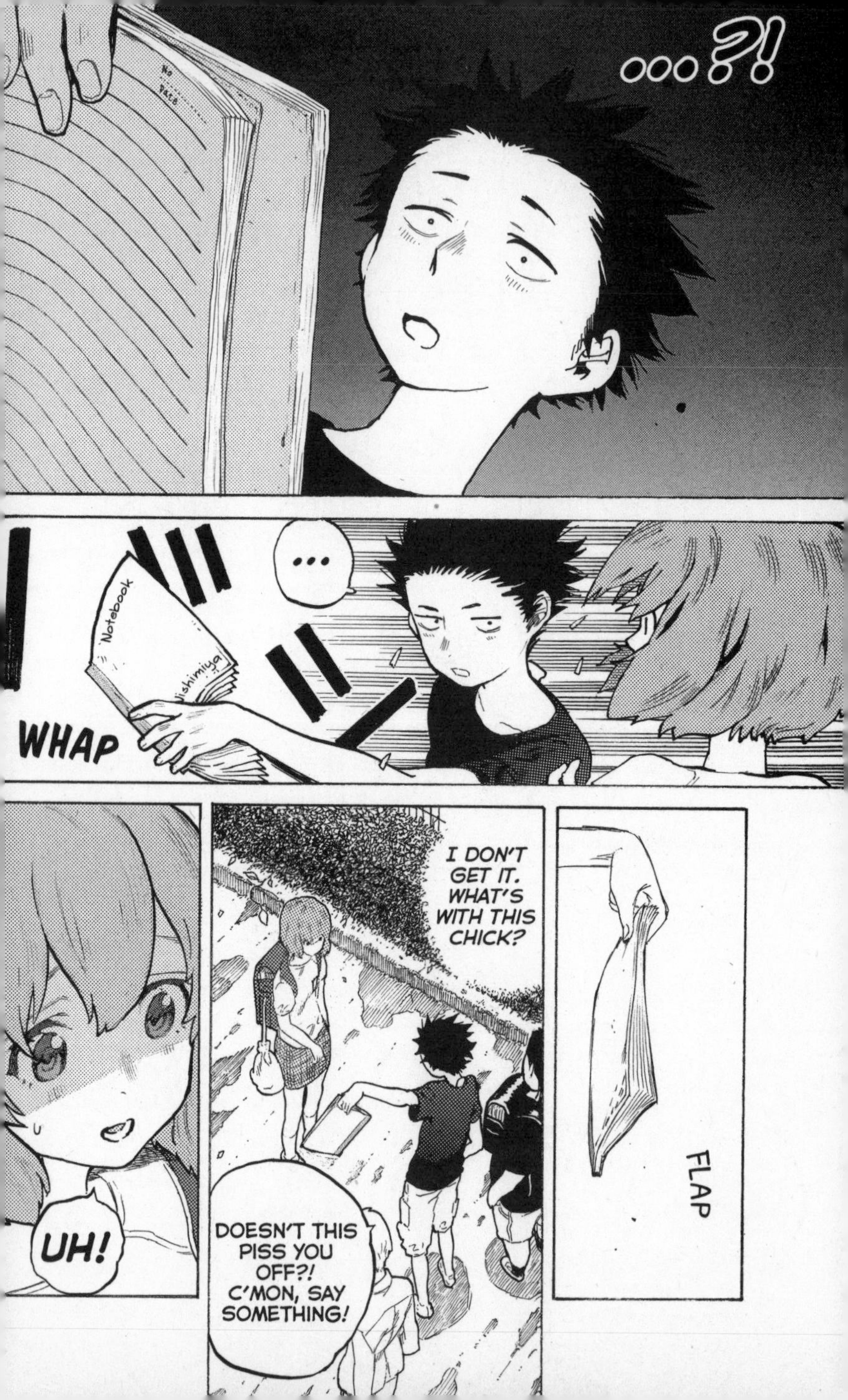
ooo?!
...
Notebook
Nishimiya
WHAP
FLAP
I DON'T GET IT. WHAT'S WITH THIS CHICK?
DOESN'T THIS PISS YOU OFF?! C'MON, SAY SOMETHING!
UH!

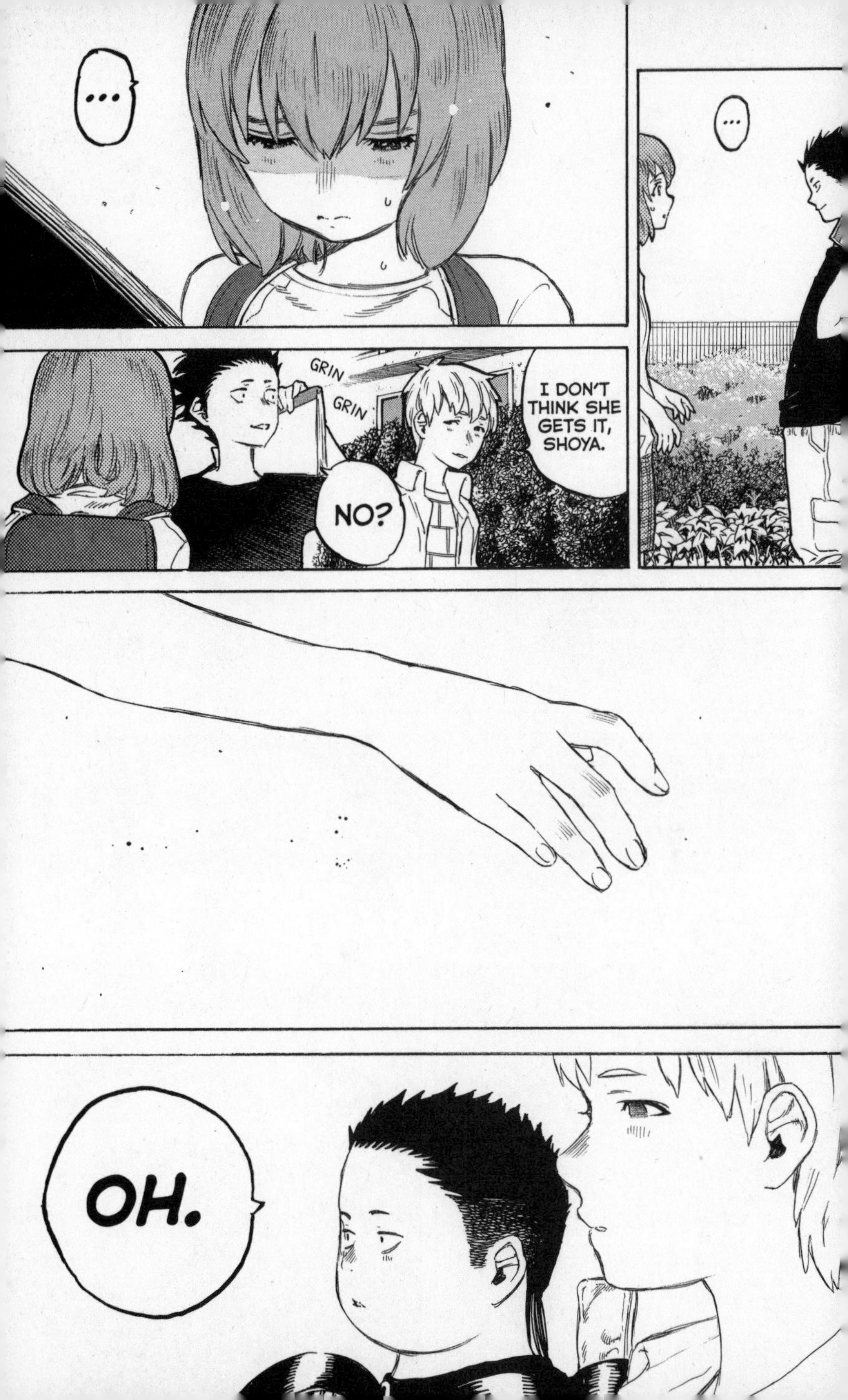
...
...
I DON'T THINK SHE GETS IT, SHOYA.
GRIN
GRIN
NO?
OH.

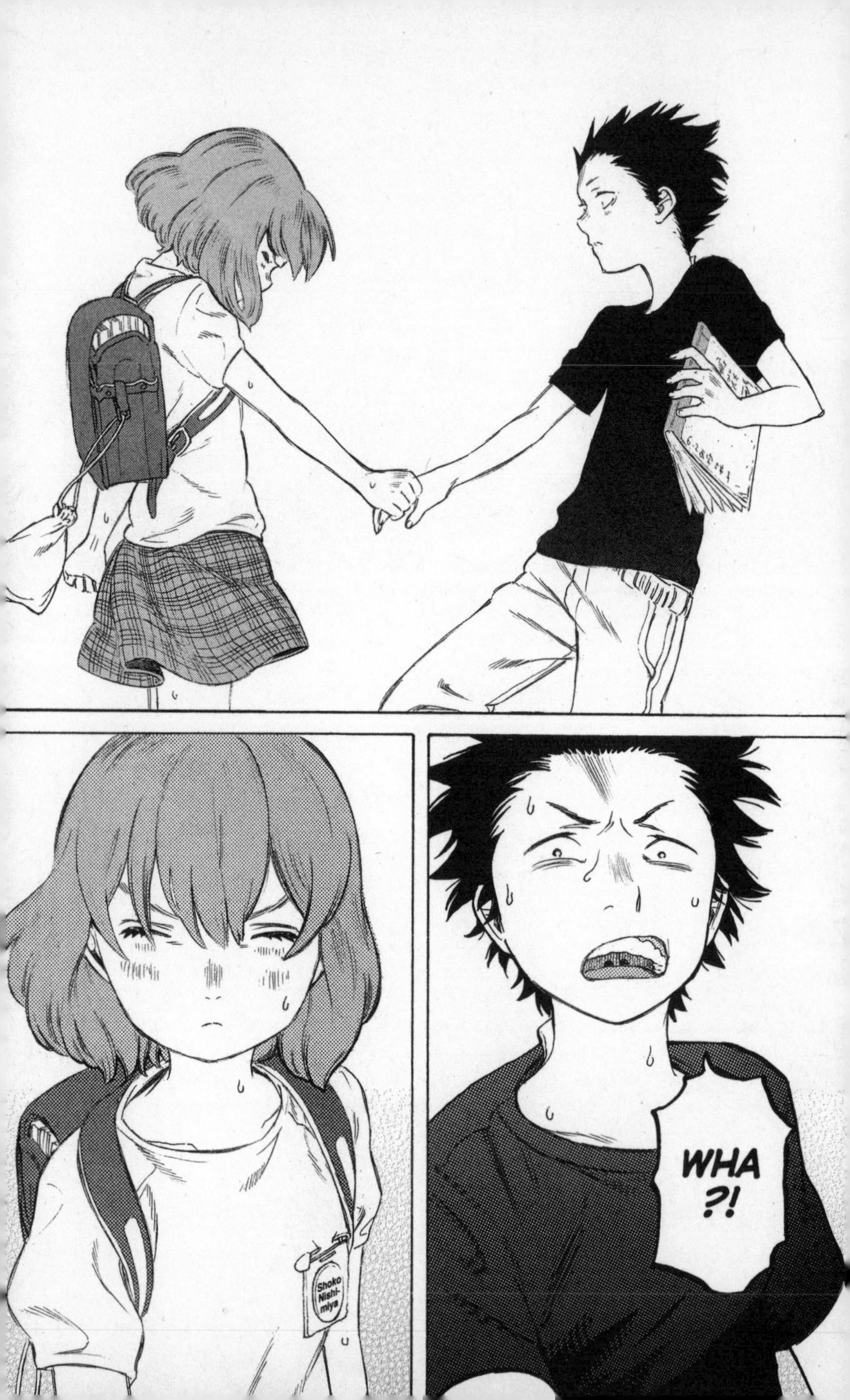
WHA ?!
Shoko Nishi-miya

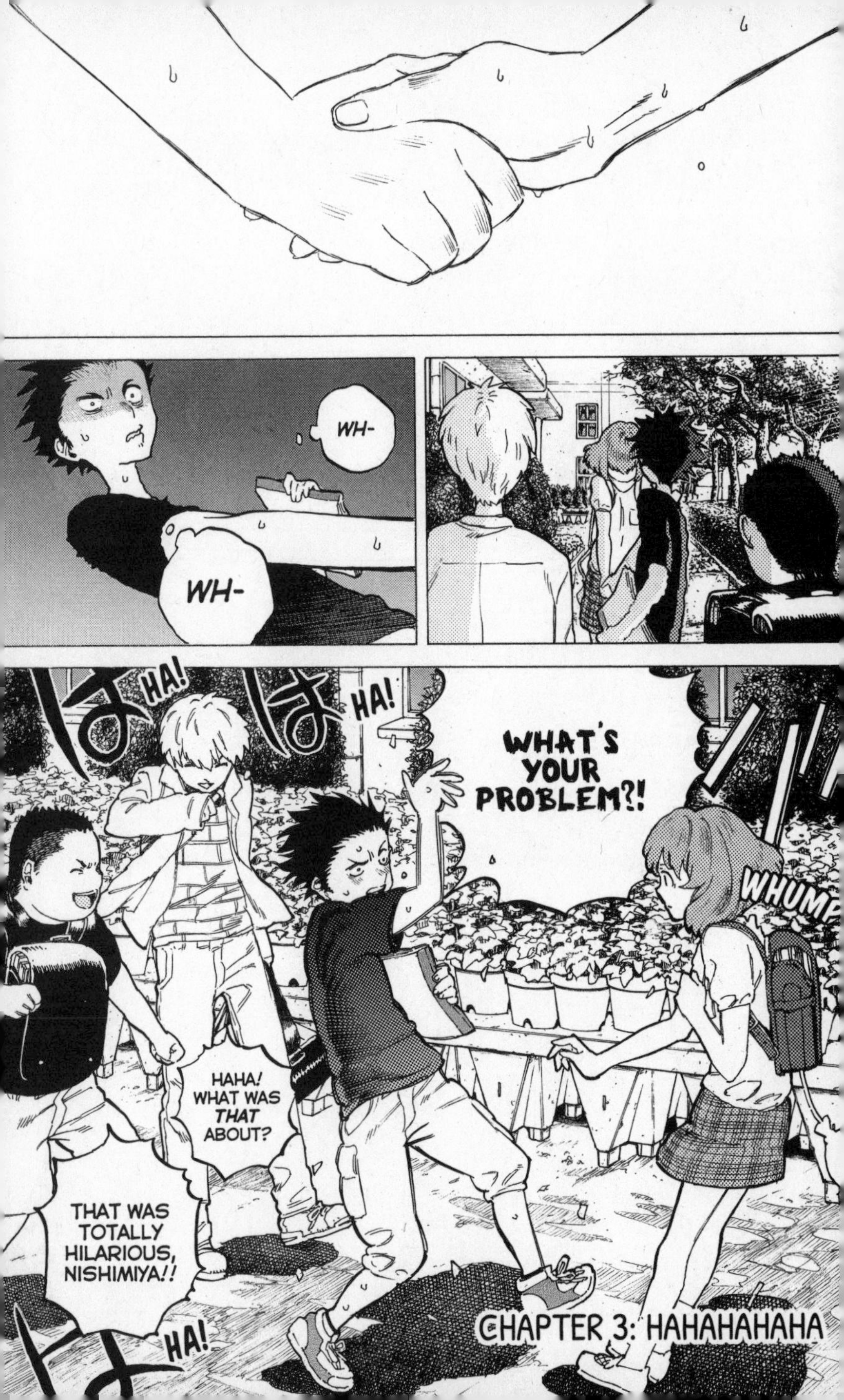
WH-
WH-
WHUMP
WHAT'S YOUR PROBLEM?!
HA!
HA!
HAHA! WHAT WAS THAT ABOUT?
THAT WAS TOTALLY HILARIOUS, NISHIMIYA!!
HA!
CHAPTER 3: HAHAHAHAHA

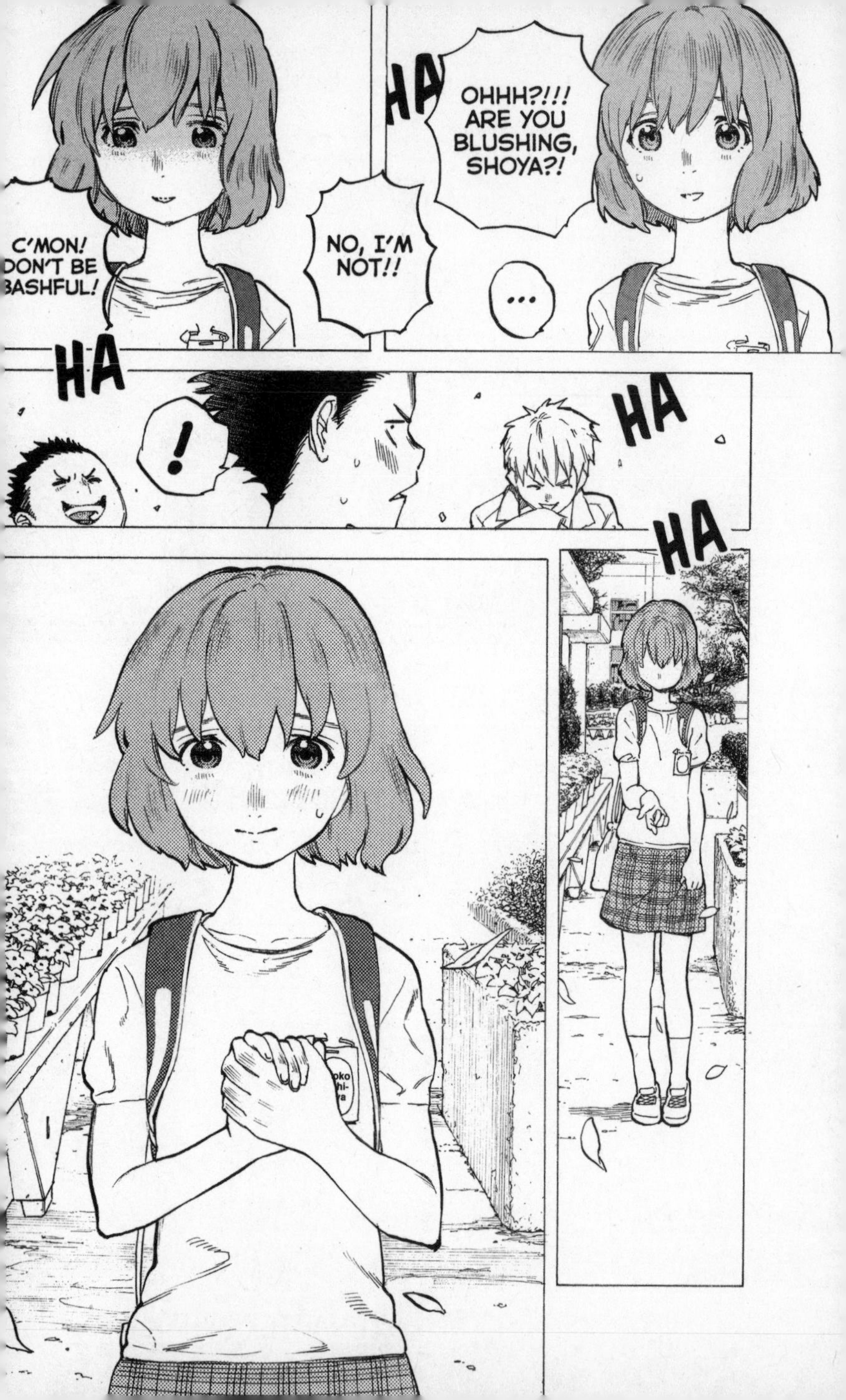
HA
OHHH?!!! ARE YOU BLUSHING, SHOYA?!
...
NO, I'M NOT!!
C'MON! DON'T BE BASHFUL!
HA
HA
!
HA

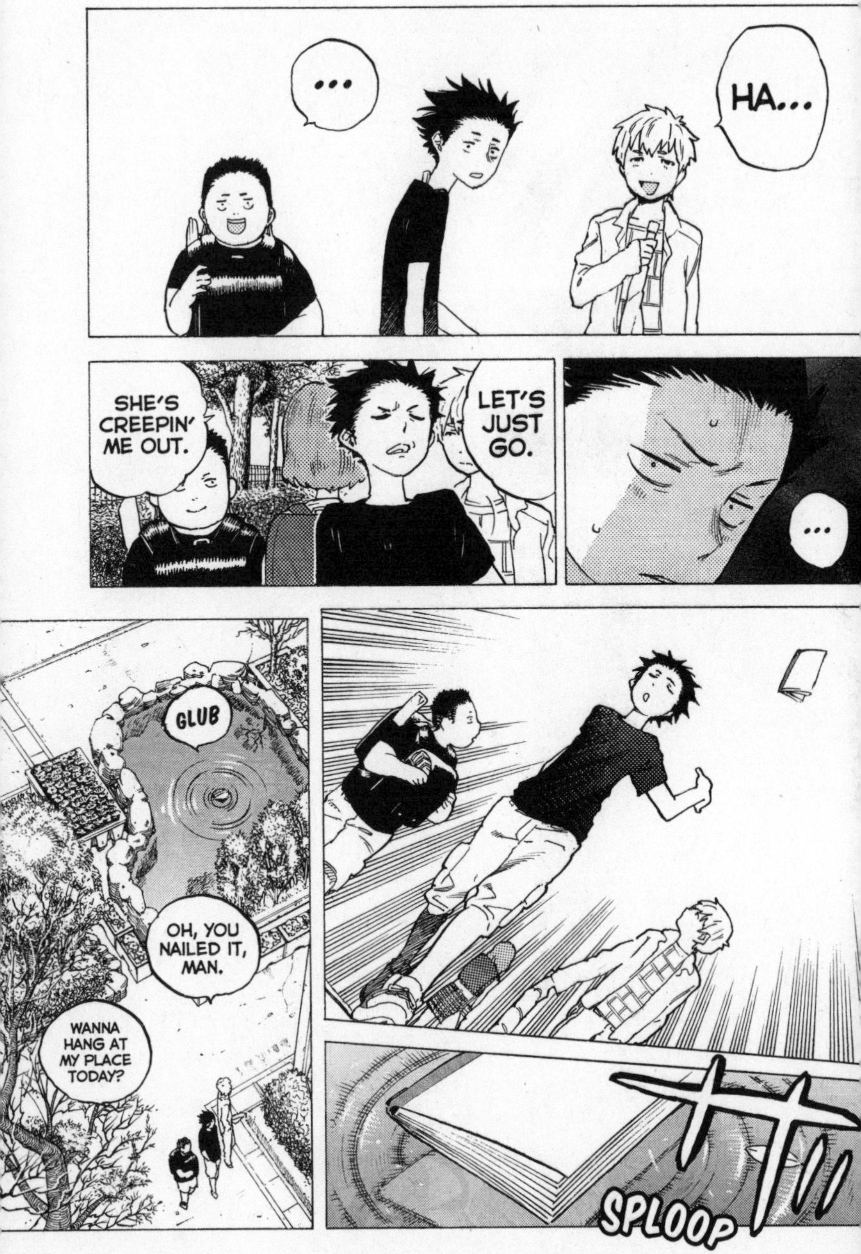
HA...
...
...
LET'S JUST GO.
SHE'S CREEPIN' ME OUT.
SPLOOP
GLUB
OH, YOU NAILED IT, MAN.
WANNA HANG AT MY PLACE TODAY?

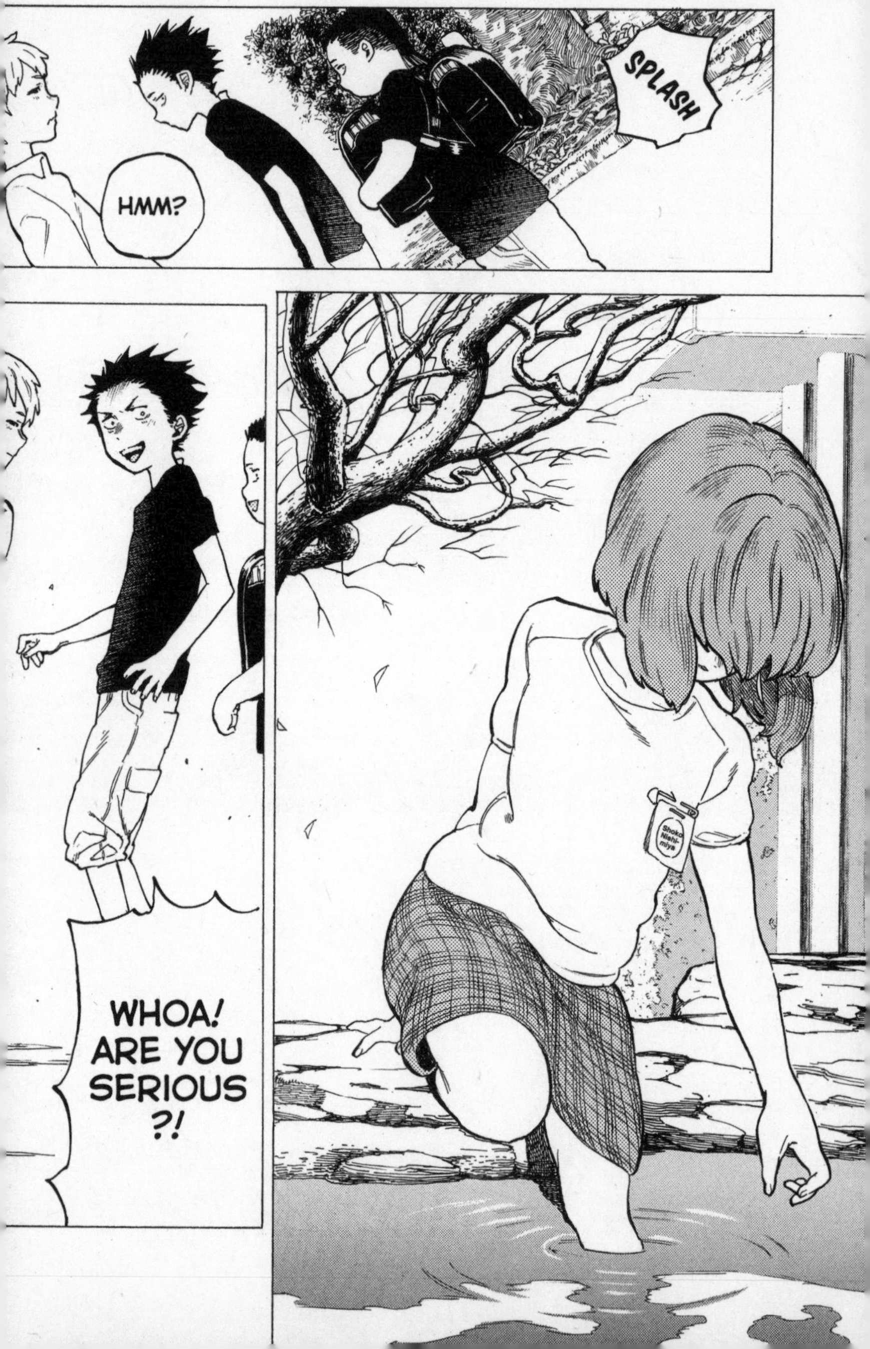
SPLASH
HMM?
Shoko Nishi-miya
WHOA! ARE YOU SERIOUS ?!

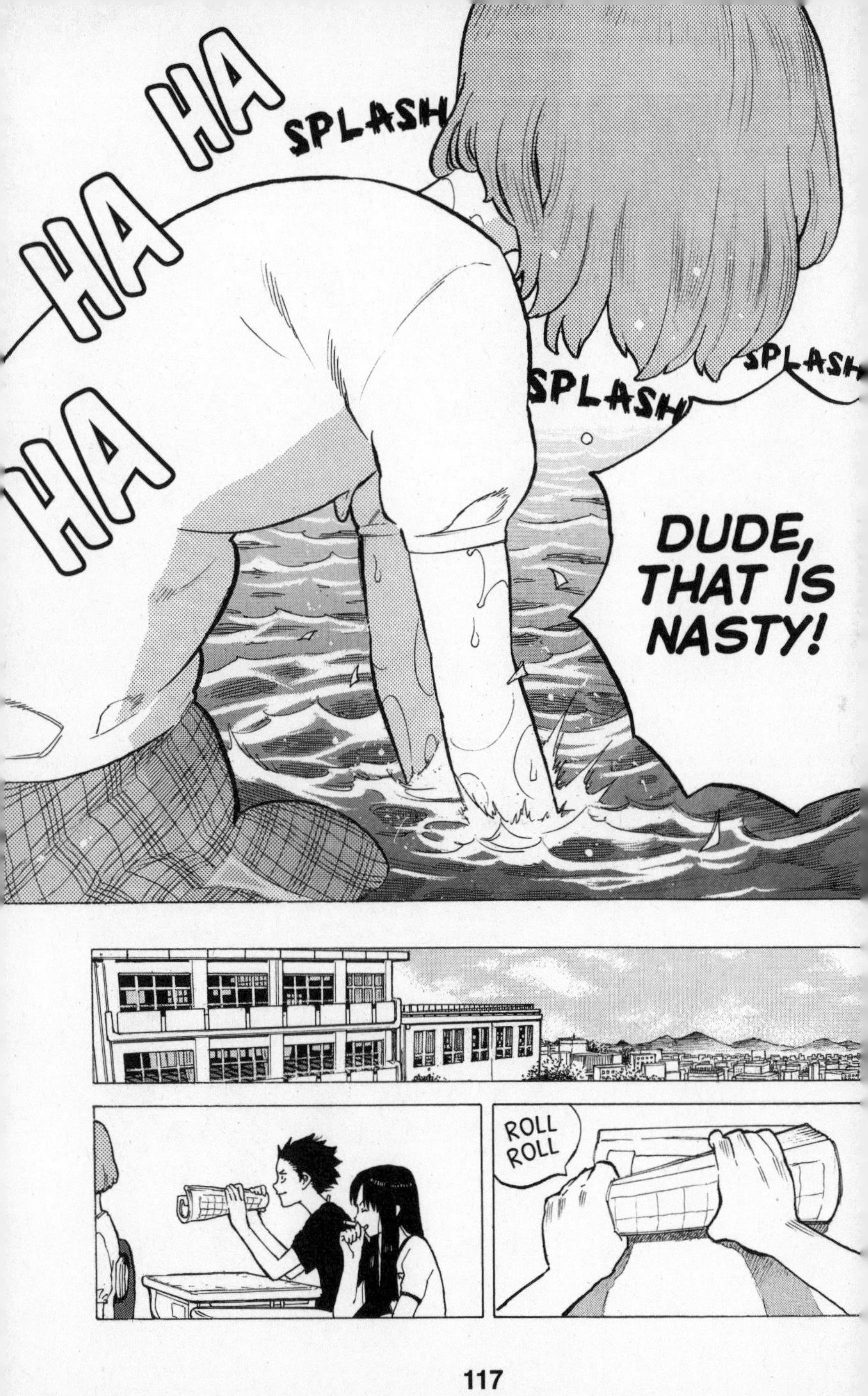
SPLASH
SPLASH
SPLASH
HA HA HA HA
DUDE, THAT IS NASTY!
ROLL ROLL

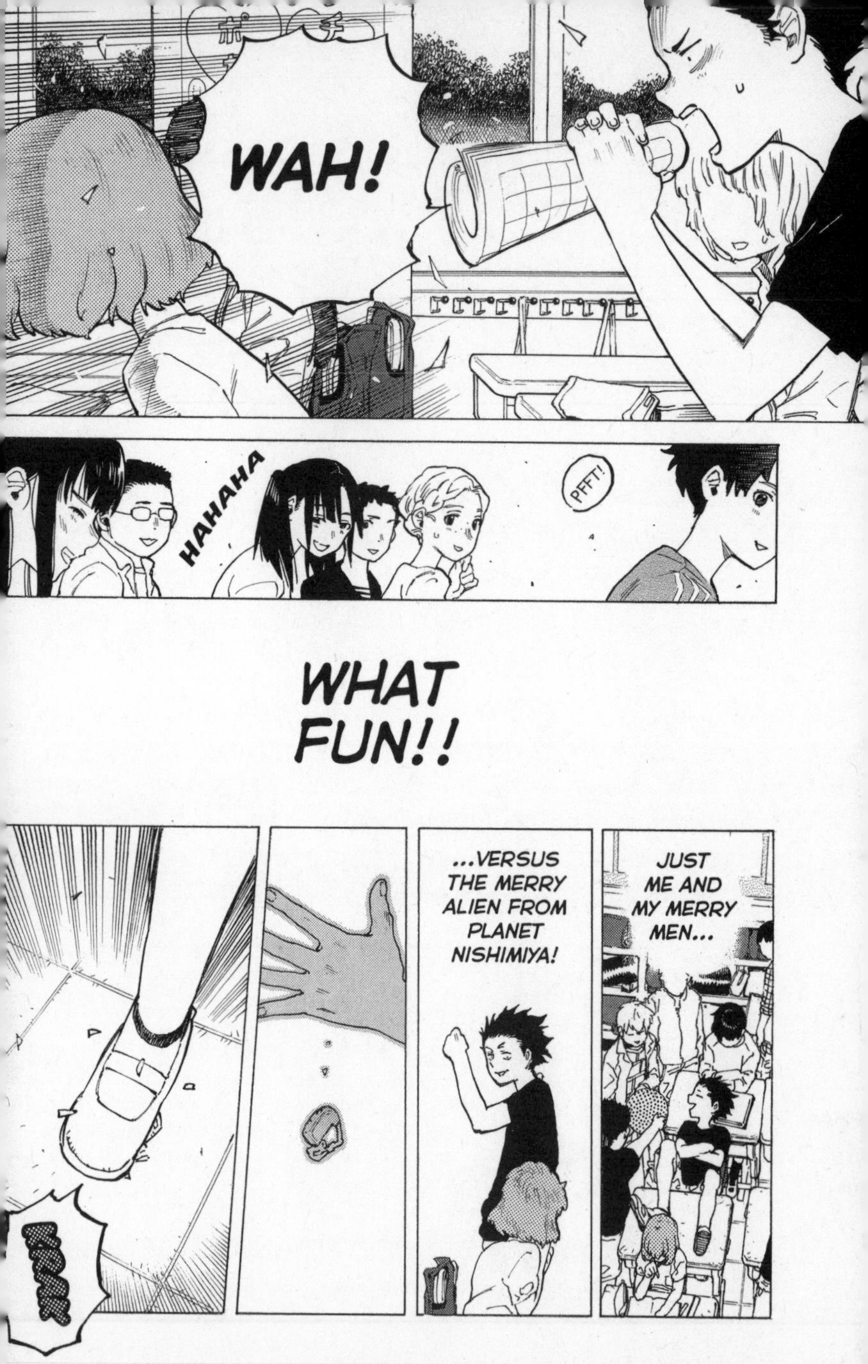
WAH!
PFFT!
HAHAHA
WHAT FUN!!
JUST ME AND MY MERRY MEN...
...VERSUS THE MERRY ALIEN FROM PLANET NISHIMIYA!

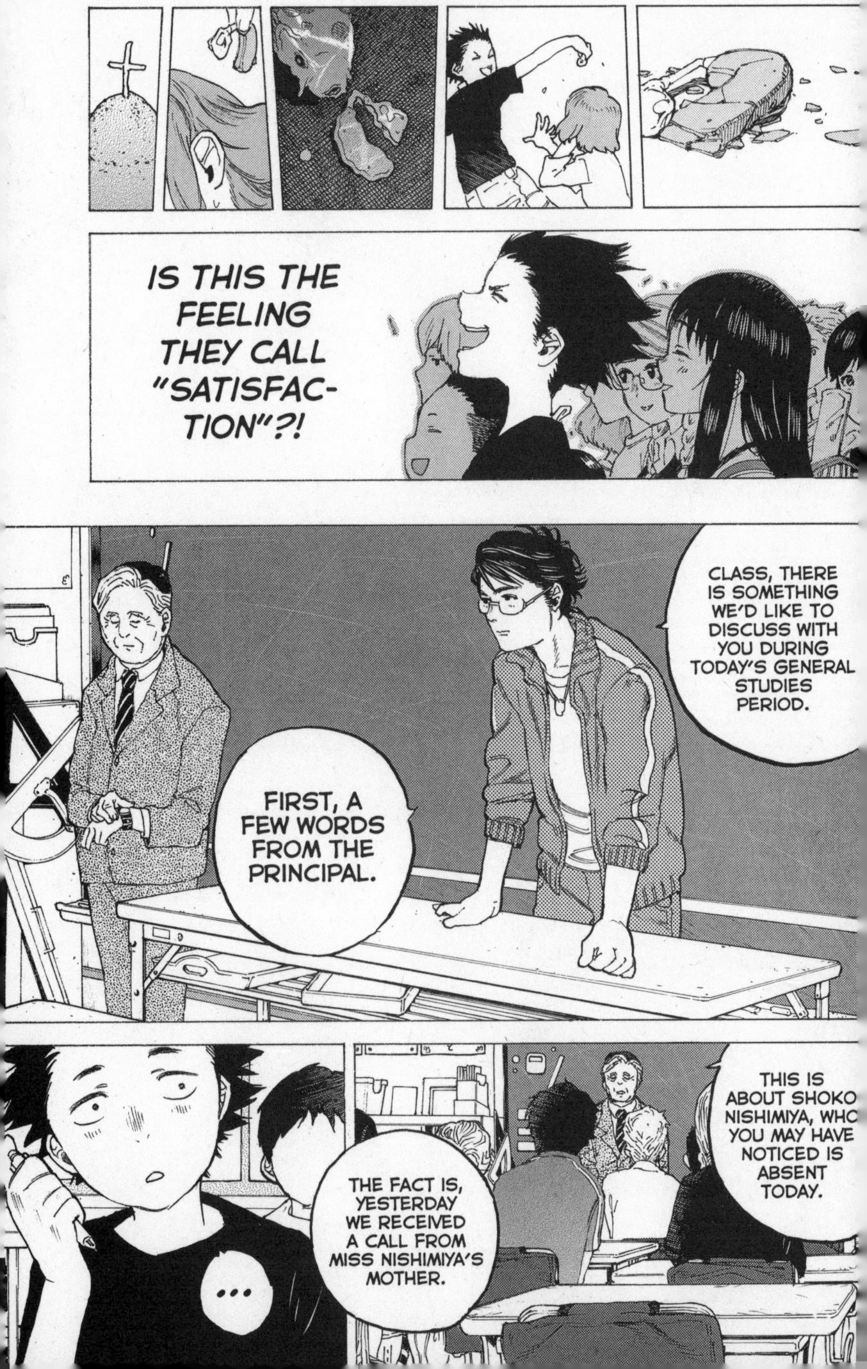
IS THIS THE FEELING THEY CALL "SATISFACTION"?!
CLASS, THERE IS SOMETHING WE'D LIKE TO DISCUSS WITH YOU DURING TODAY'S GENERAL STUDIES PERIOD.
FIRST, A FEW WORDS FROM THE PRINCIPAL.
THIS IS ABOUT SHOKO NISHIMIYA, WHO YOU MAY HAVE NOTICED IS ABSENT TODAY.
THE FACT IS, YESTERDAY WE RECEIVED A CALL FROM MISS NISHIMIYA'S MOTHER.
...

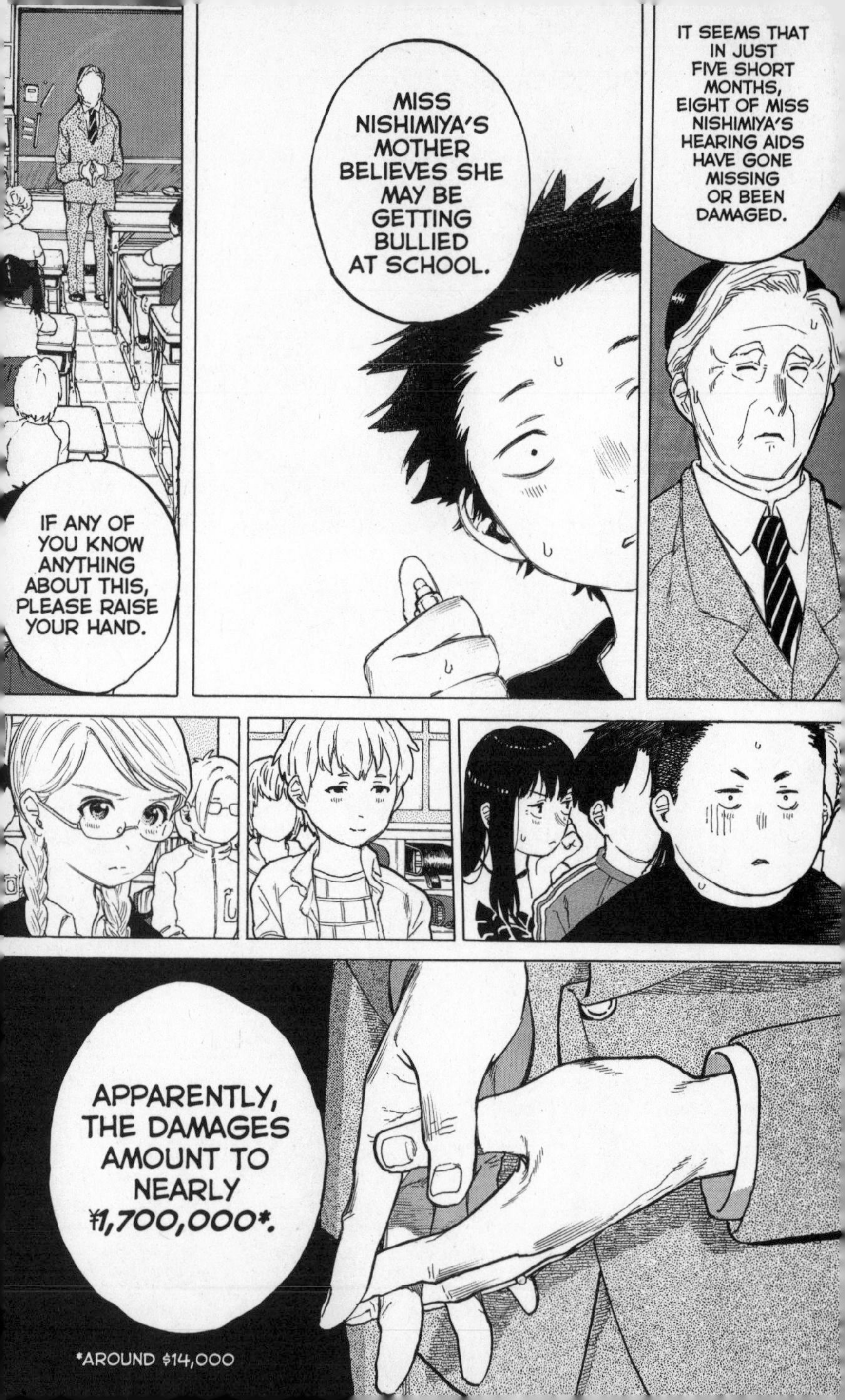
IT SEEMS THAT IN JUST FIVE SHORT MONTHS, EIGHT OF MISS NISHIMIYA'S HEARING AIDS HAVE GONE MISSING OR BEEN DAMAGED.
MISS NISHIMIYA'S MOTHER BELIEVES SHE MAY BE GETTING BULLIED AT SCHOOL.
IF ANY OF YOU KNOW ANYTHING ABOUT THIS, PLEASE RAISE YOUR HAND.
APPARENTLY, THE DAMAGES AMOUNT TO NEARLY ¥1,700,000*.
*AROUND $14,000

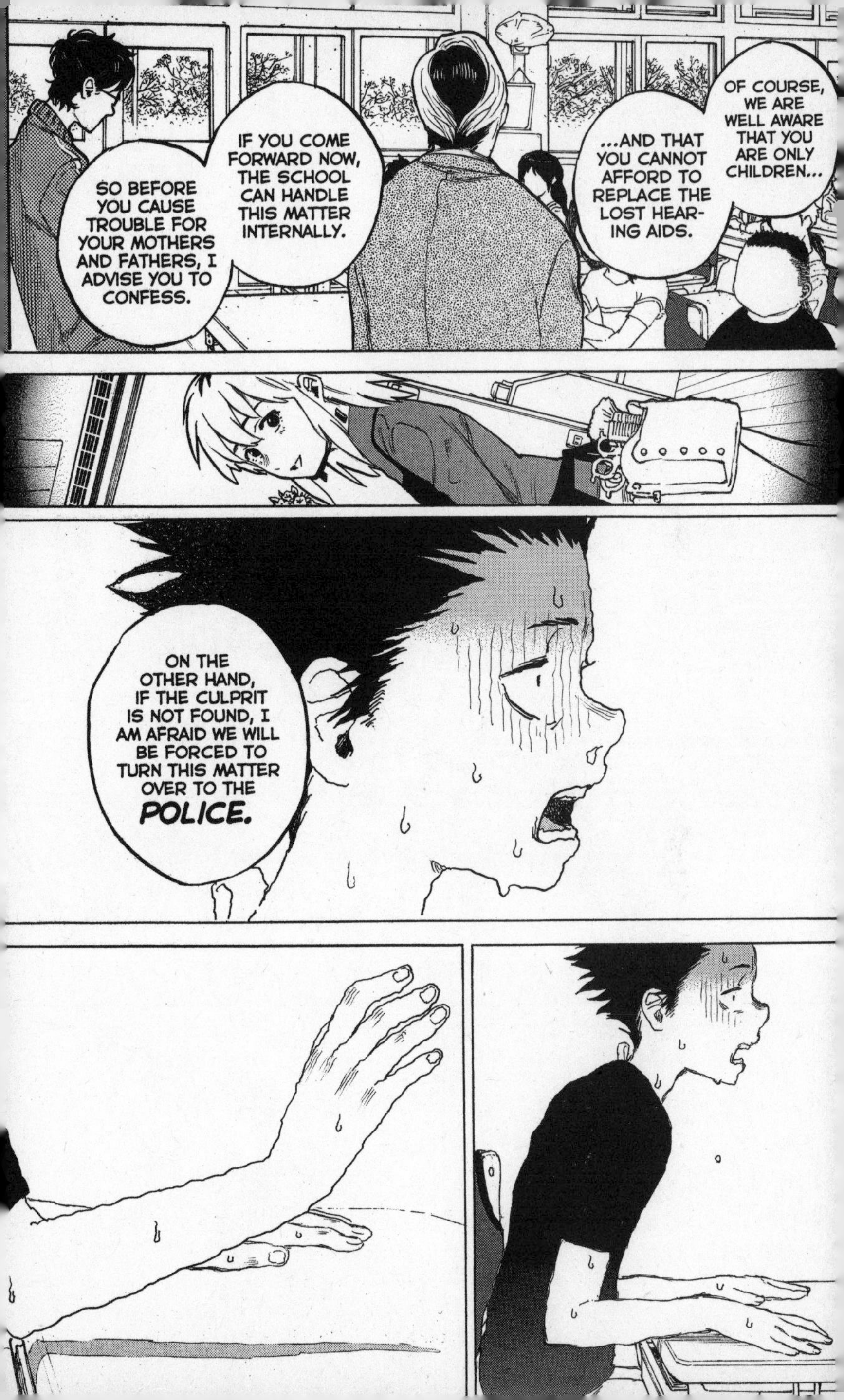
OF COURSE, WE ARE WELL AWARE THAT YOU ARE ONLY CHILDREN...
...AND THAT YOU CANNOT AFFORD TO REPLACE THE LOST HEAR-ING AIDS.
IF YOU COME FORWARD NOW, THE SCHOOL CAN HANDLE THIS MATTER INTERNALLY.
SO BEFORE YOU CAUSE TROUBLE FOR YOUR MOTHERS AND FATHERS, I ADVISE YOU TO CONFESS.
ON THE OTHER HAND, IF THE CULPRIT IS NOT FOUND, I AM AFRAID WE WILL BE FORCED TO TURN THIS MATTER OVER TO THE ***POLICE.***

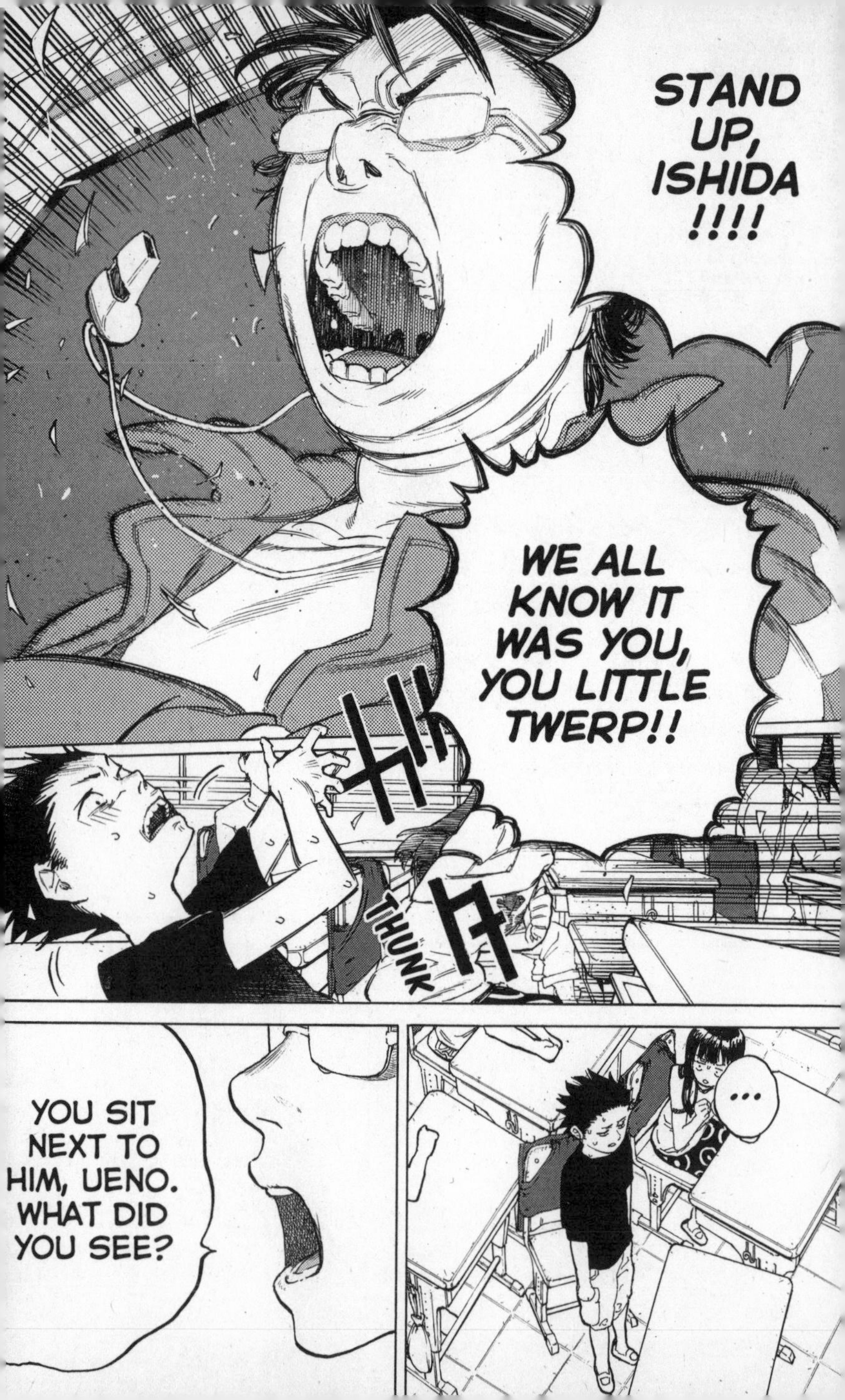
STAND UP, ISHIDA !!!!
WE ALL KNOW IT WAS YOU, YOU LITTLE TWERP!!
THUNK
...
YOU SIT NEXT TO HIM, UENO. WHAT DID YOU SEE?

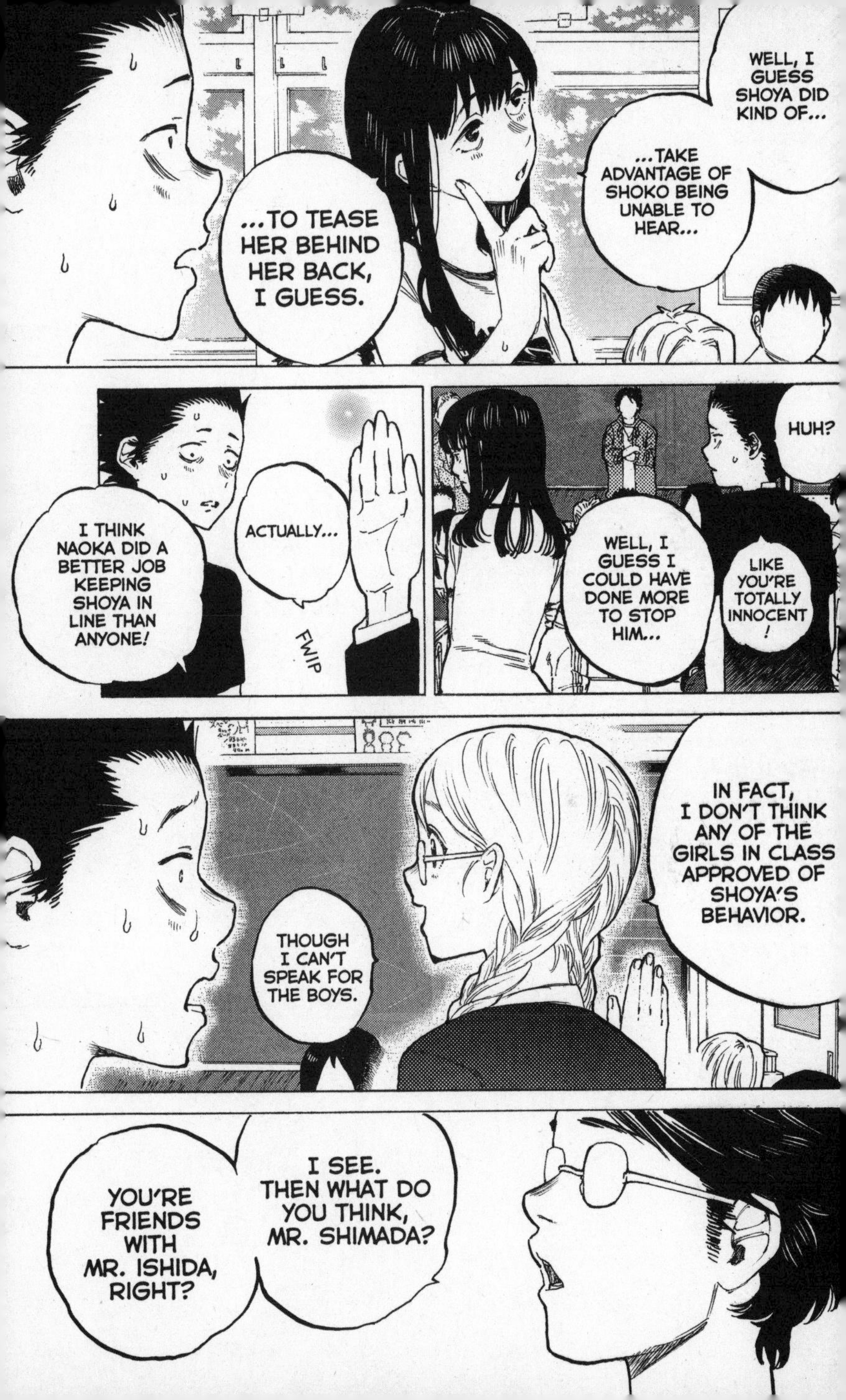
WELL, I GUESS SHOYA DID KIND OF...
...TAKE ADVANTAGE OF SHOKO BEING UNABLE TO HEAR...
...TO TEASE HER BEHIND HER BACK, I GUESS.
HUH?
LIKE YOU'RE TOTALLY INNOCENT!
WELL, I GUESS I COULD HAVE DONE MORE TO STOP HIM...
ACTUALLY...
FWIP
I THINK NAOKA DID A BETTER JOB KEEPING SHOYA IN LINE THAN ANYONE!
IN FACT, I DON'T THINK ANY OF THE GIRLS IN CLASS APPROVED OF SHOYA'S BEHAVIOR.
THOUGH I CAN'T SPEAK FOR THE BOYS.
I SEE. THEN WHAT DO YOU THINK, MR. SHIMADA?
YOU'RE FRIENDS WITH MR. ISHIDA, RIGHT?

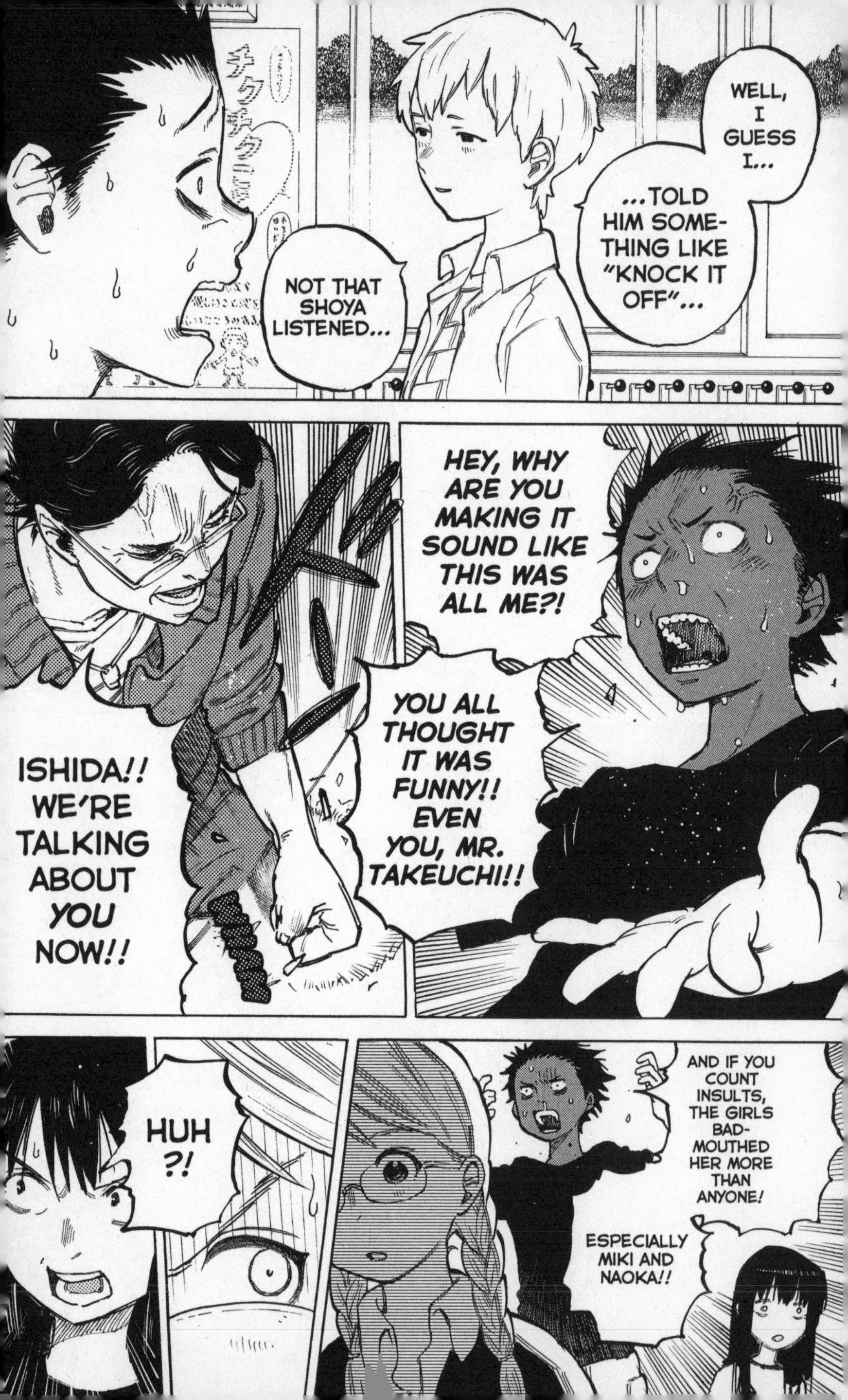
WELL, I GUESS I...
...TOLD HIM SOME-THING LIKE "KNOCK IT OFF"...
NOT THAT SHOYA LISTENED...
HEY, WHY ARE YOU MAKING IT SOUND LIKE THIS WAS ALL ME?!
YOU ALL THOUGHT IT WAS FUNNY!! EVEN YOU, MR. TAKEUCHI!!
ISHIDA!! WE'RE TALKING ABOUT YOU NOW!!
AND IF YOU COUNT INSULTS, THE GIRLS BAD-MOUTHED HER MORE THAN ANYONE!
ESPECIALLY MIKI AND NAOKA!!
HUH ?!

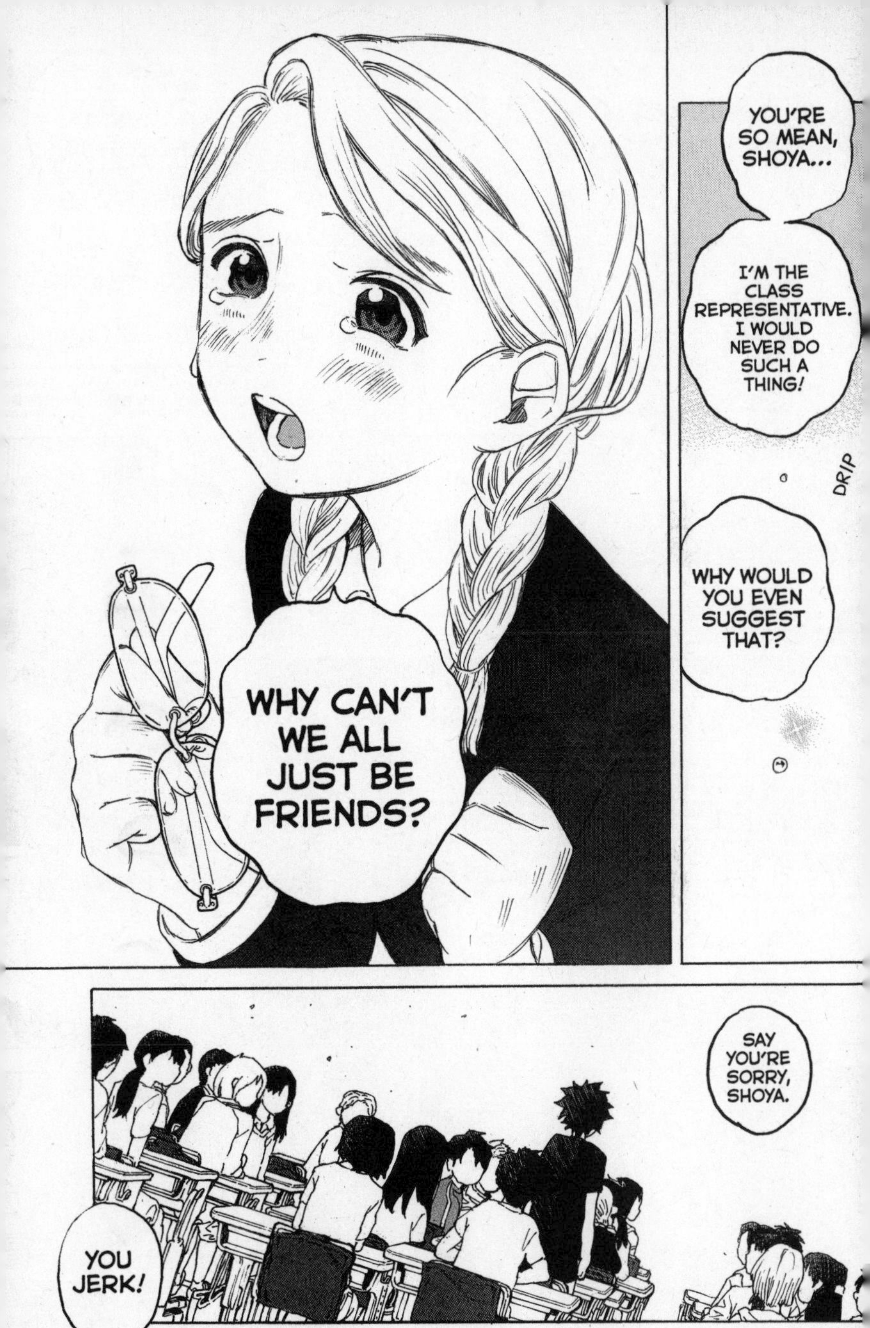
YOU'RE SO MEAN, SHOYA...
I'M THE CLASS REPRESENTATIVE. I WOULD NEVER DO SUCH A THING!
DRIP
WHY WOULD YOU EVEN SUGGEST THAT?
WHY CAN'T WE ALL JUST BE FRIENDS?
SAY YOU'RE SORRY, SHOYA.
YOU JERK!

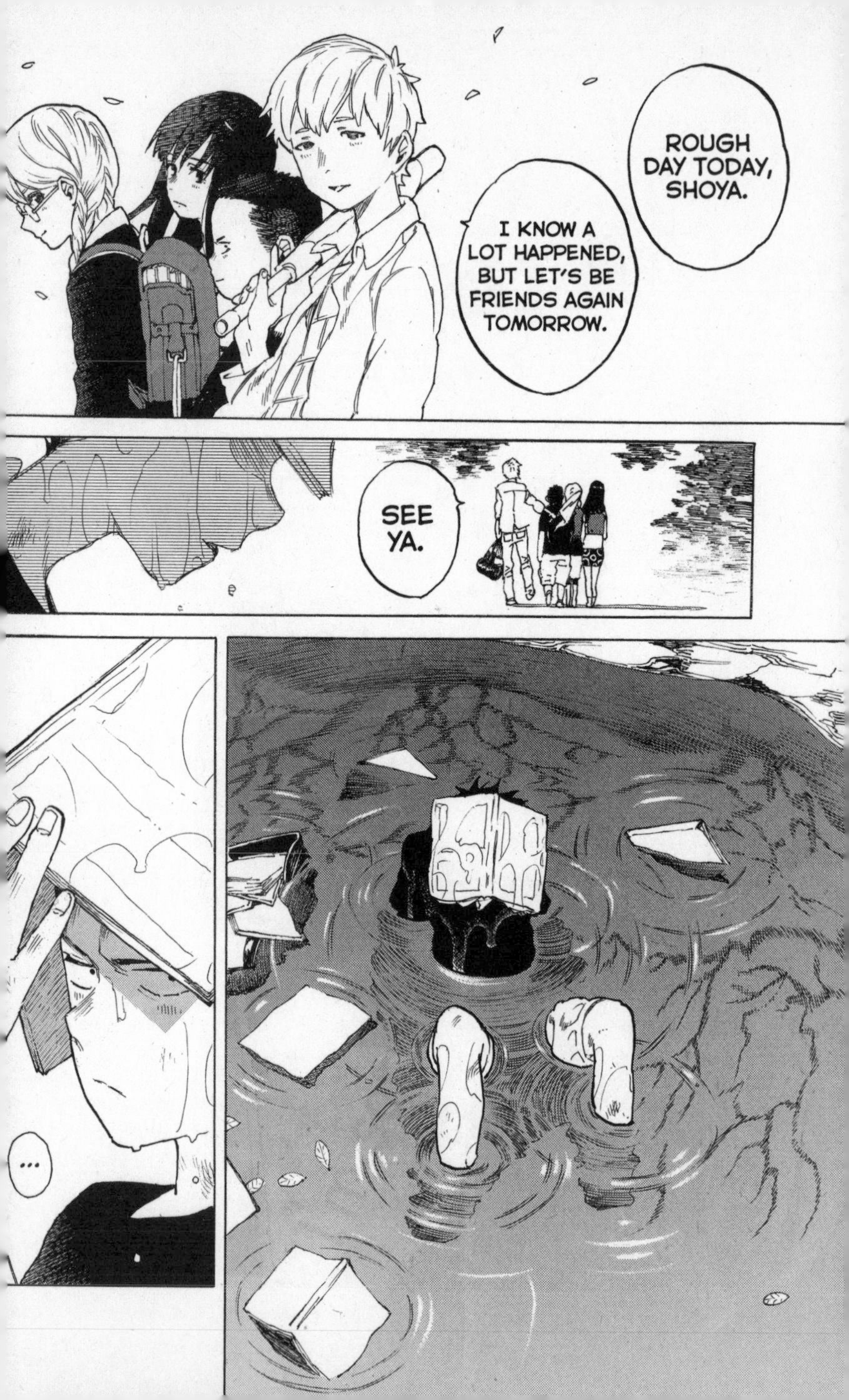
ROUGH DAY TODAY, SHOYA.
I KNOW A LOT HAPPENED, BUT LET'S BE FRIENDS AGAIN TOMORROW.
SEE YA.
...

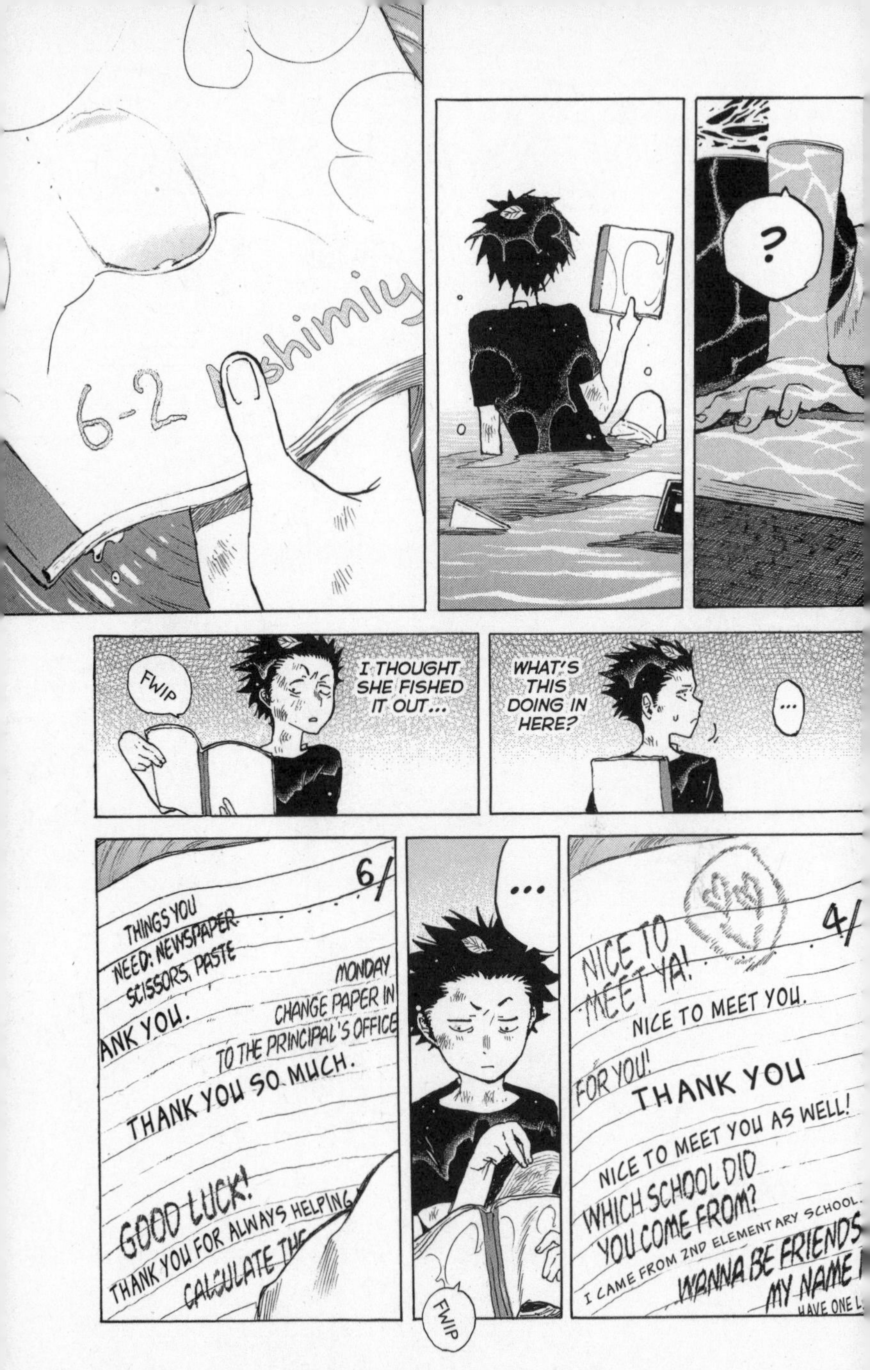
?
6-2 N shimiy
...
WHAT'S THIS DOING IN HERE?
I THOUGHT SHE FISHED IT OUT...
FWIP
4/
NICE TO MEET YA!
NICE TO MEET YOU.
FOR YOU!
THANK YOU
NICE TO MEET YOU AS WELL!
WHICH SCHOOL DID YOU COME FROM?
I CAME FROM 2ND ELEMENTARY SCHOOL.
WANNA BE FRIENDS
MY NAME I
HAVE ONE L
...
FWIP
6/
THINGS YOU NEED: NEWSPAPER SCISSORS, PASTE
MONDAY
CHANGE PAPER IN TO THE PRINCIPAL'S OFFICE
ANK YOU.
THANK YOU SO MUCH.
GOOD LUCK!
THANK YOU FOR ALWAYS HELPING
CALCULATE TH

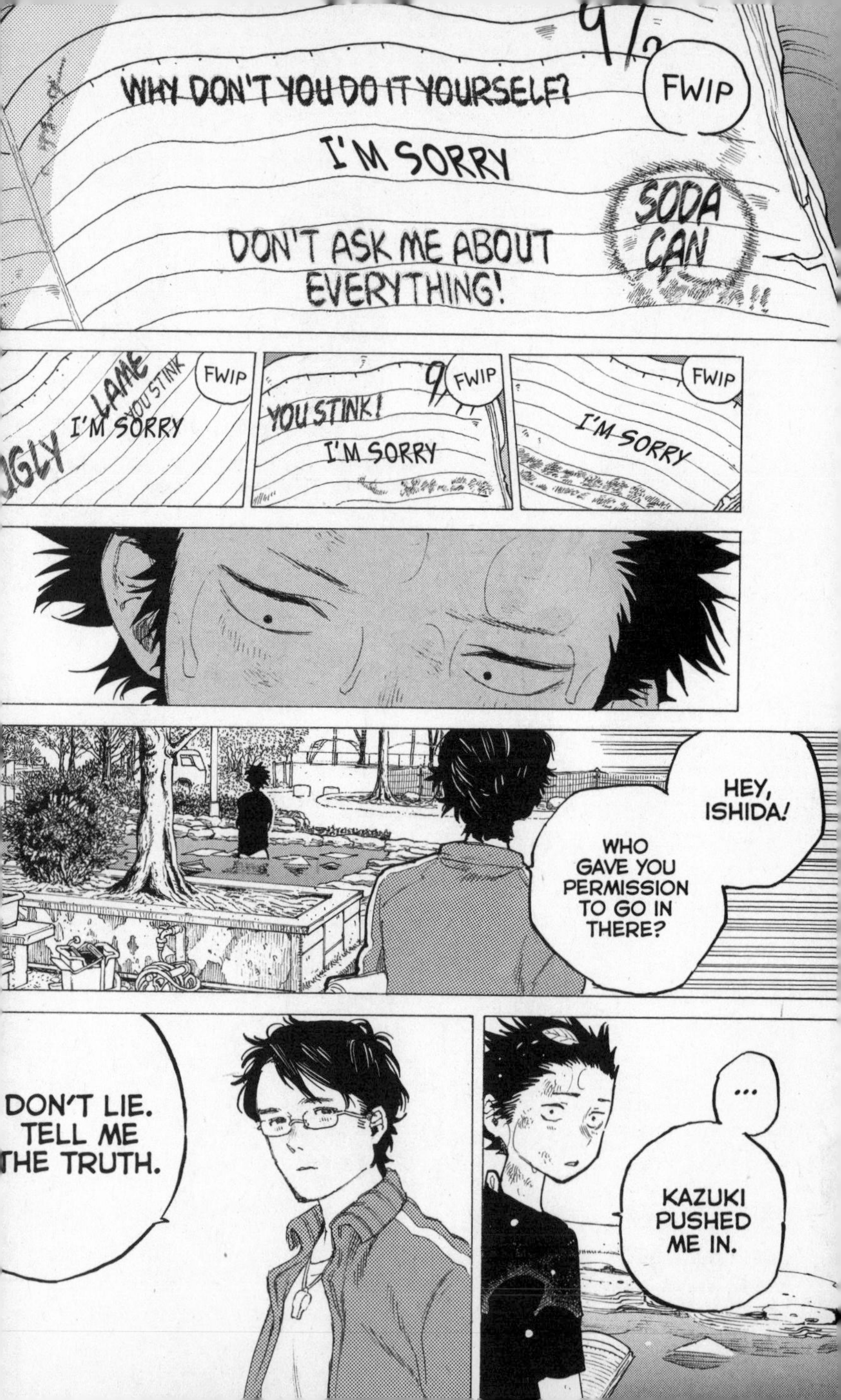
FWIP
WHY DON'T YOU DO IT YOURSELF?
I'M SORRY
SODA CAN
DON'T ASK ME ABOUT EVERYTHING!
FWIP
I'M SORRY
FWIP
YOU STINK!
I'M SORRY
FWIP
LAME
YOU STINK
UGLY
I'M SORRY
HEY, ISHIDA!
WHO GAVE YOU PERMISSION TO GO IN THERE?
...
KAZUKI PUSHED ME IN.
DON'T LIE. TELL ME THE TRUTH.

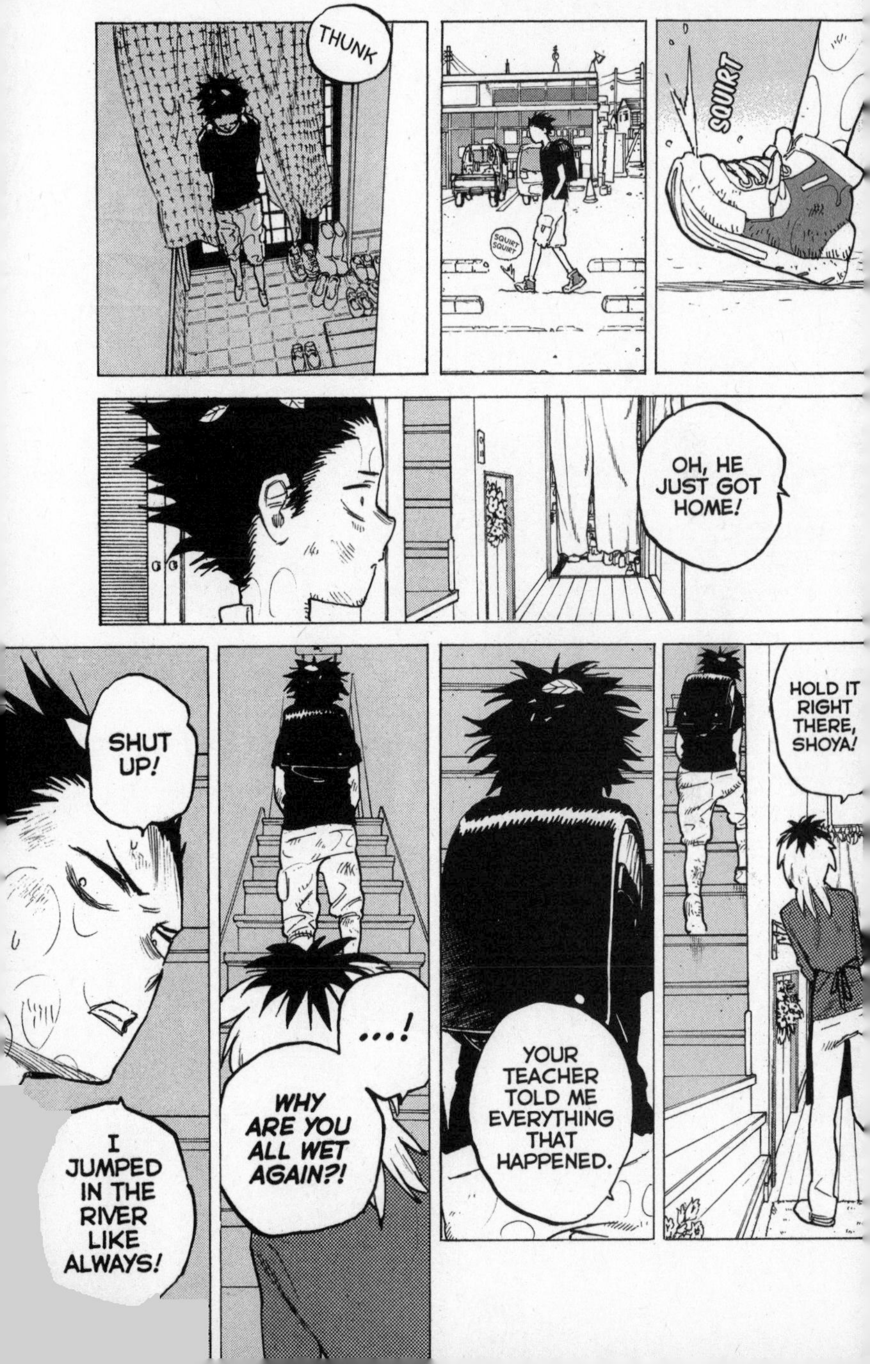
SQUIRT
SQUIRT SQUIRT
THUNK
OH, HE JUST GOT HOME!
HOLD IT RIGHT THERE, SHOYA!
YOUR TEACHER TOLD ME EVERYTHING THAT HAPPENED.
...!
WHY ARE YOU ALL WET AGAIN?!
SHUT UP!
I JUMPED IN THE RIVER LIKE ALWAYS!

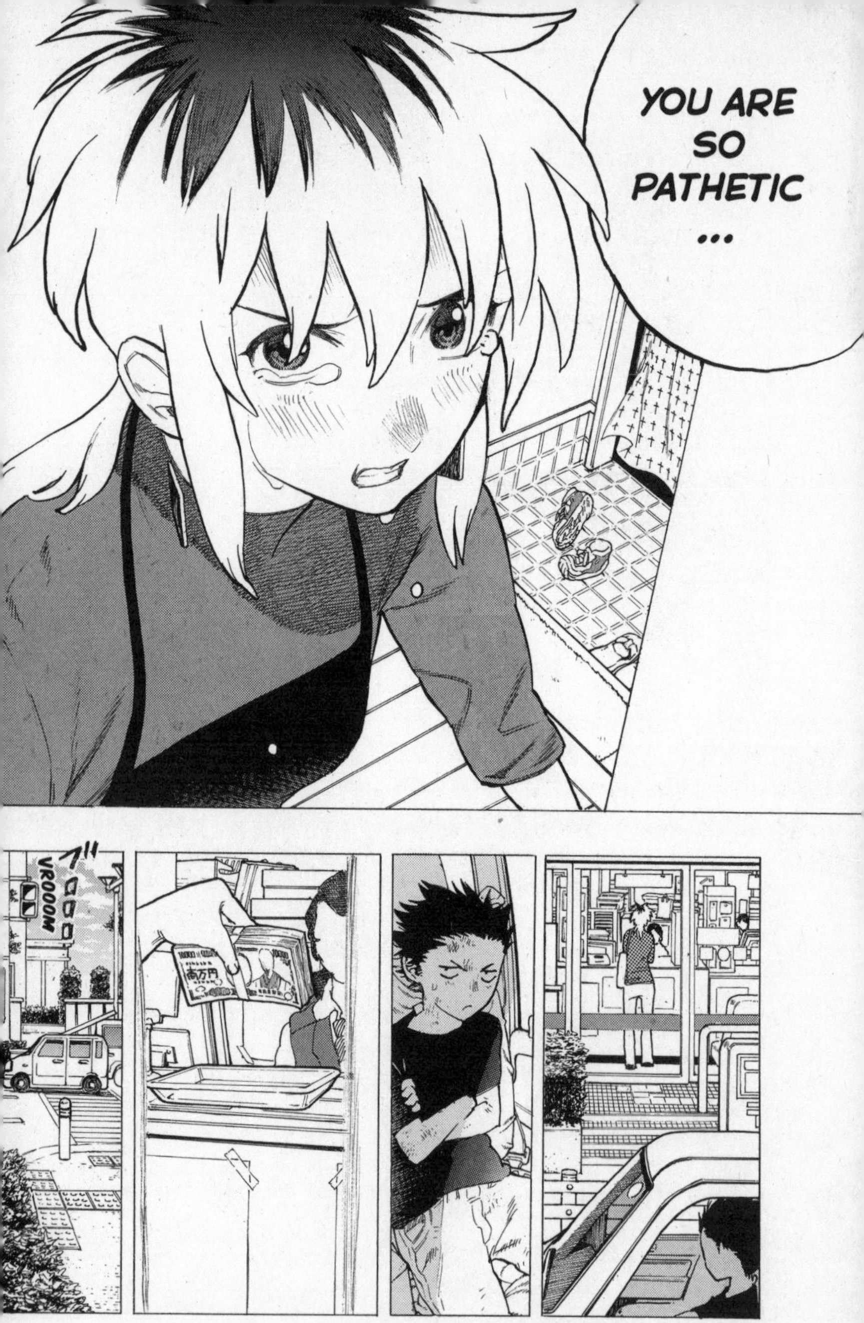
YOU ARE SO PATHETIC ...
ブロロロ
VROOOM

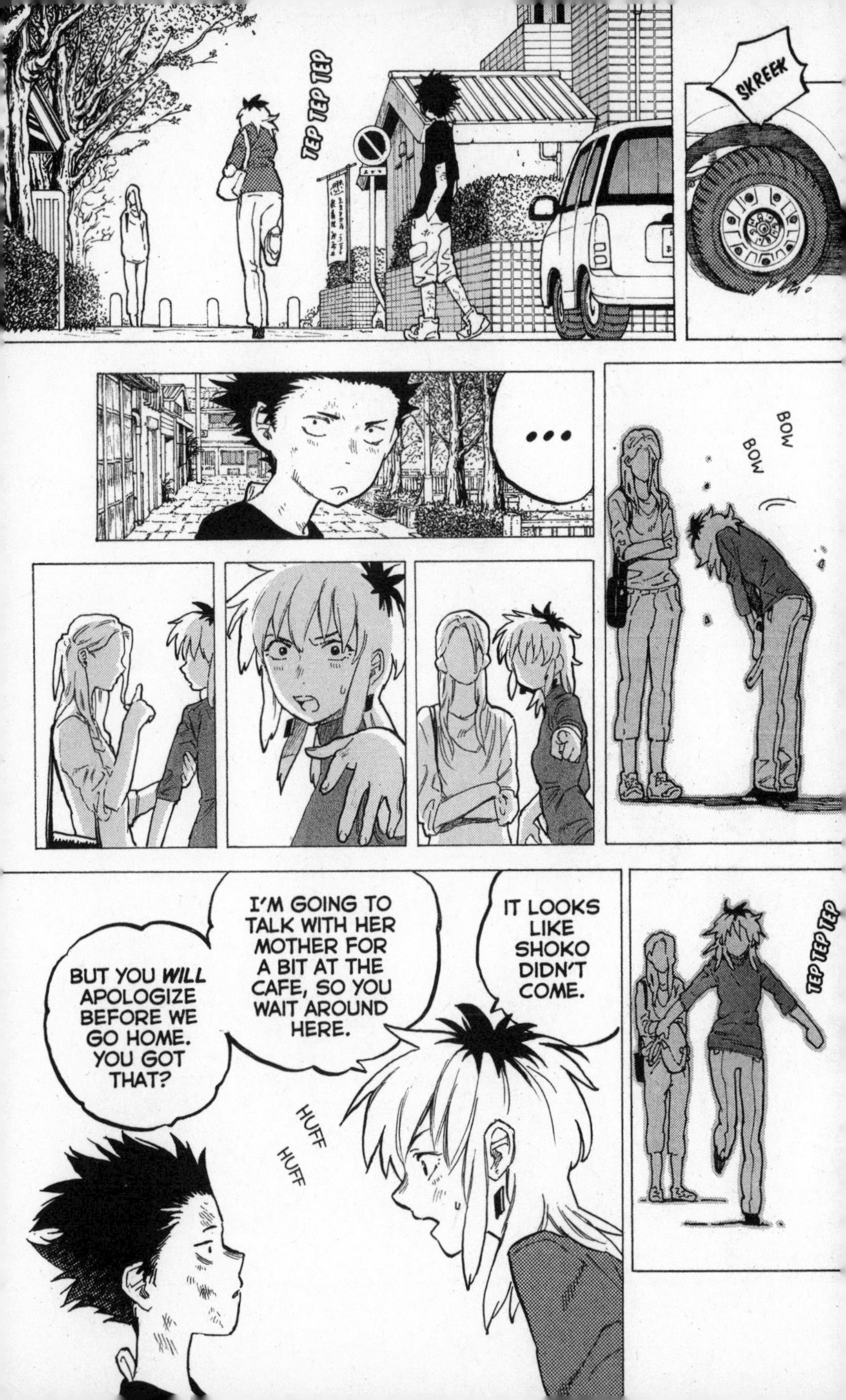
SKREEK
TEP TEP TEP
BOW
BOW
...
TEP TEP TEP
IT LOOKS LIKE SHOKO DIDN'T COME.
I'M GOING TO TALK WITH HER MOTHER FOR A BIT AT THE CAFE, SO YOU WAIT AROUND HERE.
BUT YOU *WILL* APOLOGIZE BEFORE WE GO HOME. YOU GOT THAT?
HUFF
HUFF

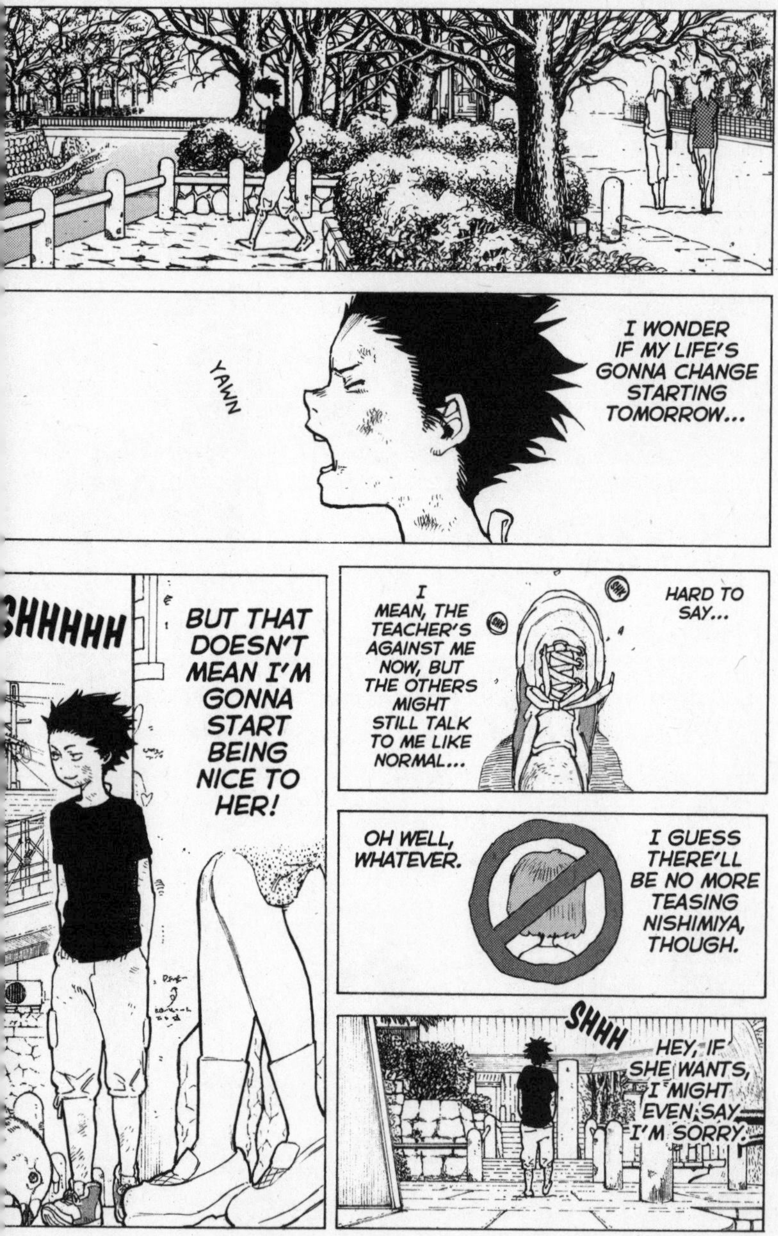
I WONDER IF MY LIFE'S GONNA CHANGE STARTING TOMORROW...
YAWN
HARD TO SAY...
I MEAN, THE TEACHER'S AGAINST ME NOW, BUT THE OTHERS MIGHT STILL TALK TO ME LIKE NORMAL...
I GUESS THERE'LL BE NO MORE TEASING NISHIMIYA, THOUGH.
OH WELL, WHATEVER.
HEY, IF SHE WANTS, I MIGHT EVEN SAY I'M SORRY.
SHHH
BUT THAT DOESN'T MEAN I'M GONNA START BEING NICE TO HER!
SHHHHHH

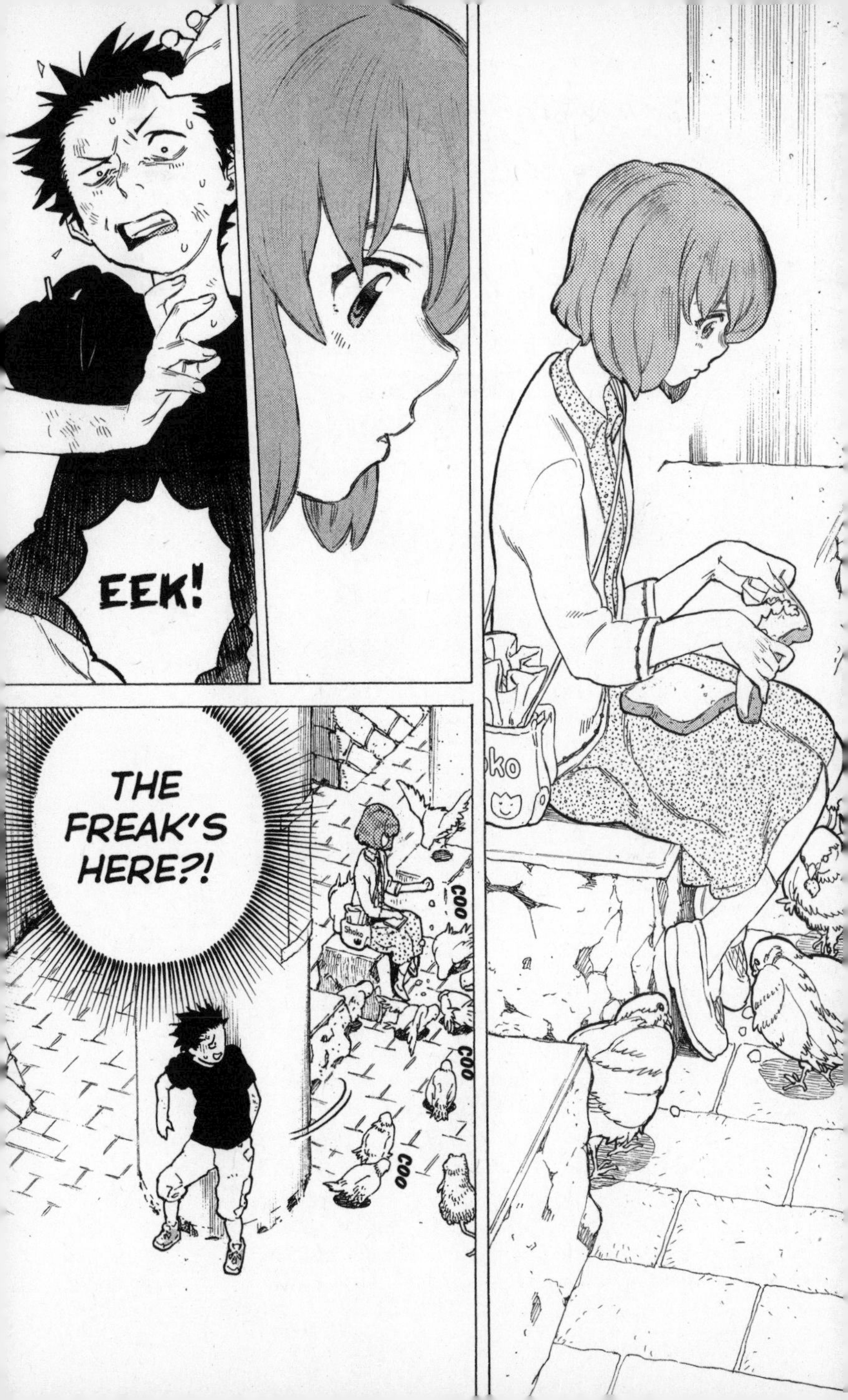

EEK!
THE FREAK'S HERE?!
COO
Shoko
COO
COO

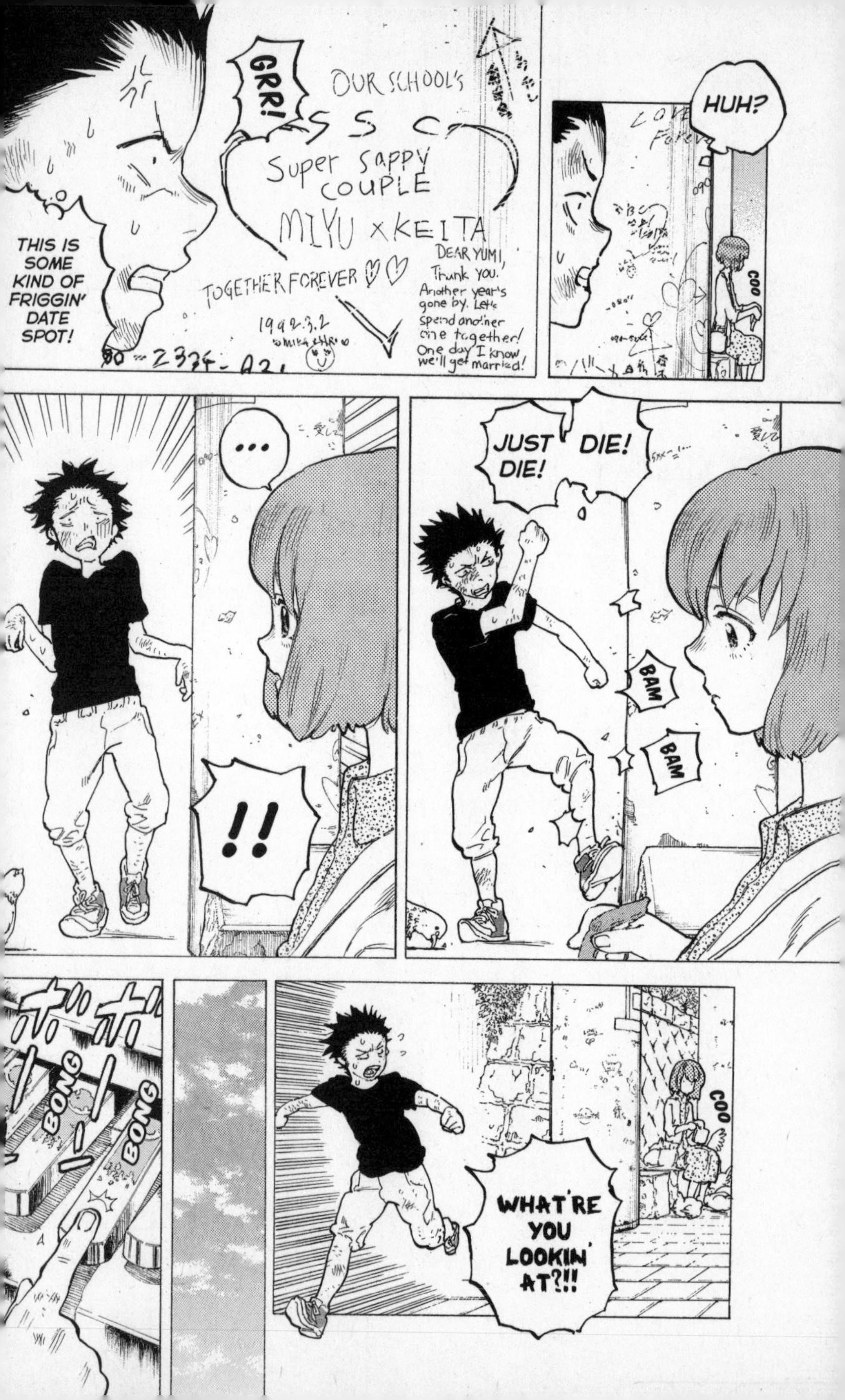
GRR!
THIS IS SOME KIND OF FRIGGIN' DATE SPOT!
OUR SCHOOL'S
SSC
Super Sappy COUPLE
MIYU x KEITA
TOGETHER FOREVER
DEAR YUMI, Thank you. Another year's gone by. Let's spend another one together! One day I know we'll get married!
1992.3.2
HUH?
COO
...
!!
JUST DIE! JUST DIE!
BAM
BAM
BONG
BONG
WHAT'RE YOU LOOKIN' AT?!!
COO

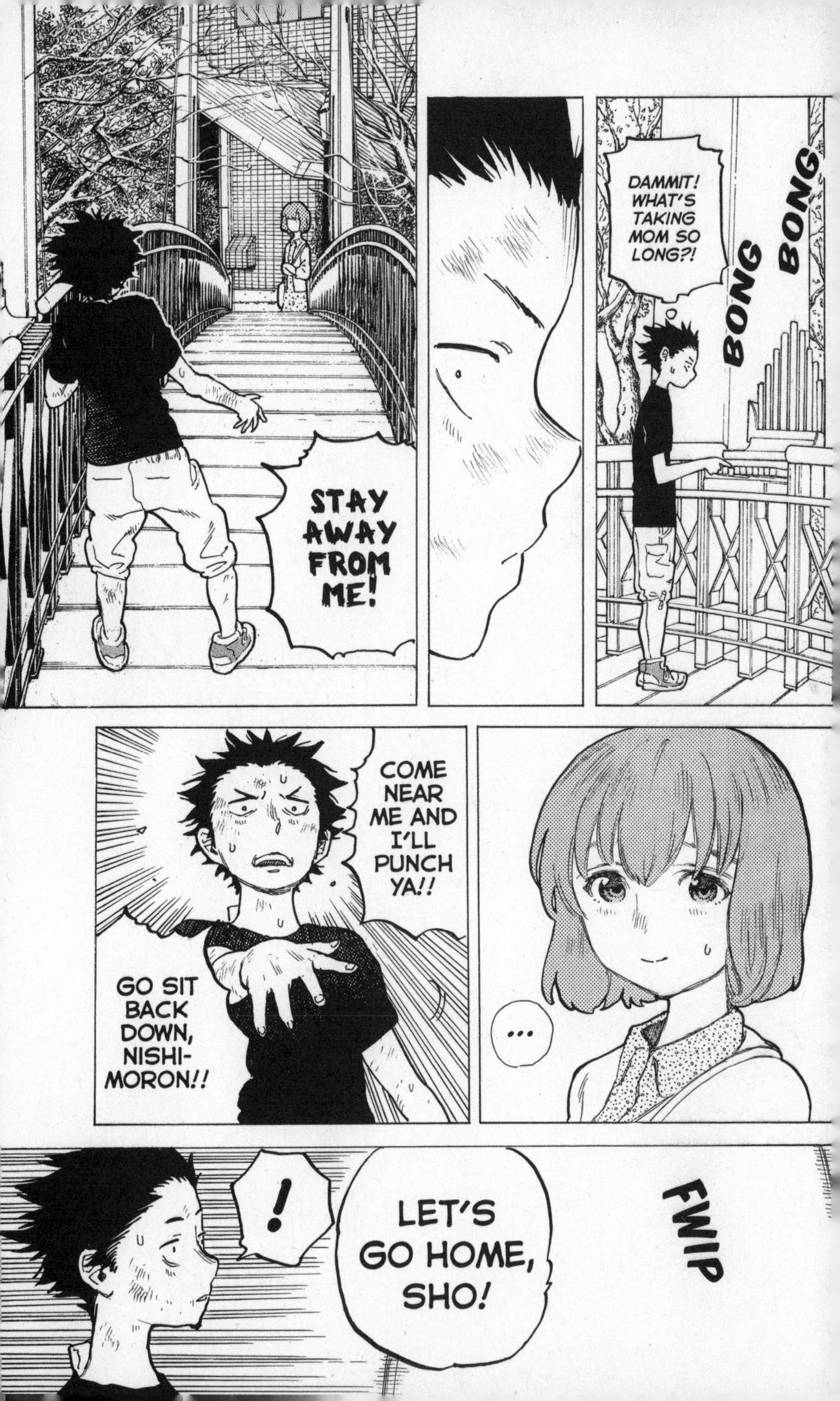
DAMMIT! WHAT'S TAKING MOM SO LONG?!
BONG
BONG
STAY AWAY FROM ME!
...
COME NEAR ME AND I'LL PUNCH YA!!
GO SIT BACK DOWN, NISHI-MORON!!
FWIP
LET'S GO HOME, SHO!
!

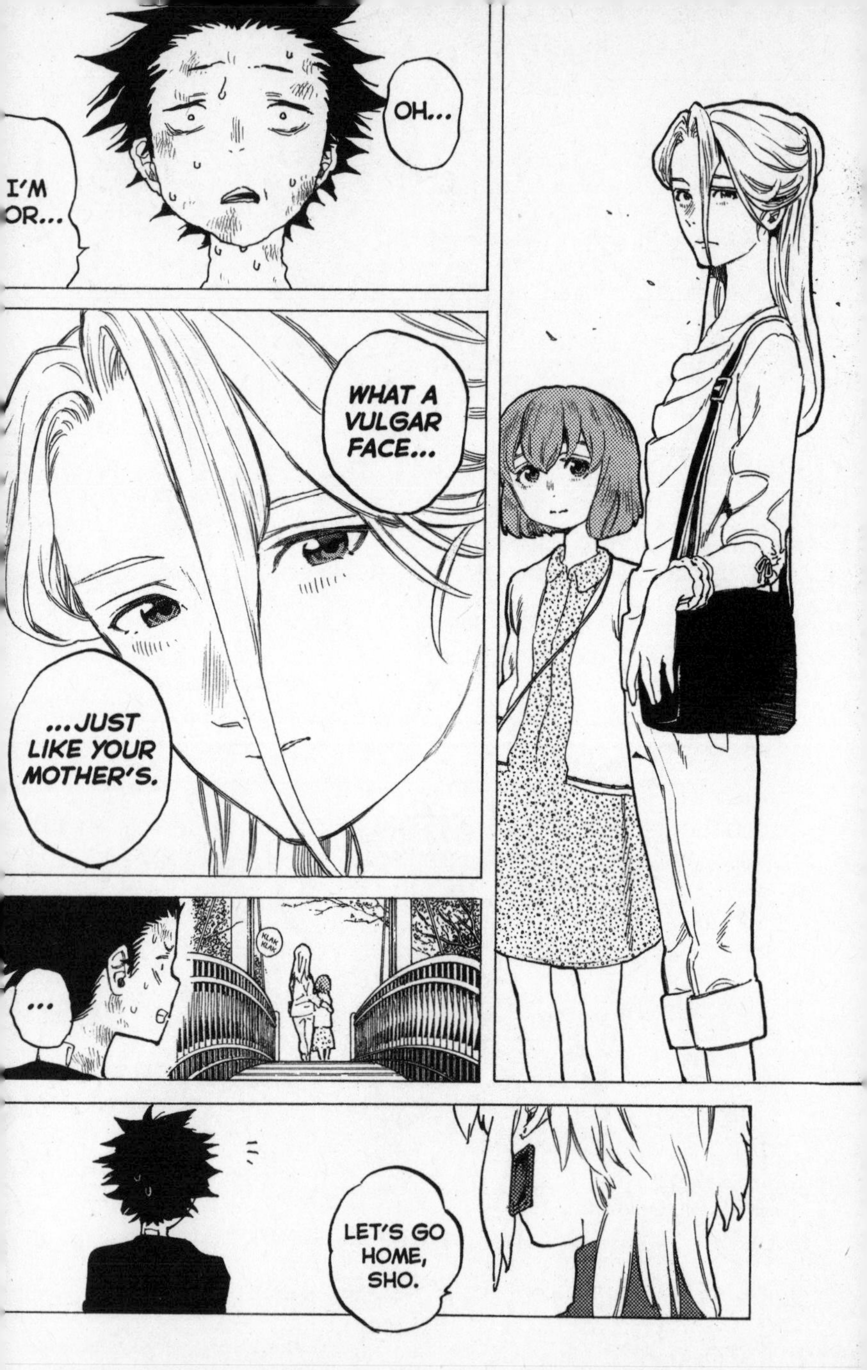
OH...
I'M
OR...
WHAT A VULGAR FACE...
...JUST LIKE YOUR MOTHER'S.
KLAK KLAK
...
LET'S GO HOME, SHO.

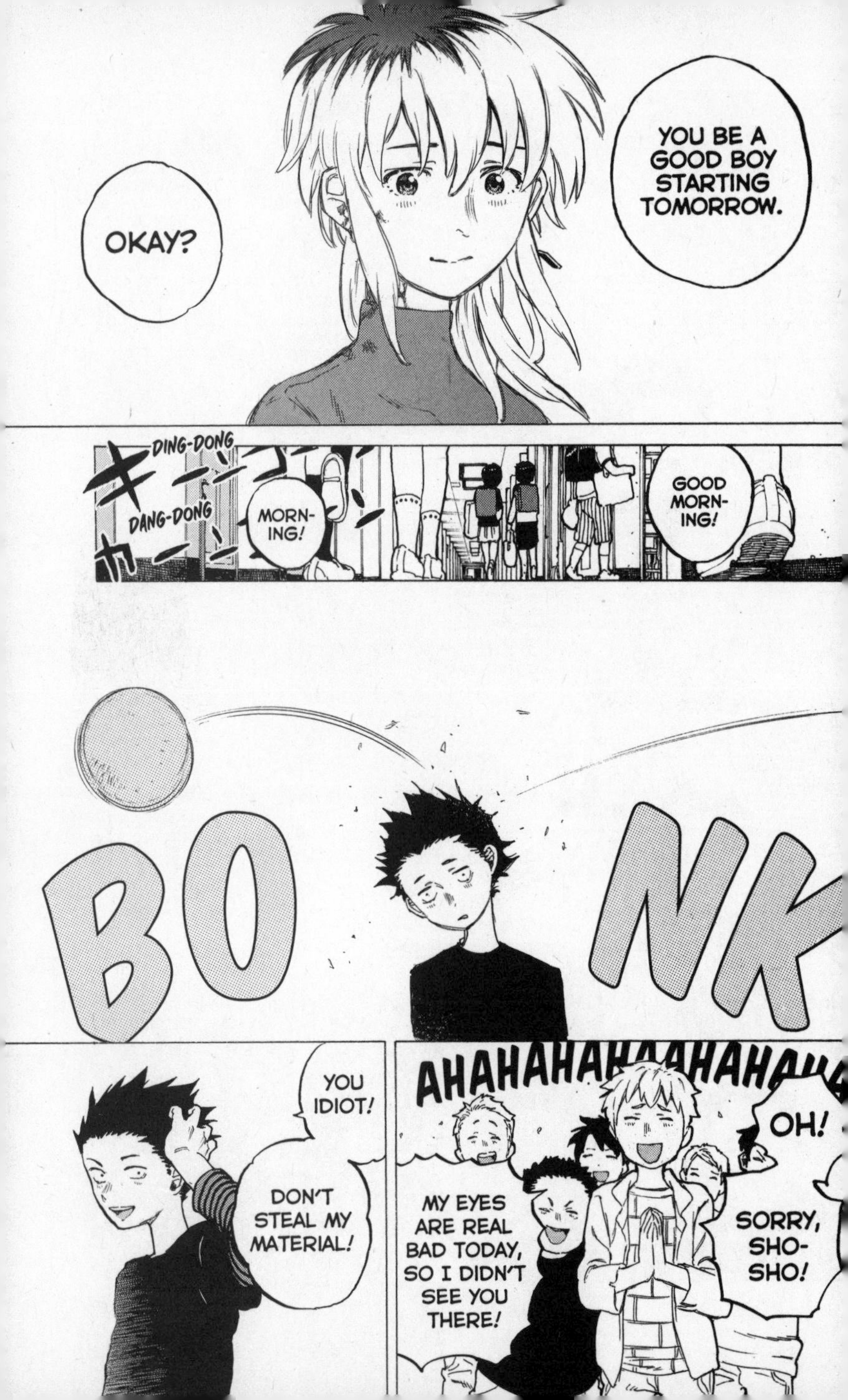
YOU BE A GOOD BOY STARTING TOMORROW.
OKAY?
GOOD MORN-ING!
MORN-ING!
DING-DONG
DANG-DONG
BONK
AHAHAHAHAHAHAHA
OH!
SORRY, SHO-SHO!
MY EYES ARE REAL BAD TODAY, SO I DIDN'T SEE YOU THERE!
YOU IDIOT!
DON'T STEAL MY MATERIAL!

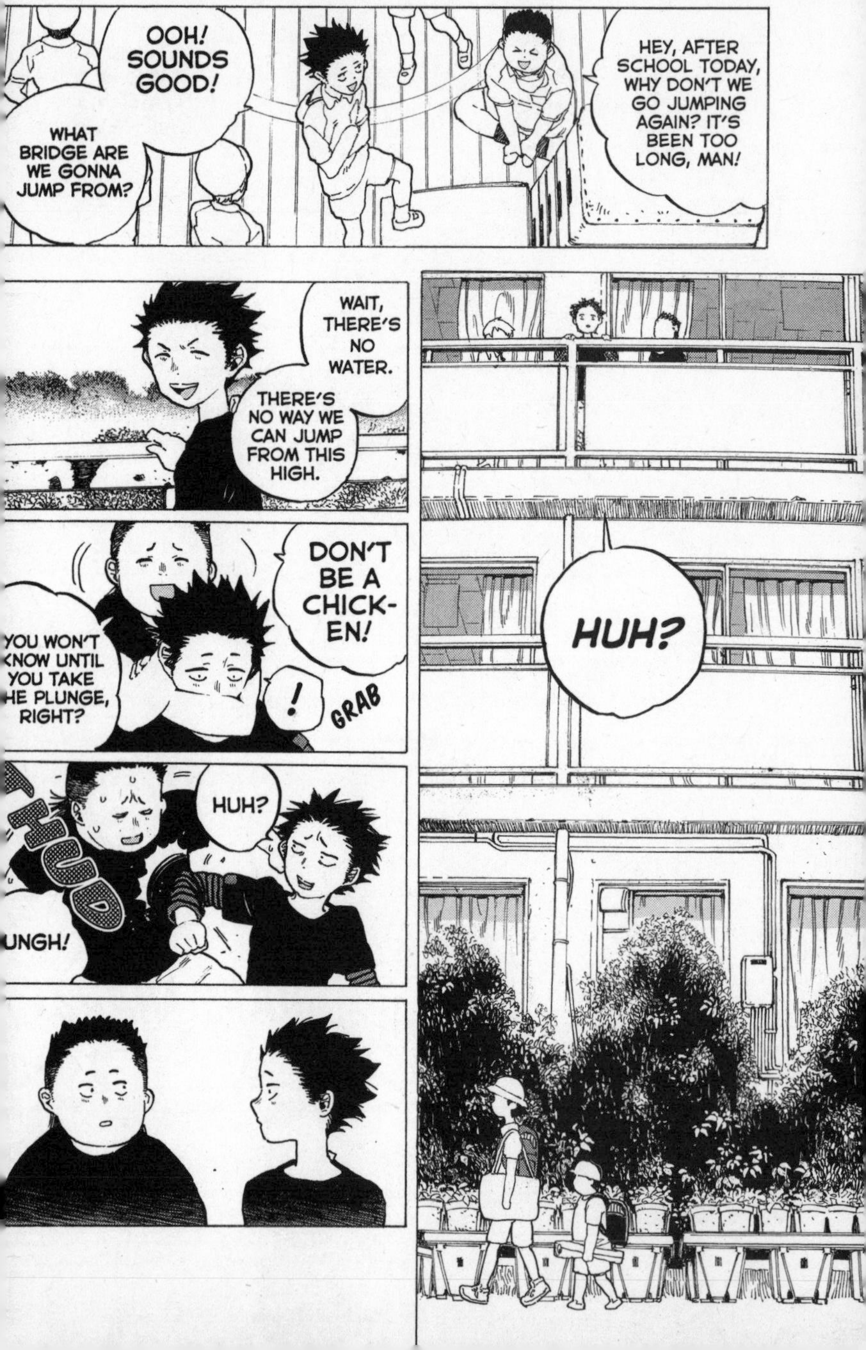
HEY, AFTER SCHOOL TODAY, WHY DON'T WE GO JUMPING AGAIN? IT'S BEEN TOO LONG, MAN!
OOH! SOUNDS GOOD!
WHAT BRIDGE ARE WE GONNA JUMP FROM?
HUH?
WAIT, THERE'S NO WATER.
THERE'S NO WAY WE CAN JUMP FROM THIS HIGH.
DON'T BE A CHICK-EN!
YOU WON'T KNOW UNTIL YOU TAKE HE PLUNGE, RIGHT?
!
GRAB
HUH?
THUD
UNGH!

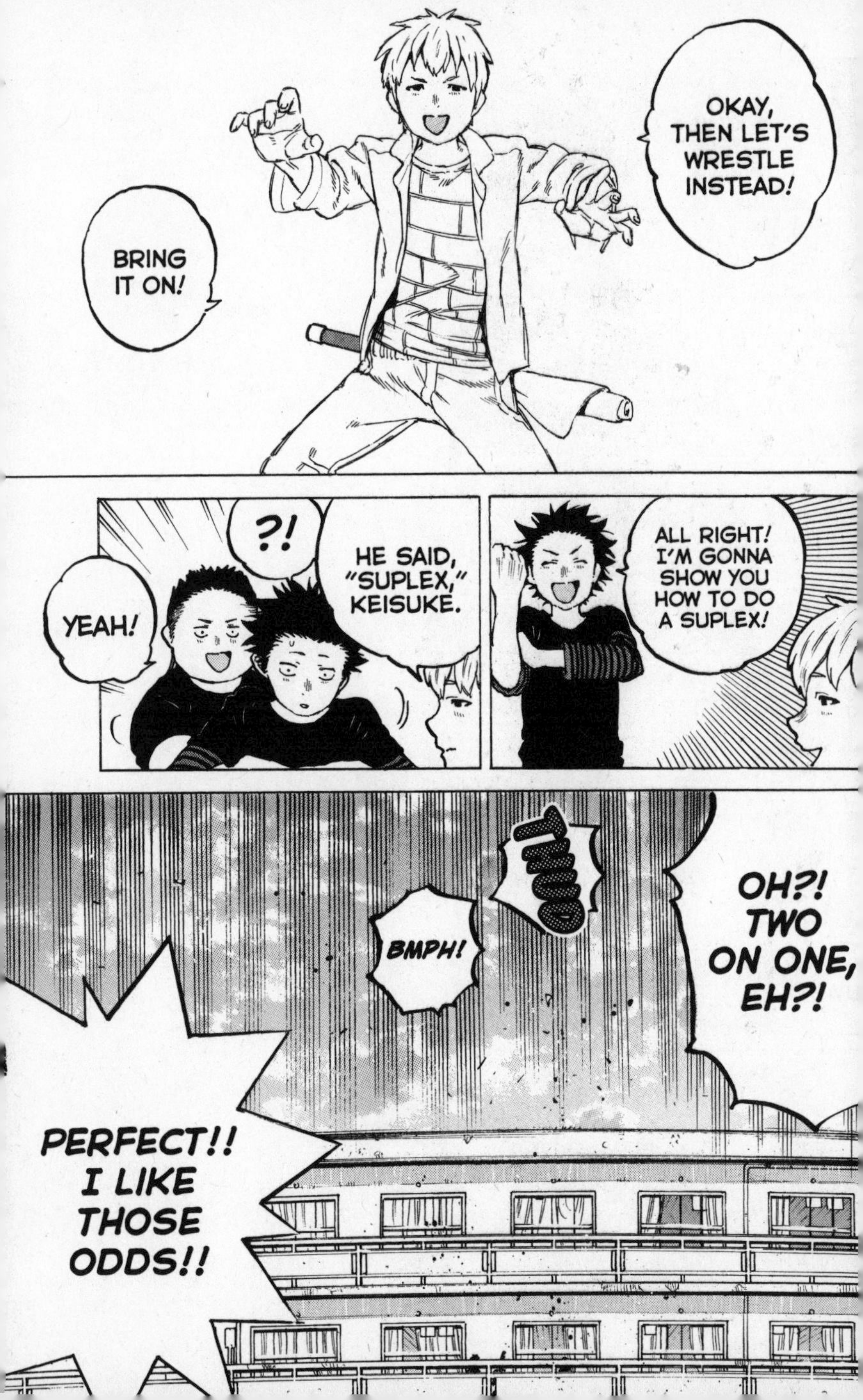
OKAY, THEN LET'S WRESTLE INSTEAD!
BRING IT ON!
ALL RIGHT! I'M GONNA SHOW YOU HOW TO DO A SUPLEX!
HE SAID, "SUPLEX," KEISUKE.
?!
YEAH!
THUD
BMPH!
OH?! TWO ON ONE, EH?!
PERFECT!! I LIKE THOSE ODDS!!

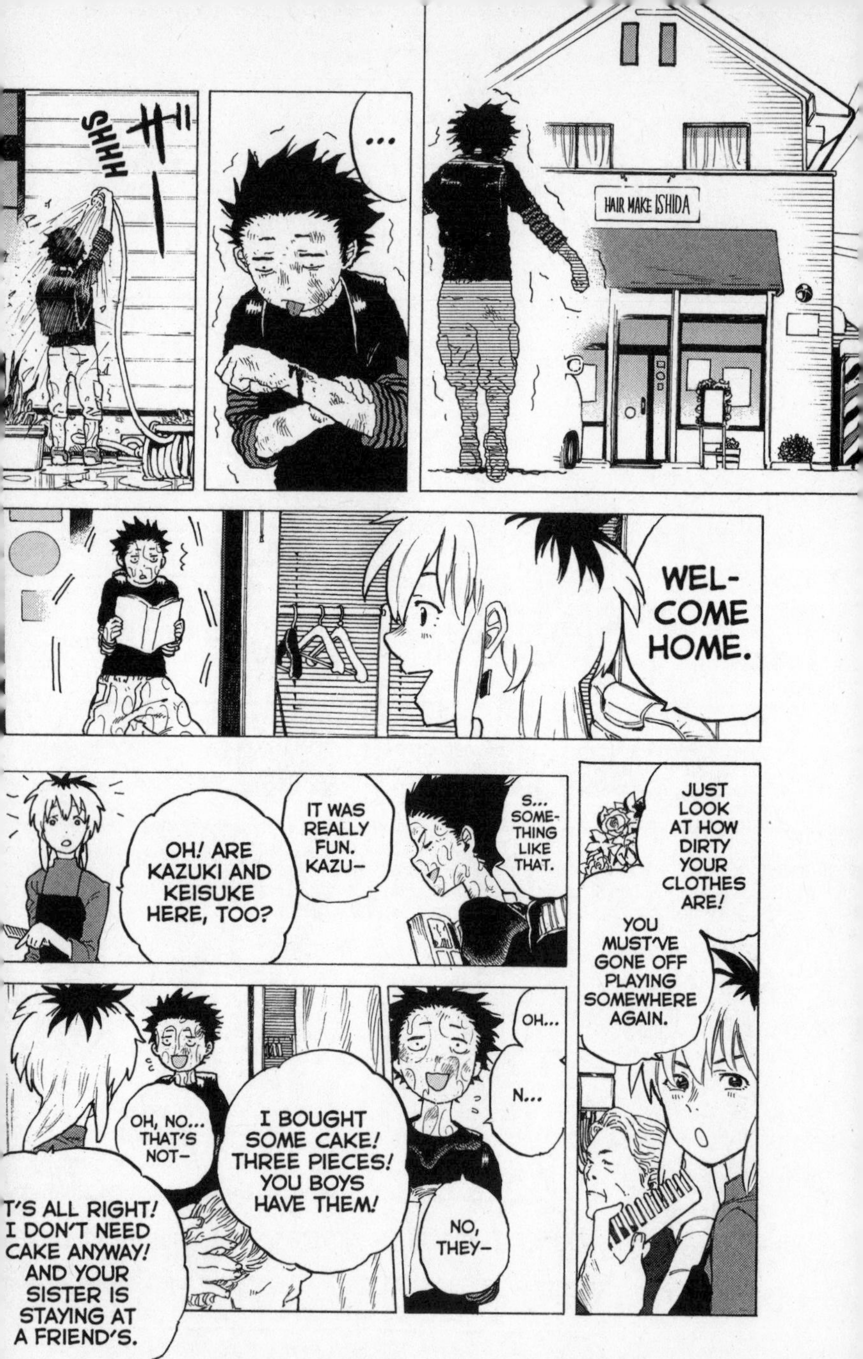
HAIR MAKE ISHIDA
...
SHHHH
WEL-COME HOME.
JUST LOOK AT HOW DIRTY YOUR CLOTHES ARE!
YOU MUST'VE GONE OFF PLAYING SOMEWHERE AGAIN.
S... SOME-THING LIKE THAT.
IT WAS REALLY FUN. KAZU-
OH! ARE KAZUKI AND KEISUKE HERE, TOO?
OH...
N...
NO, THEY-
I BOUGHT SOME CAKE! THREE PIECES! YOU BOYS HAVE THEM!
OH, NO... THAT'S NOT-
T'S ALL RIGHT! I DON'T NEED CAKE ANYWAY! AND YOUR SISTER IS STAYING AT A FRIEND'S.

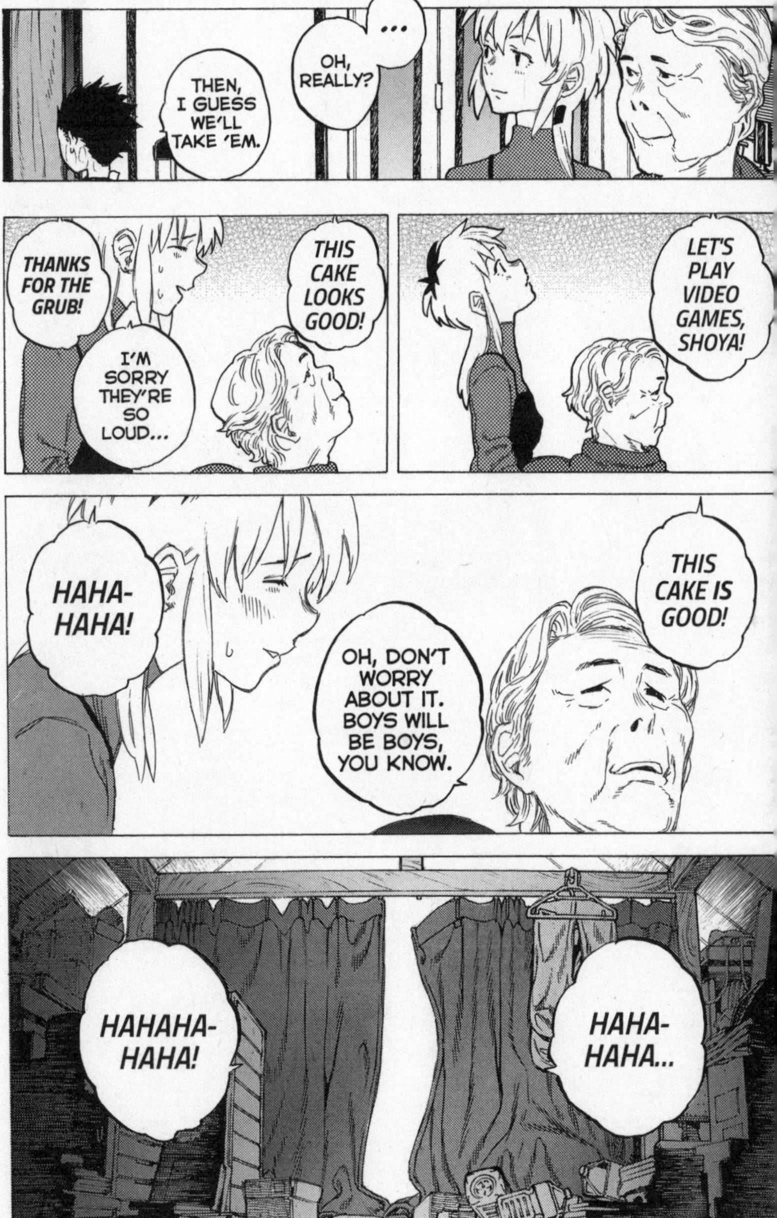
...
OH, REALLY?
THEN, I GUESS WE'LL TAKE 'EM.
LET'S PLAY VIDEO GAMES, SHOYA!
THIS CAKE LOOKS GOOD!
THANKS FOR THE GRUB!
I'M SORRY THEY'RE SO LOUD...
THIS CAKE IS GOOD!
HAHA-HAHA!
OH, DON'T WORRY ABOUT IT. BOYS WILL BE BOYS, YOU KNOW.
HAHA-HAHA...
HAHAHA-HAHA!

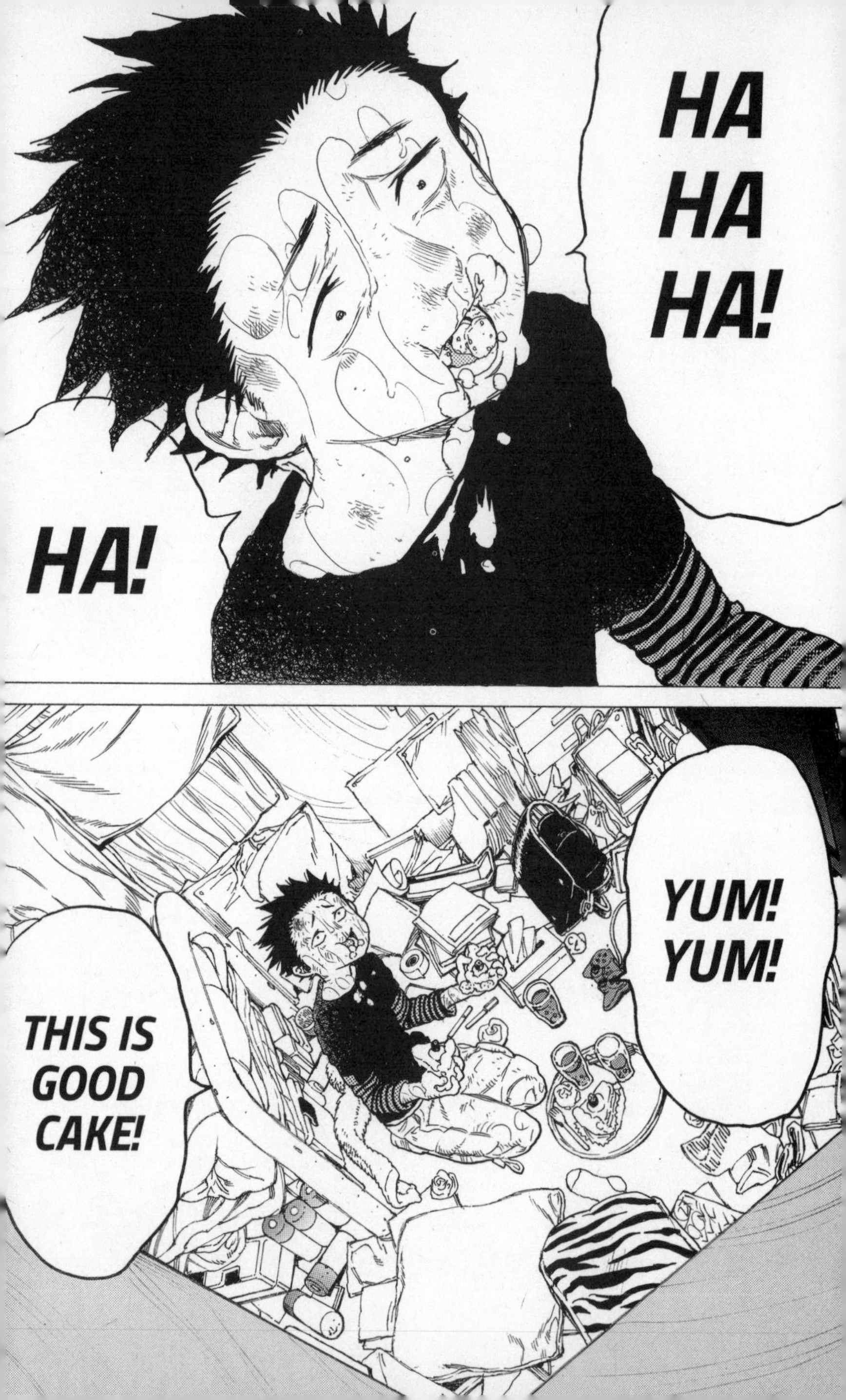
HA HA HA!
HA!
YUM! YUM!
THIS IS GOOD CAKE!

ALL I WANTED...

...WAS TO FIGHT OFF BOREDOM.

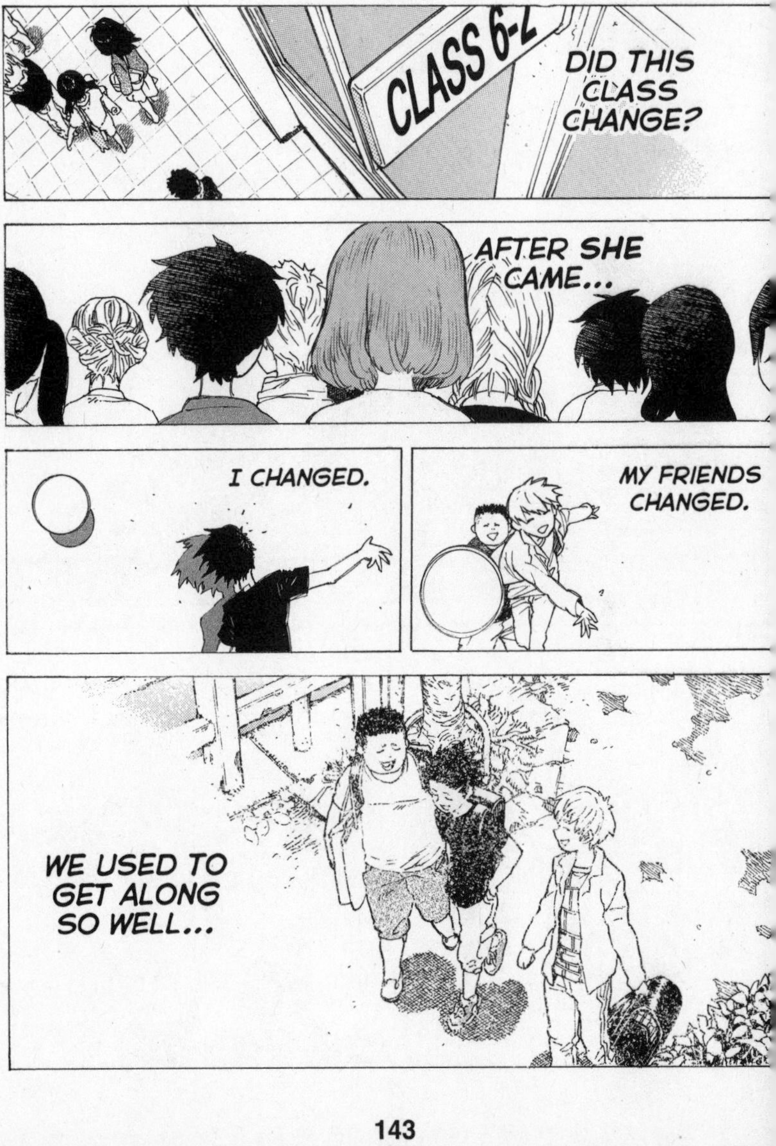
CLASS 6-2
DID THIS CLASS CHANGE?
AFTER SHE CAME...
MY FRIENDS CHANGED.
I CHANGED.
WE USED TO GET ALONG SO WELL...

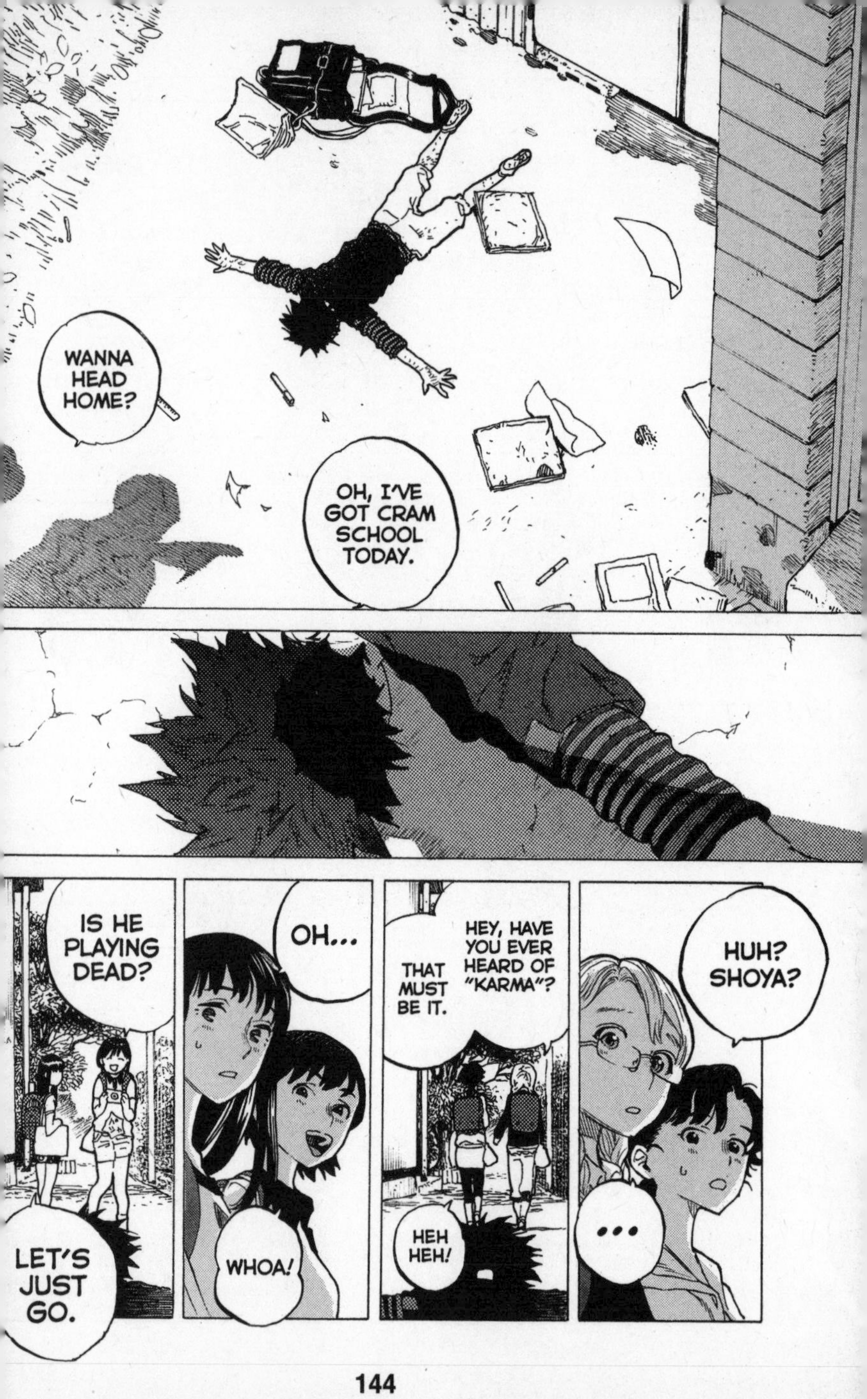
WANNA HEAD HOME?
OH, I'VE GOT CRAM SCHOOL TODAY.
HUH? SHOYA?
...
HEY, HAVE YOU EVER HEARD OF "KARMA"?
THAT MUST BE IT.
HEH HEH!
OH...
WHOA!
IS HE PLAYING DEAD?
LET'S JUST GO.

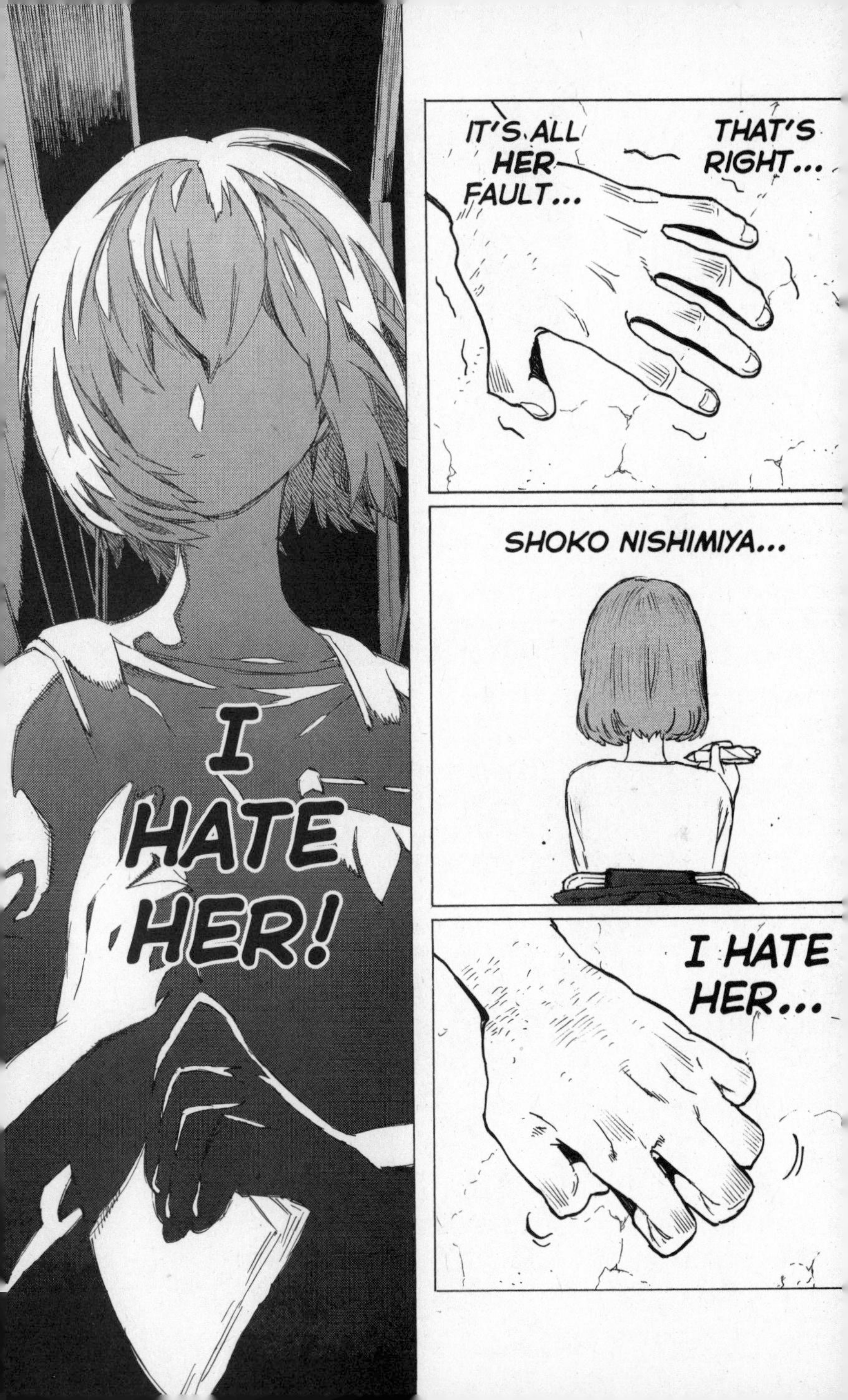
THAT'S RIGHT...
IT'S ALL HER FAULT...
SHOKO NISHIMIYA...
I HATE HER...
I HATE HER!

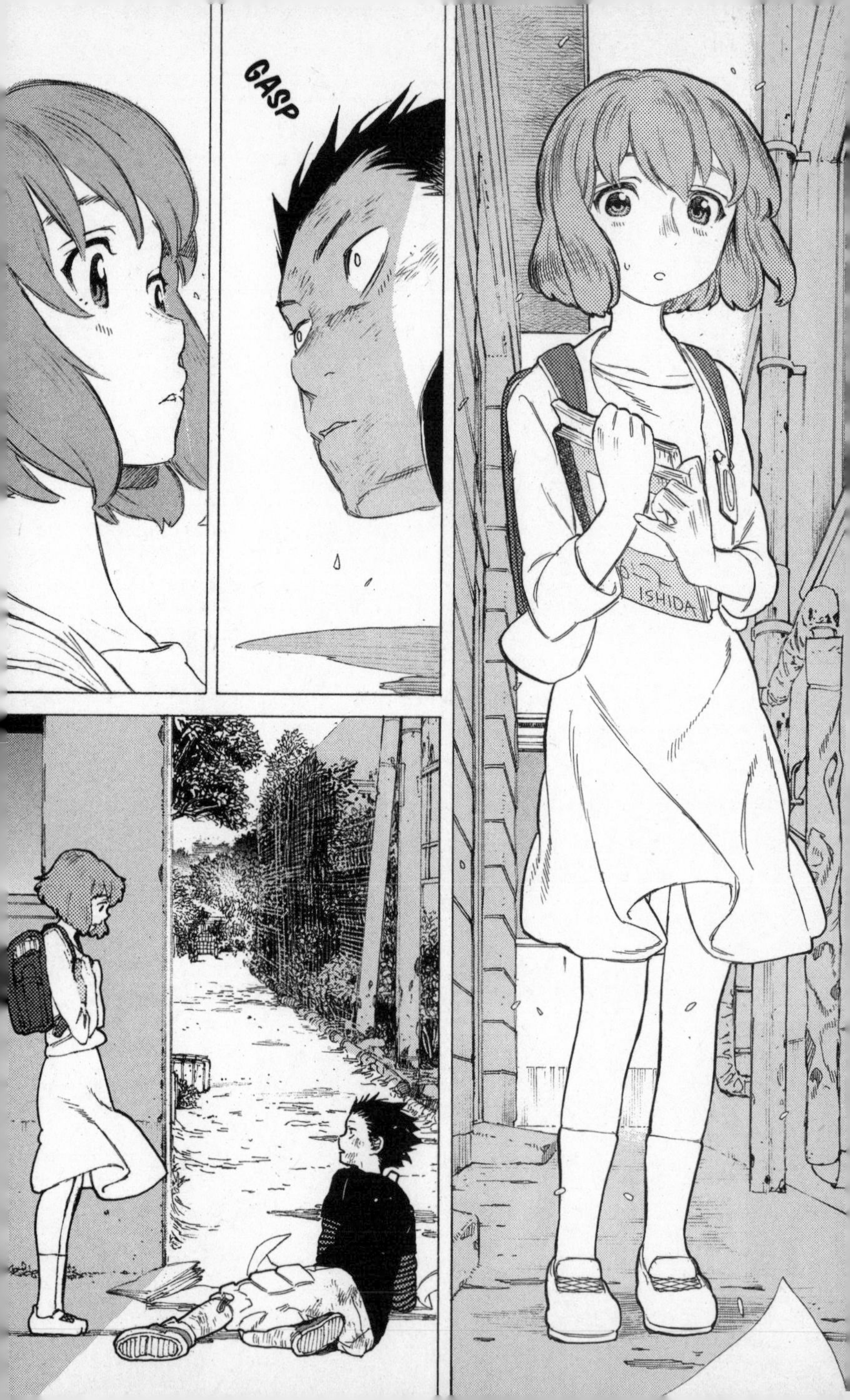

ISHIDA
GASP

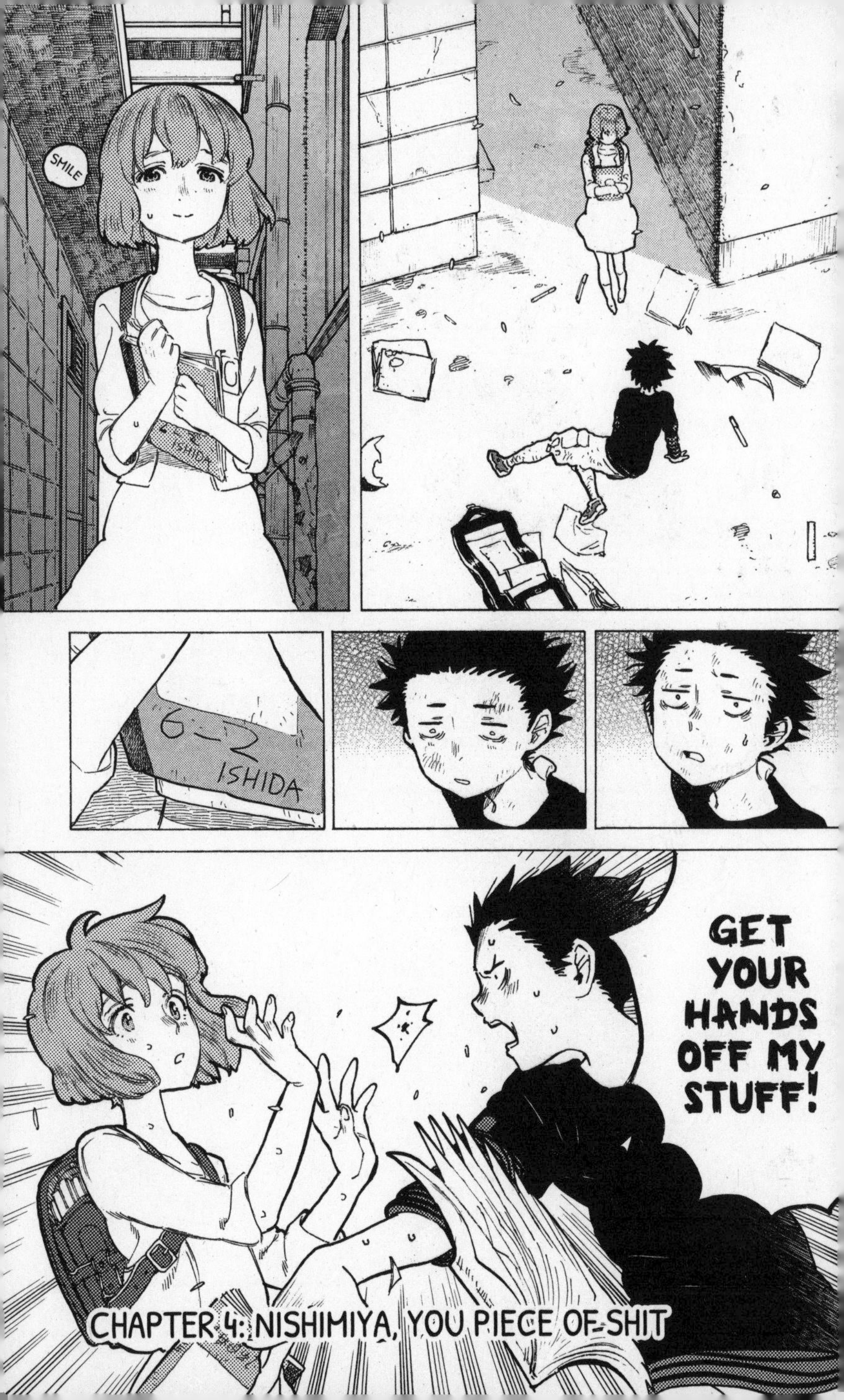
SMILE
ISHIDA
6-2
ISHIDA
GET YOUR HANDS OFF MY STUFF!

CHAPTER 4: NISHIMIYA, YOU PIECE OF SHIT

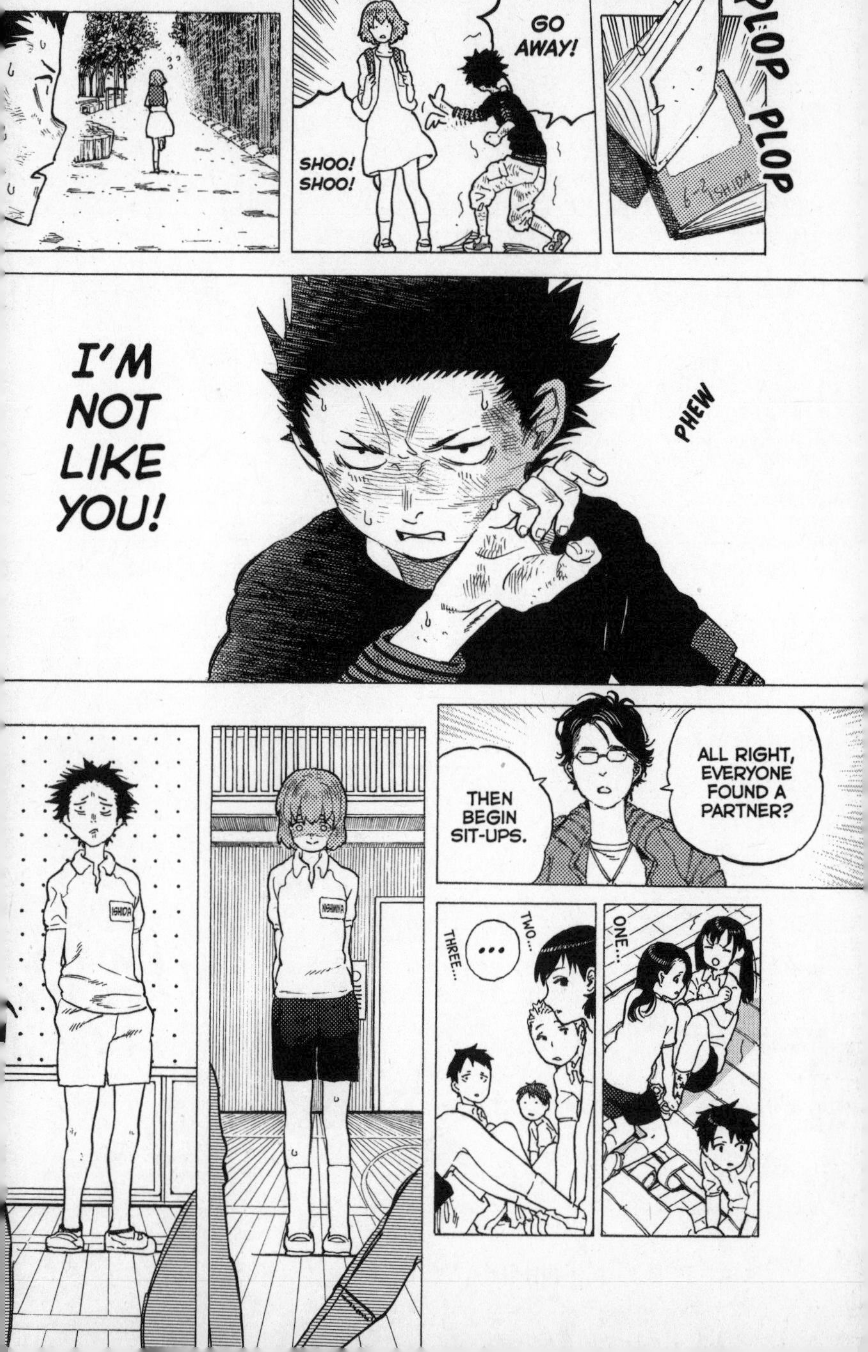
PLOP PLOP PLOP
6-2 ISHIDA
GO AWAY!
SHOO! SHOO!
I'M NOT LIKE YOU!
PHEW
ALL RIGHT, EVERYONE FOUND A PARTNER?
THEN BEGIN SIT-UPS.
ONE...
TWO...
...
THREE...
NISHIMIYA
ISHIDA

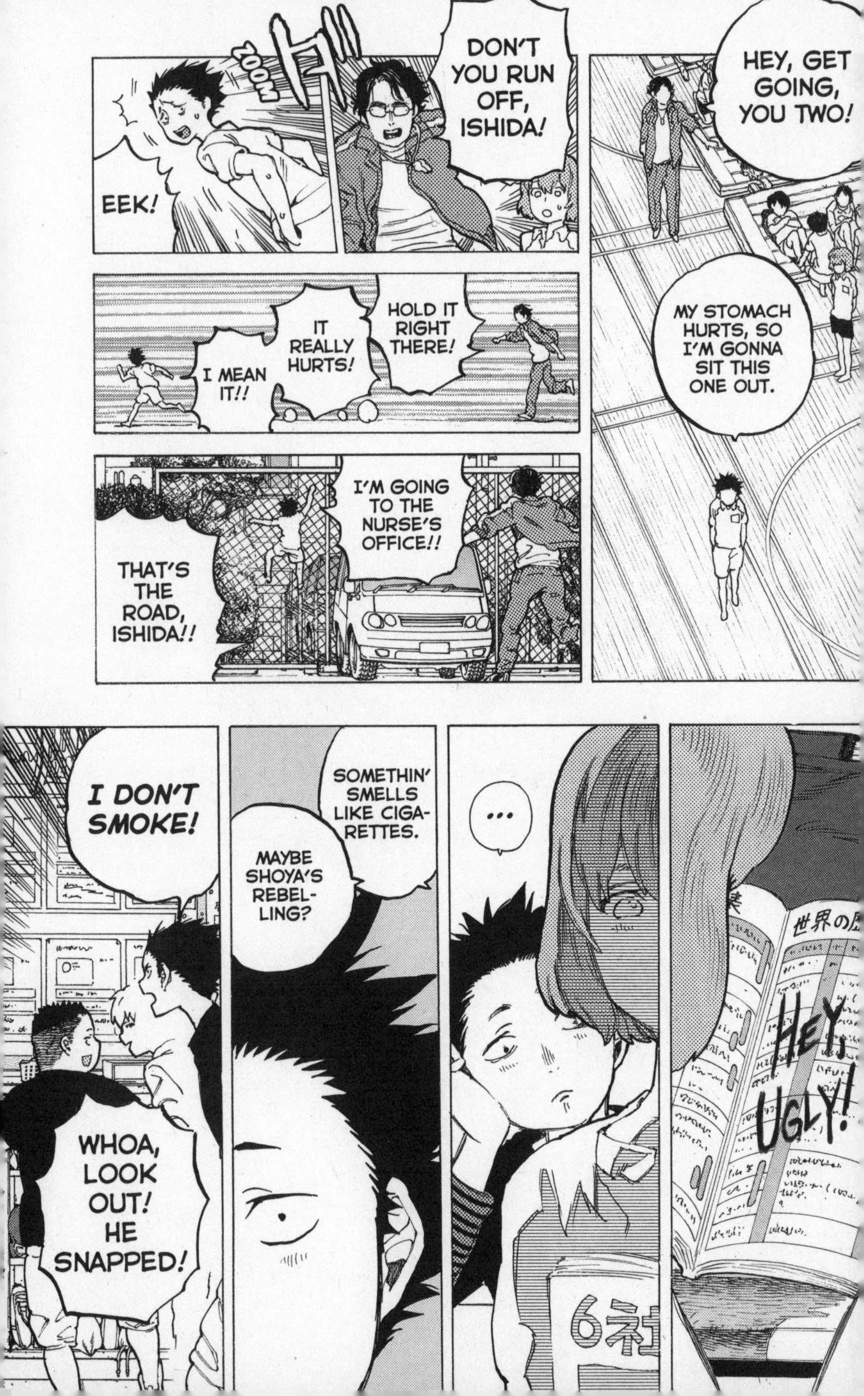
HEY, GET GOING, YOU TWO!
MY STOMACH HURTS, SO I'M GONNA SIT THIS ONE OUT.
DON'T YOU RUN OFF, ISHIDA!
ZOOM
EEK!
HOLD IT RIGHT THERE!
IT REALLY HURTS!
I MEAN IT!!
I'M GOING TO THE NURSE'S OFFICE!!
THAT'S THE ROAD, ISHIDA!!
HEY, UGLY!
...
SOMETHIN' SMELLS LIKE CIGA-RETTES.
MAYBE SHOYA'S REBEL-LING?
I DON'T SMOKE!
WHOA, LOOK OUT! HE SNAPPED!

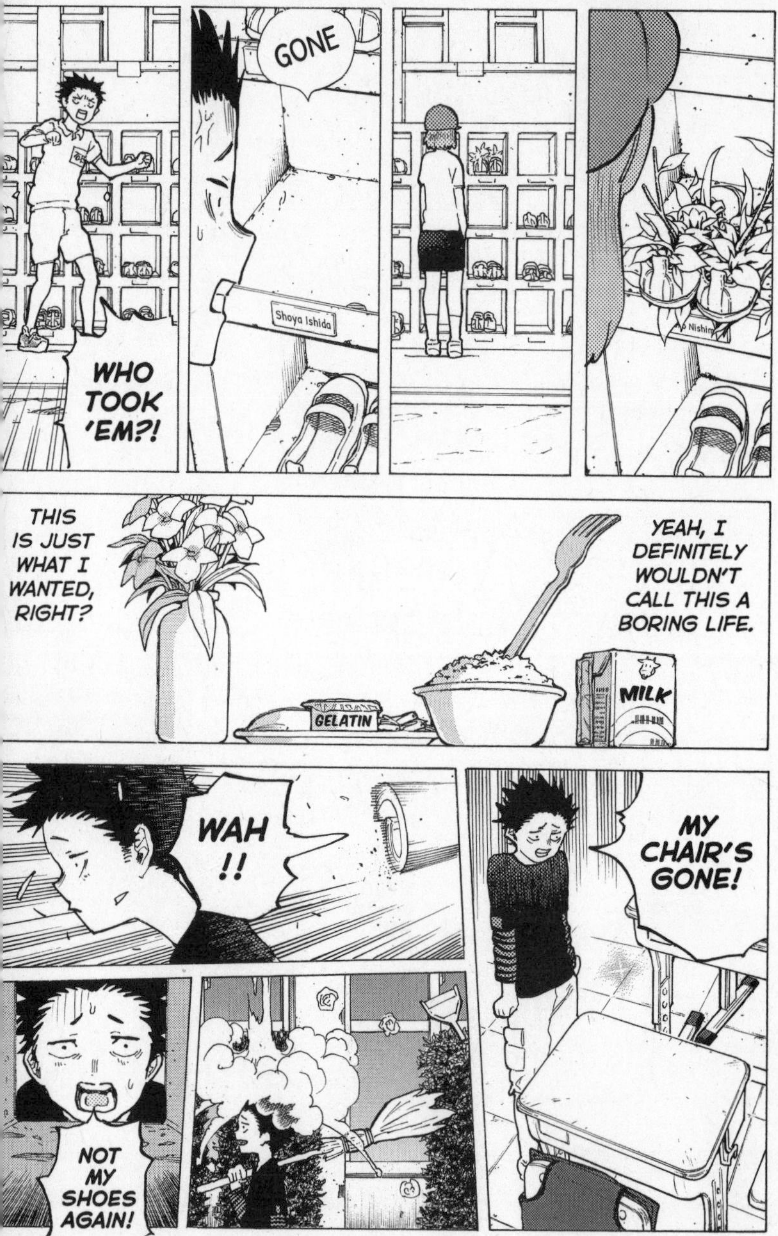
GONE
Shoya Ishida
WHO TOOK 'EM?!
YEAH, I DEFINITELY WOULDN'T CALL THIS A BORING LIFE.
MILK
GELATIN
THIS IS JUST WHAT I WANTED, RIGHT?
MY CHAIR'S GONE!
WAH !!
NOT MY SHOES AGAIN!

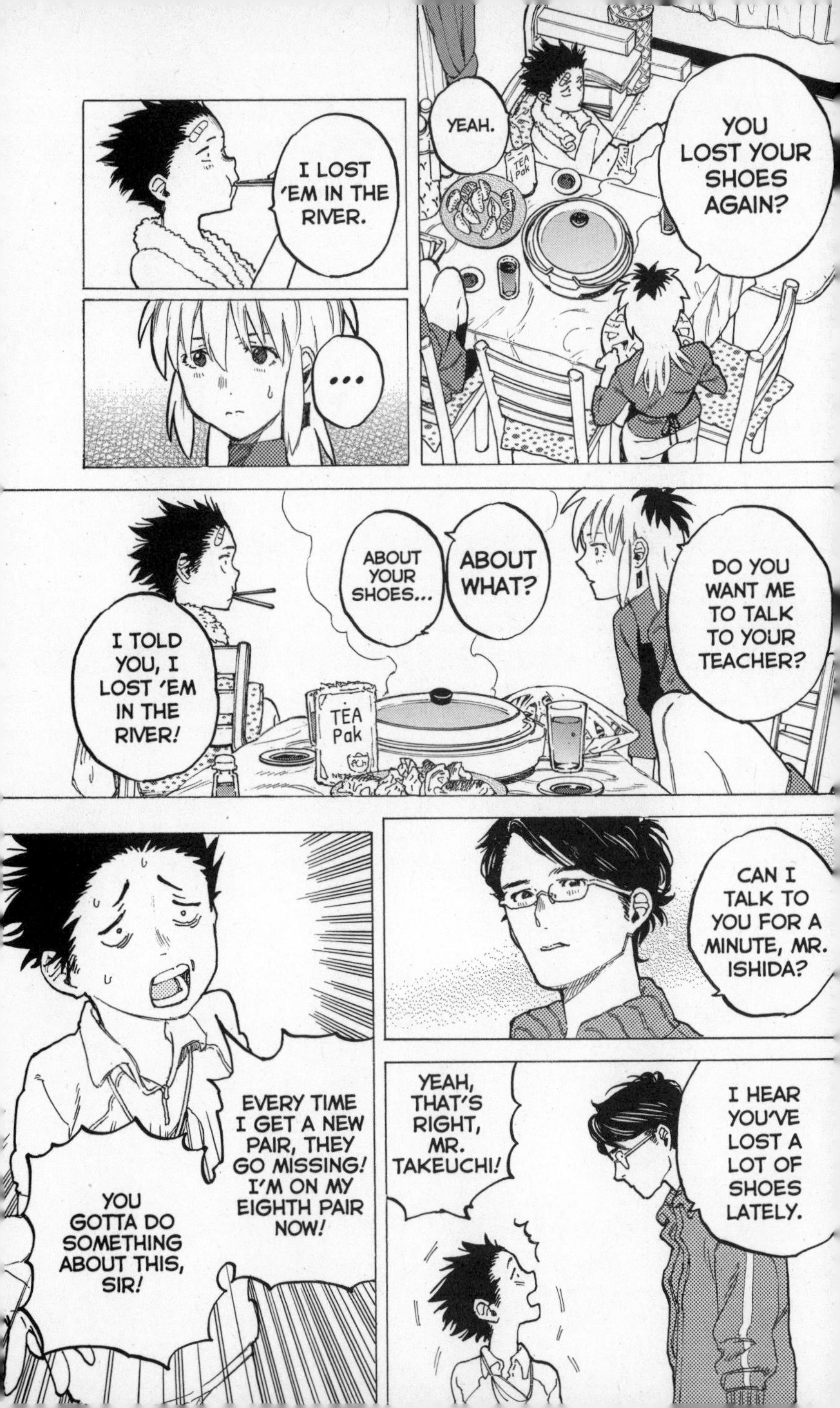
YOU LOST YOUR SHOES AGAIN?
YEAH.
I LOST 'EM IN THE RIVER.
...
DO YOU WANT ME TO TALK TO YOUR TEACHER?
ABOUT WHAT?
ABOUT YOUR SHOES...
I TOLD YOU, I LOST 'EM IN THE RIVER!
CAN I TALK TO YOU FOR A MINUTE, MR. ISHIDA?
I HEAR YOU'VE LOST A LOT OF SHOES LATELY.
YEAH, THAT'S RIGHT, MR. TAKEUCHI!
EVERY TIME I GET A NEW PAIR, THEY GO MISSING! I'M ON MY EIGHTH PAIR NOW!
YOU GOTTA DO SOMETHING ABOUT THIS, SIR!

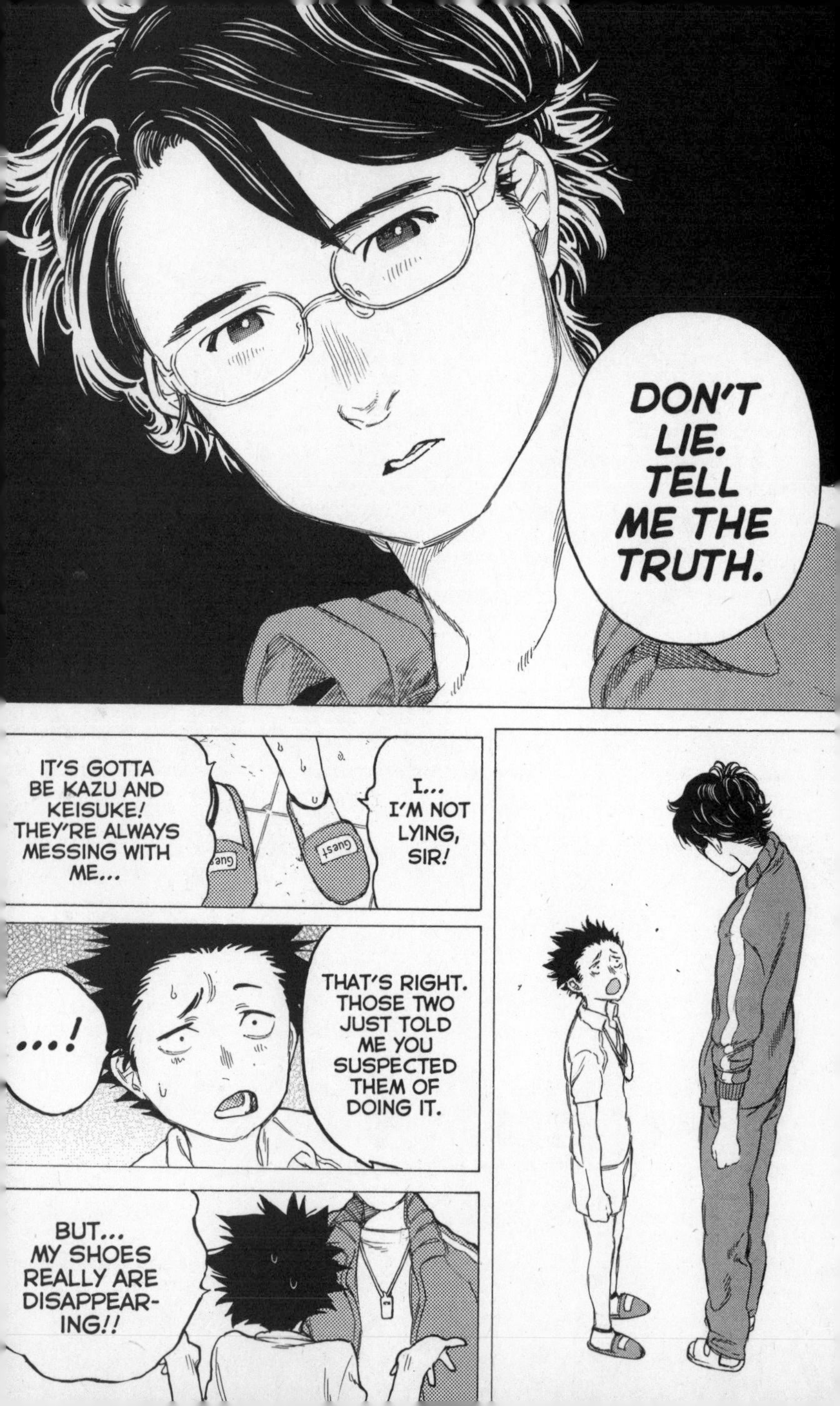
DON'T LIE. TELL ME THE TRUTH.
I... I'M NOT LYING, SIR!
Guest
Guest
IT'S GOTTA BE KAZU AND KEISUKE! THEY'RE ALWAYS MESSING WITH ME...
THAT'S RIGHT. THOSE TWO JUST TOLD ME YOU SUSPECTED THEM OF DOING IT.
...!
BUT... MY SHOES REALLY ARE DISAPPEAR-ING!!

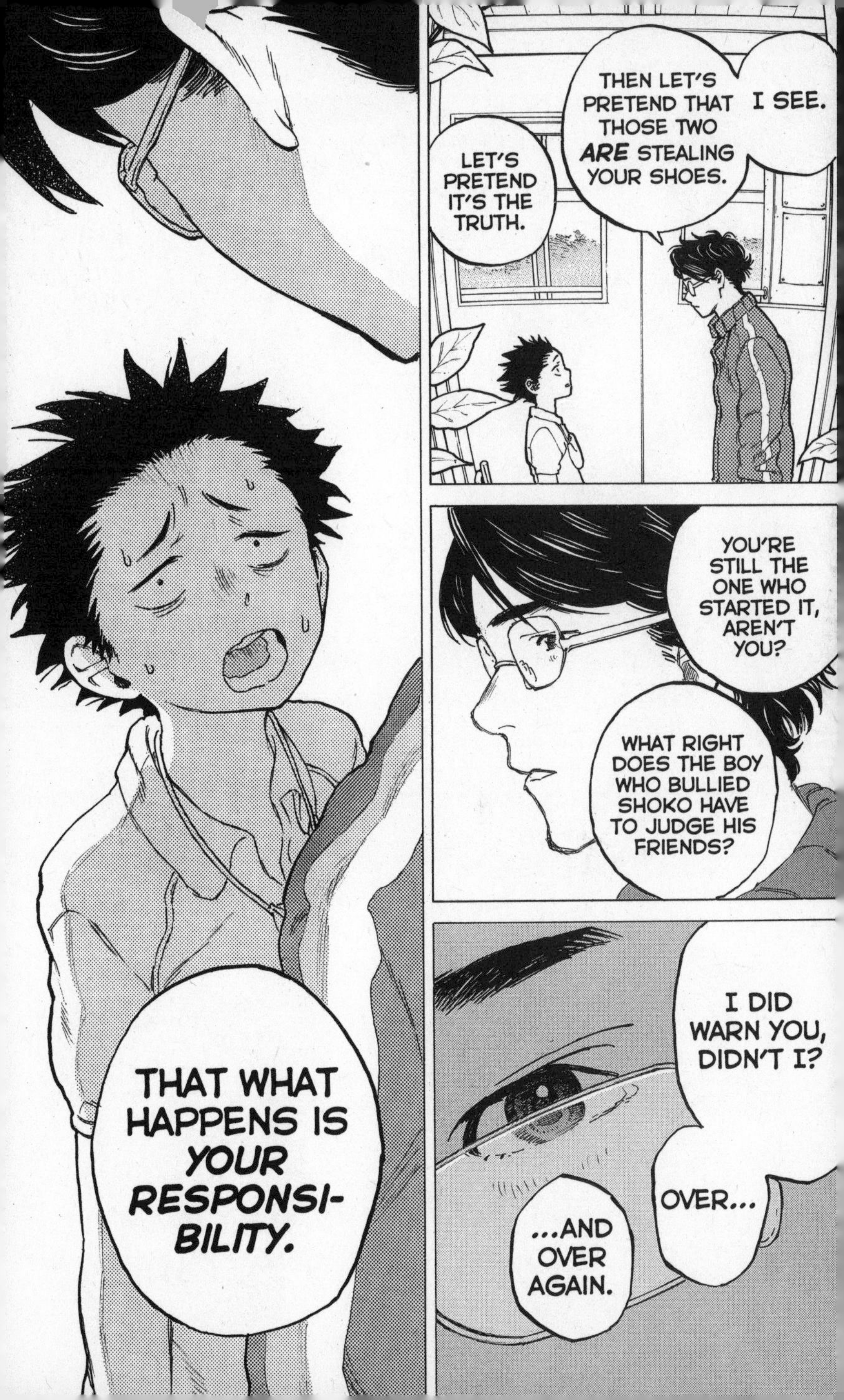
I SEE.
THEN LET'S PRETEND THAT THOSE TWO ARE STEALING YOUR SHOES.
LET'S PRETEND IT'S THE TRUTH.
YOU'RE STILL THE ONE WHO STARTED IT, AREN'T YOU?
WHAT RIGHT DOES THE BOY WHO BULLIED SHOKO HAVE TO JUDGE HIS FRIENDS?
I DID WARN YOU, DIDN'T I?
OVER...
...AND OVER AGAIN.
THAT WHAT HAPPENS IS *YOUR RESPONSIBILITY.*

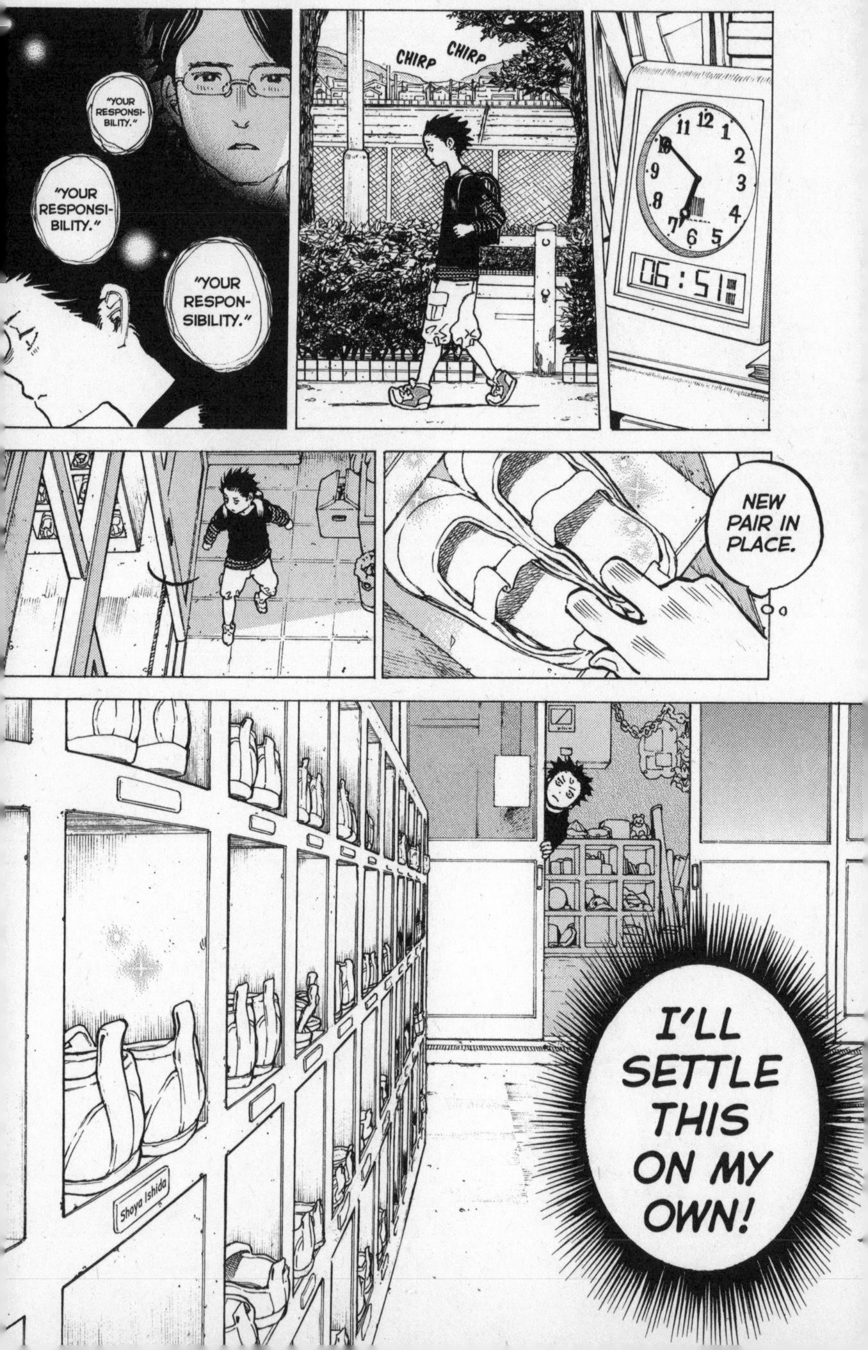
06:51
CHIRP
CHIRP
"YOUR RESPONSI-BILITY."
"YOUR RESPONSI-BILITY."
"YOUR RESPON-SIBILITY."
NEW PAIR IN PLACE.
I'LL SETTLE THIS ON MY OWN!
Shoya Ishida

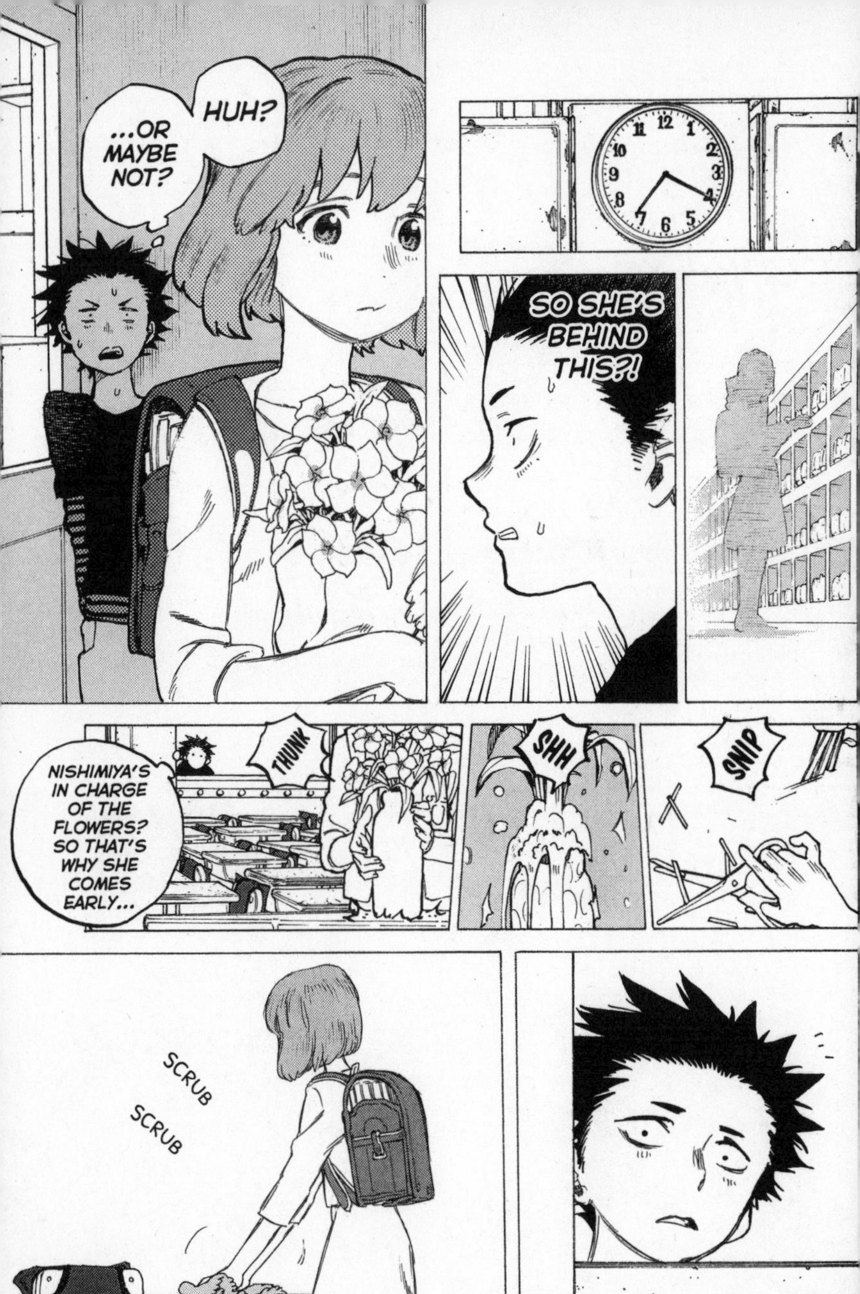
SO SHE'S BEHIND THIS?!
HUH?
...OR MAYBE NOT?
SNIP
SHH
THUNK
NISHIMIYA'S IN CHARGE OF THE FLOWERS? SO THAT'S WHY SHE COMES EARLY...
SCRUB
SCRUB

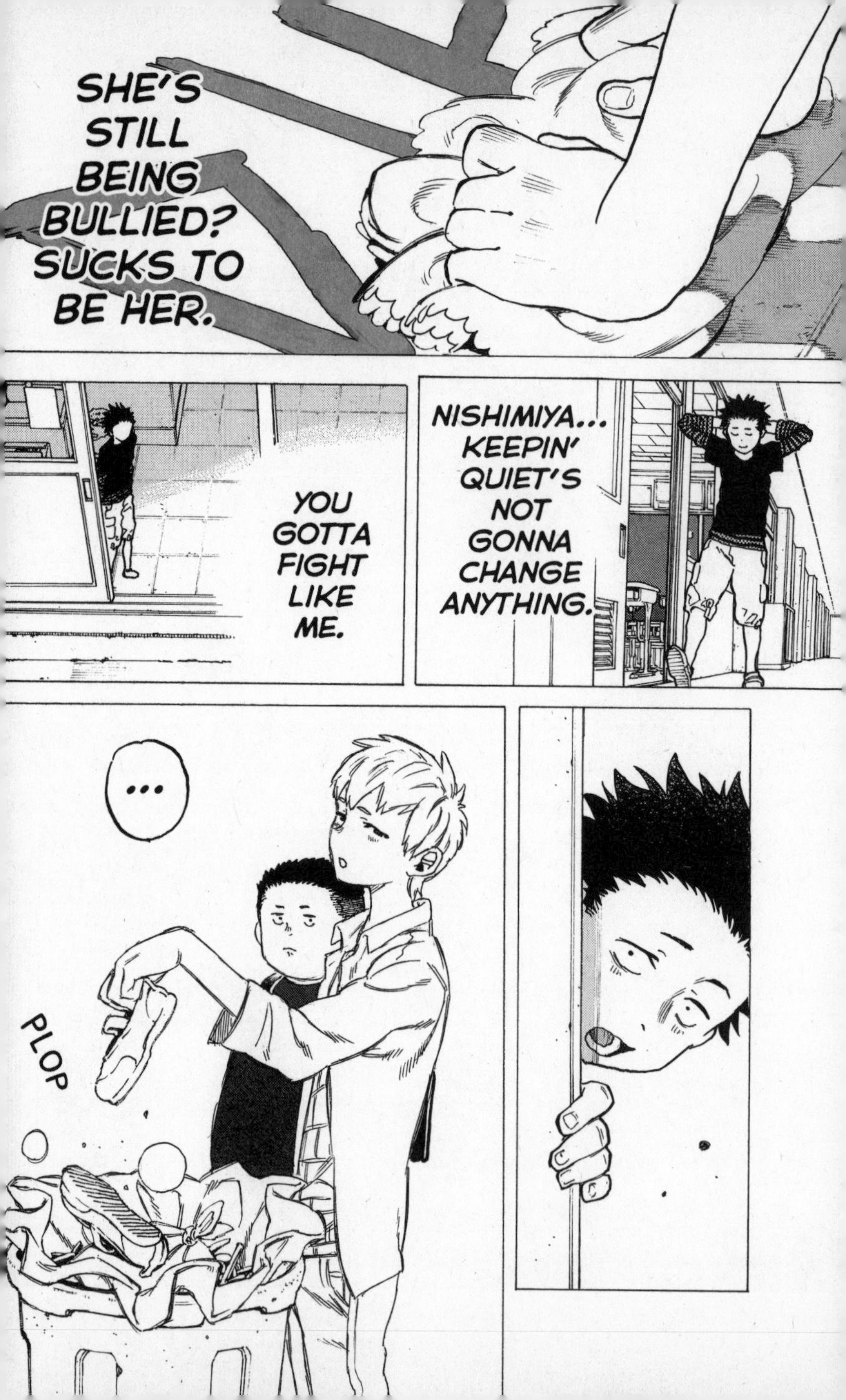
SHE'S STILL BEING BULLIED? SUCKS TO BE HER.
NISHIMIYA... KEEPIN' QUIET'S NOT GONNA CHANGE ANYTHING.
YOU GOTTA FIGHT LIKE ME.
...
PLOP

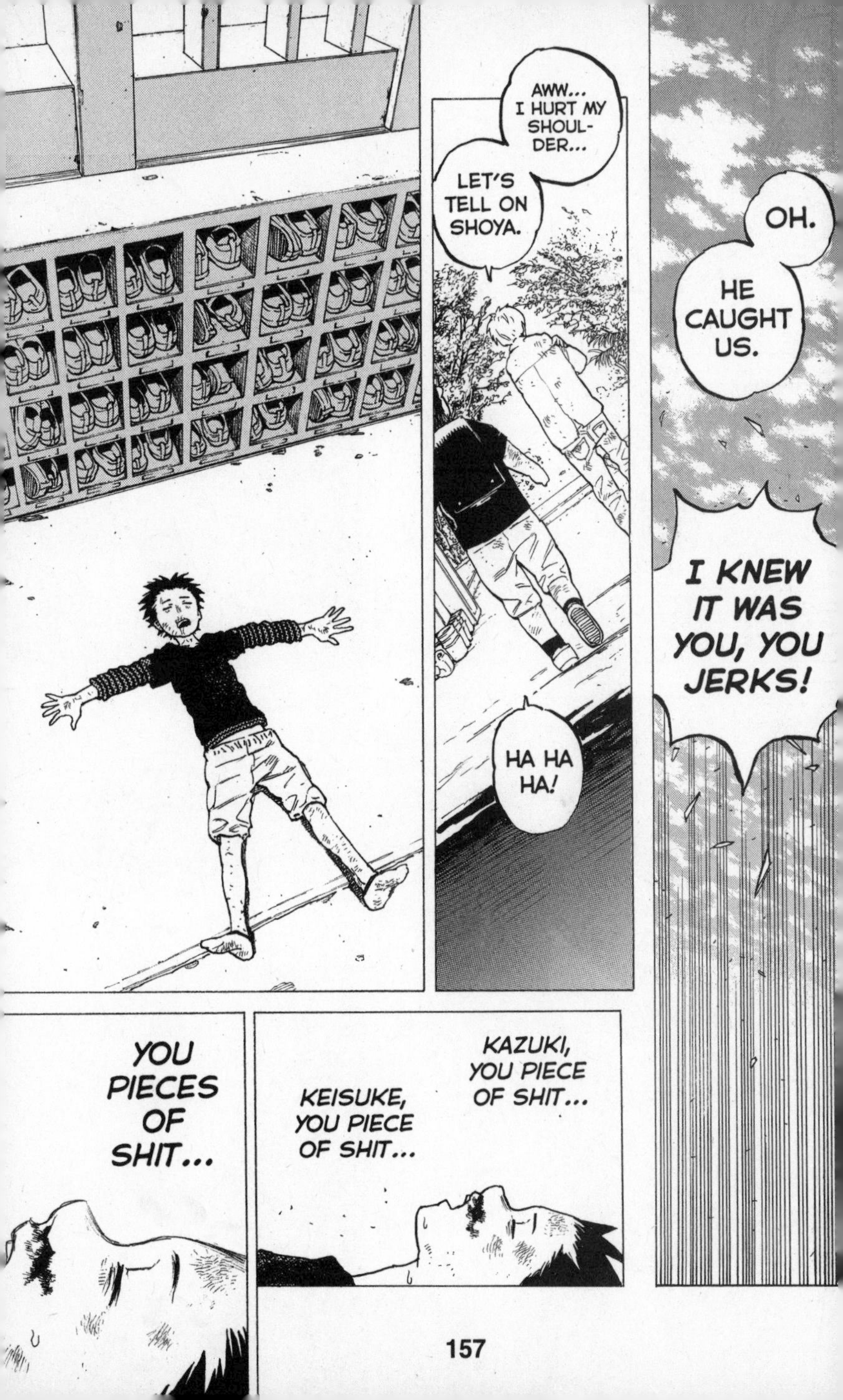
OH.
HE CAUGHT US.
I KNEW IT WAS YOU, YOU JERKS!
AWW... I HURT MY SHOUL-DER...
LET'S TELL ON SHOYA.
HA HA HA!
KAZUKI, YOU PIECE OF SHIT...
KEISUKE, YOU PIECE OF SHIT...
YOU PIECES OF SHIT...

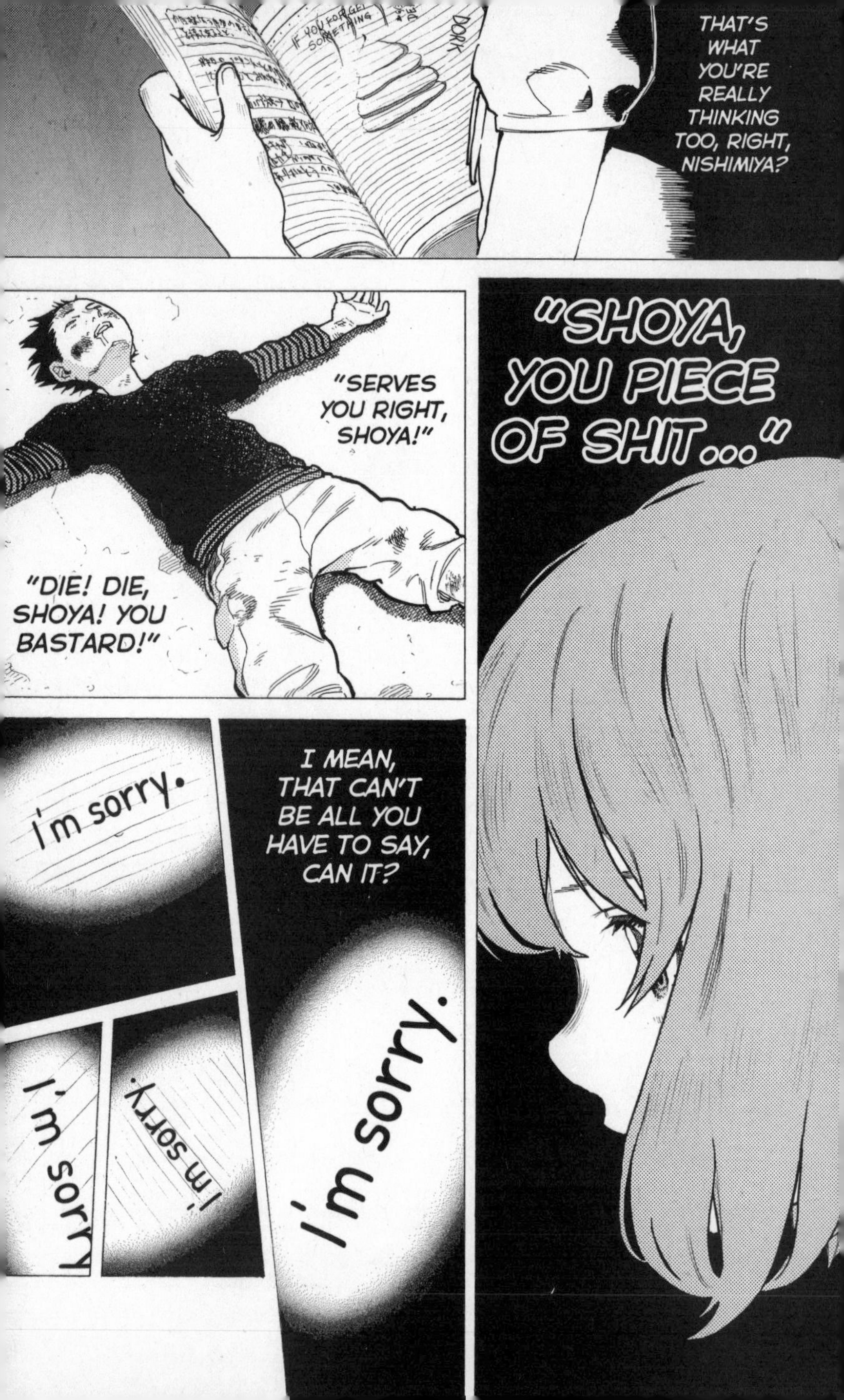
IF YOU FORGET SOMETHING
DORK
THAT'S WHAT YOU'RE REALLY THINKING TOO, RIGHT, NISHIMIYA?
"SHOYA, YOU PIECE OF SHIT..."
"SERVES YOU RIGHT, SHOYA!"
"DIE! DIE, SHOYA! YOU BASTARD!"
I MEAN, THAT CAN'T BE ALL YOU HAVE TO SAY, CAN IT?
I'm sorry.
I'm sorry.
I'm sorry
I'm sorry

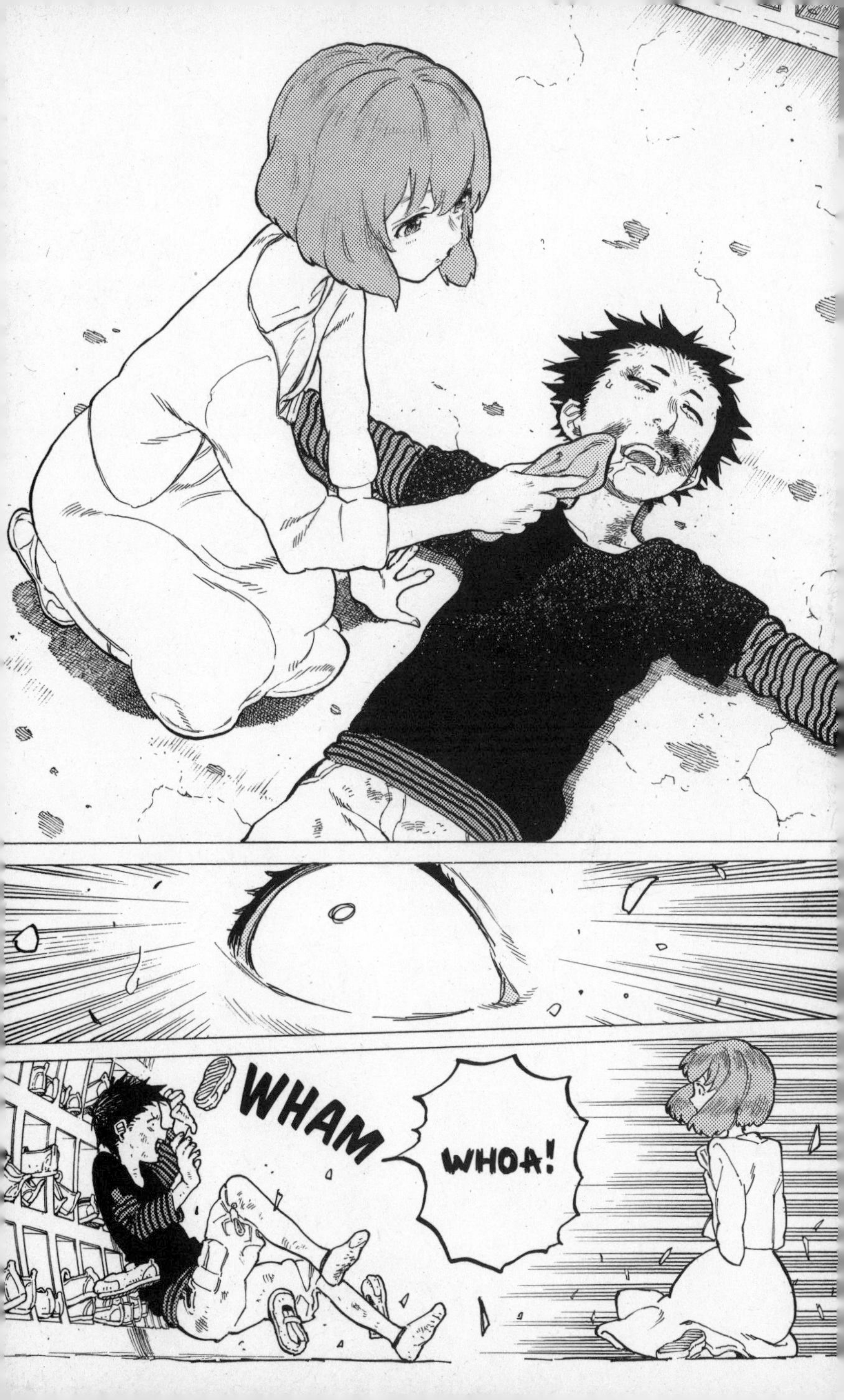
WHOA!
WHAM

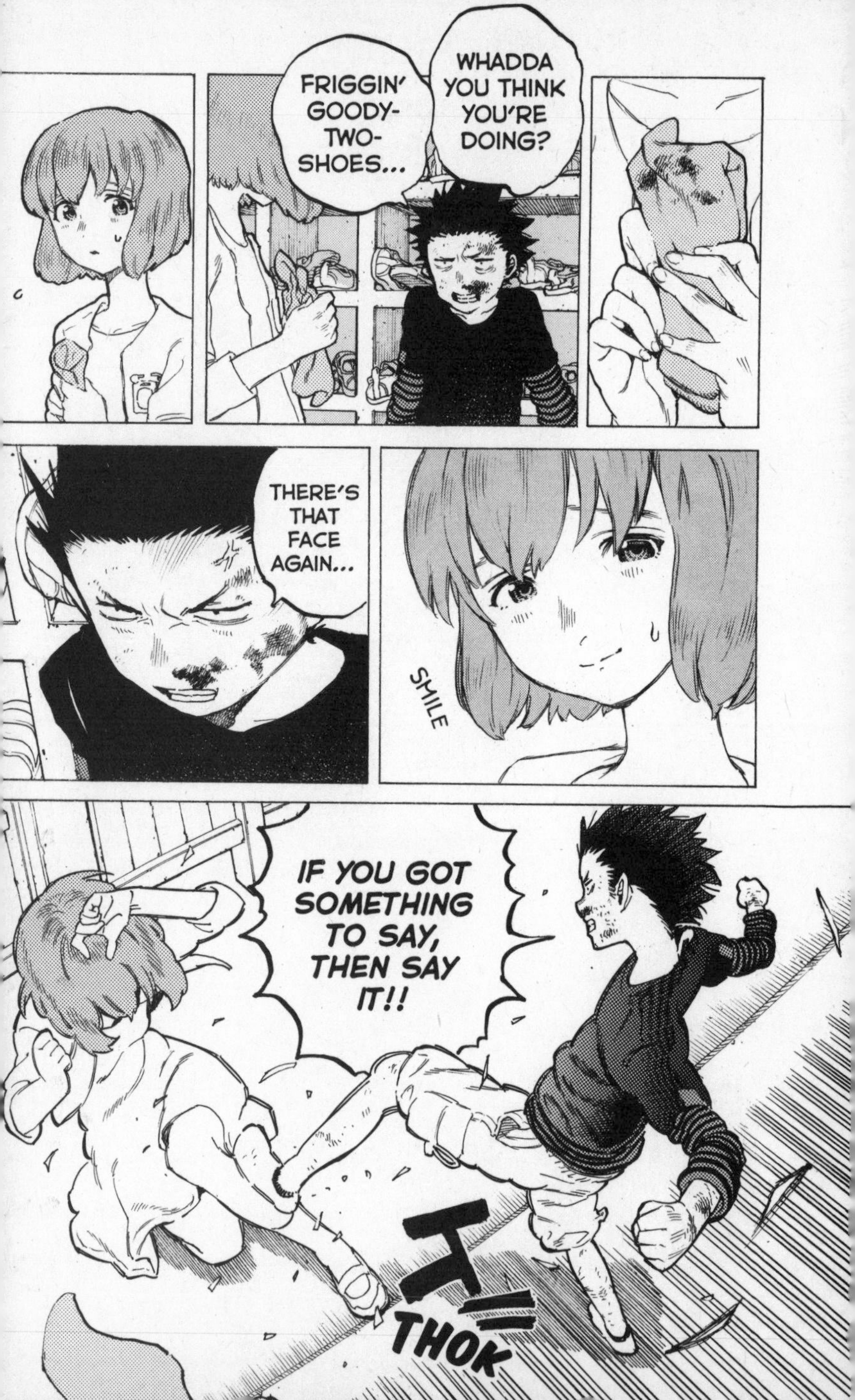
WHADDA YOU THINK YOU'RE DOING?
FRIGGIN' GOODY-TWO-SHOES...
SMILE
THERE'S THAT FACE AGAIN...
IF YOU GOT SOMETHING TO SAY, THEN SAY IT!!
THOK

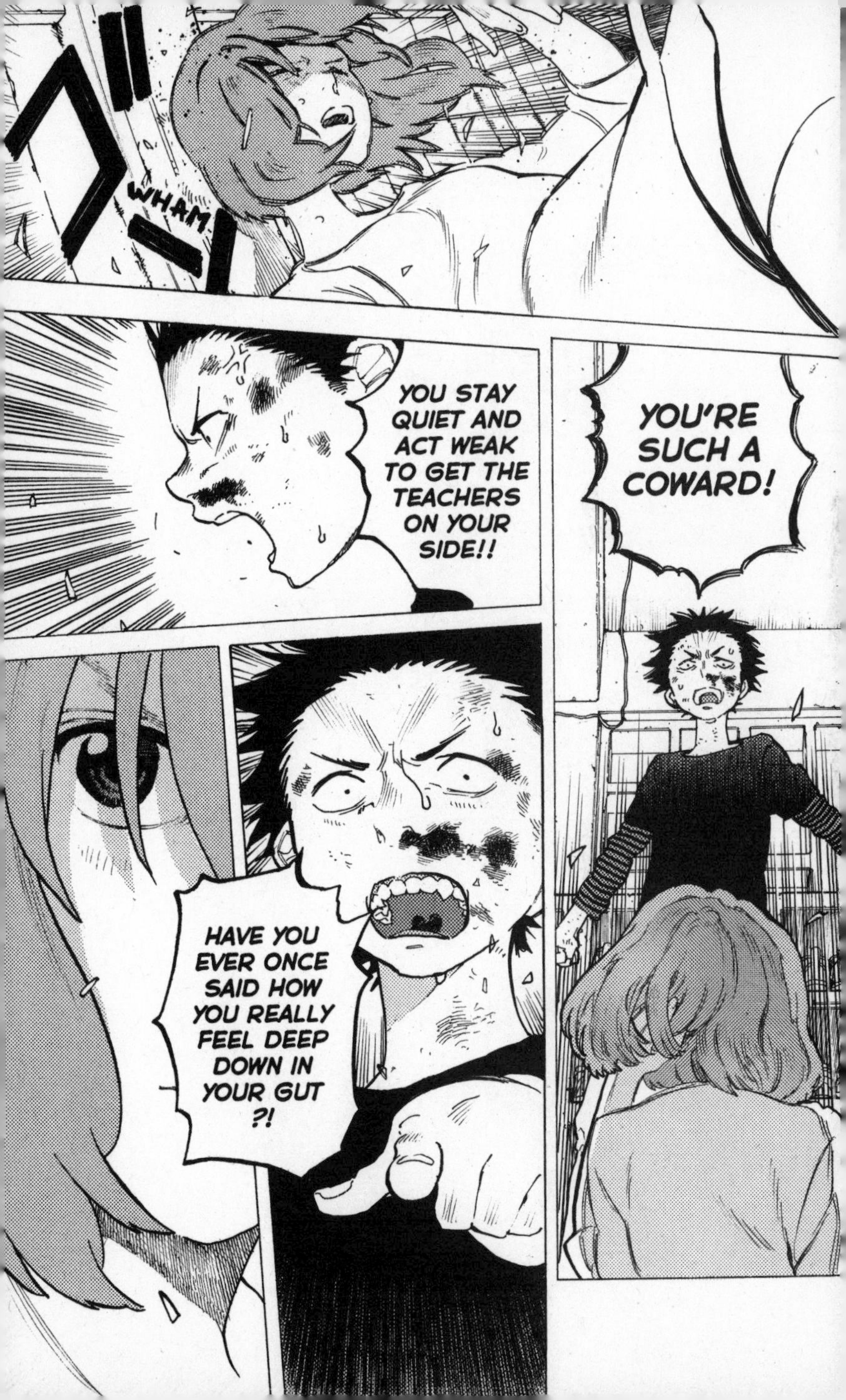
WHAM
YOU'RE SUCH A COWARD!
YOU STAY QUIET AND ACT WEAK TO GET THE TEACHERS ON YOUR SIDE!!
HAVE YOU EVER ONCE SAID HOW YOU REALLY FEEL DEEP DOWN IN YOUR GUT ?!

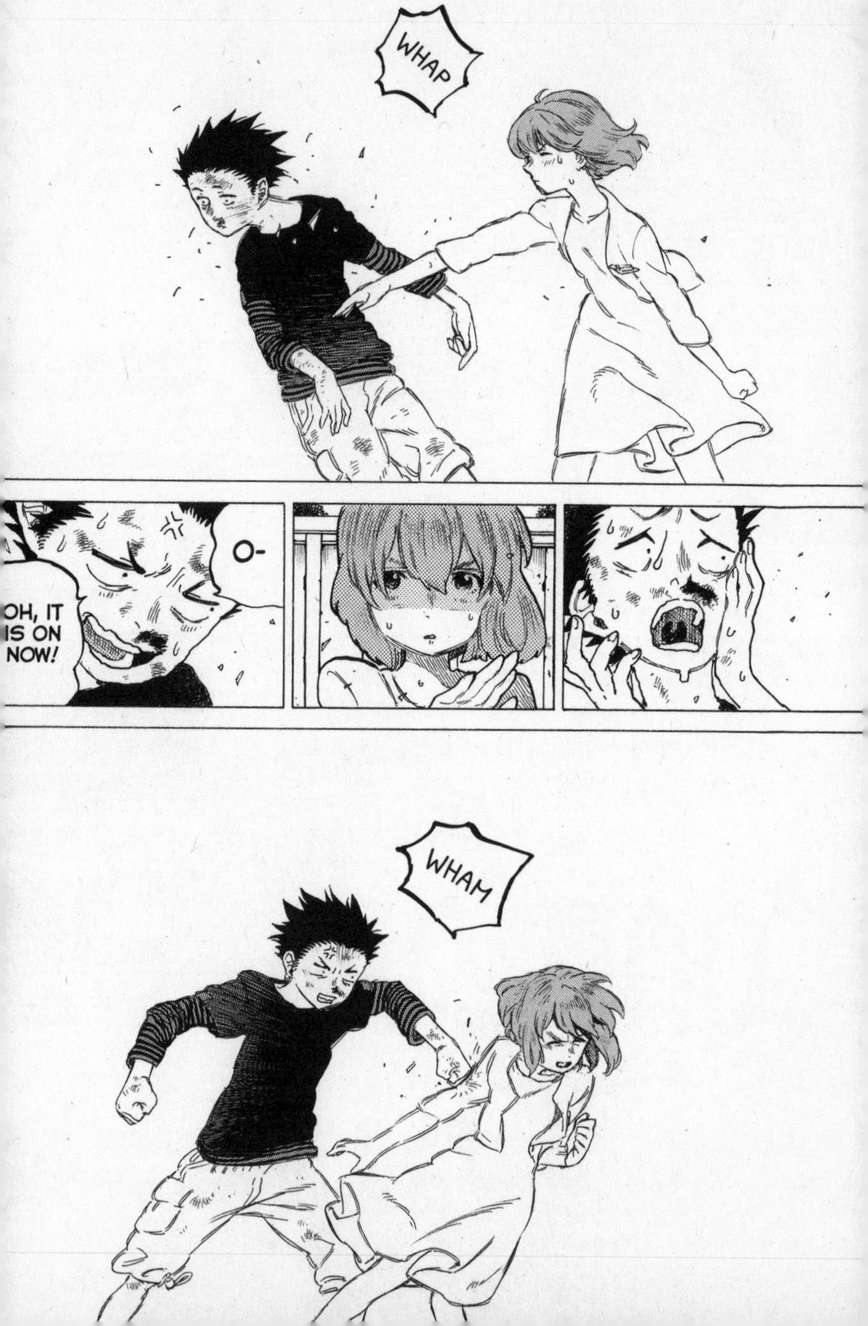
WHAP
O-
OH, IT IS ON NOW!
WHAM

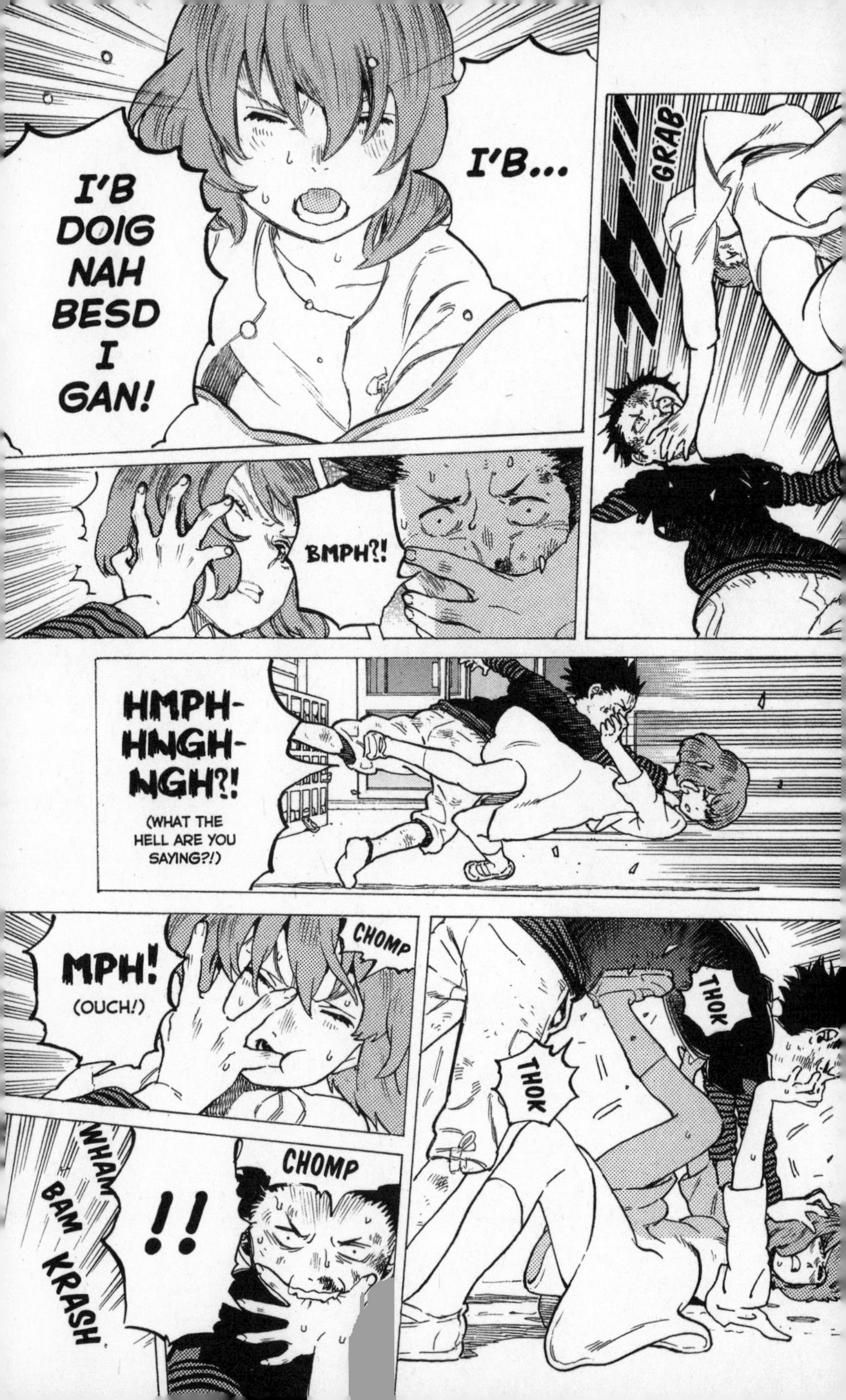
GRAB
I'B...
I'B DOIG NAH BESD I GAN!
BMPH?!
HMPH-HNGH-NGH?!
(WHAT THE HELL ARE YOU SAYING?!)
THOK
THOK
CHOMP
MPH!
(OUCH!)
CHOMP
!!
WHAM
BAM
KRASH

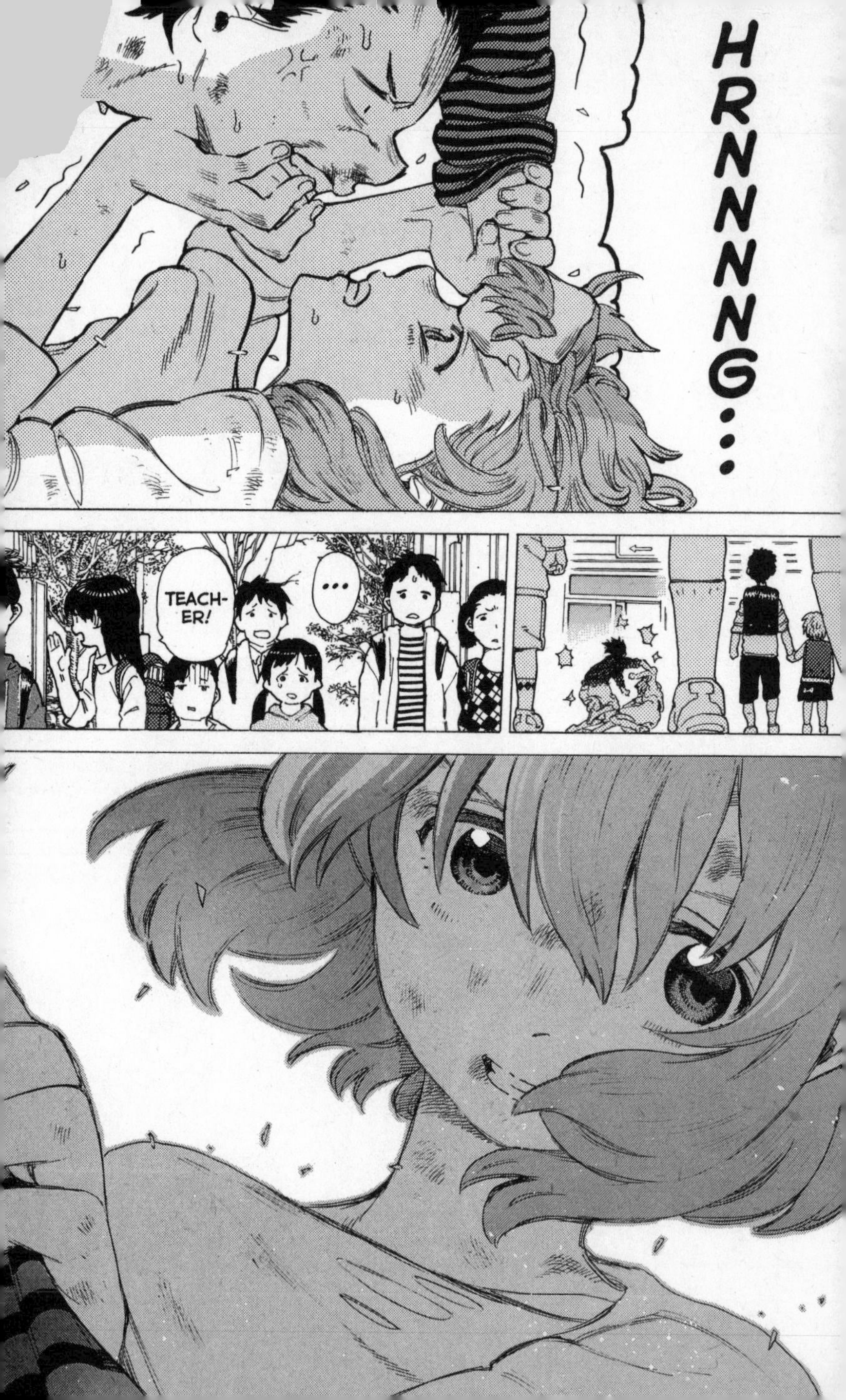
HRNNNNG...
...
TEACH-
ER!

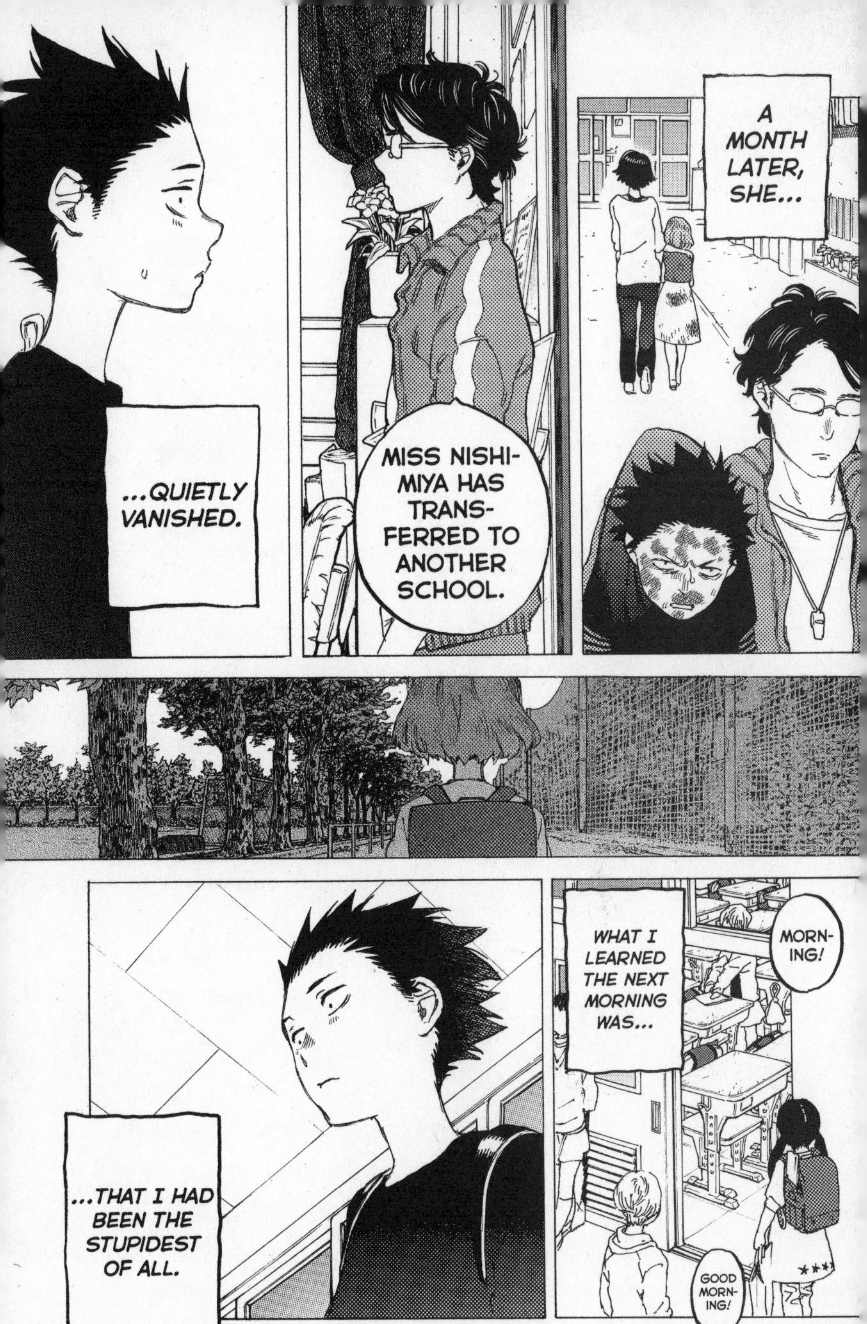
A MONTH LATER, SHE...
MISS NISHI-MIYA HAS TRANS-FERRED TO ANOTHER SCHOOL.
...QUIETLY VANISHED.
MORN-ING!
WHAT I LEARNED THE NEXT MORNING WAS...
GOOD MORN-ING!
...THAT I HAD BEEN THE STUPIDEST OF ALL.

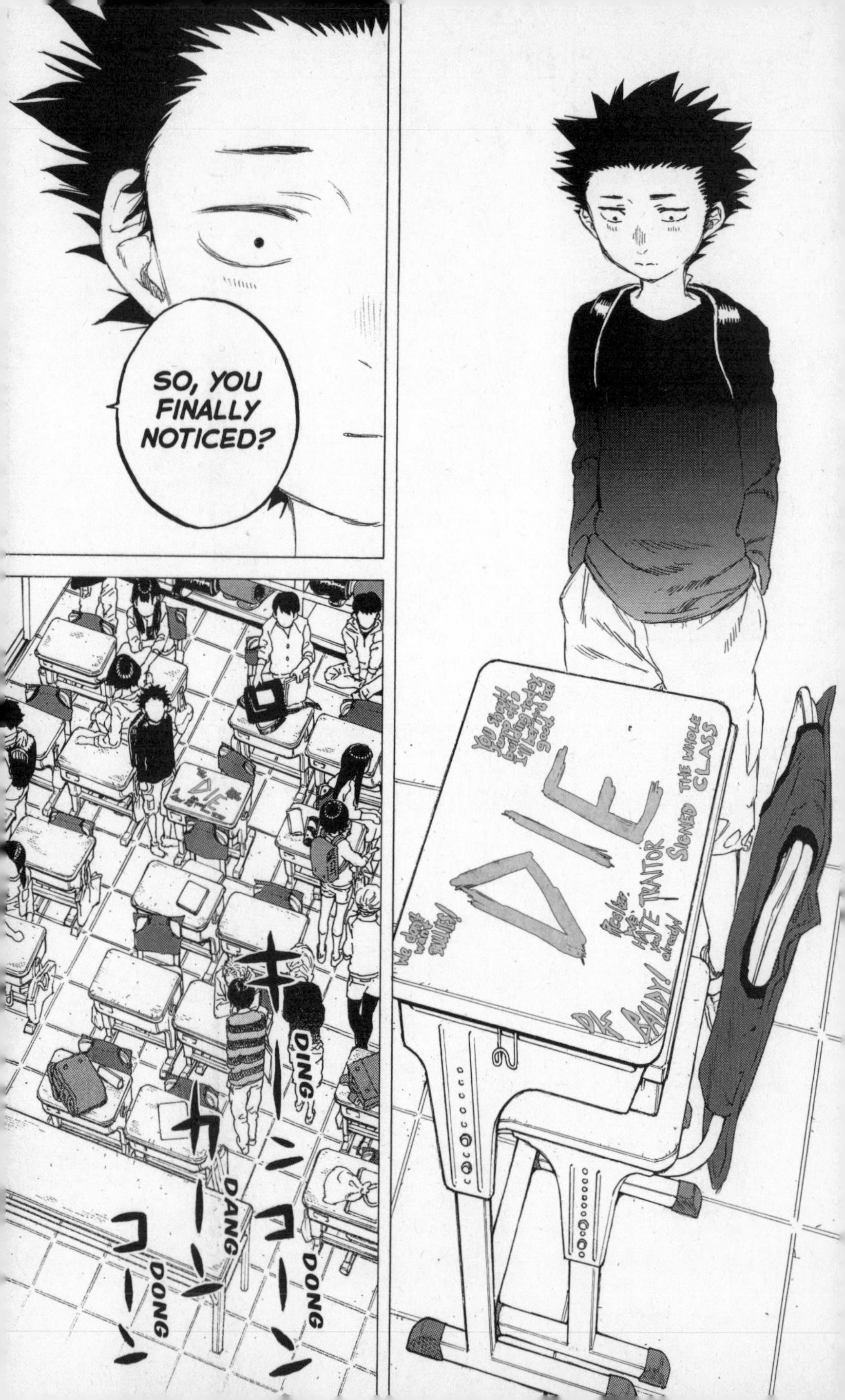
DIE
SIGNED THE WHOLE CLASS
TRAITOR
Realize we HATE you already!
We don't want BULLIES!
DIE BALDY!
SO, YOU FINALLY NOTICED?
DING
DONG
DANG
DONG

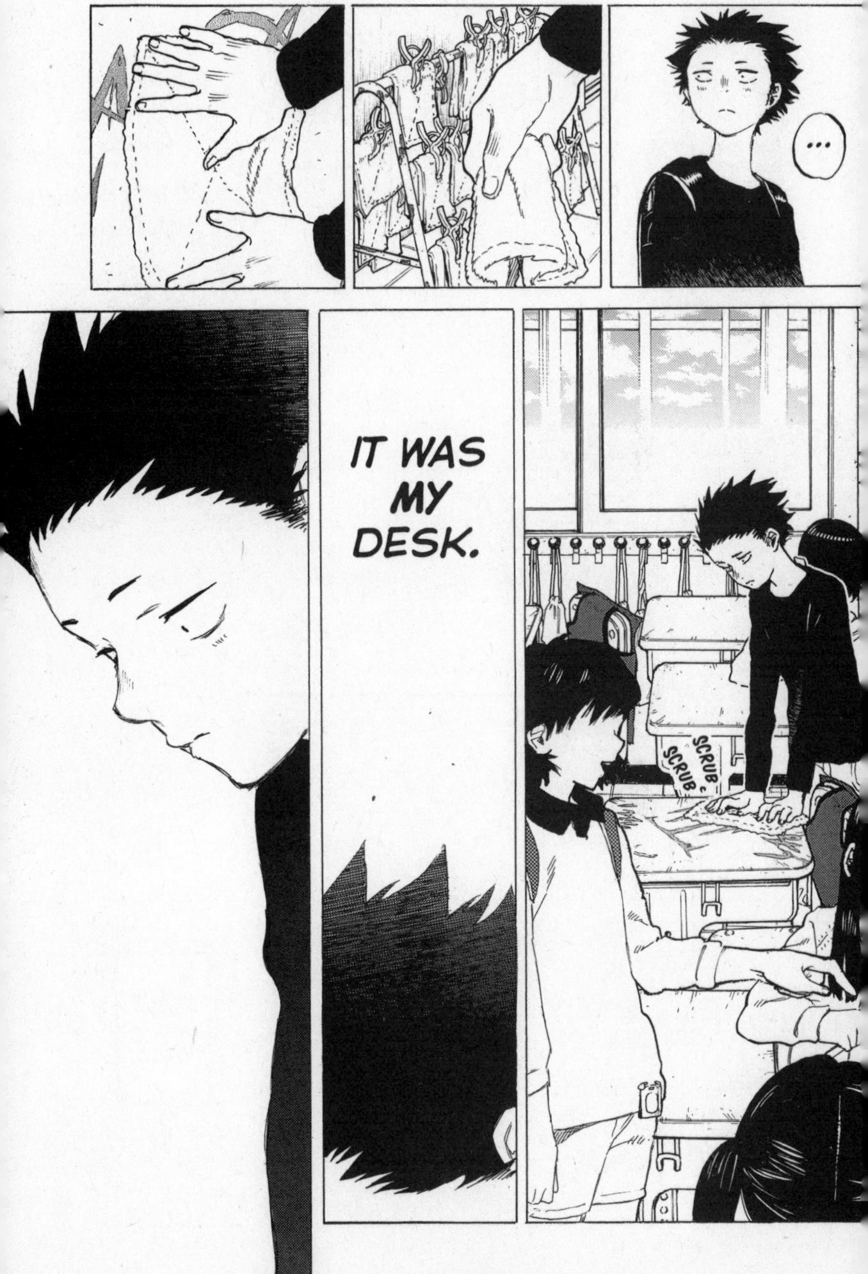
...
IT WAS MY DESK.
SCRUB SCRUB

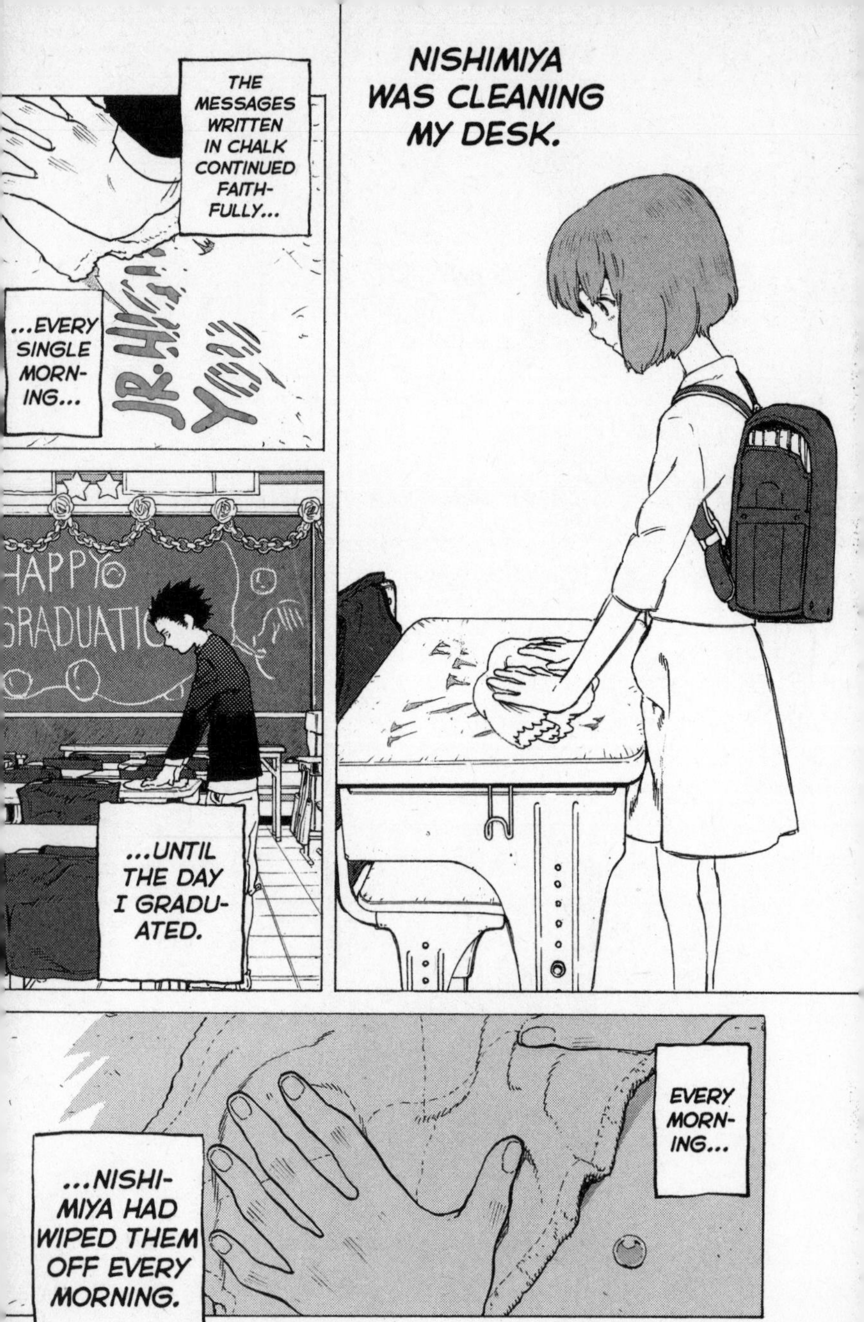
NISHIMIYA WAS CLEANING MY DESK.
THE MESSAGES WRITTEN IN CHALK CONTINUED FAITH-FULLY...
...EVERY SINGLE MORN-ING...
HAPPY
...UNTIL THE DAY I GRADU-ATED.
EVERY MORN-ING...
...NISHI-MIYA HAD WIPED THEM OFF EVERY MORNING.

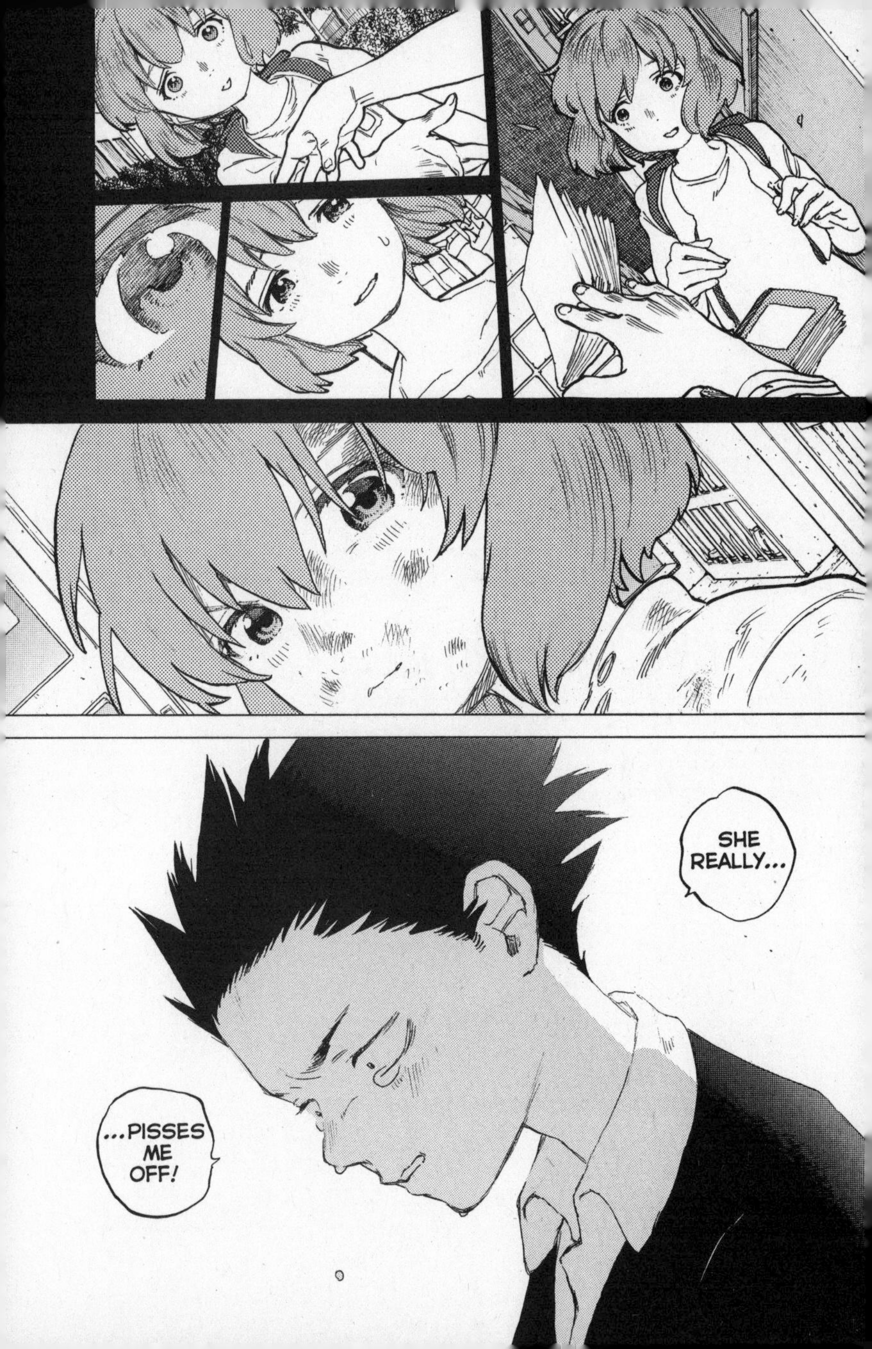
SHE REALLY...
...PISSES ME OFF!

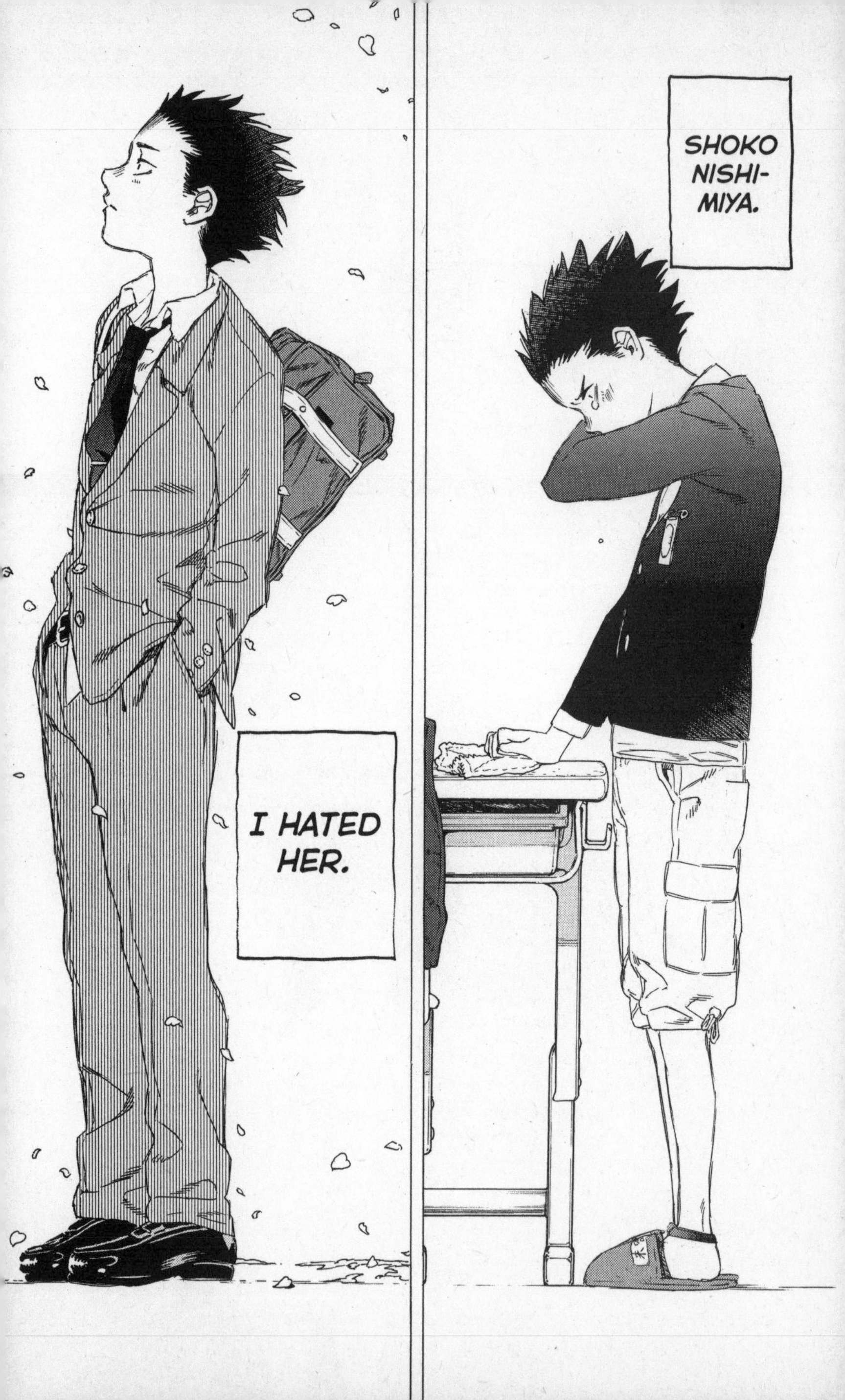
SHOKO NISHI-MIYA.
I HATED HER.

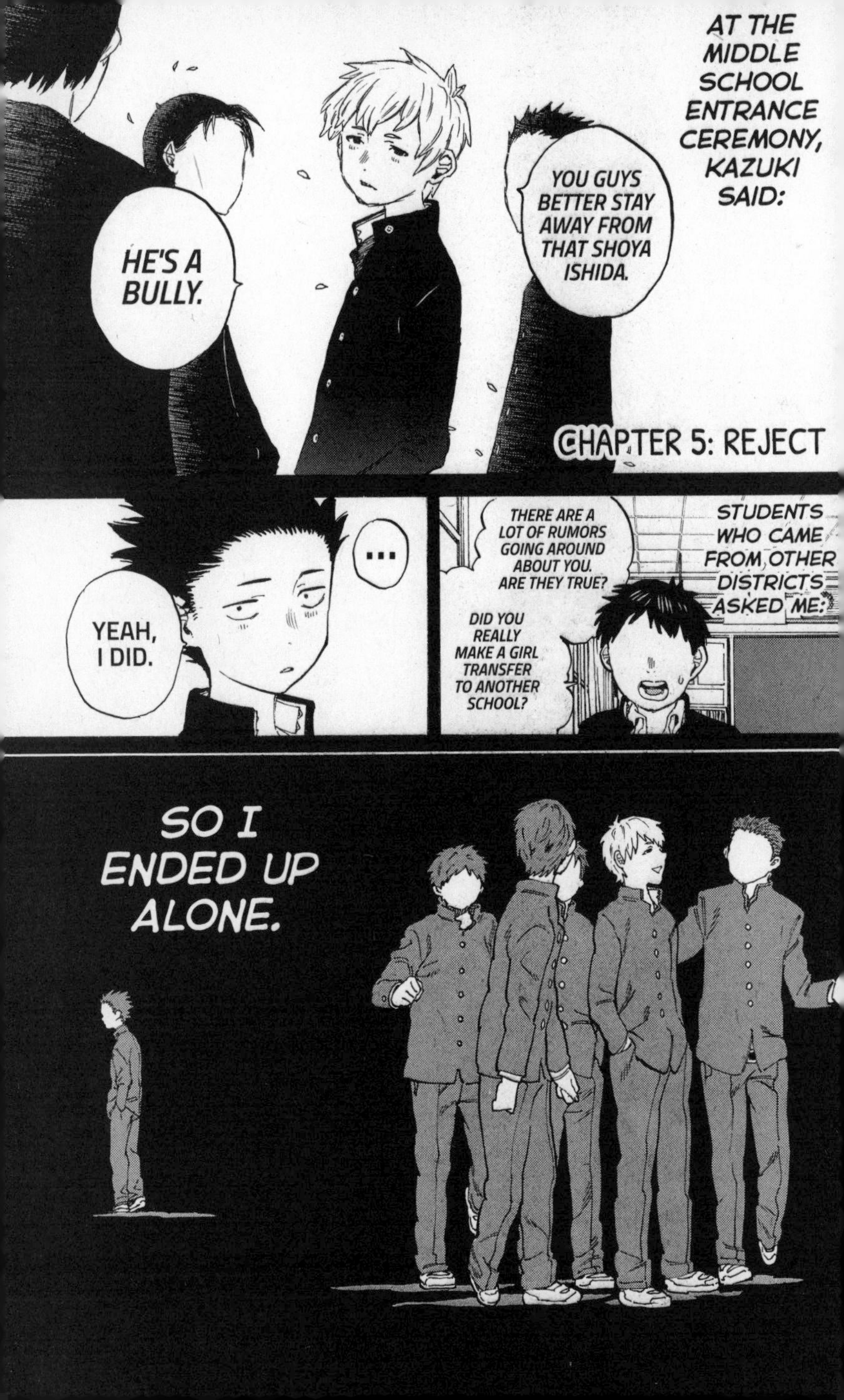
AT THE MIDDLE SCHOOL ENTRANCE CEREMONY, KAZUKI SAID:
YOU GUYS BETTER STAY AWAY FROM THAT SHOYA ISHIDA.
HE'S A BULLY.
CHAPTER 5: REJECT
STUDENTS WHO CAME FROM OTHER DISTRICTS ASKED ME:
THERE ARE A LOT OF RUMORS GOING AROUND ABOUT YOU. ARE THEY TRUE?
DID YOU REALLY MAKE A GIRL TRANSFER TO ANOTHER SCHOOL?
...
YEAH, I DID.
SO I ENDED UP ALONE.

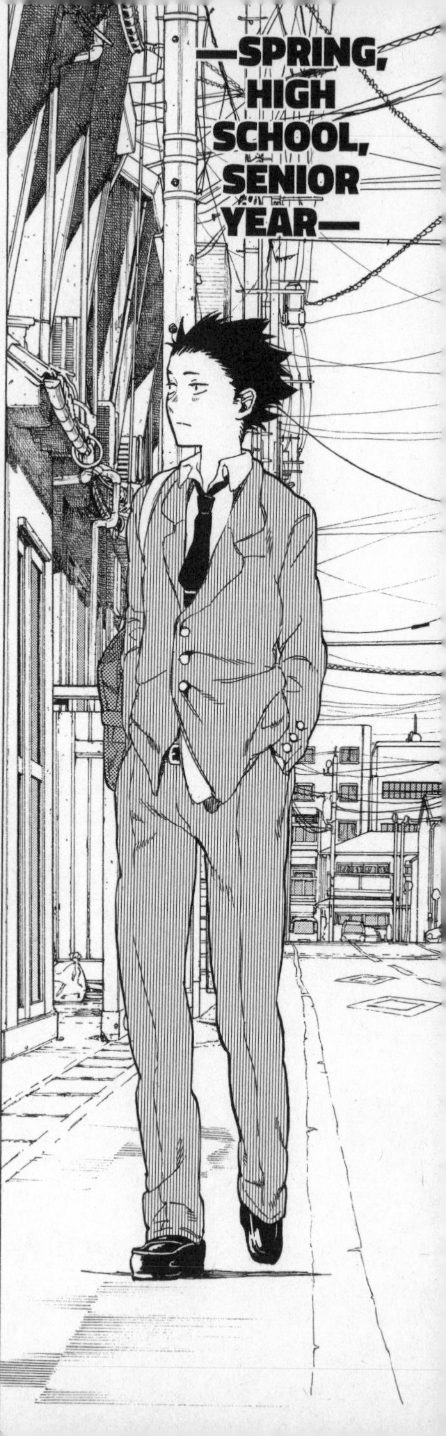
—SPRING, HIGH SCHOOL, SENIOR YEAR—

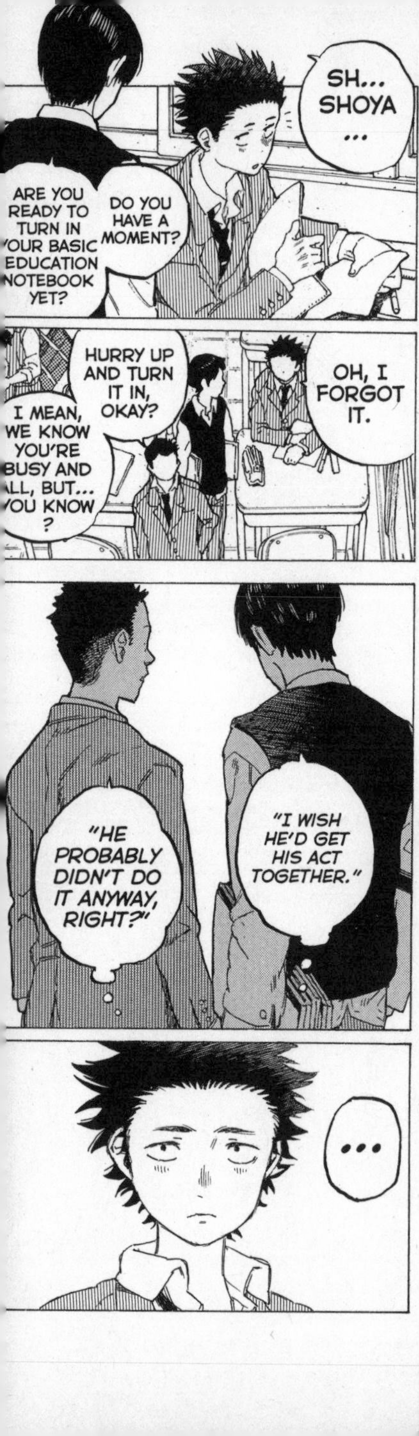
SH... SHOYA ...
DO YOU HAVE A MOMENT?
ARE YOU READY TO TURN IN OUR BASIC EDUCATION NOTEBOOK YET?
OH, I FORGOT IT.
HURRY UP AND TURN IT IN, OKAY?
I MEAN, WE KNOW YOU'RE BUSY AND LL, BUT... OU KNOW ?
"I WISH HE'D GET HIS ACT TOGETHER."
"HE PROBABLY DIDN'T DO IT ANYWAY, RIGHT?"
...

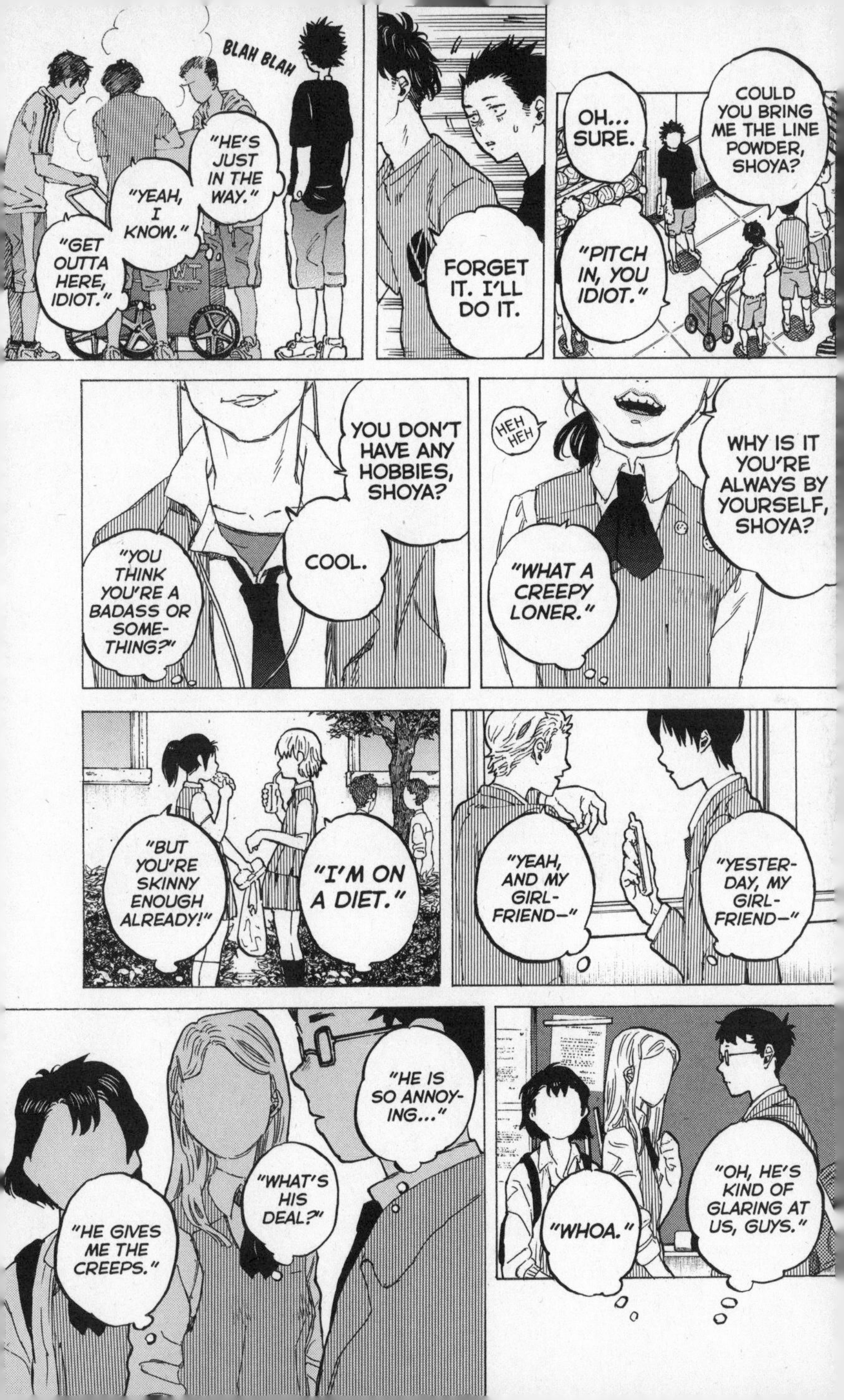
COULD YOU BRING ME THE LINE POWDER, SHOYA?
OH... SURE.
"PITCH IN, YOU IDIOT."
FORGET IT. I'LL DO IT.
BLAH BLAH
"HE'S JUST IN THE WAY."
"YEAH, I KNOW."
"GET OUTTA HERE, IDIOT."
WHY IS IT YOU'RE ALWAYS BY YOURSELF, SHOYA?
HEH HEH
"WHAT A CREEPY LONER."
YOU DON'T HAVE ANY HOBBIES, SHOYA?
COOL.
"YOU THINK YOU'RE A BADASS OR SOME-THING?"
"YESTER-DAY, MY GIRL-FRIEND—"
"YEAH, AND MY GIRL-FRIEND—"
"I'M ON A DIET."
"BUT YOU'RE SKINNY ENOUGH ALREADY!"
"OH, HE'S KIND OF GLARING AT US, GUYS."
"WHOA."
"HE IS SO ANNOY-ING..."
"WHAT'S HIS DEAL?"
"HE GIVES ME THE CREEPS."

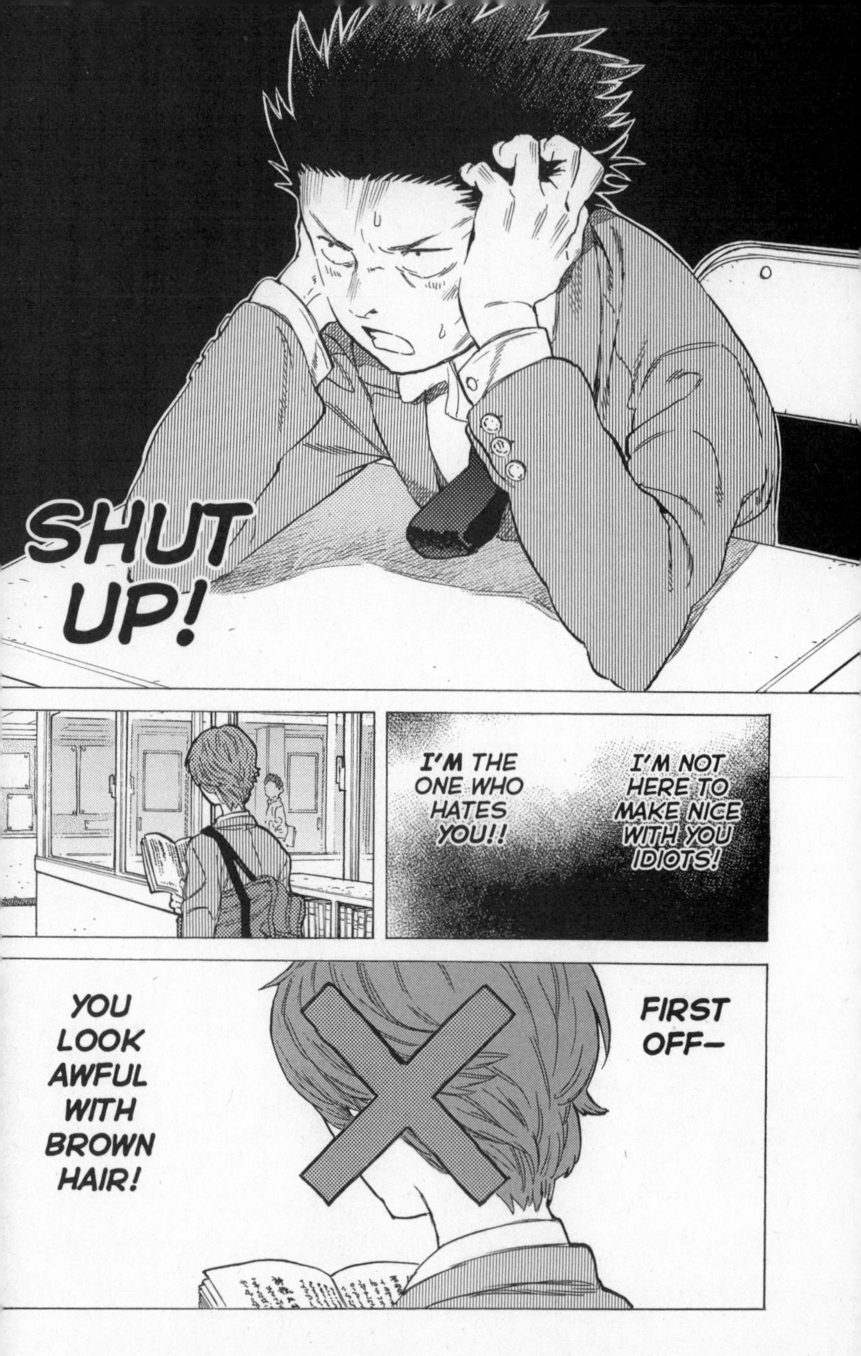
SHUT UP!
I'M NOT HERE TO MAKE NICE WITH YOU IDIOTS!
I'M THE ONE WHO HATES YOU!!
FIRST OFF—
YOU LOOK AWFUL WITH BROWN HAIR!

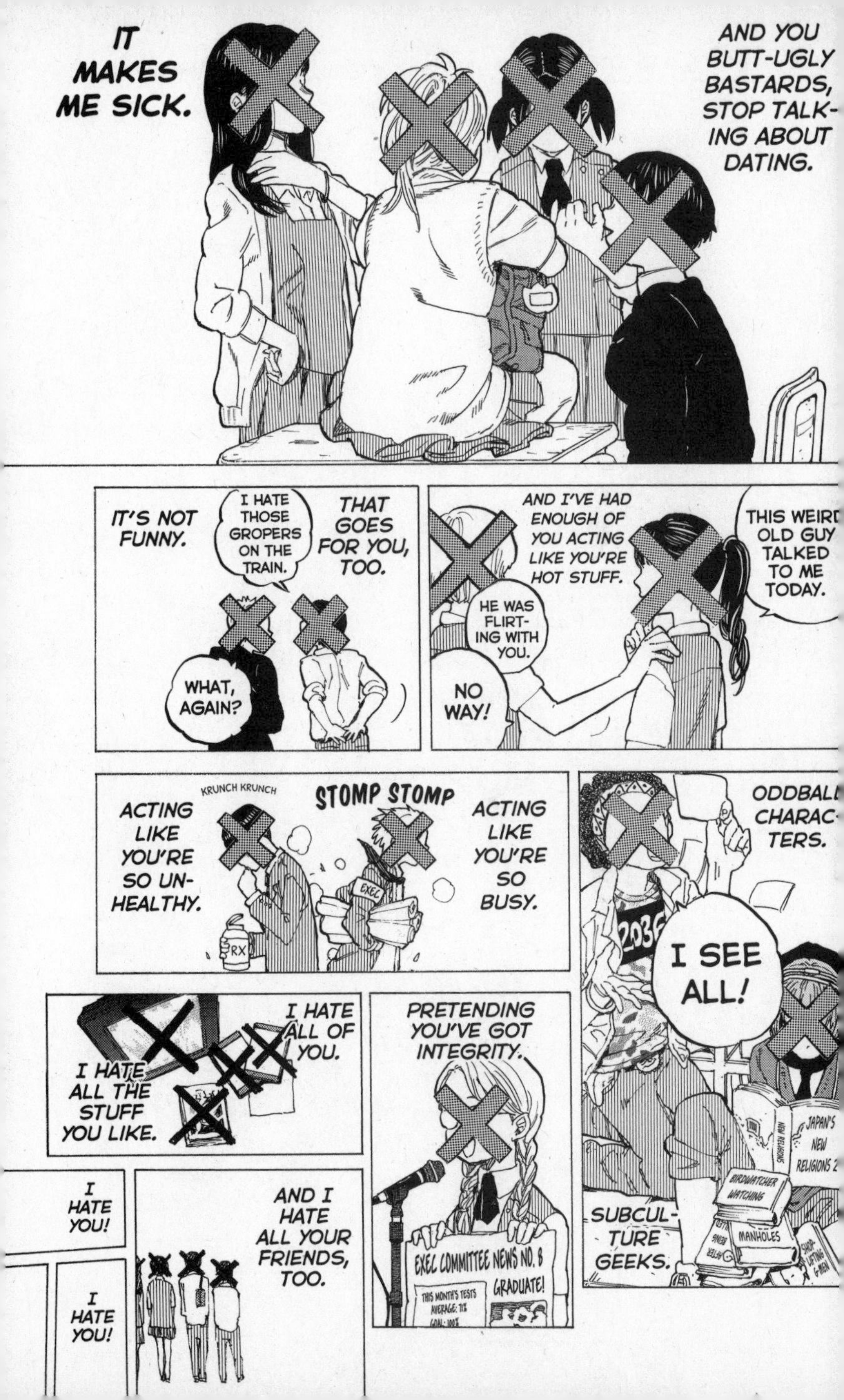
AND YOU BUTT-UGLY BASTARDS, STOP TALKING ABOUT DATING.
IT MAKES ME SICK.
THIS WEIRD OLD GUY TALKED TO ME TODAY.
AND I'VE HAD ENOUGH OF YOU ACTING LIKE YOU'RE HOT STUFF.
HE WAS FLIRTING WITH YOU.
NO WAY!
THAT GOES FOR YOU, TOO.
I HATE THOSE GROPERS ON THE TRAIN.
IT'S NOT FUNNY.
WHAT, AGAIN?
ODDBALL CHARACTERS.
I SEE ALL!
2036
JAPAN'S NEW RELIGIONS 2
NEW RELIGIONS
BIRDWATCHER WATCHING
MANHOLES
SHOPLIFTING G-MEN
SUBCULTURE GEEKS.
ACTING LIKE YOU'RE SO BUSY.
STOMP STOMP
EXEC
KRUNCH KRUNCH
ACTING LIKE YOU'RE SO UNHEALTHY.
RX
PRETENDING YOU'VE GOT INTEGRITY.
EXEC COMMITTEE NEWS NO. 8
GRADUATE!
THIS MONTH'S TESTS AVERAGE
I HATE ALL OF YOU.
I HATE ALL THE STUFF YOU LIKE.
AND I HATE ALL YOUR FRIENDS, TOO.
I HATE YOU!
I HATE YOU!

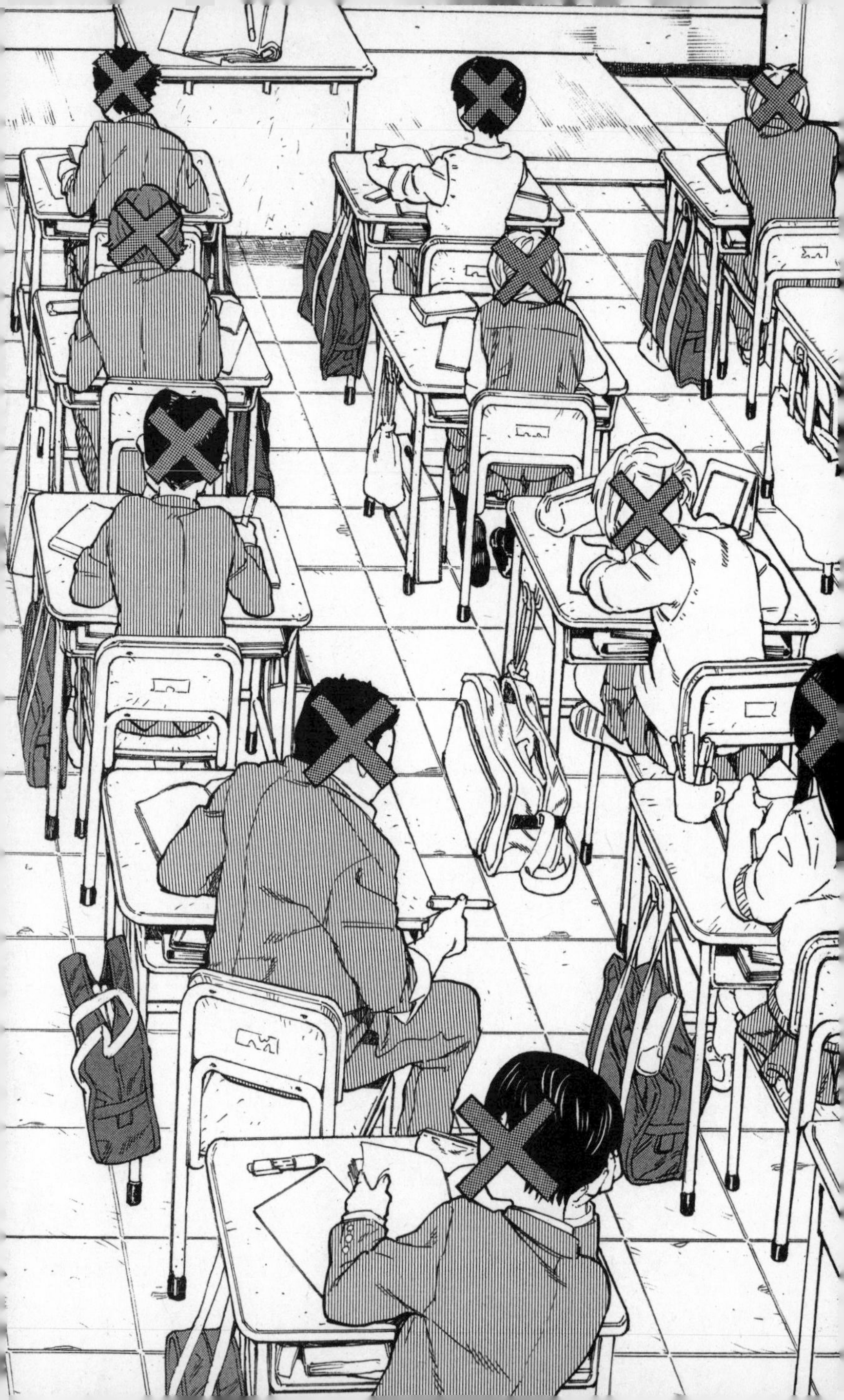

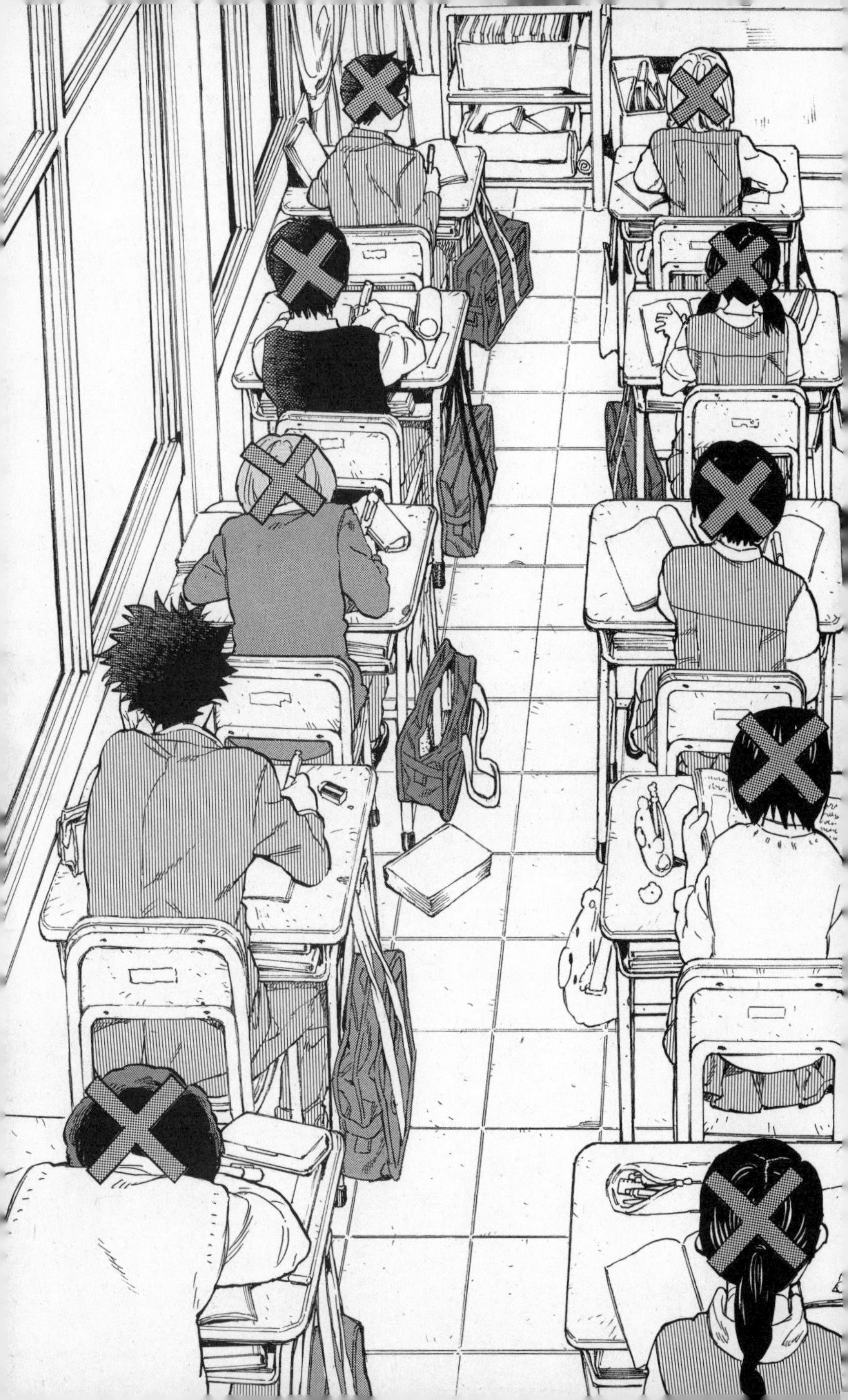

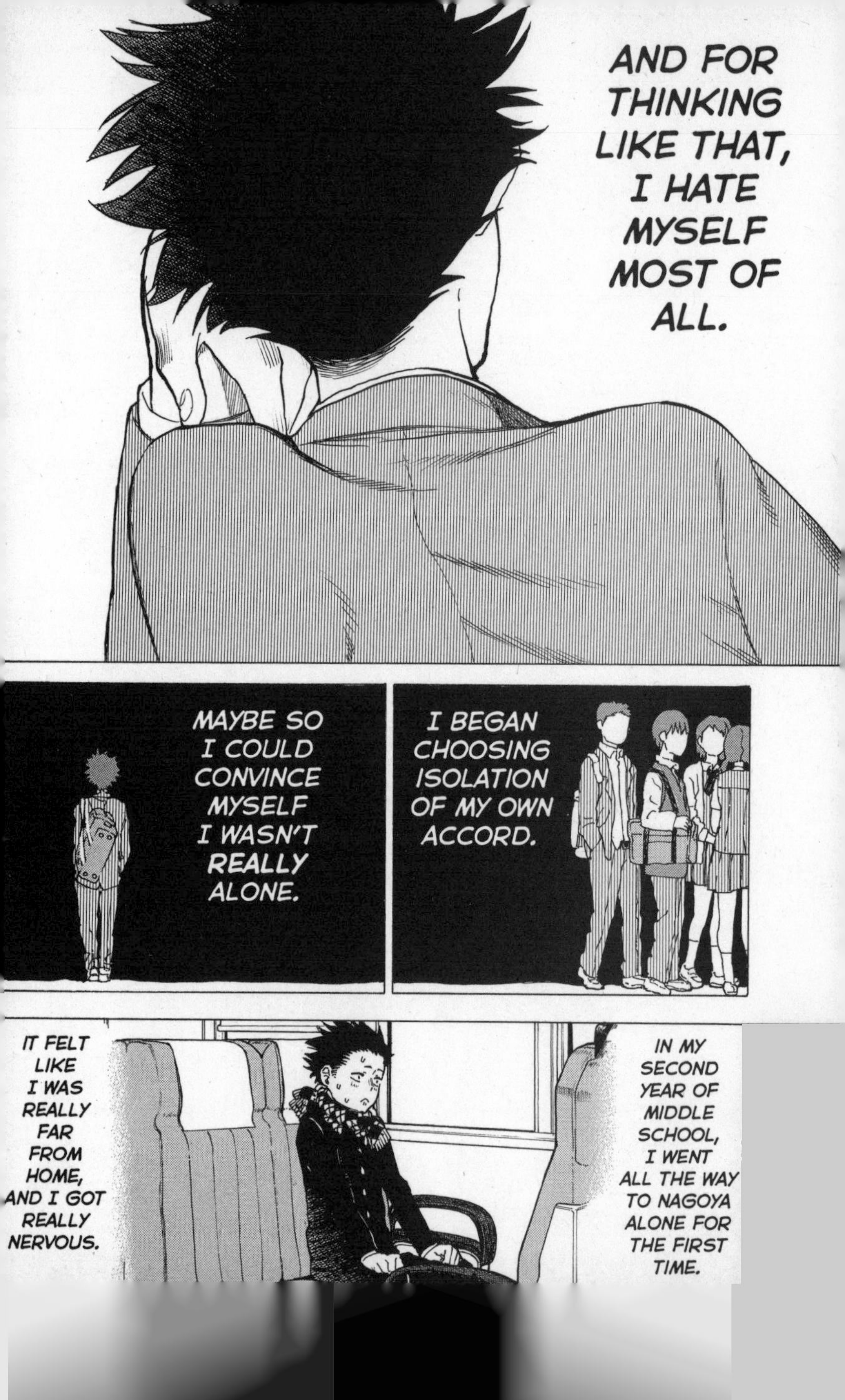
AND FOR THINKING LIKE THAT, I HATE MYSELF MOST OF ALL.
I BEGAN CHOOSING ISOLATION OF MY OWN ACCORD.
MAYBE SO I COULD CONVINCE MYSELF I WASN'T REALLY ALONE.
IN MY SECOND YEAR OF MIDDLE SCHOOL, I WENT ALL THE WAY TO NAGOYA ALONE FOR THE FIRST TIME.
IT FELT LIKE I WAS REALLY FAR FROM HOME, AND I GOT REALLY NERVOUS.

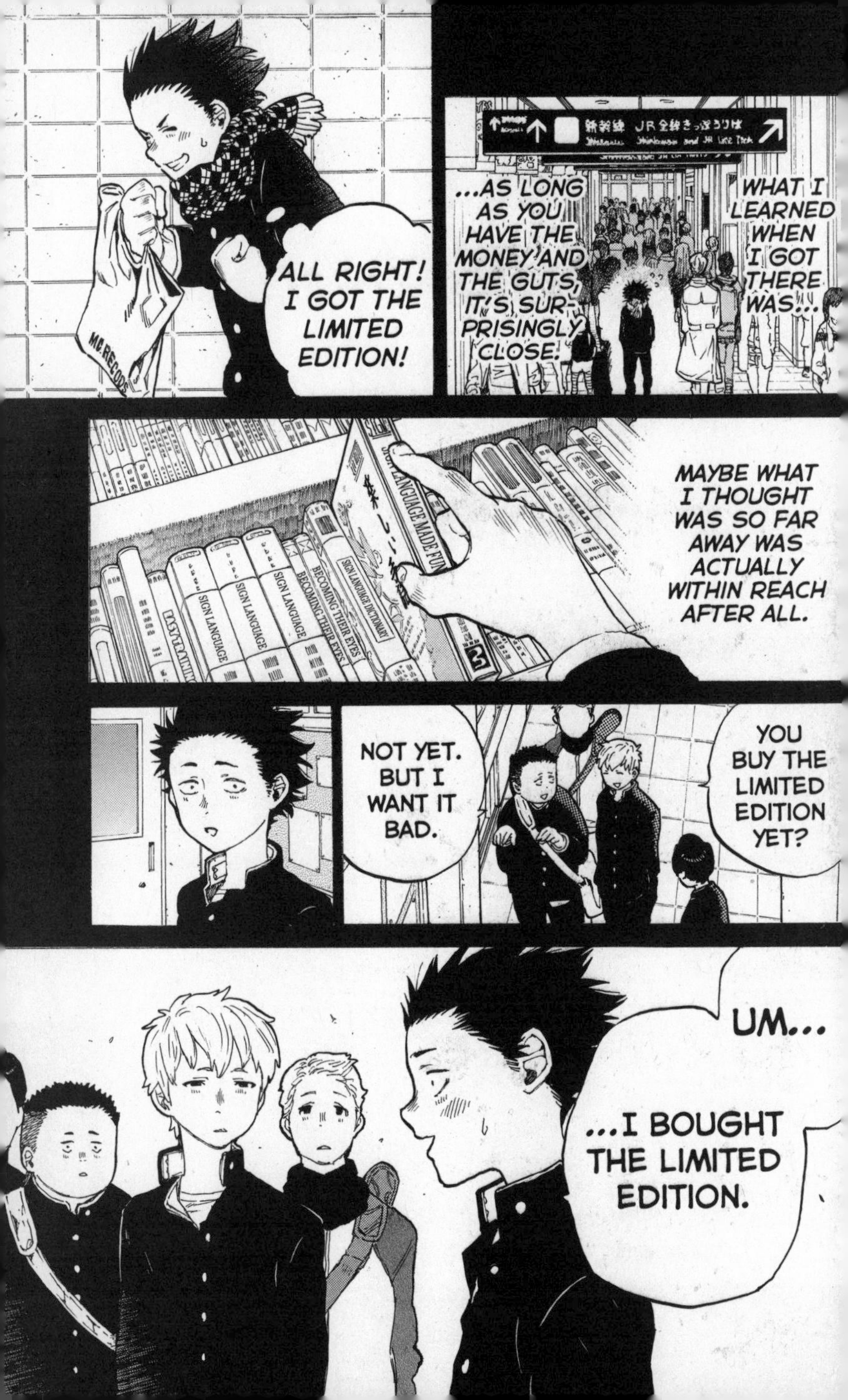
WHAT I LEARNED WHEN I GOT THERE WAS...
...AS LONG AS YOU HAVE THE MONEY AND THE GUTS, IT'S SURPRISINGLY CLOSE.
ALL RIGHT! I GOT THE LIMITED EDITION!
MAYBE WHAT I THOUGHT WAS SO FAR AWAY WAS ACTUALLY WITHIN REACH AFTER ALL.
SIGN LANGUAGE MADE FUN
SIGN LANGUAGE DICTIONARY
BECOMING THEIR EYES
BECOMING THEIR EYES
SIGN LANGUAGE
SIGN LANGUAGE
SIGN LANGUAGE
YOU BUY THE LIMITED EDITION YET?
NOT YET. BUT I WANT IT BAD.
UM...
...I BOUGHT THE LIMITED EDITION.

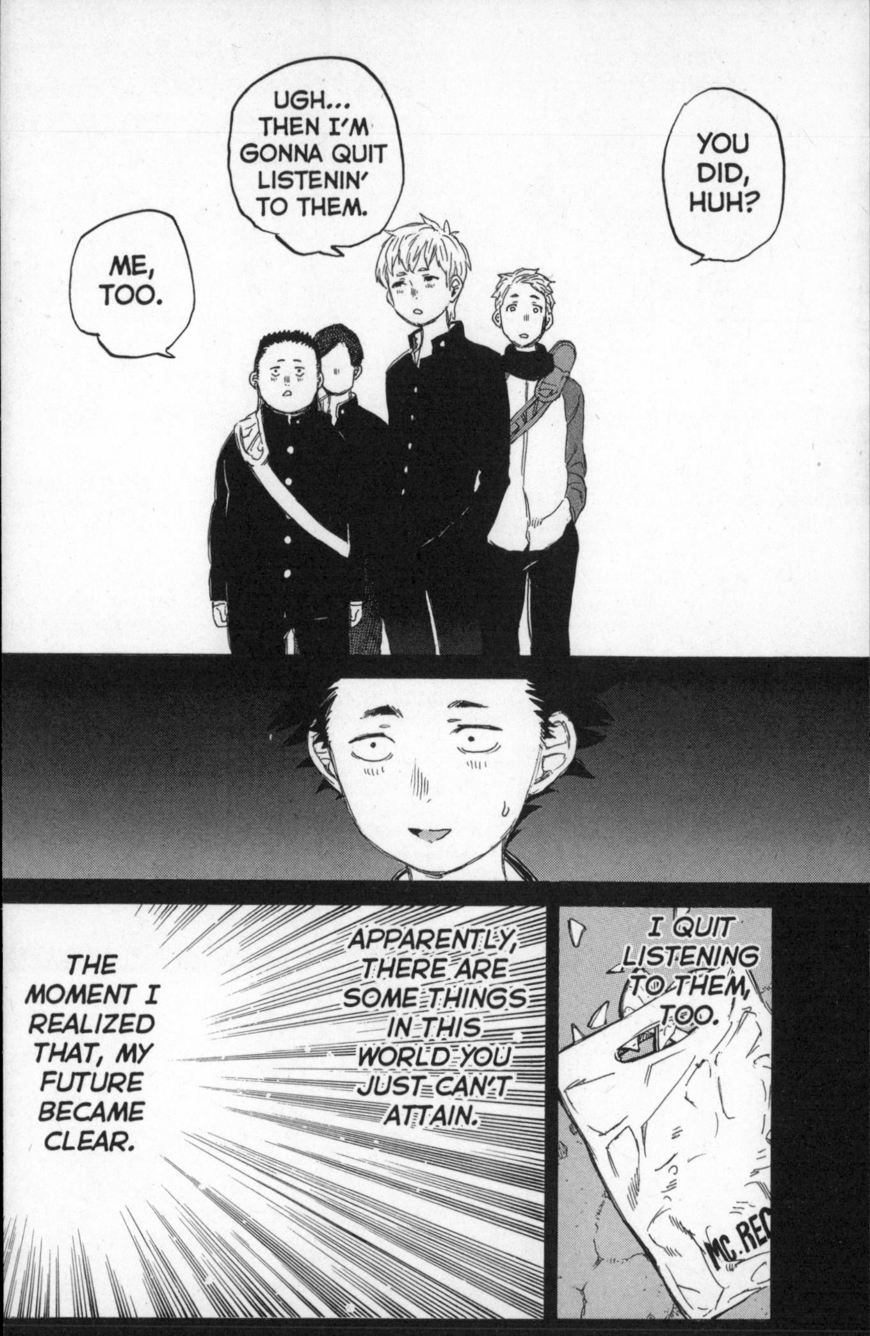
YOU DID, HUH?
UGH... THEN I'M GONNA QUIT LISTENIN' TO THEM.
ME, TOO.
I QUIT LISTENING TO THEM, TOO.
APPARENTLY, THERE ARE SOME THINGS IN THIS WORLD YOU JUST CAN'T ATTAIN.
THE MOMENT I REALIZED THAT, MY FUTURE BECAME CLEAR.

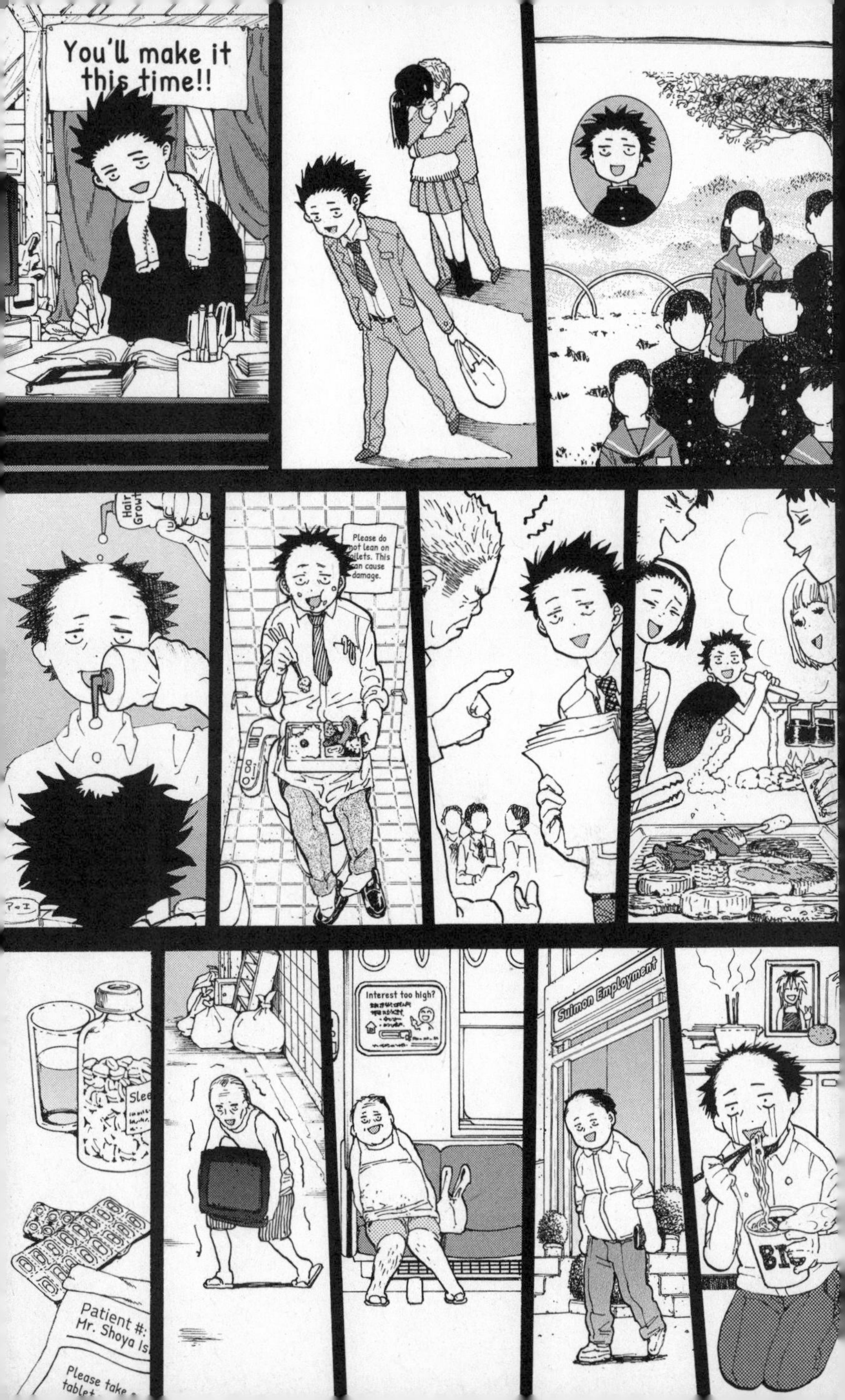

You'll make it this time!!
Please do
ot lean on
oilets. This
an cause
damage.
Hair
Grow
BI
Suimon Employment
Interest too high?
Slee
Patient #:
Mr. Shoya Is
Please take
tablet

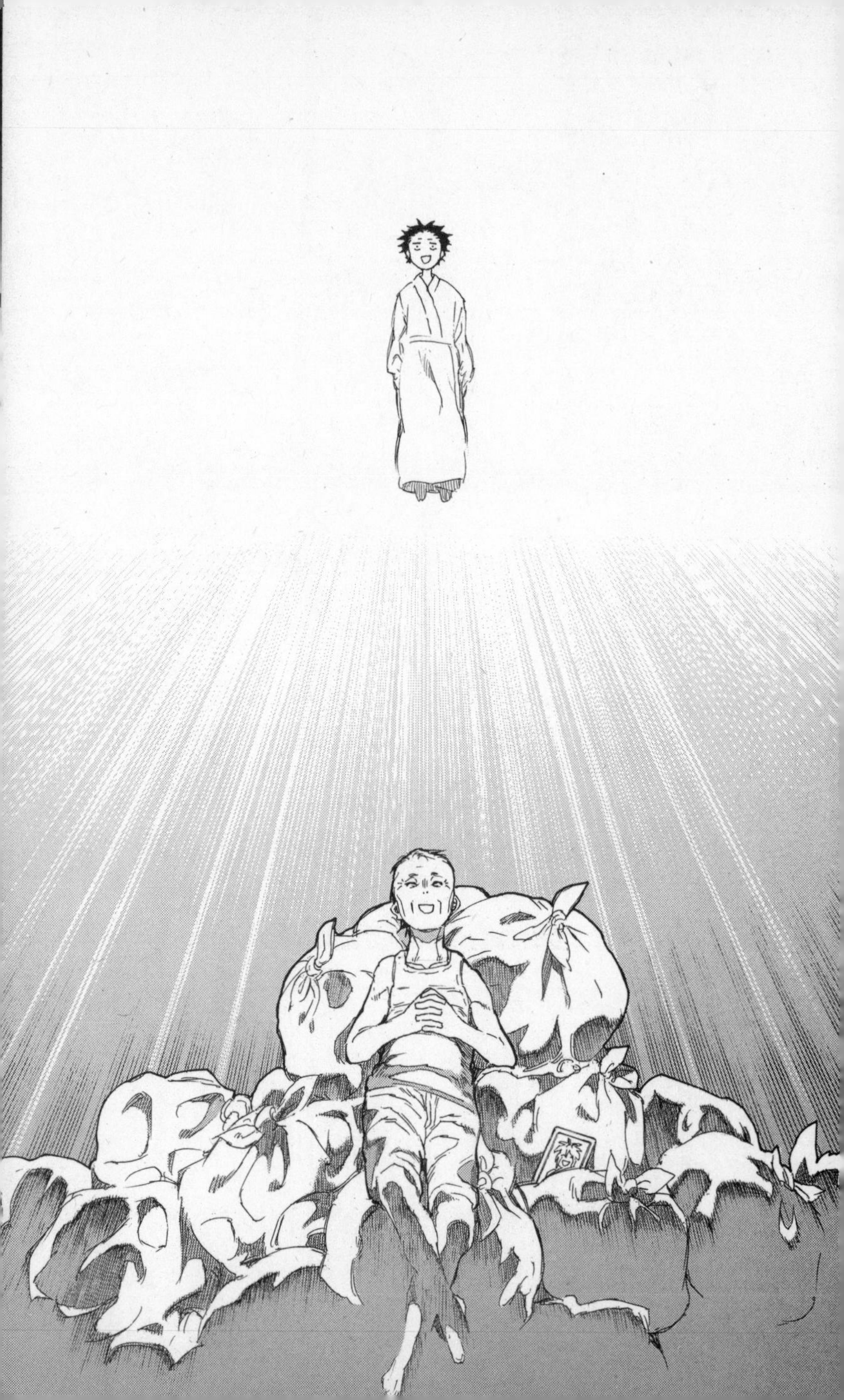

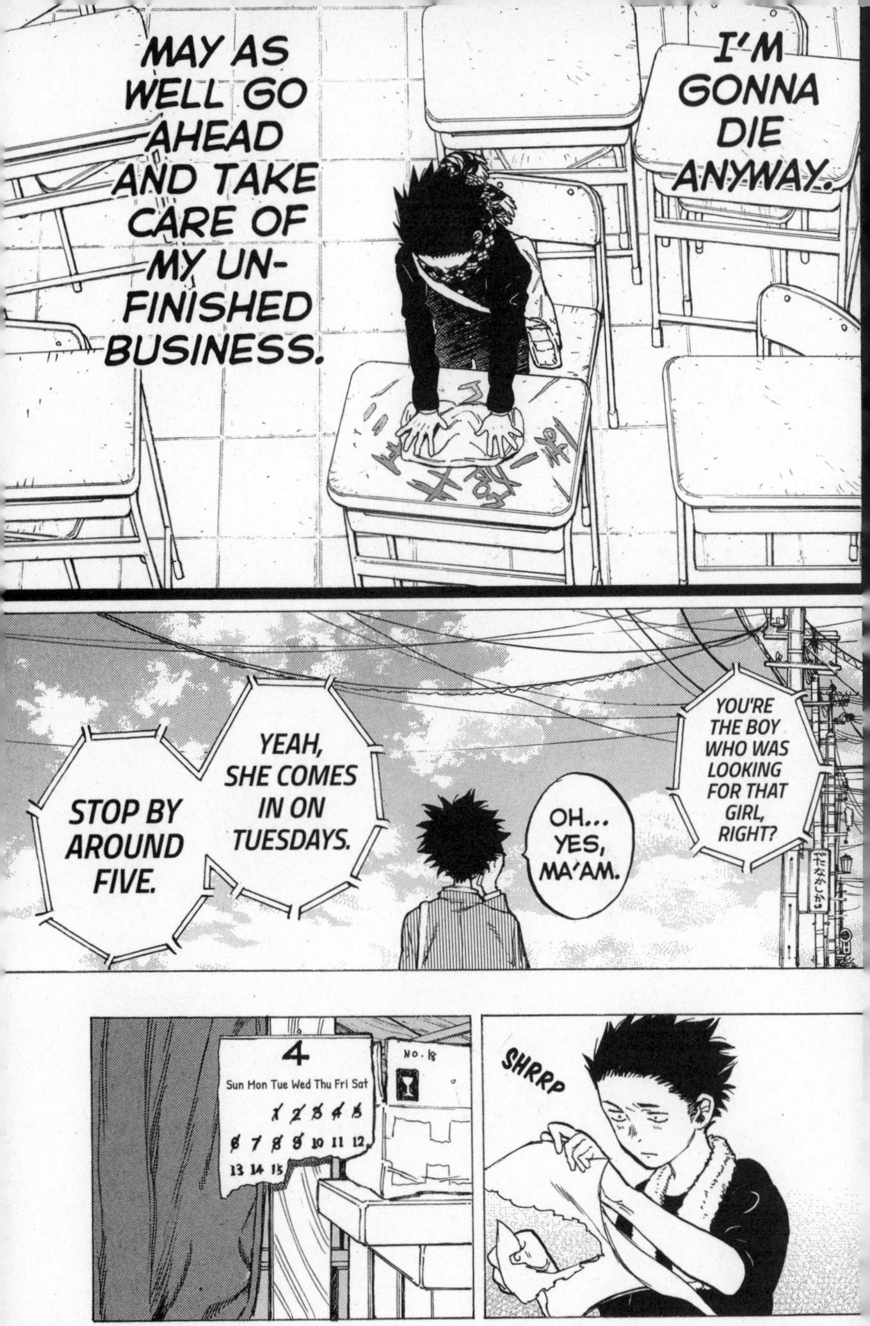
I'M GONNA DIE ANYWAY.
MAY AS WELL GO AHEAD AND TAKE CARE OF MY UN-FINISHED BUSINESS.
YOU'RE THE BOY WHO WAS LOOKING FOR THAT GIRL, RIGHT?
OH... YES, MA'AM.
YEAH, SHE COMES IN ON TUESDAYS.
STOP BY AROUND FIVE.
SHRRP
NO. 18
4
Sun Mon Tue Wed Thu Fri Sat
1 2 3 4 5
6 7 8 9 10 11 12
13 14 15

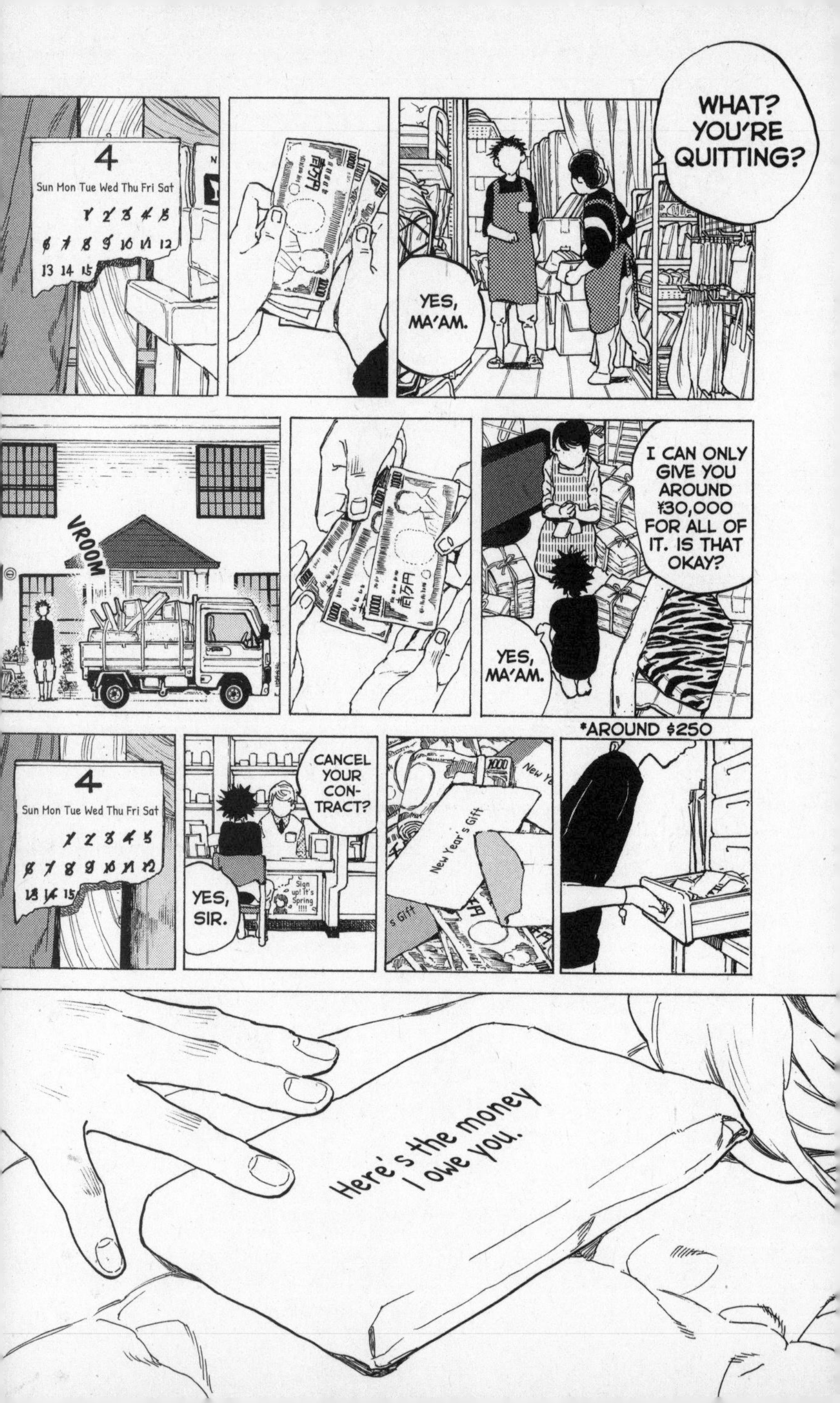

WHAT? YOU'RE QUITTING?
YES, MA'AM.
4
Sun Mon Tue Wed Thu Fri Sat
1 2 3 4 5
6 7 8 9 10 11 12
13 14 15
I CAN ONLY GIVE YOU AROUND ¥30,000 FOR ALL OF IT. IS THAT OKAY?
YES, MA'AM.
*AROUND $250
VROOM
New Year's Gift
CANCEL YOUR CON-TRACT?
YES, SIR.
Sign up! It's Spring !!!!
4
Sun Mon Tue Wed Thu Fri Sat
1 2 3 4 5
6 7 8 9 10 11 12
13 14 15
Here's the money I owe you.

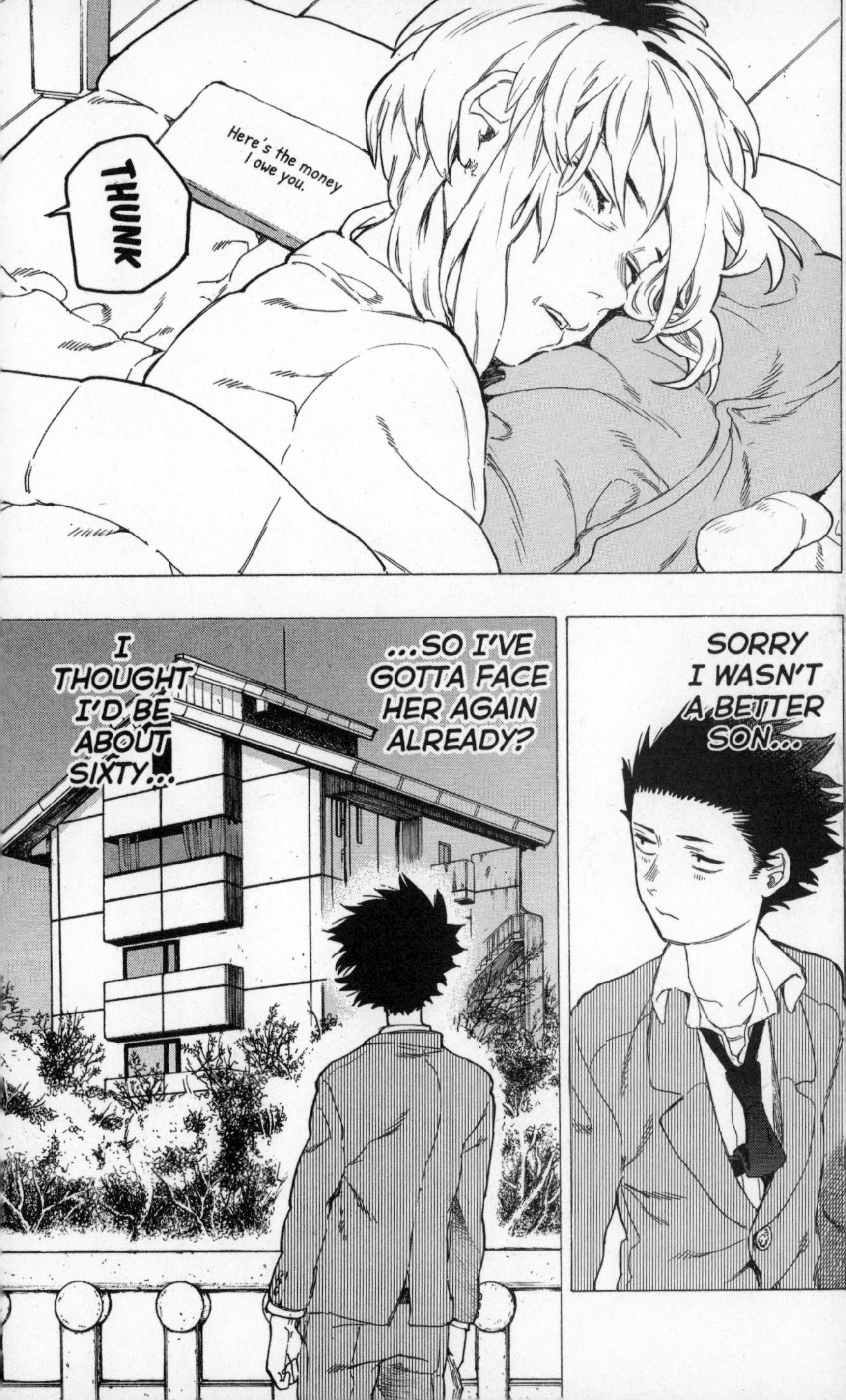
Here's the money I owe you.
THUNK
SORRY I WASN'T A BETTER SON...
...SO I'VE GOTTA FACE HER AGAIN ALREADY?
I THOUGHT I'D BE ABOUT SIXTY...

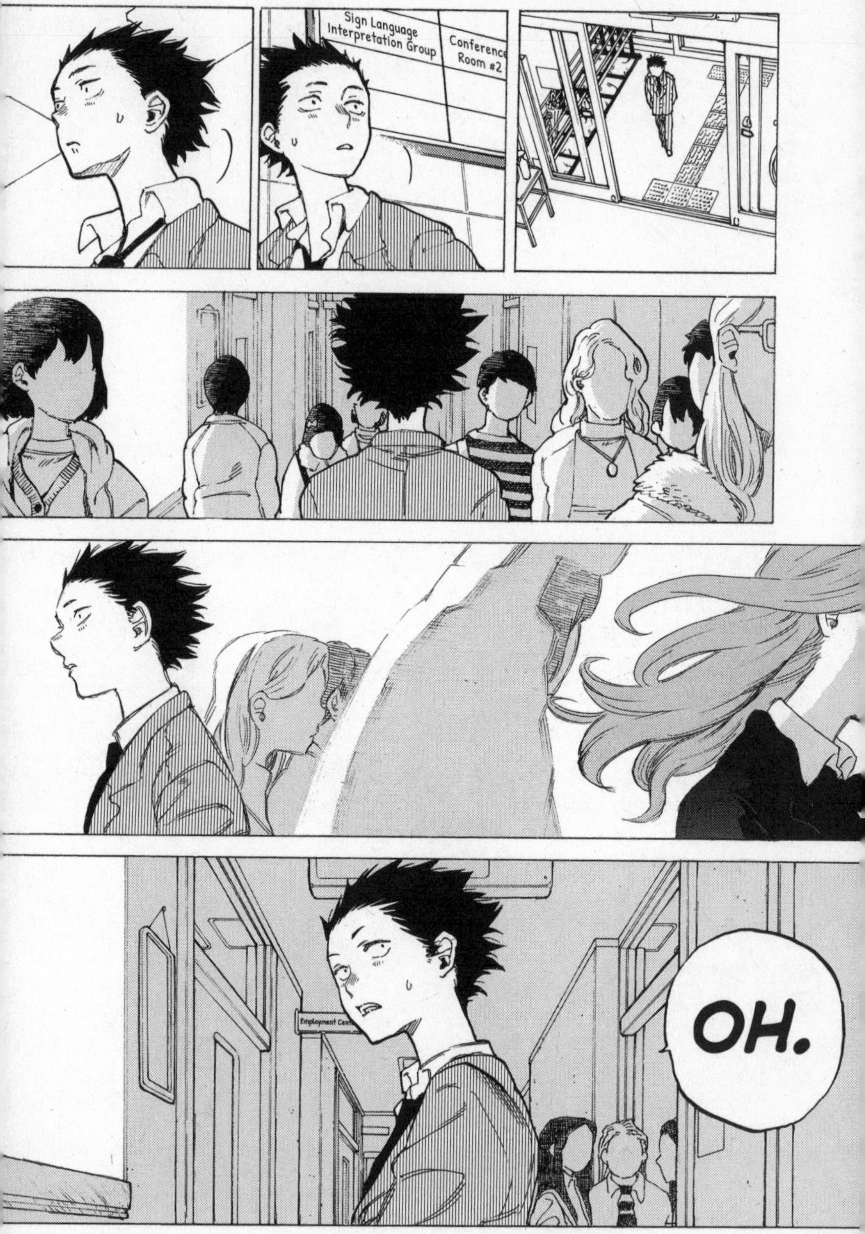
Conference Room #2
Sign Language Interpretation Group
OH.

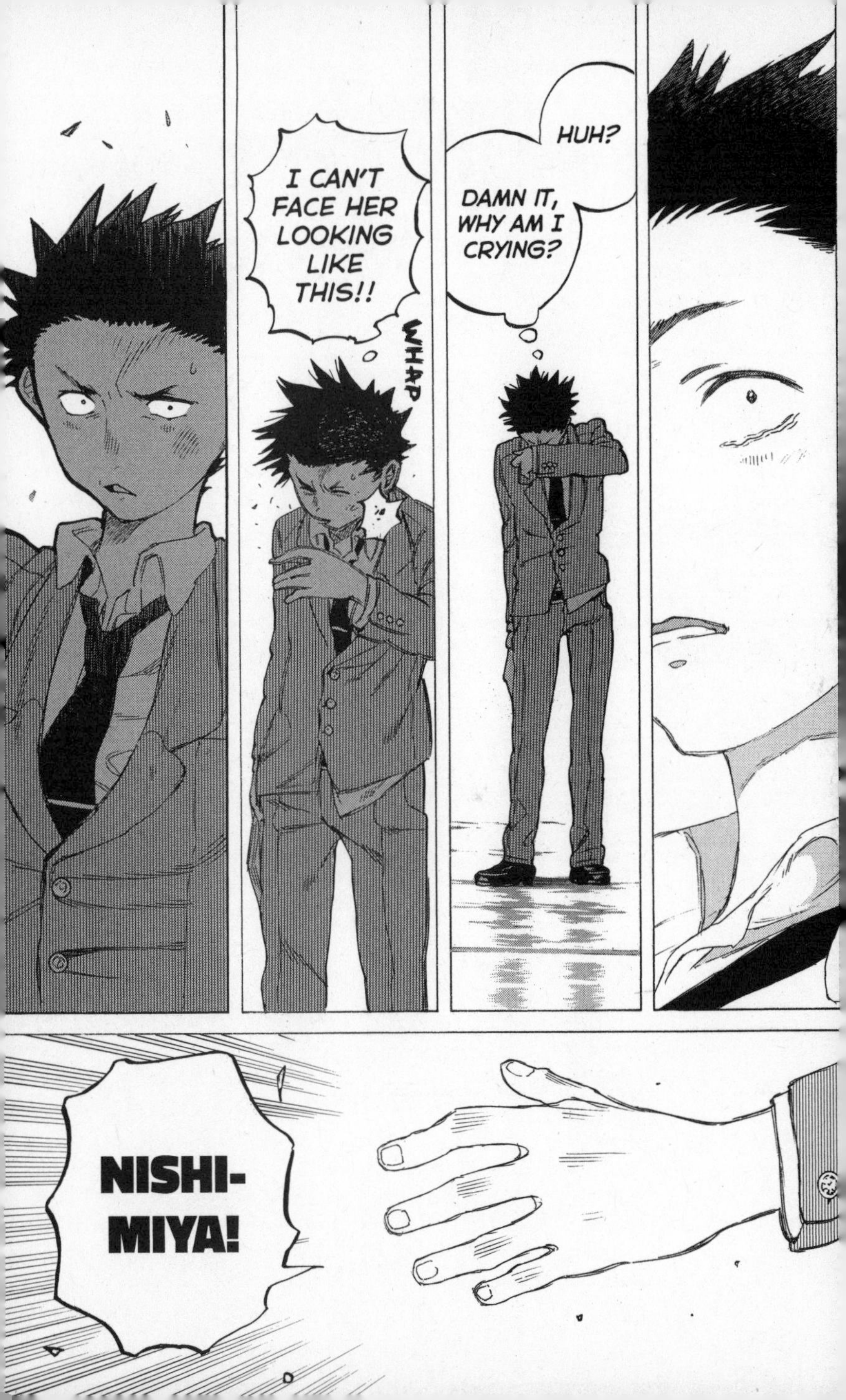
HUH?
DAMN IT, WHY AM I CRYING?
I CAN'T FACE HER LOOKING LIKE THIS!!
WHAP
NISHI-MIYA!

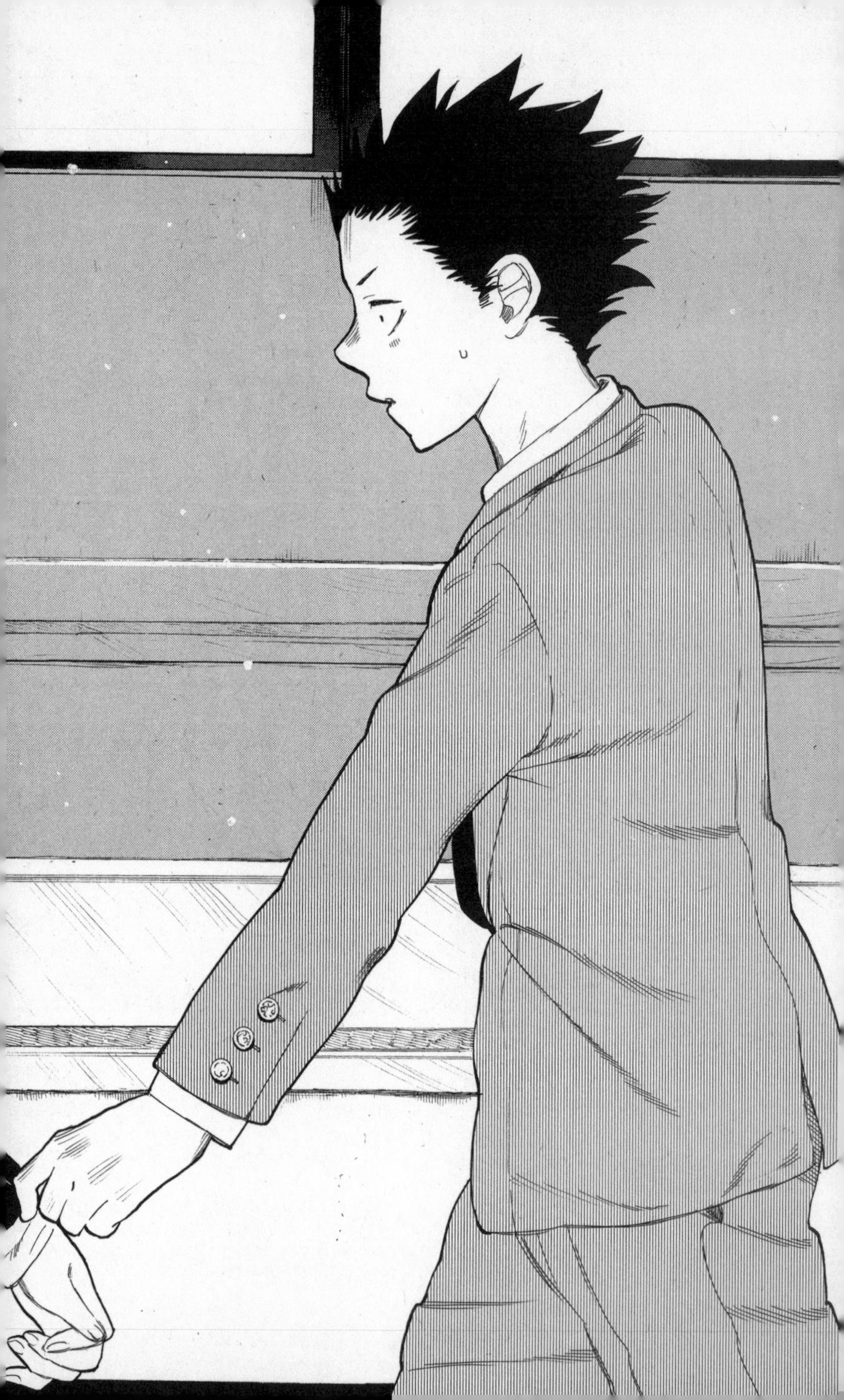

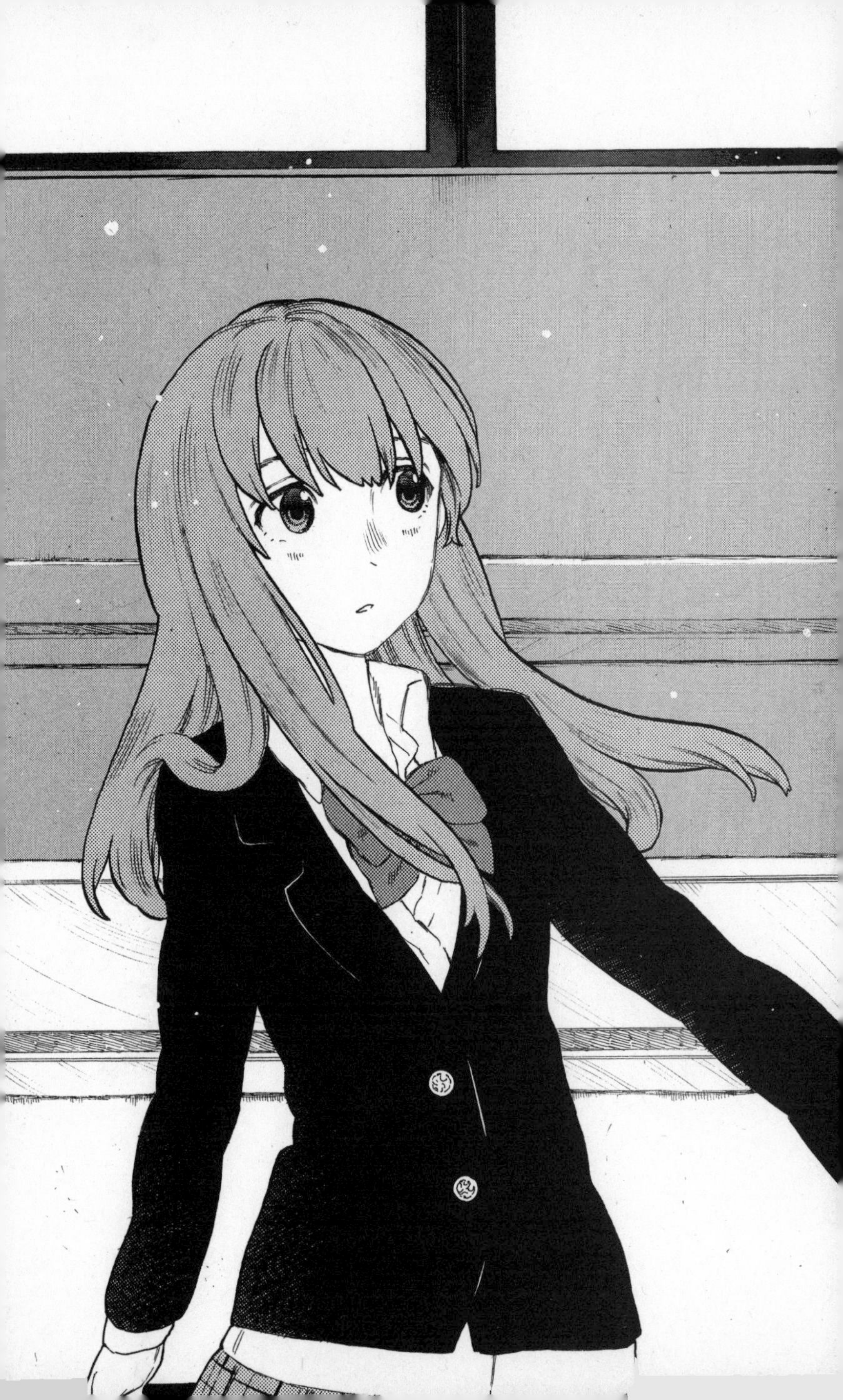

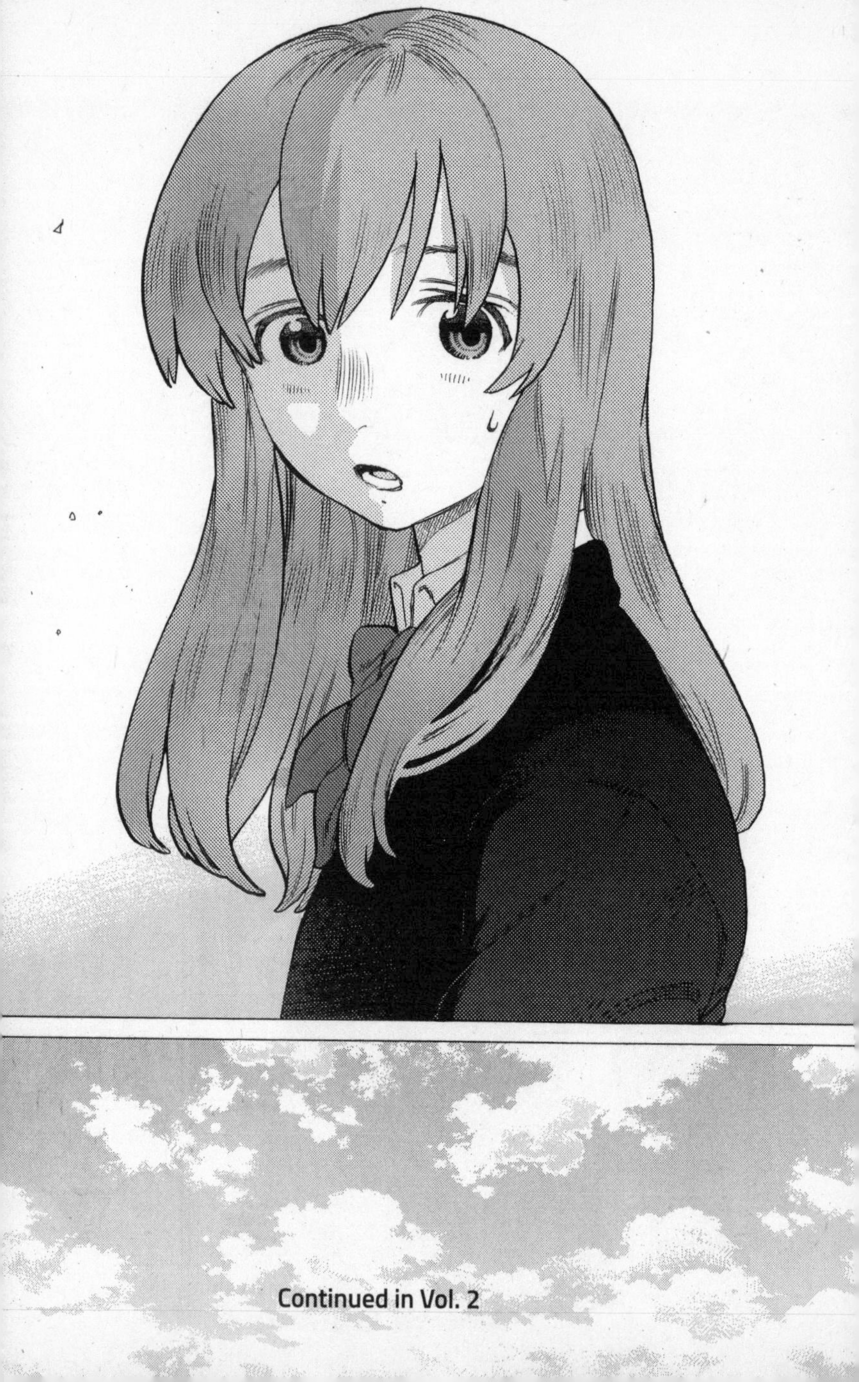
Continued in Vol. 2

a Silent Voice

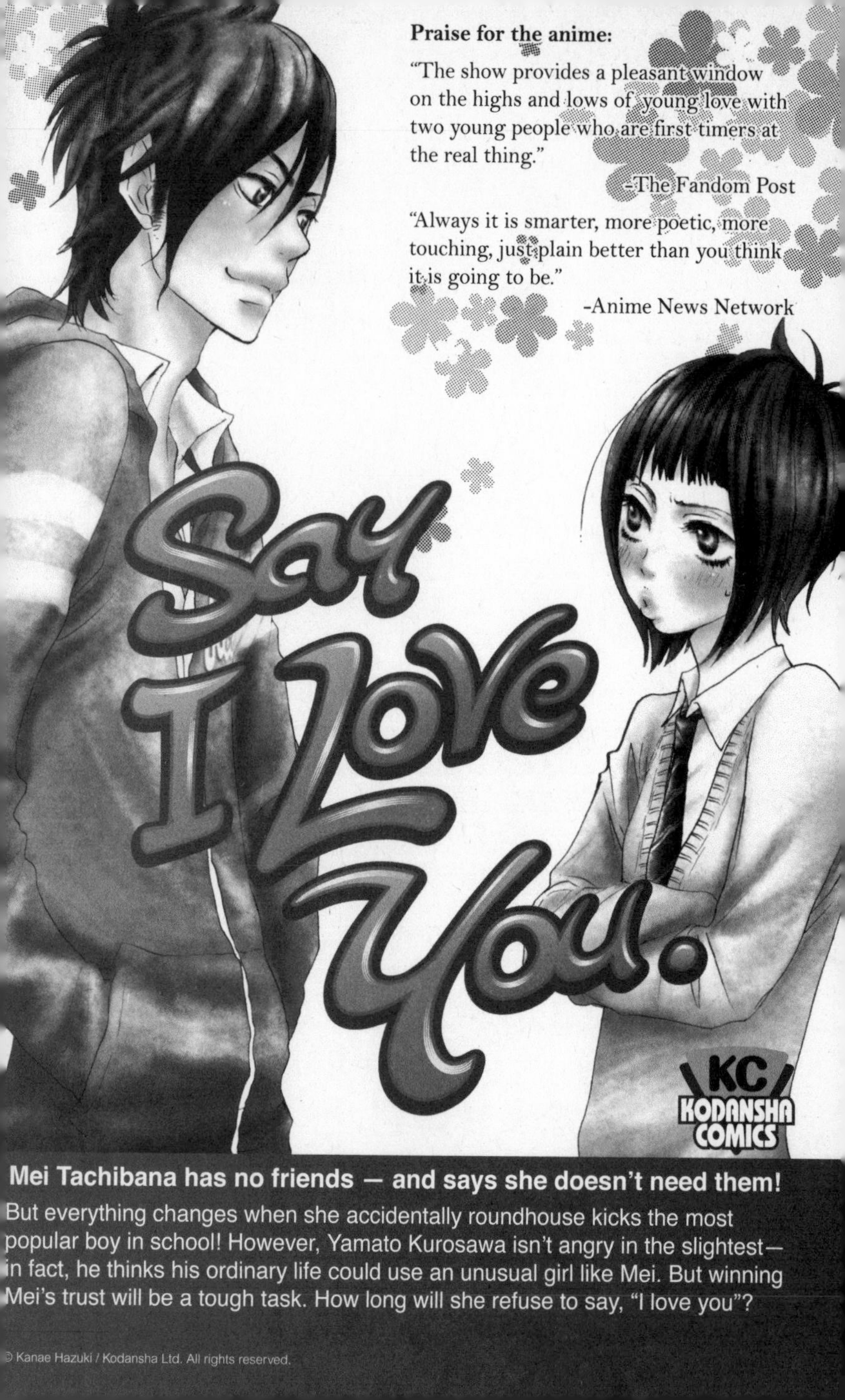
Praise for the anime:
"The show provides a pleasant window on the highs and lows of young love with two young people who are first timers at the real thing."
-The Fandom Post
"Always it is smarter, more poetic, more touching, just plain better than you think it is going to be."
-Anime News Network
Say I Love You.
KC
KODANSHA COMICS

My Little Monster

OPPOSITES ATTRACT...MAYBE?

Haru Yoshida is feared as an unstable and violent "monster." Mizutani Shizuku is a grade-obsessed student with no friends. Fate brings these two together to form the most unlikely pair. Haru firmly believes he's in love with Mizutani and she firmly believes he's insane.

KC
KODANSHA
COMICS

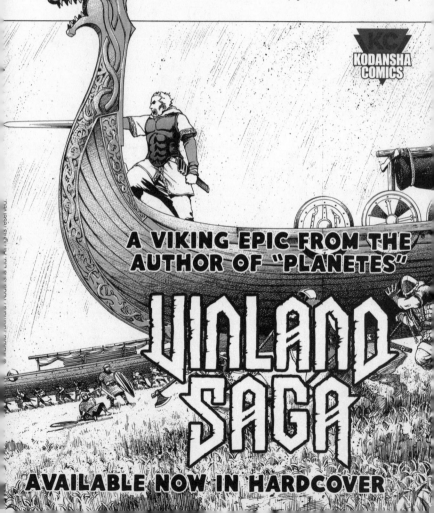

NO.6

A PERFECT LIFE
IN A PERFECT CITY

For Shion, an elite student in the technologically sophisticated city No. 6, life is carefully choreographed. One fateful day, he takes a misstep, sheltering a fugitive his age from a typhoon. Helping this boy throws Shion's life down a path to discovering the appalling secrets behind the "perfection" of No. 6.

KODAN
COMI

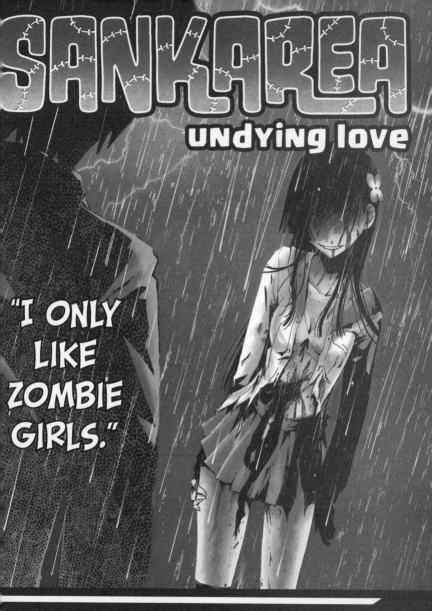

SANKAREA

undying love

"I ONLY LIKE ZOMBIE GIRLS."

Chihiro has an unusual connection to zombie movies. He doesn't feel bad for the survivors – he wants to comfort the undead girls they slaughter! When his pet passes away, he brews a resurrection potion. He's discovered by local heiress Sanka Rea, and she serves as his first test subject!

KC
KODANSHA
COMICS